Intermarket Trading Strategies

For other titles in the Wiley Trading Series
please see www.wiley.com/finance

INTERMARKET TRADING STRATEGIES

Markos Katsanos

A John Wiley and Sons, Ltd., Publication

Published by   John Wiley & Sons Ltd, The Atrium, Southern Gate, Chichester,
                    West Sussex PO19 8SQ, England

                    Telephone   (+44) 1243 779777

Email (for orders and customer service enquiries): cs-books@wiley.co.uk
Visit our Home Page on www.wiley.com

Other Wiley Editorial Offices

John Wiley & Sons Inc., 111 River Street, Hoboken, NJ 07030, USA

Jossey-Bass, 989 Market Street, San Francisco, CA 94103-1741, USA

Wiley-VCH Verlag GmbH, Boschstr. 12, D-69469 Weinheim, Germany

John Wiley & Sons Australia Ltd, 42 McDougall Street, Milton, Queensland 4064, Australia

John Wiley & Sons (Asia) Pte Ltd, 2 Clementi Loop #02-01, Jin Xing Distripark, Singapore 129809

John Wiley & Sons Canada Ltd, 6045 Freemont Blvd, Mississauga, ONT, L5R 4J3, Canada

Wiley also publishes its books in a variety of electronic formats. Some content that appears in print may
not be available in electronic books.

Library of Congress Cataloging-in-Publication Data

Katsanos, Markos.
   Intermarket trading strategies / Markos Katsanos.
      p. cm.
   Includes bibliographical references and index.
   ISBN 978-0-470-75810-6
1. Investment analysis.   2. Portfolio management.   I. Title.
   HG4529.K376 2008
   332.64—dc22
                                                     2008040290

British Library Cataloguing in Publication Data

A catalogue record for this book is available from the British Library

ISBN 978-0-470-75810-6 (HB)

Typeset in 10/12pt Times by Aptara Inc., New Delhi, India

To my wife Erifili

Contents

Acknowledgments

I am particularly indebted to Dr Evangelos Falaris, Professor of Economics at the University of Delaware, who took the time to review selected chapters and offered both technical and expositional comments.

Many thanks also to Murray Ruggiero, one of the world's leading experts in intermarket analysis, who contributed to improving the final version of the book by making valuable comments and suggestions on a preliminary manuscript. Murray is Vice President of Research and Development of TradersStudio, contributing editor for *Futures Magazine* and author of several books on trading systems.

Special thanks to my wife, Erifili, for her love and patient support, and for putting up with late nights, despite having no actual interest in the subject.

I also want to thank Jayanthi Gopalakrishnan, the editor of *Technical Analysis of Stocks & Commodities* magazine, for encouraging me to write the articles for the magazine and helping me later with the task of finding the best publisher for the book. Many thanks also to Caitlin Cornish, my editor at John Wiley & Sons, and to her assistant Aimée Dibbens, for their guidance and support during the publication process.

It is difficult to appreciate the effort and hours that go into researching and writing a book of this nature until you've had a chance to work on one yourself. The correlation studies involved a huge amount of historical data and I would like to thank Peter Day for helping out with the VBA to manage the data in Excel and Rubi Cabal, marketing director at CSI data, for allowing me access to CSI's correlation reports.

Finally, I would like to thank the technical support staff at Ward Systems Inc., and also Lynn Dufrenne, Lead Support Representative at Equis Technical Support for their help in solving the unavoidable software problems.

Introduction

With the emergence of the internet and international cross border trading, the world's futures and equity markets started to converge, making intermarket analysis an essential constituent of technical analysis.

Single market technical analysis indicators were designed in the 1980s for national markets, and are no longer sufficient nor can be relied upon for analyzing the constantly changing market dynamics.

But how do markets interact and influence each other and how can we use intermarket relationships to construct a viable technical system?

Because the answers have been so elusive, they became the motivation for my research. The more I looked into it, the more I became convinced that there is clear and incontrovertible evidence that the markets are linked to each other, and incorporating intermarket correlations into a trading discipline can give a trading advantage. Two years of research later, I finally came up with some rules and mathematical formulae for intermarket trading.

It has been more than 15 years since John Murphy, a pioneer on the subject, wrote his first book on intermarket analysis. The material in my book is based on original research not published anywhere else and, unlike Murphy's intuitive chart-based approach, I am going to use mathematical and statistical principles to develop and design intermarket trading systems appropriate for long- and short-term and even day trading.

Although the book makes extensive use of market statistics obtained from hundreds of correlation studies, the data and empirical findings are not its heart. They serve as a background in developing the trading systems presented in the second part of the book, as well as help shape our thinking about the way the financial markets work.

The key difference between *Intermarket Trading Strategies* and other books on trading lies in its philosophy. I believe that knowing how the markets work is, in the end, more important than relying on a "black box" mechanical system that produced profitable trades in the past but not even the creator of the system can fully explain why. The focus of this book is how intermarket analysis can be used to forecast future equity and index price movements by introducing custom indicators and intermarket-based systems. A total of 29 conventional and five neural network trading systems are provided to trade gold, the S&P ETF (SPY), S&P e-mini futures, DAX and FTSE futures, gold and oil stocks, commodities, sector and international ETF, and finally the yen and the euro.

Naturally, past results are no guarantee of future performance.

Even so, the results of out-of-sample back-testing are compelling enough to merit attention. Some results are more compelling. The multiple regression gold system, presented in Chapter 11, returned an amazing $1.2 million of profits on a $100 000 initial equity. The stock index trading systems also produced impressive profits. The profitability of the Standard & Poor's e-mini intraday system was neither standard nor poor, producing a 300 % profit during the test duration. Investors who prefer to trade only stocks will find intermarket systems for trading oil and gold stocks in Chapter 15. My favorite is the oil stock system which made more than $1.6 million on an initial equity of only $100 000.

The foreign exchange (or Forex) market, which until recently was dominated by large international banks, is gaining popularity among active traders, because of its superior liquidity and 24-hour trading. Readers who are interested in forex trading will find, in Chapter 17, an intermarket system for trading the yen which made over $70 000 on an initial $3000 account. The EUR/USD is the most popular currency pair among forex traders and the chapter on forex wouldn't be complete without a system for trading the euro. The next section in Chapter 17 presents two systems: a conventional and a hybrid system. The latter is an excellent example of how you can enhance a classic system by adding intermarket conditions. The hybrid system improved considerably on the profitability of the traditional trend-following system, almost doubling the profit factor while reducing drawdown.

The system design is fully described from the initial concept to optimization and actual implementation. All systems are back-tested using out-of-sample data and the performance statistics are provided for each one.

The MetaStock code for all systems is provided in Appendix A and a detailed procedure for recreating the artificial neural network systems in NeuroShell Trader is included in Appendix B.

The benefits of diversification, and an example of static portfolio diversification by optimizing the portfolio allocation based on the desired risk and return characteristics, are discussed in the first chapter and a dynamic portfolio allocation method, based on market timing and relative strength, is included in Chapter 16.

The book is divided into two parts. Part I serves as a background to Part II and includes an overview of the basics of intermarket analysis, correlation analysis in Chapter 2 and custom intermarket indicators in Chapter 9.

Part II uses many of the concepts presented in Part I to develop custom trading systems to trade popular markets like US and European stock index futures, forex and commodities.

The chapters in this book are divided as follows.

- The book begins with a discussion of the basic principles of intermarket analysis and the benefits of portfolio diversification by including uncorrelated assets such as commodities and foreign currencies.
- Chapter 2 explains the concept of correlation and the basic assumptions used.
- Chapter 3 explains the linear regression method used for predicting one security based on its correlation with related markets. An example using the S&P, the VIX and the Euro Stoxx is also included. Nonparametric regression (involving nonlinear relationships) is also briefly discussed.
- Chapter 4 is an overview of major international financial, commodity and equity indices including the DAX, the CAC 40, the FTSE, the Euro Stoxx 50, the Nikkei 225, the Hang Seng, the dollar index, the oil index, the CRB index, the Goldman Sachs Commodity Index, the XAU, the HUI, and the Volatility Index (VIX).
- Chapter 5 examines the correlation between the S&P 500 and major US and international equity, commodity and other indices.
- Chapter 6 examines long-term, short-term and even intraday correlations between major European indices and stock index futures and explains how they can be applied to develop trading systems.
- Chapter 7 is about gold and its correlation with other commodities, indices and foreign exchange rates with special emphasis on leading/lagging analysis.
- In Chapter 8 of this book I examine intraday correlations, especially useful for short-term traders. A leading/lagging correlation analysis between the S&P e-mini, the Dow e-mini, DAX and Euro Stoxx futures is also included.
- Chapter 9 presents various custom intermarket indicators and explains how each one can be used within the framework of a trading system. These include eight new custom intermarket indicators, published for the first time in this book. The MetaStock code for all indicators is included in Appendix A.
- The personal computer has revolutionized the creation and testing of trading systems. The inexpensive software takes out much of the work needed for testing, allowing the trader to test endless permutations of rules and parameters. In Chapter 10, I present some techniques for developing a trading system and evaluating the test results. I suggest methods of avoiding curve fitting and the illusion of excellence created by optimization. I also discuss stop-loss and other money management techniques. Finally, a brief introduction to neural network systems will explain the basic principles of this alternative approach for designing trading systems.
- Chapter 11 compares the performance of 15 intermarket systems for trading gold based on the intermarket indicators in Chapter 9 and using gold's correlations with the dollar index, the XAU and silver.
- Chapter 12 describes a long-term market timing system for trading the S&P ETF (SPY) using a market breadth indicator, and for traders who prefer the emotionally charged world of short-term trading, a hybrid system for trading the S&P e-mini using 5-minute intraday correlation with Euro Stoxx 50 futures.

- Chapter 13 presents intermarket systems for trading DAX futures based on its correlation with Euro Stoxx and S&P 500 futures.
- Artificial neural network systems are gaining popularity but are they the panacea that software vendors claim them to be? A comparison between a conventional rule-based system and a neural network strategy for trading the FTSE in Chapter 14 will shed some light on this innovative trading method, exposing the advantages and disadvantages of using neural network-based systems in predicting future price movements using intermarket relationships.
- Oil and gold have been so far (through June 2008) two of the best performing commodities in 2007–2008. For the benefit of readers who prefer to trade only stocks, Chapter 15 presents examples of intermarket trading systems for trading oil and gold stocks, using their correlation with the corresponding sector indices.
- Chapter 16 presents a dynamic asset allocation strategy by trading across different asset classes according to their relative strength.
- Forex trading is also gaining popularity and the final chapter (which is, by the way, the longest chapter of the book) is all about forex. Chapter 17 is divided into four parts. The first part discusses fundamental and technical factors affecting the foreign exchange markets and intermarket correlations between currencies, commodities, interest rates and equities, with a brief explanation of the carry trade. The correlation analysis included in the first part is used to develop an intermarket system to trade the yen and a hybrid system for trading the euro. The Australian dollar has received considerable attention lately as it is the favorite currency of "yen carry" traders. The last part of this chapter contains fundamental factors affecting the Australian dollar and its correlation with major international indices, commodities and other currencies.

The systems presented in this book are by no means exhaustive, and they are limited by space and the author's imagination and experience. They are presented as a challenge to the serious trader to reevaluate intermarket techniques as a working tool and to introduce a testing framework which amalgamates both intermarket and classic technical analysis indicators.

This book does not require any mathematical skills beyond those taught in high school algebra. Statistical and correlation analysis is used throughout the book but *all* of the theoretical tools are introduced and explained within. All other concepts (such as indicators, trading system evaluation, neural networks, etc.) are motivated, defined, and explained as they appear in the book.

Although all systems (except neural networks) are written in the MetaStock formula language it is not necessary to purchase MetaStock in order to use them, as they are fully explained in English and the MetaStock functions used are explained in the Glossary.

Not long ago, I ran into an acquaintance who asked me why I need to write a book about trading systems if I can make more money by trading in a day than by the royalties from the book in a year. I don't think that it makes a lot of sense to write a book for money and I don't know any author who became rich from writing (unless the book is a huge success). There are, of course, other valid reasons that motivate people to write books, like impressing your friends or establishing yourself as an expert in the subject or even visibility and media coverage. Although I have to admit that all these have crossed my mind, my main reason was the motivation to research the highly complex subject of intermarket relationships and write down my findings in an orderly, methodical and timely manner (which I wouldn't have done had I not had the deadlines imposed by my contract with the publisher).

I hope that readers will find the information useful and exploit my intermarket indicators and strategies in order to detect profitable trading opportunities.

Part I

1
Intermarket Analysis

It's not that I am so smart; it's just that I stay with the problems longer.
                                                                    –Albert Einstein

The basic premise of intermarket analysis is that there is both a cause and effect to the movement of money from one area to another. Consider, for example, the price of gold and the dollar. Because gold is denominated in US dollars, any significant fluctuation of the dollar will have an impact on the price of gold, which in turn will affect the price of gold mining stocks.

The strength and direction of the relationship between two markets is measured by the correlation coefficient which reflects the simultaneous change in value of a pair of numeric series over time.

Highly positively correlated markets can be expected to move in similar ways and highly negatively correlated markets are likely to move in opposite directions. Knowing which markets are positively or negatively correlated with a given market is very important for gaining an understanding of the future directional movement of the market you propose to trade.

Advancements in telecommunications have contributed to the integration of international markets. Sophisticated traders are starting to incorporate intermarket analysis in their trading decisions through a variety of means ranging from simple chart analysis to correlation analysis. Yet the intermarket relationships hidden in this data are often quite complex and not readily apparent, while the scope of analysis is virtually unlimited.

But what is intermarket analysis?

The financial markets comprise of more than 500 000 securities, derivatives, currencies, bonds, and other financial instruments – the size of a small city. All interact with each other to some extent and a seemingly unimportant event can cause a chain of reactions causing a landslide of large-scale changes to the financial markets.

Consider the following example: Let's suppose that the Bank of Japan decides to buy dollars in order to push the yen down. As a result Japanese stock prices will go up as a weak yen will help boost profits for exporters. A sharp rise of the Nikkei will in turn have a positive effect on all other Asian markets. The next morning European markets, in view of higher Asian markets and in the absence of other overnight news, will open higher. This will in turn drive US index futures higher and boost US markets at open. In addition lower yen prices will encourage the "yen carry trade", i.e. borrowing yen at lower or near zero interest rates and buying higher yielding assets such as US bonds or even emerging market equities, which in turn will push bonds and equities higher. On the other hand, a scenario for disaster will develop if the opposite happens and the yen rises sharply against the dollar. This will cause a sharp unwinding of the "yen carry trade", triggering an avalanche of sharp declines in all financial markets.

But what might cause the yen to rise? The following is a possible scenario: As we head into the economic slowdown, the carry trade money that has flowed into risky cyclical assets is likely to fall in value. As a result, speculators in these assets will cut their losses, bail out and repay their yen debts. This is a scenario for disaster because when the yen rebounds against the dollar, it often snaps back very fast and carry trades can go from profit to loss with almost no warning.

A popular chaos theory axiom (known as the "butterfly effect" because of the title of a paper given by the mathematician Edward Lorenz in 1972 to the American Association for the Advancement of Science in Washington, D.C. entitled "Predictability: Does the Flap of a Butterfly's Wings in Brazil Set Off a Tornado in Texas?") stipulates that a small change in the initial condition of the system (the flapping of the wing) causes a chain of events leading to large-scale phenomena. Had the butterfly not flapped its wings, the trajectory of the system might have been vastly different.

A financial series would appear to be chaotic in nature, but its statistics are not because, as well as being orderly in the sense of being deterministic, chaotic systems usually have well defined statistics.

The rapid progress of global communications has contributed to the integration of all international financial markets as the world has gotten smaller due to the ability to communicate almost instantaneously. Relationships that were dismissed as irrelevant in the past cannot be ignored any more as the globalization of the markets contributes to a convergence of formerly unrelated markets.

Take a look at the comparison chart in Fig. 1.1. The S&P 500 is depicted with a bold thick line. The second one however is not even a stock index. It is the Japanese yen exchange rate (USD/JPY).

The next composite chart in Fig. 1.2 is of three stock indices. The first two (depicted with a bar chart and thick line) are of the S&P 500 and the Nasdaq Composite respectively. The third chart (thin line) is the Athens General Index which, surprisingly, correlates better with the S&P 500 than its compatriot, the Nasdaq Composite.

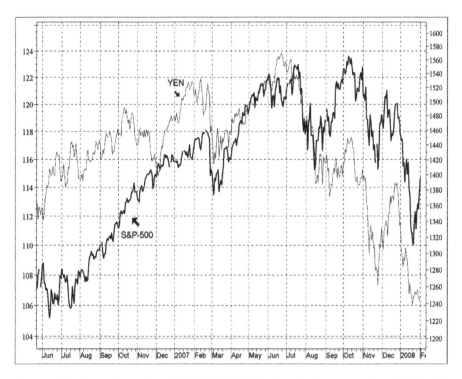

Figure 1.1 Comparison chart of the S&P 500 (in bold with the scale on the right Y-axis) and the yen (USD/JPY) (with the scale on the left axis) from June 2006 to January 2008.

The above examples are included to illustrate that the integration of global markets can extend beyond the obvious relations.

I often hear CNBC guests suggesting investing in international markets as a means of diversifying one's portfolio away from the US equity markets. Although some emerging markets may have relatively medium to low correlation with US markets, one important question to ask is whether diversification works when it is needed most. Evidence from stock market history suggests that periods of negative shocks and poor market performance were associated with high, rather than low, correlations. The events of 21 January 2008 are still fresh in my mind, when a 2.9 % correction in the S&P 500 was followed the next day by a devastating 7.2 % drop in the German DAX, wiping out nine months of profits in a day. Emerging markets sunk even more with the Jakarta Composite falling more than 12 % in two days while Brazil's Bovespa lost more than 8.5 %. Indeed, investors who have apparently relied upon diversification in the past to protect them against corrections of the market have been frequently disappointed.

Figure 1.2 Weekly comparison chart of the S&P 500 (thick line with the scale on the right Y-axis), the Nasdaq (in bold with the scale on the left axis) and the Greek Athens General Index (ATG) from 1999 to 2008.

The only effective method of diversifying one's portfolio is by including asset classes with low or negative correlation to stocks such as cash, foreign exchange or commodities. Whatever the relationship is – leading, lagging, or divergent responses to economic conditions – a strong negative correlation coefficient between two markets is a suggestion that these markets will move against each other sometime in the future. And, of course, the higher the absolute value of the coefficient of correlation, the higher the diversity of their performances.

Although intermarket analysis has been classified as a branch of technical analysis, it has not been embraced fully by analysts. The majority of traders continue to focus on only one market at a time and they tend to miss the forest for the trees. No market exists in a vacuum, and traders who focus on the bigger picture portrayed through all international markets tend to be the ones that deliver better performance.

Traditional technical analysis indicators such as moving averages are lagging indicators calculated from past data and are limited in assessing the current trend. Regardless of the hours spent in back-testing, there is a limit beyond which a system based on a lagging indicator can be improved further. Thus the addition of leading indicators that anticipate reversals in trend direction is essential and beneficial to the system's performance. These can only be created by taking into consideration directional movements of correlated markets.

The use of intermarket correlation analysis can help you improve on your trading system by avoiding trades against the prevailing direction of correlated markets, but can also be used on its own to develop a complete system based on divergences between two or more highly correlated markets. Knowing the correlation of the market you propose to trade with other markets is very important for predicting its future direction. In addition, short-term traders can take advantage of the time difference between world markets and anticipate the next day's movement. Asian markets are the first to start trading, followed by the European markets. For a US trader the insight gained from all preceding markets is a valuable tool in predicting at least the opening in his local market.

I have found that the most accurate economist is the market itself. It is far easier to forecast economic activity from the behavior of markets themselves than it is to forecast the capital markets from lagging economic statistics such as the unemployment index. The market is a discounting mechanism. It interprets the impact of economic news some time in the future. Of course, this is only a guess and guesses are not always right. But the truth is that the market is a much better guesser than any of us are, as it represents the average opinion of all the economists in the world.

There appears to be no end to the conclusions that can be drawn if a little understanding, imagination, and pure common sense are applied. Major changes in commodity prices affect the bond markets of different countries in different ways, depending upon their economic structure.

What sectors are affected first? Which asset class will provide the best potential profits? If opportunities dry up in one sector, where is the money heading to take advantage of the next cycle? This is what intermarket analysis can tell you if you learn what to look for, which makes it a grand endeavor and a continuing challenge but always worth the effort.

Intermarket analysis can also be useful in estimating the duration and state of the business cycle by watching the historic relationship between bonds, stocks and commodities as economic slowing favors bonds over stocks and commodities.

Near the end of an economic expansion bonds usually turn down before stocks and commodities and the reverse is true during an economic expansion. Bonds are usually the first to peak and the first to bottom and can therefore provide ample warning of the start or the end of a recession. Bonds have an impressive record as a leading indicator for the stock market, although this information cannot be used in constructing a trading system as the lead times can be quite long, ranging from one to two years.

You can see in Fig. 1.3 that bonds peaked in October 1998, 18 months before stocks peaked in March 2000 and 29 months before the official start of the recession in March 2001. The Commodity Research Bureau (CRB) index was the last to peak, making a complex triple top formation with the last peak coinciding with the start of the recession.

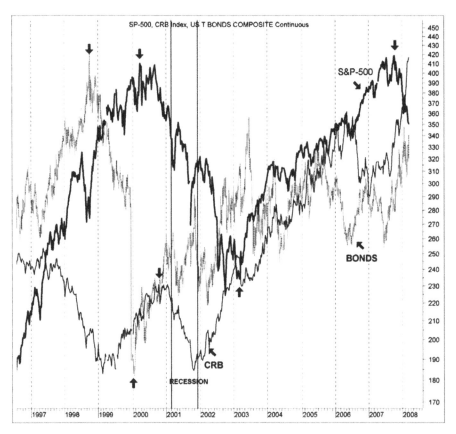

Figure 1.3 Weekly composite chart of the S&P 500 (thick line), the CRB index (thin line with the scale on the right Y- axis) and US Treasury Bonds (grey bar chart) from 1997 to 2008. Down arrows indicate major tops in stocks and bonds and up arrows bottoms.

Bonds were also the first to bottom in anticipation of the recovery, followed by commodities and then stocks. From the beginning of 2003 until the middle of 2005 all three were rising together. Commodities are usually the last to bottom during a recovery but this was not the case here as they were boosted by the weakness in the dollar. The dollar made a final peak in January 2002 and reversed direction, dropping like a rock against the euro and other major currencies. This triggered a secular bull market in gold which spread to the rest of the commodities and has continued until the end of June 2008, almost nine months after stocks peaked in September 2007.

More information on the business cycle, including sector rotation during economic cycles, can be found in John Murphy's excellent book *Intermarket Analysis: Profiting from Global Market Relationships* (see Bibliography).

1.1   DETERMINING INTERMARKET RELATIONS

The simplest and easiest method of intermarket analysis is a visual inspection of a comparison chart of one security superimposed on the chart of another. A custom indicator can also be calculated from the ratio of prices, to help assess their past relation and anticipate future direction. Both of the above methods, however, are limited to two markets and the use of the correlation coefficient is essential for an analysis of multiple markets. For predictive purposes, we wish to detect correlations that are significantly different from zero. Such relationships can then be used to predict the future course of events in trading systems or forecasting models.

In addition, linear regression can be used to predict the future price trend of a market based on its correlation with multiple related markets.

When assessing intermarket relations you should always keep in mind that these are neither fixed nor static in time. Instead they fluctuate continuously in strength and time. It is usually very difficult to determine which market is leading or lagging. A lead can shift over time and become a lag, with the markets switching positions as follower and leader. In addition, a weak positive correlation can sometimes become negative and vice versa. For this reason it is always prudent to look at the prevailing rate of change of the correlation between two related markets before reaching any important conclusions or trading decisions.

The variability of the correlation over time is more evident in Fig. 1.4, where yearly correlations between the S&P 500 and four major international indices are plotted against time from 1992 up to the end of 2007. You can see that correlations before 1996 were inconsistent and unpredictable but started to converge during the last ten-year period. The most incongruous relationship is that between the S&P 500 and Japan's Nikkei (in white) as it fluctuated from negative to positive values over time.

The recent integration of global markets has also been accelerated by a flurry of mergers, acquisitions and alliances between international exchanges, the most important being the merger between the New York Stock Exchange and Euronext, Europe's leading cross-border exchange, which includes French, Belgian, Dutch and Portuguese national markets. A few months later the Nasdaq, after a failed bid for the London Stock Exchange, announced a takeover of the OMX, which owns and operates stock exchanges in Stockholm, Helsinki, Copenhagen, Reykjavik (Iceland) and the Baltic states.

1.2   USING INTERMARKET CORRELATIONS FOR PORTFOLIO DIVERSIFICATION

The benefits of diversification are well known: most investment managers diversify by including international equities, bonds and cash in their US stock portfolio. Less common, however, is the diversification into other asset classes such as commodities or foreign currencies (forex).

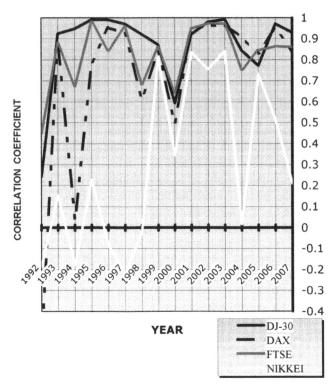

Figure 1.4 Yearly correlation variation between the S&P 500 and leading international indices from 1992–2007. The correlation with the DJ-30 is depicted by a black line, with Germany's DAX by a dashed line, with the FTSE by a grey line, and with the Nikkei by a white line. Notice the correlation volatility, especially before 1996. The Nikkei had the weakest and most volatile correlation with the S&P 500.

There is a widely held belief that, because commodities and currencies are traded on very thin margins, they are just too risky and can lead to financial ruin. Visions of wheat being delivered to the trader's front yard, margin calls or stories of consecutive "limit down days" add fuel to the fire. Claims that "over 90 % of all futures traders lose money over time" do not help either.

Because of their low correlation to equities, most commodities are attractive diversification candidates as they can lead to a large increase in return while simultaneously reducing risk. Furthermore, futures diversification is particularly effective in declining stock markets, just where it is needed most. During periods of very low or negative stock returns, commodities (except industrial metal futures) dominate the portfolio return, acting as a hedge, or buffer, in falling markets. The benefit of including foreign stocks is not so clear as the world has gotten smaller due to the ability to communicate almost instantaneously.

Unfortunately, the approach of most novice investors or even fund managers is to have no risk management at all and it becomes obvious too late that this is an extremely dangerous omission. A fund or portfolio manager should not be evaluated only by the return he has achieved. Another important criterion of his performance is the portfolio risk exposure over time. A good benchmark of that risk is the standard deviation of returns. This is a measure of how far apart the monthly or yearly returns are scattered around the average.

Correlation is a relatively simple concept but absolutely mandatory in the use of investments. It basically refers to whether or not different investments or asset classes will move at the same time for the same reason and in the same direction. To be effective, diversification must involve asset classes that are not correlated (that is, they do not move in the same direction at the same time). High positive correlation reduces the benefits of diversification. On the other hand, selecting uncorrelated or negatively correlated asset classes not only reduces the downside volatility in the performance curve of the portfolio to a minimum but can also increase overall profitability as well. An example will help illustrate the basics of diversification.

Suppose you are considering diversifying your stock portfolio by adding an uncorrelated commodity future from the energy complex. If you invest your entire equity in either stocks or crude oil futures, and returns vary in the future as they have in the past, your equity line (in points) will be similar to the charts in the bottom window of Fig. 1.5. If, however, you invest 70 % of your initial capital in stocks and 30 % in crude oil futures, your equity line will be similar to the top chart in Fig. 1.5. You can clearly see that the portfolio's returns are not nearly as volatile as are those of the individual investments.

The reason for the reduction in volatility is that stocks did not move in the same direction at the same time with crude oil futures. Thus, a crucial factor for constructing portfolios is the degree of correlation between investment returns. Diversification provides substantial risk reduction if the components of a portfolio are uncorrelated.

In fact, it is possible to reduce the overall risk of the portfolio to almost zero if enough investment opportunities having non-correlated returns are combined together!

Maximum return, however, is also proportional to risk. Low risk investments produce low returns and speculative or riskier investments can produce higher returns. Thus reducing risk can also reduce return. Like everything else in life, the best solution is a compromise between risk and return.

The problem is therefore reduced to finding an efficient portfolio that will maximize expected return according to one's individual risk preferences. The following example will help illustrate the basics of selecting an appropriate portfolio of securities or asset classes.

Let's suppose that we want to invest in international equities but also diversify into futures and forex. For simplicity's sake I include only one sample from each asset class, for example crude oil futures to represent commodities, gold to represent

Figure 1.5 Monthly comparison chart of the S&P 500 (bar chart with the scale on the right Y-axis) and light sweet crude oil futures continuous contract (NYMEX:CL) (line chart below) from January of 1994 to January of 2008. The equity line of a composite portfolio consisting of 70 % equities (represented by the S&P 500) and 30 % oil futures is plotted in the top window. The composite portfolio produced better returns with less volatility.

precious metals and the British pound to represent foreign exchange. International equities are represented by the S&P 500 (or a stock selection tracking the S&P), one European (the FTSE 100) and one Asian (the Hang Seng) index. In Table 1.1, I have prepared the average yearly percentage returns and standard deviation of returns. I have also calculated, at the bottom of the table, the total average 10-year return and the standard deviation of returns using Excel's STDEV function.

The correlation coefficients between the selected asset classes or indices are listed in Table 1.2. These coefficients are based on monthly percentage yields and are calculated, as part of this study, over the same 10-year period. As discussed later, the correlation coefficients play a role in selecting the asset class allocation.

You can see from Table 1.2 that the S&P 500 is correlated only with international indices. Among the other asset classes, the British pound is weakly correlated with gold ($r = 0.36$) and negatively correlated with the FTSE ($r = -0.30$) so it might be beneficial to include the pound together with the FTSE but not with gold. Gold is

Table 1.1 All stock index returns include dividends. Also foreign index returns were converted to US dollars. The bond returns were obtained from the Lehman Brothers website (http://www.lehman.com/fi/indices/) and concerned aggregate returns of the US Bond Index. British pound (GBP/USD) returns include price appreciation versus the USD and also interest income. Oil returns were obtained from the historical continuous light sweet crude oil contract (NYMEX:CL).

				Annual returns				
Year	S&P 500	FTSE	Hang Seng	Bonds	GBP	Gold	Crude oil	Cash
1997	33.36	23.98	−17.3	9.65	2.31	−21.8	−31.9	5.25
1998	28.58	17.02	−2.15	8.69	6.47	−0.26	−31.7	5.06
1999	21.04	17.22	71.51	−0.82	2.37	0.00	112.4	4.74
2000	−9.10	−15.6	−8.96	11.63	−1.85	−5.55	4.69	5.95
2001	−11.9	−17.6	−22.0	8.44	1.39	2.48	−26.0	4.09
2002	−22.1	−8.79	−15.1	10.26	13.56	24.80	57.3	1.70
2003	28.68	27.60	38.55	4.10	14.35	19.09	4.23	1.07
2004	10.88	18.43	16.30	4.34	12.25	5.58	33.61	1.24
2005	4.91	9.70	7.82	2.43	−5.78	18.00	40.48	3.00
2006	15.79	27.77	37.35	4.33	18.85	23.17	0.02	4.76
Mean	10.02	9.97	10.61	6.31	6.39	6.55	16.31	3.69
St Dev	19.14	17.53	30.35	4.00	8.02	14.73	45.67	1.80

also very weakly correlated with crude oil ($r = 0.18$). As you will see later, however, in the case of low correlations the volatility and not the correlation coefficient is the dominant factor to consider in reducing portfolio risk. Bonds had very low correlation with the British pound ($r = 0.10$) and crude oil ($r = 0.11$) but were not particularly correlated with the others.

Table 1.2 Pearson's correlation of monthly percentage yields for the 10-year period from 1997 to 2006.

			Correlation of monthly returns				
	S&P 500	FTSE	Hang Seng	Bonds	GBP	Gold	Crude oil
S&P 500	1	0.81	0.57	−0.06	−0.09	−0.04	−0.03
FTSE	0.81	1	0.57	−0.02	−0.30	−0.06	0.03
Hang Seng	0.57	0.57	1	0.05	0.00	0.11	0.18
Bonds	−0.06	−0.02	0.05	1	0.10	0.08	0.11
GBP	−0.09	−0.30	0.00	0.10	1	0.36	0.00
Gold	−0.04	−0.06	0.11	0.08	0.36	1	0.18
Oil	−0.03	0.03	0.18	0.11	0.00	0.18	1

Table 1.3 Risk reduction associated with asset allocation and correlations. The standard deviation of each portfolio was calculated in a separate spreadsheet by adding the annual returns of each asset class according to their percentage weights in the portfolio and then calculating the standard deviation of the annual returns for the entire 10-year period of the study.

Portfolio allocation	US stocks only	Stocks & bonds	International stocks & bonds	Stocks, bonds & futures	Minimum risk	Maximum return
S&P 500	100 %	70 %	50 %	40 %	10 %	60 %
Cash		10 %	10 %			
FTSE			10 %			
Hang Seng			10 %			10 %
Bonds		20 %	20 %	40 %		
GBP					55 %	
Gold				10 %		
CRB						
Oil				10 %	15 %	30 %
Average % Return	10.0	8.64	8.69	8.81	8.92	11.96
Standard deviation	19.1	13.1	12.5	6.86	6.38	18.70
Risk adj. return	0.52	0.66	0.70	1.28	1.40	0.64

A comparison of the returns, standard deviation and risk adjusted return of the four hypothetical passive portfolios shows the real effect of diversification (Table 1.3). The first portfolio (in the third column of Table 1.3) contained a typical allocation of asset classes found in an average US fund, i.e. 70 % equities, 20 % bonds and 10 % money market. By including uncorrelated assets such as bonds and cash (with zero correlation with the S&P), a risk reduction of 31 % was achieved with only 1.4 % reduction in returns. A further 5 % risk reduction was accomplished by including international equities (10 % British and 10 % Hong Kong equities). The main reason for including international equities was to improve on US equity returns, but this was not the case in the hypothetical portfolio as the Hang Seng underperformed the S&P 500 during the 1997–1998 Asian financial crisis. Commodities, however, were the real star of the show as they played an important role in significantly reducing risk and, at the same time, increasing return.

This is evident from the standard deviation of returns of the third hypothetical portfolio. A huge 64 % reduction in risk was achieved by including gold (10 %) and crude oil futures (10 %), even though the standard deviation (and risk) of investing in crude oil alone was more than double that of the S&P.

The fourth portfolio was obtained by finding the best allocation (highest return) with the minimum risk. This produced a portfolio consisting of 30 % US equities, 55 % bonds and 15 % oil futures. The relatively high percentage allocation of bonds was to be expected as their standard deviation was the lowest of the group. The presence of the highly volatile oil futures in the minimum risk portfolio, however, was certainly a surprise.

This portfolio reduced risk by an astonishing 64 %, sacrificing only 1.2 percentage points in return compared to the equities only portfolio.

The relatively low performance of this portfolio was no surprise as the standard deviation is proportional to returns: the smaller the standard deviation, the smaller the risk and, of course, the smaller the potential magnitude of the return. There is therefore a limit beyond which the expected return cannot be increased without increasing risk.

Finally I used Excel's Solver to maximize return without increasing the risk more than the first (equities) portfolio. This portfolio (last column in Table 1.3) included 60 % US stocks, 10 % international equities and 30 % crude oil futures. It outperformed the S&P 500 by almost 2 percentage points with slightly less risk. Typically, futures can be added up to a maximum 30 % allocation while maintaining a risk advantage over a portfolio without futures.

In maximizing the return I had to constrain the risk to lower than the first portfolio, otherwise the solver produced a portfolio consisting of 100 % oil futures which is unacceptable. Similarly in minimizing risk (fourth portfolio) I had to specify a minimum return otherwise the solution also produced an unacceptable portfolio consisting mostly of cash and bonds. I also had to constrain the allocation percentages to positive values otherwise the solution occasionally included negative allocations indicating selling the asset short rather than buying.

Of course future performance rarely measures up fully to past results. While historical relations between asset classes may provide a reasonable guide, rates of return are often less predictable. In addition, as you can see from Fig. 1.4, correlations can also change over time.

One solution is to rebalance the portfolio on a set time period to take into account the most recent correlations in order to maintain the desired level of risk exposure. This method of asset allocation, is not the only one, however.

A different, dynamic rather than static, approach would involve changing asset weights depending on market conditions. This can be accomplished by reducing the allotment of equities in favor of cash, precious metals or foreign exchange in a down market. A dynamic asset allocation trading system is also discussed in Chapter 16 of this book.

2
Correlation

2.1 THE CORRELATION COEFFICIENT

2.1.1 Pearson's Correlation

The correlation coefficient measures the strength and direction of correlation or co-relation between two variables.

There are several methods, depending on the nature of data being studied, for calculating the correlation coefficient, but the best known is Pearson's product-moment correlation coefficient, usually denoted by r, which is obtained by dividing the covariance of the two variables by the product of their standard deviations. The formula for calculating Pearson's r is:

$$r = \frac{\sigma_{XY}}{\sigma_X \sigma_Y} \tag{2.1}$$

where σ_{XY} is the covariance of variables X and Y and σ_X, σ_y are their standard deviations. The covariance is the cross product of the deviations from the mean and is calculated by the following formula:

$$\sigma_{XY} = \frac{\sum (x - \bar{x})(y - \bar{y})}{n - 1}. \tag{2.2}$$

Unfortunately the size of the covariance depends on the values of measurement of each variable and is not normalized between -1.0 and $+1.0$ as is the correlation coefficient.

Substituting for the covariance in (1.1) we get:

$$r = \frac{\sum z_x z_y}{\sigma_x \sigma_y (n-1)} \tag{2.3}$$

which is the average product of the z-scores, where $z_x = \sum (x_i - \bar{x})$ and $z_y = \sum (y_i - \bar{y})$.

The correlation coefficient varies between -1 and 1. A value of $+1$ indicates a perfect linear relationship with positive slope between the two variables; a value of -1 indicates a perfect linear relationship with negative slope between the two variables and a correlation coefficient of 0 means that there is no linear relationship between the variables. Values in between indicate the degree of correlation and their interpretation is subjective depending to some extent on the variables under consideration.

The interpretation is different for medical research, social, economic or financial time series data. In the case of financial time series the interpretation can again be different depending on whether we compare raw price data or percent changes (yields), as the direct calculation of the correlation based on absolute prices tends to overestimate the correlation coefficient as relations between financial price series are seldom linear. Correlations based on price percent changes, on the other hand, produce more realistic values for the correlation coefficient as they deviate less from linearity.

Therefore, although the correlation coefficient between two time series is unique, two different interpretations are included in Table 2.1, according to the method used for the calculation, in order to take into account the error resulting from the violation of the linearity assumption.

Table 2.1 Interpretation of Pearson's correlation coefficient. The second column applies to the correlation between raw price data and the last column to percent weekly changes or yields. The interpretation for negative values of Pearson's correlation is exactly the same.

Correlation coefficient r	Interpretation	
Absolute value	Price comparison	Percent changes
0.9 to 1	Extremely strong	Extremely strong
0.8 to 0.9	Very strong	Very strong
0.7 to 0.8	Strong	Very strong
0.6 to 0.7	Moderately strong	Strong
0.5 to 0.6	Moderate	Moderately strong
0.4 to 0.5	Meaningful	Moderate
0.3 to 0.4	Low	Meaningful
0.2 to 0.3	Very low	Low
0.1 to 0.2	Very slight	Very low
0 to 0.1	Non-existent	Non-existent

A more precise interpretation arising from the correlation coefficient is recommended by some statisticians and requires one further calculation. If the correlation coefficient is squared, the result, commonly known as r^2 or r square or coefficient of determination (see also Section 2.1.2), will indicate approximately the percent of the "dependent" variable that is associated with the "independent" variable or the proportion of the variance in one variable associated with the variance of the other variable. For example, if we calculated that the correlation between the S&P 500 and the 10-year Treasury yield (TNX) is 0.50 then this correlation squared is 0.25, which means that 25 % of the variance of the two indices is common. In thus squaring correlations and transforming the result to percentage terms we are in a better position to evaluate a particular correlation.

There is also another factor we must consider when we try to interpret the correlation coefficient – the number of points we have used.

If we plotted only two points, then we would be bound to get a straight line between them. With three points there is still a chance that the points will lie close to a straight line, purely by chance. Clearly, a high correlation coefficient on only a few points is not very meaningful.

Traders often need to know if time series of commodity or stock prices are cyclic and, if they are, the extent of the cycle. The correlation coefficient can also be used in this case by testing for auto-correlation at different lags (testing whether values in a given series are related to other values in the same series). By doing many correlations with differing lags, the extent or duration of the cycle can be determined.

2.1.2   Coefficient of determination

The coefficient of determination r^2 is the square of Pearson's correlation coefficient. It represents the percent of the data that is the closest to the line of best fit. For example, if $r = 0.922$, then $r^2 = 0.850$, which means that 85 % of the total variation in y can be explained by the linear relationship between x and y (as described by the regression equation). The other 15 % of the total variation in y remains unexplained and stems from other exogenous factors. In regression, the coefficient of determination is useful in determining how well the regression line approximates the real data points but it can also be used (as explained above) to interpret the correlation coefficient.

2.1.3   Spearman's ρ

The best known non-parametric correlation coefficient is Spearman's rank correlation coefficient, named after Charles Spearman and often denoted by the Greek letter ρ (rho). Unlike Pearson's correlation coefficient, it does not require the assumption that the variables are normally distributed but, like Pearson's correlation, linearity is still an assumption.

The main advantage of using the Spearman coefficient is that it is not sensitive to outliers because it looks at ranks as opposed to actual values.

The formula for calculating Spearman's correlation, ρ is:

$$\rho = 1 - \frac{6 \sum d^2}{n(n^2 - 1)} \tag{2.4}$$

where d is the difference between paired ranks on the same row.

Similar to Pearson's correlation coefficient, Spearman's ρ takes values between -1 and $+1$. In calculating Spearman's coefficient some information is lost because the prices are converted to ranks. Therefore, when two variables appear to be normally distributed it is better to use Pearson's correlation coefficient.

The concept of correlation will be discussed extensively in the rest of the book and should be fully understood by the readers, so I have included an example of calculating both Pearson's and Spearman's correlation coefficients in the Excel worksheets in Tables 2.2 and 2.3 respectively.

2.2 ASSUMPTIONS

2.2.1 Linearity

The formula used when calculating the correlation coefficient between two variables makes the implicit assumption that a linear relationship exists between them. When this assumption is not true, the calculated value can be misleading. In practice this assumption can virtually never be confirmed; fortunately, the correlation coefficient is not greatly affected by minor deviations from linearity. However, it is always prudent to look at a scatterplot of the variables of interest before making important conclusions regarding the relation between two variables.

To understand what a linear relationship is, consider the scatterplots in Figs. 2.1, 2.2 and 2.3.

The first scatterplot in Fig. 2.1, between the S&P 500 and the British FTSE 100, illustrates an approximate linear relationship, as the points fall generally along a straight line. Keep in mind that in the financial markets there is no such thing as a perfect linear relationship. In contrast, the plot in Fig. 2.2 between the S&P 500 and the Nasdaq 100 exhibits a curvilinear relationship. In this case increasingly greater values of the Nasdaq 100 are associated with increasingly greater values of the S&P 500 up to a certain value (approximately 1200 on the Nasdaq scale).

A statistician, not knowing what each variable represents, would try to fit a cubic line of the form

$$SP = a + b.NDX + c.NDX^2 + d.NDX^3$$

and predict future values of the S&P 500 using the cubic equation above.

Table 2.2 Example of calculating Pearson's r in Excel. The variables X and Y are the daily percent change in gold and the dollar index respectively from 8 December 2006 to 29 December 2006.

A	B	C	D	E	F	G	H	1
Date	X	Y	$X-\mu$	$(X-\mu)^2$	$Y-\mu$	$(Y-\mu)^2$	$(X-\mu)(Y-\mu)$	2
12-8-06	−1.344	0.640	−1.386	1.921	0.570	0.325	−0.790	3
12-11-06	0.929	−0.132	0.887	0.787	−0.202	0.041	−0.179	4
12-12-06	−0.008	−0.289	−0.050	0.003	−0.359	0.129	0.018	5
12-13-06	−0.325	0.470	−0.367	0.135	0.400	0.160	−0.147	6
12-14-06	−0.430	0.444	−0.472	0.223	0.374	0.140	−0.176	7
12-15-06	−1.664	0.406	−1.706	2.910	0.336	0.113	−0.573	8
12-18-06	0.163	−0.036	0.121	0.015	−0.106	0.011	−0.013	9
12-19-06	1.088	−0.667	1.046	1.094	−0.737	0.543	−0.771	10
12-20-06	−0.402	0.096	−0.444	0.197	0.026	0.001	−0.011	11
12-21-06	−0.250	0.072	−0.292	0.085	0.002	0.000	−0.001	12
12-22-06	0.332	0.263	0.290	0.084	0.193	0.037	0.056	13
12-26-06	0.613	0.298	0.571	0.326	0.228	0.052	0.130	14
12-27-06	0.401	−0.107	0.359	0.129	−0.177	0.031	−0.064	15
12-28-06	1.133	−0.179	1.091	1.190	−0.249	0.062	−0.272	16
12-29-06	0.394	−0.227	0.352	0.124	−0.297	0.088	−0.105	17
Σ	0.630	1.052		9.223		1.733	−2.897	18
N	15	15					−0.207	19
mean μ	0.042	0.070			Covariance $\sigma_{xy}=$		−0.725	20
σ	0.812	0.352			Pearson's Correlation **r**			21

Excel Formula

ROW				19	20	21
COLUMN						
B	17			COUNT(B3:B17)	B18/B19	SQRT(E18/(B19−1))
C				COUNT(C3:C17)	C18/C19	SQRT(G18/(C19−1))
D	B17−B$20					
E	D17*D17					
F	C17−C$20					
G	F17*F17					
H	D17*F17			H18/(B19−1)	H19/B21/C21	

Table 2.3 Example of calculating Spearman's ρ in Excel. The variables X and Y are the daily percent change in gold and the dollar index respectively from 8 December 2006 to 29 December 2006.

	A	B	C	D	E	F	
							1
	Date	X	Y	Rank	Rank	d^2	2
	12-8-06	-1.344	0.640	14	1	169	3
	12-11-06	0.929	-0.132	3	11	64	4
	12-12-06	-0.008	-0.289	9	14	25	5
	12-13-06	-0.325	0.470	11	2	81	6
	12-14-06	-0.430	0.444	13	3	100	7
	12-15-06	-1.664	0.406	15	4	121	8
	12-18-06	0.163	-0.036	8	9	1	9
	12-19-06	1.088	-0.667	2	15	169	10
	12-20-06	-0.402	0.096	12	7	25	11
	12-21-06	-0.250	0.072	10	8	4	12
	12-22-06	0.332	0.263	7	6	1	13
	12-26-06	0.613	0.298	4	5	1	14
	12-27-06	0.401	-0.107	5	10	25	15
	12-28-06	1.133	-0.179	1	12	121	16
	12-29-06	0.394	-0.227	6	13	49	17
Σ		0.630	1.052			956.00	18
N		15					19
				Spearman's Correlation ρ =		-0.707	20

Excel Formula

ROW			
COLUMN			
B	17		SUM(B3:B17)
C		18	SUM(C3:C17)
D	RANK(B17,B$3:B$17)		
E	RANK(C17,C$3:C$17)		
F	(D17−E17)^2	20	SUM(F3:F17)
			1−6*F18/B19/(B19^2−1)

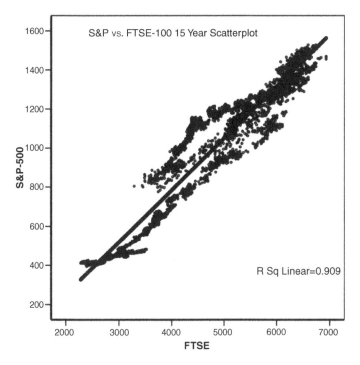

Figure 2.1 Scatterplot of the S&P 500 and the British FTSE 100, for the last 15-year period. The relationship is approximately linear, as the points fall generally along a straight line.

A chart of the two indices in Fig. 2.4, however, reveals the true reason of discontinuity of the linear relationship: a decoupling of the two indices which started in the middle of 1998, with the Nasdaq outperforming the S&P until the bubble peak of March 2000, and its subsequent devastating collapse which happened to coincide for values of the Nasdaq greater than 1200. This is the reason for the breakout of the linear relationship as depicted in Fig. 2.2 by the vertical line AB.

The third scatterplot in Fig. 2.3 plots the S&P 500 vs. Japan's Nikkei 225.

Pearson's coefficient of correlation is -0.445 and Spearman's ρ is -0.4, suggesting a negative correlation for the period from 1 January 1992 to 13 December 2006. Both values are, however, meaningless for making any useful predictions for the Nikkei based on the S&P 500 as their relationship is not linear.

A closer examination of the scatterplot, however, reveals that the scatter is clustered around three distinct areas, each having completely different slopes: Area A at the top left of the chart exhibits a distinct positive correlation with the S&P; area B in the center of the chart with a negative correlation; and area C at the bottom right with no correlation at all. The time period of the above different correlations can be identified more precisely by superimposing a chart of the Nikkei on the S&P (Fig. 2.5). The period from 1992 to 2007 under study can be divided into six types.

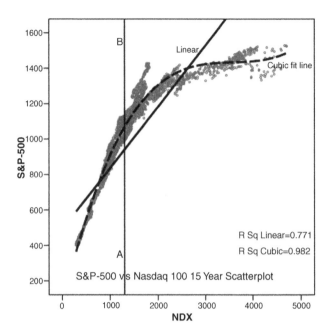

Figure 2.2 Scatterplot of the S&P 500 and the Nasdaq 100, for the last 15-year period. The relationship is not linear, as the best fit line is curvilinear.

The first five from 1992 to 1999 (marked A, B, C, D and E) feature alternate positive and negative correlations and the last one (marked F in Fig. 2.5) a distinct positive correlation for the period from 1999 to 2007. The positive correlation periods can be allocated to area A in Fig. 2.3 and the negative correlated periods to area B.

Area C consists of smaller periods with zero or near zero correlation enclosed inside the longer periods.

In view of the above, it is evident that neither Pearson's nor Spearman's correlation coefficients are appropriate for analyzing nonlinear relationships. In these cases, mathematicians use the so-called coefficient of nonlinear correlation or Eta (denoted by the Greek letter η) which is computed by splitting one of the variables into groups of equal width according to their rank. Eta is then calculated by dividing the group by the total variance. Eta can be used to measure the degree of linearity of a relationship, as the extent to which Eta is greater than r is an estimate of the extent to which the data relationship is nonlinear. Unfortunately, Eta is not particularly useful for analyzing financial markets because, in the case of time series, the groups should be categorized according to time and not rank.

In cases of minor deviations from linearity (for example the relation between the FTSE and the S&P 500), transforming raw prices into percentage yields usually enhances the linear relationship between two variables, resulting in a more reliable correlation and regression analysis.

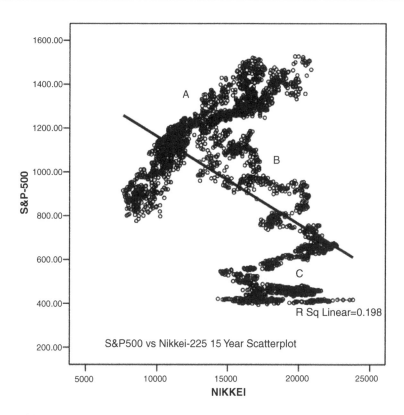

Figure 2.3 Scatterplot of the S&P 500 and the Nikkei, for the last 15-year period. The relationship is not linear, as the points deviate significantly from the best fit line.

Fortunately there are methods more appropriate for analyzing the nonlinear nature of the financial markets: artificial neural networks and kernel regression. Neural networks are nonparametric models which are inherently nonlinear in their computational elements and provide potentially the greatest opportunity for exploiting time series with low correlation dimension estimates by analyzing complex nonlinear relationships without making prior assumptions about the data distribution. More information on neural networks is provided in Chapters 10 and 14.

2.2.2 Normality

A correlation coefficient derived using Pearson's formula makes the implicit assumption that the two variables are jointly normally distributed. In the case of most financial series this assumption is not justified, and a nonparametric measure such as the Spearman rank correlation coefficient might be more appropriate.

Figure 2.4 Weekly chart of the S&P 500 (thick line) with the Nasdaq 100 superimposed (thin black line) from 1990 to 2007. The relative strength between the S&P 500 and the NDX is plotted in the top window.

Consider the histogram of 15-year S&P daily changes in Fig. 2.6. Overlaying the normal (Gaussian) distribution we notice that these are not fully described by the Gaussian model. There are two problems with approximating S&P returns with the normal distribution model. The first is that the vast majority of the returns tend to be located near the center of the distribution and the second – and most important – is that the actual distribution has fatter and longer tails. This means that the probability of a larger movement in the index is much higher than that predicted by the normal distribution. The Gaussian model predicted a virtually nil (0.000027) probability of a one day 4 % decline in the index whereas such events occurred six times during the period from 1 January 1992 to 31 December 2006. This is more obvious in the normal plot in Fig. 2.8 where it can be seen that for daily changes greater than 2 % or less than −2 % the distribution deviates significantly from normality. The volatility and hence the deviation from the normal curve has been exacerbated since the "uptick rule" (a regulation that prohibited short selling following downticks) was abolished by the SEC on 6 July 2007. The effect of the abolition of the uptick rule can be seen

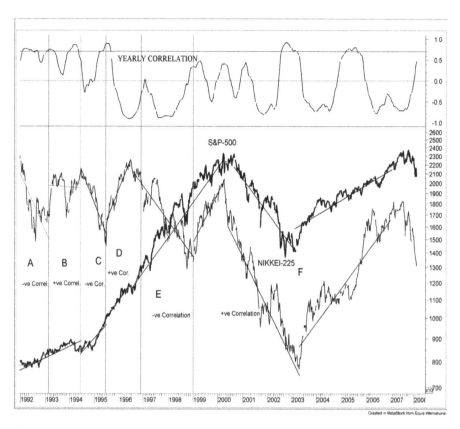

Figure 2.5 Weekly composite chart of the S&P 500 (thick line) with Japan's Nikkei superimposed (thin black line) from 1990 to 2007. The 52-week Pearson's correlation strength between the S&P 500 and the Nikkei is plotted in the top window.

graphically in Fig. 2.9 which has "fatter" tails (that is, higher frequency at extreme values) than the distribution in Fig. 2.6. In addition, the standard deviation of daily changes, which was only 1.0 before the uptick was abolished, increased by more than 30 % to 1.3 after the uptick rule was eliminated. It is not certain, however, that the increased volatility can be wholly contributed to the repeal of the uptick rule as it coincided with the sub prime mortgage financial upheaval and the collapse of Bear Stearns. At the time of writing, the situation with the financials has not yet normalized but it would be interesting to see the net effect of this rule on the distribution of daily changes of the S&P 500 as soon as enough data are available for such a study.

In any case, if we have to use statistical metrics that assume normality, it is preferable to use daily or weekly changes instead of raw index values. A comparison of the distribution of raw S&P values in Fig. 2.7 with that of daily returns in Fig. 2.6 will make this more obvious. In fact, Fig. 2.7 bears no resemblance to a normal distribution at all.

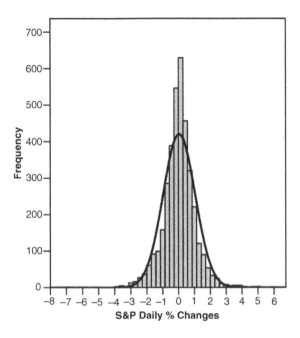

Figure 2.6   Distribution of S&P 500 daily % returns for the 15-year period from 1992–2006.

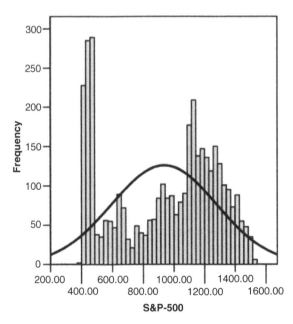

Figure 2.7   Distribution of S&P 500 daily prices for the 15-year period from 1992–2006.

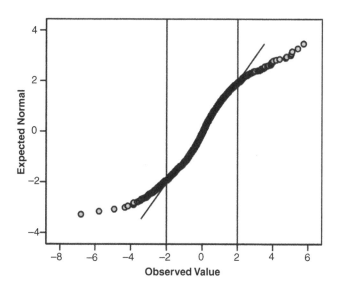

Figure 2.8 Normality plot of the S&P 500 15-year daily % returns.

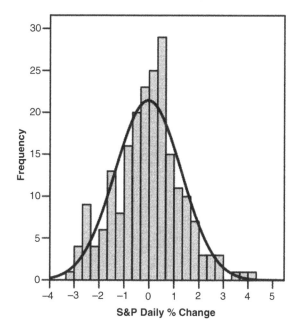

Figure 2.9 Distribution of S&P 500 daily % returns since the elimination of the uptick rule (from 9 July 2007 until 5 May 2008). Notice the unusually high frequency of more than −2.5 % daily declines during the relatively short period of 210 trading days. The standard deviation also increased by more than 30 % and the kurtosis (which is the variance due to infrequent extreme deviations) increased by more than 700 % from 0.43 to 3.77.

2.3   OUTLIERS

Because of the way in which the regression line is determined (especially the fact that it is based on minimizing the sum of the *squares* of distances of data points from the line and not the sum of simple distances) outliers have a significant influence on the slope of the regression line and, consequently, on the value of the correlation coefficient. This is more of a problem when working with financial series with small samples (less than a year's data).

A single outlier is capable of changing the slope of the regression line considerably and, consequently, the value of the correlation, as demonstrated in the following example in Fig. 2.10 of the six month scatterplot of the Amex oil index (XOI) vs. the Nymex oil futures daily changes. By removing just one outlier (on the far right of the graph), the correlation improved from 0.523 to 0.568 and the coefficient of determination (r^2) from 0.283 to 0.323.

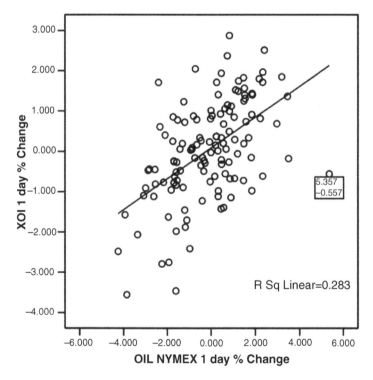

Figure 2.10   Six month scatterplot of the Amex oil index (XOI) vs. Nymex oil futures. By removing just one outlier (enclosed in the square on the far right of the graph), the correlation improved from 0.523 to 0.568.

2.4   HOMOSCEDASTICITY

In calculating Pearson's correlation coefficient or the regression coefficients, the variance is assumed to be the same at any point along the linear relationship. Otherwise the correlation coefficient is a misleading average of points of higher and lower correlation. A set of random variables having the same variance is called homoscedastic.

Serious violations in homoscedasticity (assuming a distribution of data is homoscedastic when in actuality it is heteroscedastic) result in underemphasizing the Pearson coefficient. Heteroscedasticity does not invalidate the analysis and can be usually rectified by transforming the price data to yields or logarithms. An example of heteroscedasticity is depicted in Fig. 2.11 of the scatterplot of the S&P vs. Canada's TSX index, where the variance is greater for larger values of the indices at the top right of the graph.

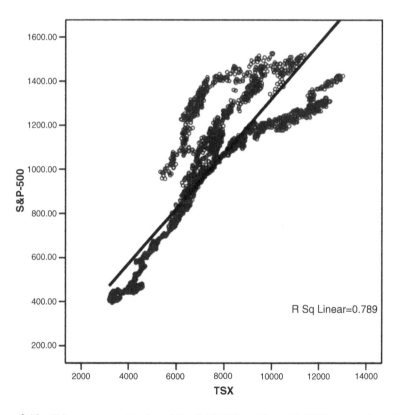

Figure 2.11   Fifteen year scatterplot of the S&P 500 vs. Canada's TSX composite index. The plot shows a violation of the assumption of homoscedasticity. For lower values on the TSX-axis, the points are all very near the regression line, while for higher values the variability around the regression line increases dramatically.

3
Regression

Man loves company, even if only that of a small burning candle.
–Georg Christoph Lichtenberg

Regression involves the use of the concept of correlation in predicting future values of one security (dependent variable), in terms of another (independent or predictor variable). For example, if there is high correlation between the S&P 500 and the Euro Stoxx 50 index we can use the linear regression equation to predict future values of the S&P by extending the least squares or linear regression line into the future.

The mere fact that we use our knowledge of the relationship between the two indices to predict values of the S&P 500 from the Euro Stoxx doesn't imply that changes in the Euro Stoxx cause changes in the S&P. These could be caused by a number of economic or geopolitical reasons which affect both indices.

3.1 THE REGRESSION EQUATION

The general form of a simple linear regression is:

$$y = bx + a \qquad (3.1)$$

where a (regression constant) is the intercept and b (regression coefficient) is the slope of the line, y is the dependent variable and x is the independent variable. Estimates for the values of a and b can be derived by the method of ordinary least squares. The method is called "least squares" because estimates of a and b minimize the sum of squared error estimates for the given data set. The regression constant a and the coefficient b are calculated using the following formulae:

$$b = \frac{\sum (x_i - \bar{x})(y_i - \bar{y})}{\sum (x_i - \bar{x})^2} = \frac{n \sum xy - \sum x \sum y}{n \sum x^2 - \left(\sum x\right)^2} \quad (3.2)$$

$$a = \frac{\sum y - b \sum x}{n} = \bar{y} - b\bar{x} \quad (3.3)$$

where $\bar{x}$ is the mean of the x values, and $\bar{y}$ is the mean of the y values.

The formula for the regression coefficient b can be alternatively expressed in terms of Pearson's correlation coefficient r:

$$b = r \frac{s_y}{s_x} \quad (3.4)$$

where s_x is the standard deviation of the predictor variable x and s_y is the standard deviation of the dependent variable y.

Table 3.1 shows an Excel sheet of one day changes between gold and the dollar index, illustrating the calculation of the regression coefficient and the constant.

Thus the regression equation to predict the dollar index in terms of gold is Y (dollar) $= -0.314 * X$ (gold) $+ 0.083$

In the following example only 15 data sets were used but in practice more than two years' data need to be taken into account for a reliable prediction.

3.2   MULTIPLE REGRESSION

The concept of linear regression with a single predictor variable can be extended for more than one variable combined into the following equation:

$$y = b_1 x_1 + b_1 x_1 + \ldots + b_k x_k + a \quad (3.5)$$

In single regression we fitted a straight line to the scatterplot of points in a two dimensional graph. Extending this concept, the geometry of multiple regression (where two or more predictor variables are involved), would involve fitting a plane in multi-dimensional space.

However, since we live in a three-dimensional world, we cannot visualize the geometry when more than two independent variables are involved. We can extend, however, the same method only mathematically.

The practical problem in multiple linear regression is to select an effective set of predictor variables which will maximize the coefficient of determination, r squared, which is the proportion of variance in the dependent variable that can be explained by the variance of the predictor variables. Therefore, we want to include predictor variables that are highly correlated with the dependent variable but have low correlations among themselves.

Table 3.1 Example of calculating the regression coefficient b and the intercept a using Excel. The formula for calculating the other statistical metrics can be found in Table 2.2 (Chapter 2). The Greek letter μ depicts the mean for both the X and Y variables. The variables X and Y are the one day percentage change of gold (spot) and the dollar index respectively from 8 December 2006 to 29 December 2006.

A	B	C	D	E	F	G	H	
								1
Date	X	Y	$X - \mu$	$(X - \mu)^2$	$X - \mu$	$(Y - \mu)^2$	$(X - \mu)(Y - \mu)$	2
12/8/06	-1.344	0.640	-1.386	1.921	0.570	0.325	-0.790	3
12/11/06	0.929	-0.132	0.887	0.787	-0.202	0.041	-0.179	4
12/12/06	-0.008	-0.289	-0.050	0.003	-0.359	0.129	0.018	5
12/13/06	-0.325	0.470	-0.367	0.135	0.400	0.160	-0.147	6
12/14/06	-0.430	0.444	-0.472	0.223	0.374	0.140	-0.176	7
12/15/06	-1.664	0.406	-1.706	2.910	0.336	0.113	-0.573	8
12/18/06	0.163	-0.036	0.121	0.015	-0.106	0.011	-0.013	9
12/19/06	1.088	-0.667	1.046	1.094	-0.737	0.543	-0.771	10
12/20/06	-0.402	0.096	-0.444	0.197	0.026	0.001	-0.011	11
12/21/06	-0.250	0.072	-0.292	0.085	0.002	0.000	-0.001	12
12/22/06	0.332	0.263	0.290	0.084	0.193	0.037	0.056	13
12/26/06	0.613	0.298	0.571	0.326	0.228	0.052	0.130	14
12/27/06	0.401	-0.107	0.359	0.129	-0.177	0.031	-0.064	15
12/28/06	1.133	-0.179	1.091	1.190	-0.249	0.062	-0.272	16
12/29/06	0.394	-0.227	0.352	0.124	-0.297	0.088	-0.105	17
Σ	0.630	1.052		9.223		1.733	-2.897	18
n	15	15		Covariance σ_{xy} =			-0.207	19
mean μ	0.042	0.070		Pearson's Correlation **r**			-0.725	20
σ	0.812	0.352		Regression Coef. b (formula 3.2)			-0.314	21
				Regression Coef. b (formula 3.4)			-0.314	22
				Regression Constant a =			0.083	23
				Regression Constant a =			0.083	24

Formula for Column H

Row	
21	H18/E18
22	H20*C21/B21
23	(C18-H21*B18)/B19
24	C20-H22*B20

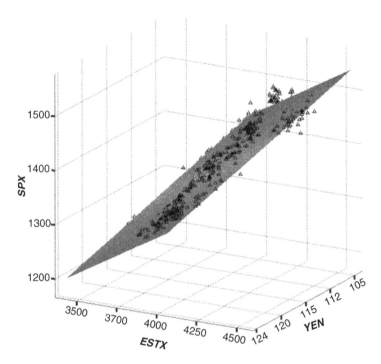

Figure 3.1 Three-dimensional scatterplot visualizing the relationship between the S&P 500 (on the Y-axis) vs. the Euro Stoxx 50 (on the X-axis) and the yen (on the Z-axis) for the 2-year period from 1 January 2006 to 31 December 2007. The more points fall inside the regression plane the better the predictive power of the regression model.

As a rule of thumb, intercorrelation among the independents above 0.80 signals a possible problem and may cause the system to become unstable. The statistically preferred method of assessing multicollinearity is to calculate the tolerance coefficient for each independent variable.

Tolerance is $1 - r^2$ (one minus the coefficient of determination) for the regression of each independent variable on all the other independents, ignoring the dependent. There will be as many tolerance coefficients as there are independents. The higher the intercorrelation of the independents, the more the tolerance will approach zero. As a rule of thumb, if tolerance is less than 0.20, a problem with multicollinearity is indicated.

High multicollinearity can be ignored when two or more independents are components of an index, and high intercorrelation among them is intentional and desirable. These are usually combined in an index prior to running regression, but when this is not practically possible they can be entered individually. For example, if data for an obscure index are not readily available some of the component stocks can be used instead of the index itself.

Table 3.2 Correlation matrix of weekly % yields of major international indices, the CBOE volatility index (VIX,) the Utility Index (UTY) and the 10-year Treasury yield (TNX) with the S&P 500 for the 5-year period from 1 January 2001 to 31 December 2006.

	S&P 500	ESTX	DAX	CAC 40	FTSE	Nikkei	VIX	UTY	TNX
S&P 500	1	0.81	0.80	0.80	0.74	0.42	−0.72	0.60	0.39
ESTX	0.81	1	0.94	0.97	0.88	0.49	−0.57	0.43	0.45
DAX	0.80	0.94	1	0.92	0.82	0.51	−0.56	0.39	0.49
CAC 40	0.80	0.97	0.92	1	0.89	0.49	−0.56	0.43	0.46
FTSE	0.74	0.88	0.82	0.89	1	0.45	−0.54	0.40	0.42
Nikkei	0.42	0.49	0.51	0.49	0.45	1	−0.36	0.21	0.29
VIX	−0.72	−0.57	−0.56	−0.56	−0.54	−0.36	1	−0.43	−0.25
UTY	0.60	0.43	0.39	0.43	0.40	0.21	−0.43	1	0.04
TNX	0.39	0.45	0.49	0.46	0.42	0.29	−0.25	0.04	1

Perhaps this is better understood with an example. Let's say that we want to design an intermarket system to trade the S&P 500. The first step is to calculate the correlation between the S&P 500 with major international equity, commodity and financial indices.

Because of normality and linearity problems associated with raw index prices, these are converted to weekly percentage yields and the correlation matrix is calculated (depicted in Table 3.2). The next step is to add to the regression equation the predictor variables one at a time and calculate the coefficient of determination (r squared) and the tolerance for each variable. As you can see in Table 3.3, including more than three variables will only improve r squared marginally or not at all and the tolerance

Table 3.3 The coefficient of determination (r^2), the r^2 change and the tolerance are depicted for each model. The first model includes only the Euro Stoxx, the second includes the Euro Stoxx and the VIX and one more index is added for each subsequent model.

Model	r^2	r^2 change	Tolerance							
			ESTX	VIX	UTY	TNX	DAX	FTSE	CAC 40	Nikkei
1	0.65	0.65	1.00							
2	0.75	0.10	0.67	0.67						
3	**0.79**	**0.05**	**0.63**	**0.63**	**0.77**					
4	0.80	0.01	0.52	0.63	0.74	0.77				
5	0.81	0.01	0.12	0.62	0.74	0.74	0.12			
6	0.81	0.00	0.08	0.62	0.74	0.73	0.12	0.21		
7	0.81	0.00	0.05	0.62	0.73	0.73	0.11	0.19	0.05	
8	0.81	0.00	0.05	0.60	0.73	0.73	0.11	0.19	0.05	0.72

drops below 0.2 for a number of cross correlated variables. Thus the first step is to exclude the DAX, FTSE and CAC 40 since they are highly correlated with the ESTX (Euro Stoxx). The Nikkei is then dropped from the analysis as it doesn't improve the r squared coefficient at all. The remaining variables are the ESTX, VIX and UTY (model 3) and the regression equation becomes:

$$SP = 0.366^*ESTX - 0.067^*VIX + 0.206^*UTY + 0.045 \qquad (3.6)$$

where SP, ESTX, VIX, TNX and UTY are weekly percentage changes of the corresponding indices.

Substituting the values for ESTX, VIX and UTY for 11/7/06 in (3.6):

$$SP = 0.366^*1.7 - 0.067^*(-0.09) + 0.206^*(-1.6) + 0.045 = 0.343\,\% \text{ vs } 0.36\,\%$$

the actual S&P 500 weekly change for the specific week.

3.3   ASSUMPTIONS

The correlation assumptions discussed in Chapter 2 are also valid for regression, since according to (3.4) regression is directly proportional to correlation.

The most important assumption is that of linearity. Checking that the linearity assumption is met is an essential task before using a regression model, as substantial violation of linearity means regression results may be more or less unusable.

Simple inspection of scatterplots is a common, if non-statistical, method of determining if nonlinearity exists in a relationship. An alternative is to fit a preliminary linear regression and to use the appropriate diagnostic plots to detect departures from linearity. Transforming one of the variables (for example by taking differences or logs) can sometimes help linearize a nonlinear relationship between two financial series.

Normality is also a problem when considering raw stock or index prices but it is less of a problem when taking log differences or percentage yields. The problem of the longer tails (discussed in Chapter 2) can be partially overcome by removing some of the most extreme outliers.

Normality can be visually assessed by looking at a histogram of frequencies. Alternatively you can use a formal normality test such as the Shapiro-Wilks W test or the Kolmogorov-Smirnov D test.

3.4   NONPARAMETRIC REGRESSION

Nonparametric regression relaxes the usual assumption of linearity and makes no assumptions about the population distribution.

A more accurate estimate of the prediction is usually obtained by using nonparametric regression in cases of severe violations of linearity at the expense of much greater computation and a more difficult-to-understand result.

Two common methods of nonparametric regression are kernel regression and smoothing splines. The smoothing splines method minimizes the sum of squared residuals, adding a term which penalizes the roughness of the fit. The kernel regression algorithm falls into a class of algorithms called "SVMs" or "Support Vector Machines". SVM-based techniques typically use a kernel function to find an optimal separating hyperplane so as to separate two classes of patterns with maximal margin. SVM models are closely related to neural network models.

In recent years, SVMs have received considerable attention because of their superior performance in forecasting high noise and non-stationary financial time series. A major advantage of SVMs over other nonparametric methods is that they can have good performance even in problems with a large number of inputs. However, unlike other nonparametric methods the major difficulty of the SVM approach lies in the selection of its kernel, as choosing different kernel functions will produce different SVMs.

4
International Indices and Commodities

To conquer fear is the beginning of wisdom.

–Bertrand Russell

Before proceeding with intermarket correlation, and for the benefit of US readers, I thought it might be useful to say a few words about the international indices used in the next chapters. I presume that readers who have bought this book are familiar with the Standard & Poor 500 and the Nasdaq so I will start with European stock indices.

4.1 THE DAX

The leading index of the Deutsche Börse, the DAX (symbol: GDAXI) comprises of the 30 largest and most actively traded German equities (blue chips). The criteria for weighting the stocks in the index are trading volume and market capitalization. The DAX is a performance index, which means that all income from dividends and bonus distributions is reinvested into the index.

In addition to the DAX, the Deutsche Börse calculates a number of other indices, the most important being:

- The MDAX, which consists of the 50 largest companies from the classic sector of the Frankfurt Stock Exchange, that rank below the DAX components in terms of market capitalization and trading volume.
- The TecDAX, which consists of the 30 largest companies from the technology sector of the Frankfurt Stock Exchange, that rank below the DAX components in terms of market capitalization and trading volume. The TecDAX is equivalent to the US Nasdaq 100 index.

- The SDAX (small cap) which consists of 50 shares from the classic sector that rank directly below the MDAX in terms of market capitalization and trading volume. The SDAX is equivalent to the US Russell 2000 index.
- The HDAX, which is a large cap index and includes the 110 largest German equities from all sectors of the economy. This is equivalent to the US Russell 1000 index.
- The L-DAX (symbol: GDAXIL) is a late index, indicating the price development of DAX 30 index's performance after the Xetra electronic-trading system closes and is based on the floor trading at the Frankfurt Stock Exchange. The L-DAX index is computed daily between 17:30 and 20:00 CET and takes over after the DAX closes at 17:30 hours CET.
- The Dax Volatility Indices: VDAX (symbol: VDAX) and VDAX-NEW (symbol: V1X). These are the German equivalents to the CBOE volatility index (VIX) and track the implied volatility of the DAX index. In simpler terms the volatility indices measure in percentage terms whether the DAX options are selling above or below their fair values (as generally estimated by the Black-Scholes formula).

  The calculation of the new V1X index is based on DAX option contracts, which are quoted both "at the money" and "out of the money". Thus, VDAX-NEW has a broader volatility surface than the VDAX, which only takes into account options that are "at the money". The VDAX-NEW will replace VDAX in the medium-term.

Each September the Deutsche Börse decides whether changes are to be made to the composition of the index. More information about German indices can be found at the Deutsche Börse's website at http://boerse-frankfurt.com.

The DAX is a highly cyclical index that now (May 2008) faces a potential downturn as fully one-fifth of the index is made up of financial stocks, which are sinking to multi-year lows.

Futures and options on the DAX trade in the Eurex Exchange (symbol: FDAX) from 8:00–22:10 CET; they have a contract value of 25 euro per index point of the DAX index and are highly liquid with an average volume of more than 200 000 contracts per day.

4.2 THE CAC 40

The CAC 40 index (symbol: FCHI), which takes its name from the Paris Bourse's early automation system "Cotation Assistée en Continu" (Continuous Assisted Quotation), is the main benchmark of the Euronext Paris. Tracking a sample of blue chip stocks, its performance is closely correlated to that of the market as a whole. The index contains 40 stocks selected from among the top 100 by market capitalization and the most active stocks listed on Euronext Paris, and it is the underlying asset for options and futures contracts. The base value was 1000 on 31 December 1987 and historical data are not available prior to that date.

The CAC 40 is a market value-weighted index. Since 1 December 2003, this index is no longer weighted by the total market capitalization of the component stocks but by their free float adjusted market capitalization. This method of calculation, already used for other major indices around the world, ensures greater coherence between the real allocation of companies on the market and how it is expressed in the indices. It also limits the manifestation of volatility caused by too much of an imbalance between the weight of a stock in the index and the corresponding free float or available shares in the market. The index composition is reviewed quarterly by an independent Index Steering Committee and a capping factor is used to limit an individual stock weight to 15 %.

CAC 40 futures trade under the symbol FCE at the Euronext (MONEP) and they have a contract value of 10 euro per index point.

MONEP handles equity options, long- and short-term options, and index futures. Futures are liquid for trading purposes. An average of 120 000 contracts per day changed hands for the earliest expiring contract.

Listed below are the top 10 companies currently (as of 31 December 2007) contained within the index and below that a breakdown by industry group:

CAC 40 top 10 Constituents

1	Total – Oil & Gas	12.6 %
2	Sanofi-Aventis – Pharmaceuticals	6.7 %
3	BNP Paribas – Banking	6.2 %
4	Suez – Utilities	5.6 %
5	France Telecom – Telecommunications	4.7 %
6	Axa – Insurance	4.5 %
7	ArcelorMittal – Steel	4.5 %
8	Société Générale – Banking	4.3 %
9	Vivendi – Entertainment	3.6 %
10	Carrefour – Retail	3.6 %

CAC 40 breakdown by industry

1	Financials	19.2 %
2	Industrials	12.6 %
3	Consumer Goods	12.6 %
4	Oil & Gas	12.5 %
5	Utilities	11.9 %
6	Consumer Services	9.6 %
7	Health Care	7.6 %
8	Basic Materials	6.7 %
9	Telecommunications	5.2 %
10	Technology	2.1 %

Financials at 19.2 % are the most heavily weighted group followed by Industrials and Consumer Goods (which includes famous French luxury goods manufacturer Louis Vuitton, Moet Hennessy (LVMH) and beauty products producer L'Oréal).

4.3   THE FTSE

The FTSE 100 index (pronounced "footsie") is a share index of the 100 largest companies listed on the London Stock Exchange, weighted by market capitalization.

The index calculation began on 3 January 1984 and historical data are not available prior to that date. Component companies must meet a number of requirements set out by the FTSE Group, including having a full listing on the London Stock Exchange and meeting certain tests on free float and liquidity. The constituents of the FTSE 100 are reviewed and changed four times a year.

Trading lasts from 08:00–16:29 (when the closing auction starts), and closing values are taken at 16:35. The highest value of the index to date was 6950.6, set on 30 December 1999 at the height of the internet bubble.

Though it only contains the top 100 companies, the FTSE correlates closely with the All Share Index and, indeed, some broad US stock market indices.

Listed below are the top 10 companies currently (31 August 2007) contained within the index and below that a breakdown by industry group:

FTSE 100 top 10 constituents

1	BP Plc – Oil	7.1 %
2	HSBC Holdings – Banking	7.0 %
3	Vodafone Group – Telecommunications	5.6 %
4	Glaxosmithkline – Pharmaceuticals	4.9 %
5	Royal Dutch Shell Plc – A Shares – Oil	4.7 %
6	Royal Bank Of Scotland – Banking	3.6 %
7	Royal Dutch Shell Plc – B Shares – Oil	3.6 %
8	Barclays – Banking	2.7 %
9	Anglo American – Mining	2.6 %
10	Astrazeneca – Pharmaceuticals	2.5 %

FTSE 100 breakdown by industry

1	Financials	27.7 %
2	Oil & Gas	17.2 %
3	Consumer Services	10.5 %
4	Consumer Goods	10.3 %
5	Basic Materials	10.1 %
6	Heath Care	8.2 %
7	Telecommunications	7.6 %
8	Utilities	4.7 %
9	Industrials	3.5 %
10	Technology	0.2 %

With oil and gas stocks making up almost 17 % of the index at the moment, the FTSE is very sensitive to oil prices. However, financials at 27.6 % are the most heavily weighted group and the reason for the precipitous decline during the sub-prime crisis in 2007–2008, despite rising oil prices.

The FTSE 100 index reached a 5-year high on 13 July 2007; this was partly caused by the increase in the price of oil and the resultant increase in the share prices of BP and Shell.

The index is seen as a barometer of success of the British economy and is a leading share index in Europe. It is maintained by the FTSE Group, a now independent company which originated as a joint venture between the *Financial Times* and the London Stock Exchange (hence the abbreviation Financial Times Stock Exchange). According to the FTSE Group's website, the FTSE 100 companies represent about 81 % of the UK share market.

FTSE futures trade at the London International Futures & Options Exchange (LIFFE) from 8:00–21:00 GMT (9:00–22:00 CET) under the symbol Z.

4.4   THE DOW JONES STOXX 50 AND EURO STOXX 50

The Stoxx 50 (STXX50) tracks the performance of the 50 most important and most actively traded shares in the pan-European area, while the Euro Stoxx 50 (STOXX50E or ESTX50) tracks the 50 most important stocks in the Eurozone. The Euro Stoxx covers 50 stocks from 12 Eurozone countries: Austria, Belgium, Finland, France, Germany, Greece, Ireland, Italy, Luxembourg, the Netherlands, Portugal and Spain.

The criteria for including a company in the index are market capitalization and trading volume of the European companies. Both indices are market capitalization-weighted.

Futures for both are highly liquid and trade at the Eurex (DTB) from 8:00–22:10 CET under the symbols FSTX and FESX respectively.

The Dow Jones Euro Stoxx 50 (Price) was developed with a base value of 1000 as of 31 December 1991 and uses float shares.

4.5   THE NIKKEI

The Nikkei 225 (N225) is Japan's most widely watched index of stock market activity in the Tokyo Stock Exchange (TSE) and has been calculated continuously since 7 September 1950 by the *Nihon Keizai Shimbun* (Nikkei) newspaper. It is a price-weighted average (the unit is yen), and the components are reviewed once a year.

The Nikkei Stock Average is the average price of 225 stocks traded on the first section of the Tokyo Stock Exchange, but it is different from a simple average in that the divisor is adjusted to maintain continuity and reduce the effect of external factors not directly related to the market.

The Nikkei average hit its all-time high on 29 December 1989 when it reached an intra-day high of 38 957 before closing at 38 916. Thirteen years later, the Nikkei had plunged more than 80 % from its 1989 highs.

The Nikkei's devastating decline was triggered by a real estate crisis similar to the one experienced in the United States in 2007–08. At the height of the Japanese market in 1989, Japanese banks were lending money secured by real estate. Investors took the borrowed money and ploughed it into the stock market. A snowball effect began when the real estate market crashed, pressuring further property and stock prices.

The Nikkei finally made a bottom on 28 April 2003 at 7608.

On 12 August 2005 it broke out from a 20-month rectangle formation and on 26 February 2007 rose to a six-year high of 18 215.

Nikkei futures trade in Osaka (symbol: N225), in the Chicago Mercantile Exchange (CME) in US dollars (symbol: NKD), in yen (symbol: NIY) and in Singapore (symbol: SGXNK). The Osaka exchange has recently introduced the Nikkei 225 mini contract (symbol: N225M).

4.6 THE HANG SENG

The Hang Seng (HSI) is a barometer of the Hong Kong stock market and includes companies from Finance, Utilities, Properties and Commerce, and Industry sub-indexes. The index calculation began on 24 November 1969 and Hang Seng Index futures (symbol: HSI) were introduced by the Hong Kong Futures Exchange in 1986.

Only companies with a primary listing on the Main Board of the Stock Exchange of Hong Kong (SEHK) are eligible as constituents. Mainland enterprises that have an H-share listing in Hong Kong will be eligible for inclusion in the Hang Seng Index (HSI) only when the H-share company has 100 % of its ordinary share capital listed on the Hong Kong Stock Exchange.

Hang Seng futures trade in Hong Kong (symbol: HSI) from 9:45–12:30 (first trading session) and 14:30–16:30 Hong Kong time (second trading session). The multiplier is HK$50 per index point. Mini contracts are also available with a multiplier of HK$10 per index point.

4.7 TRADING HOURS, SYMBOLS AND VOLATILITY

In Table 4.1 you can find European and US trading hours of the major exchanges.

You can see that trading in some Asian markets is not very convenient for European traders as they open too late at night and close too early in the morning.

You can find current quotes and historical prices for most of the international indices in Yahoo Finance http://finance.yahoo.com which is free for 20-minute de-layed quotes. I thought it would be useful to include a list of symbols used by the most popular data providers or brokers for some international indices in Table 4.2

Table 4.1 Trading hours in local, US Eastern time (EST) and Central European time (CET) for major world exchanges. All the times shown are standard winter times. Please note that Japan and China do not currently observe the daylight saving time (DST) or summer time and consequently the CET and EST opening and closing time indicated should be moved forward by one hour. The transition to summer time starts on 25 March and ends on 28 October in Europe. In the United States the transition starts two weeks earlier, on 11 March and ends on 4 November.

Country	Exchange	Local Open	Local Close	ET Open	ET Close	CET Open	CET Close
USA	NYSE, Nasdaq	9:30	16:00	9:30	16:00	15:30	22:00
Canada	Toronto	9:30	16:00	9:30	16:00	15:30	22:00
Germany	XETRA	9:00	17:30	3:00	11:30	9:00	17:30
Germany	Frankfurt	9:00	20:00	3:00	14:00	9:00	20:00
France	Paris	9:00	17:30	3:00	11:30	9:00	17:30
Britain	LSE	7:00	15:30	2:00	10:30	8:00	16:30
Japan	Tokyo	9:00	15:00	19:00	1:00	1:00	7:00
Hong Kong	Hong Kong	10:00	16:00	21:00	3:00	3:00	9:00
Australia	ASX	10:00	16:00	18:00	0:00	0:00	6:00

as each one uses a different symbol for the same index. You will notice that US brokers are still of the old fashioned mentality that foreign markets are irrelevant to US investors and do not provide any data for non-US indices. Of course US markets do not exist in a vacuum and it would be very helpful for US investors to check how the international markets are doing before the US market opens for trading. International indices would be also useful for traders of international ETFs or ADRs that are trading in the US exchanges.

I thought it would be useful for international traders to include the most likely daily percentage changes for some of the major international indices and commodities in order to assess risk adjusted positions in each market accordingly (see Table 4.3). Each value in Table 4.3 indicates the daily change that was exceeded by the percentile in the top row. For example the S&P 500 was up by more than 1.57 % only 5 % of the time. Frequency distribution values are included instead of standard deviations because, as discussed in Chapter 2, none of the indices conform to the normality assumption.

An interesting comparison between actual observations and theoretical probabilities as predicted by the normal distribution is depicted in Table 4.4. It can be seen that there is an exponential shift from the middle to the tails of the distribution making predictions beyond the 0.02 level of significance totally unreliable.

Since 6 July 2007 the Securities and Exchange Commission (SEC) have abolished the "uptick rule", a regulation that prohibited short selling following downticks. This

Table 4.2 Symbols for the major world indices used by different data providers and brokers. They usually differ from provider to provider by a prefix or a suffix. Blank cells indicate that the index was not available at that broker or data provider.

Index name	Reuters	Yahoo Finance	TC200	CSI Data	E*Trade/ Schwab	Interactive Brokers
S&P 500	.SPX	^SPX	SP-500	SPX-I	$SPX	SPX
S&P 100	.OEX	^OEX	OEX	OEX-I	$OEX	OEX
Dow Jones Industrials	.DJI	^DJI	DJ-30	DJIA-I	$DJI	INDU
Dow Jones Transports	.DJT	^DJT	DJ-20	DJAT-T	$DJT	TRAN
Nasdaq 100	.NDX	^NDX	NDX–X	NDX-I	$NDX	NDX
Nasdaq Composite	.IXIC	^IXIC	COMPQX	COMP-I	$COMPX	COMP
Russell 2000	.RUT	^RUT	RUT-X	RUT-I	$RUT	RUT
NYSE Composite	.NYA	^NYA	NYSE	NYA-I	$NYA	NYA
Canada TSX	.GSPTSE	^GSPTSE	TSX–X	TCMP-I	–	TSX
DAX	.GDAXI	^GDAXI	FDAC-X	GDAX-F	–	DAX
CAC 40	.FCHI	^FCHI	PCAC-X	FCHI-I	–	CAC40
DJ Euro Stoxx 50	.STOXX50E	^STOXX50E	–		–	ESTX50
DJ Stoxx 50	.STOXX50	^STOXX50	–		–	STX
FTSE 100	.FTSE	^FTSE	FTSE-X	FTSE-F	–	Z
Greece General	.ATG	–	–	ATG-F	–	–
Nikkei 225	.N225	^N225	NIKI-X	N225-F	–	N225
Hang Seng	.HSI	^HSI	HKHS-X	HSI-F	–	HSI
Korea KOSPI	.KS11	^KS11	–	KS11-F	–	–
Australia All Ordinaries	.AORD	^AORD	–	AORD-F	–	–
Brazil BOVESPA	.BVSP	^BVSP	–	BVSP-F	–	–
Mexico IPC	.MXX	^MXX	–	MXX-F	–	–
10 Yr Treasury Yield	.TNX	^TNX	TNX–X	TNX-I	$TNX	TNX
Amex Oil Index	.XOI	^XOI	XOI	XOI-I	$XOI	XOI
CRB Index	.CRB	–	CRY0	@CR	–	–
Euro	RD-EUR=	EURUSD=X	–	–	–	EUR.USD
Dollar Index	.DXY	NA	DXY0	–	–	–
Gold	XAU=	XAUUSD=X	XGLD	MAU0	–	–
Volatility Index	.VIX	^VIX	VIX–X	VIX-I	$VIX	VIX
Crude Oil	–	NA	XOIL	–	–	CL
Silver	XAG=	XAGUSD=X	XSLV	–	–	–
PHLX Gold/Silver	.XAU	^XAU	XAU	XAU-I	$XAU	XAU

Table 4.3 Frequency distribution of daily yields of major stock market indices and commodities from 1992 to 2006. The daily changes are divided by percentiles according to values below which certain percentages of cases fall. So, for example, the 5 % percentile of the S&P 500 daily change is −1.59 % which means that the S&P 500 declined by −1.59 % or less only 5 % of the time.

Daily Change %	Percentiles						
	5	10	25	50	25	10	5
S&P	−1.59	−1.08	−0.46	0.04	0.55	1.13	1.57
DJ-30	−1.52	−1.06	−0.47	0.05	0.57	1.13	1.56
Russell 2000	−1.84	−1.33	−0.50	0.11	0.60	1.25	1.78
NDX	−3.10	−2.18	−0.90	0.12	1.03	2.17	3.06
TSX	−1.34	−0.92	−0.39	0.06	0.52	0.99	1.32
Euro Stoxx	−2.40	−1.68	−0.76	0.05	0.82	1.69	2.36
DAX	−2.26	−1.58	−0.65	0.08	0.78	1.58	2.22
CAC	−2.12	−1.47	−0.68	0.02	0.77	1.52	2.10
FTSE	−1.60	−1.15	−0.51	0.02	0.57	1.15	1.62
ATG	−2.35	−1.59	−0.72	0.02	0.80	1.80	2.55
Nikkei	−2.34	−1.72	−0.80	0.00	0.79	1.69	2.27
Hang Seng	−2.43	−1.66	−0.70	0.04	0.83	1.79	2.47
10 Yr Tr Note Yield	−1.75	−1.34	−0.68	0.00	0.60	1.35	1.93
XOI	−1.99	−1.35	−0.63	0.05	0.76	1.50	2.01
OIL	−3.48	−2.50	−1.15	0.06	1.28	2.56	3.45
Canada Venture	−1.50	−1.02	−0.39	0.14	0.68	1.18	1.58
XAU	−3.47	−2.66	−1.41	−0.07	1.40	2.90	3.94
Silver	−2.46	−1.66	−0.71	0.00	0.82	1.81	2.48
Gold	−1.34	−0.89	−0.38	0.00	0.43	0.99	1.38
CRB	−1.06	−0.75	−0.37	0.02	0.39	0.76	1.09
Dollar Index	−0.86	−0.65	−0.31	0.01	0.31	0.64	0.86
Euro	−1.02	−0.74	−0.37	0.00	0.37	0.79	1.07
Yen	−1.07	−0.77	−0.37	0.00	0.39	0.80	1.06
Corn	−2.23	−1.76	−0.90	0.00	0.84	1.84	2.58
Wheat	−2.49	−1.95	−1.13	−0.07	1.09	2.22	2.85

rule was created after the 1929 stock market crash in order to prevent short-sellers from adding to the downward momentum of a sharp decline by requiring every short sale to be executed on a higher price than a previous trade. This rule has been in effect for 78 years. But can the recent volatility in the markets be blamed entirely on the rescinding of the uptick rule?

At the time of writing, not enough data were available for such a study as the recent volatility has been exaggerated by the combination of the housing and related financial upheavals. It would be interesting to see the effect that this rule had on the probabilities of daily changes of the S&P 500 (in Table 4.4).

Table 4.4 Probabilities of S&P daily declines as predicted by the normal distribution vs. frequency distribution of observed actual values on 15-year data from 1992 to 2006.

S&P 500 daily % change	Actual probability	Normal probability
−5.10 %	0.1 %	0.000 %
−3.08 %	0.5 %	0.091 %
−2.60 %	1.0 %	0.418 %
−2.22 %	2.0 %	1.200 %
−1.90 %	3.0 %	2.636 %
−1.75 %	4.0 %	3.695 %
−1.59 %	5.0 %	5.219 %
−1.08 %	10.0 %	13.253 %
−0.46 %	25.0 %	30.983 %
0.04 %	50.0 %	50.225 %

4.8 THE DOLLAR INDEX

Just as the S&P 500 provides a general indication of the value of the US stock market, the US dollar index (symbol: DXY) provides a general indication of the international value of the US dollar and it is a measure of the value of the dollar relative to its most significant trading partners. Similar in many respects to the Federal Reserve Board's trade-weighted index, the dollar index does this by averaging the exchange rates between the US dollar and six major world currencies.

The dollar index is calculated by taking the geometric weighted average of the dollar's value against a basket of six major world currencies and is calculated by taking the product of each currency spot rate raised to the corresponding weight according to the following formula:

$$\text{USDXY} = 50.14348112 \times \text{EURO}^{-0.576} \times \text{YEN}^{-0.136} \times \text{GBP}^{-0.119}$$
$$\times \text{CAD}^{-0.091} \times \text{SEK}^{-0.042} \times \text{CHF}^{-0.036} \quad (4.1)$$

In the formula above all currencies are expressed in USD per unit of the foreign currency.

To express the yen, Canadian dollar, Swedish krona and Swiss franc in their more familiar format in yen per US dollar, CAD per US dollar, SEK per US dollar and CHF per US dollar you only need to change the sign of the weight exponent. The above formula (4.1) then becomes:

$$\text{USDXY} = 50.14348112 \times \text{EURO}^{-0.576} \times \text{USDJPY}^{0.136} \times \text{GBP}^{-0.119}$$
$$\times \text{USDCAD}^{0.091} \times \text{USDSEK}^{0.042} \times \text{USDCHF}^{0.036} \quad (4.2)$$

Table 4.5 Contracts to trade based on either equal profit/loss or historical volatility. The fourth and fifth columns are daily % changes exceeded only 10 % of the time during a 5-year observation period. The sixth column is the Wilder's average daily true range, the seventh and eighth columns are the suggested number of contracts to trade for equal profit/loss based on the expected historical 10th percentile of daily changes or based on the historical volatility respectively. The last column is the 50-day average volume as of April 2007.

Name	Symbol	Multiplier	Max % daily change 10th percentile		ATR	Contracts to trade		Average volume
						For equal profit/loss	Volat. adjusted	
S&P 500	SPX	250	−1.1	1.1	12.2	1	1	49 000
S&P 500 mini	ES	50	−1.2	1.1	12.4	5	5	929 000
DJ-30	DD	25	−1.1	1.1	104	1	1	7323
DJ-30 mini	YM	5	−1.1	1.1	106	6	6	91 890
Nasdaq 100	NDX	100	−1.9	1.8	25.2	1	1	7600
Nasdaq 100 mini	NQ	20	−1.9	1.8	25.3	6	6	314 000
Russell 2000 mini	ER2	100	−1.6	1.6	11.1	3	2	16 000
Nikkei	NKD	5	−1.6	1.7	204	3	2	7500
Nikkei	JNI	1000	−1.6	1.7	214	2	2	83 000
DAX	FDAX	25	−1.7	1.7	71.5	1	1	152 635
CAC 40	FCE	10	−1.5	1.4	59.3	4	3	146 530
Euro Stoxx 50	FESX	10	−1.6	1.5	46.0	5	4	863 522
Euro	6E	125 000	−0.7	0.8	0.01	3	3	171 000
Gold	ZG	100	−1.2	1.3	7.2	5	2	44 000
Gold mini	YG	33.2	−1.2	1.3	7.2	14	6	5200
10 Year Note	ZN	1000	−0.5	0.5	0.5	8	8	919 000
10 Year Bund	GBL	1000	−0.4	0.4	0.5	7	6	1 115 000
Crude Oil	CL	1000	−2.6	2.8	1.7	2	2	430 000
Crude Oil mini	QM	500	−2.6	2.8	1.8	4	4	30 000
Wheat	ZW	5000	−2.1	2.3	0.1	7	4	57 000
Corn	ZC	5000	−1.8	1.9	0.1	10	5	204 000

Table 4.6 Suggested number of shares to trade based on either equal profit/loss or historical volatility. The number of shares to trade for equal profit/loss is based on the expected historical 10th percentile of daily changes during the last 5-year period (at the time of writing) and the volatility adjusted quantity is based on the yearly historical volatility.

Symbol	Underlying Index/Commodity	Shares to trade		Average volume
		For equal profit/loss	Volatility adjusted	
SPY	S&P 500	500	500	200 000 000
DIA	DJ-30	600	600	17 000 000
QQQQ	Nasdaq-100	1000	1000	170 000 000
IWM	Russell 2000	600	500	100 000 000
EWJ	Nikkei 225	3000	2500	24 000 000
EWG	DAX	1500	1500	2 200 000
EWQ	CAC 40	1500	1300	500 000
EZU	EURO STOXX 50	500	400	640 000
FXE	Euro	800	700	200 000
GLD	GOLD	900	400	10 000 000
IEF	7–10 Year Treasury Bond	2000	2000	360 000
USO	CRUDE OIL	600	600	13 000 000
DBA	Agricultural Commodities	1500	800	1 500 000

The constant, currently equal to 50.14348112, was set back at the initiation of the index in order to make the index equal to 100.00 at that time.

An example of calculating the dollar index on 8 February 2008 using formula (4.1) is depicted in Table 4.7. The FX rates (from Bloomberg) are raised to the negative of their weight, and the product, when multiplied by the index constant of 50.14348112, yields the dollar index level of 76.67 on that date.

The index was calibrated to par or 100 in March 1973 when the world's major trading nations abandoned the 25-year-old Bretton Woods agreement to fix their currency rates. Thus a quote of 84 means the dollar's value has declined 16 % since the base period.

The dollar index component currencies and their weightings are: Euro (57.6 %); yen (13.6 %); British pound (11.9 %); Canadian dollar (9.1 %), Swedish krona (4.2 %); and Swiss franc (3.6 %). These are depicted in the pie chart in Fig. 4.1 and in Table 4.7.

Intraday values for the dollar index are generally not available from data providers. However, a rough indication of the dollar index intraday change can be estimated by the EUR/USD FX rate because, as you can see from Table 4.8, three of the dollar index components – the British pound, the Swedish krona and the Swiss franc – are highly correlated with the euro.

Table 4.7   Shows the FX rates of the dollar index constituent currencies on 8 February 2008 (from Bloomberg). The weights applied to the FX rates are shown in the third column, and the FX rate raised to (the negative of) that weight in the last column. This product, when multiplied by the constant of 50.14348112, yields the dollar index of 76.67 on 8 February 2008. All FX rates are expressed in USD per unit of the foreign currency.

Currency	FX rate	Weight	(FX rate) $^{-\text{Weight}}$
Euro	1.4507	0.576	0.8071073384
Yen	0.0093	0.136	1.8892364628
Sterling	1.9460	0.119	0.9238298752
Canadian dollar	1.0008	0.091	0.9999272318
Swedish kroner	0.1540	0.042	1.0817430901
Swiss franc	0.9065	0.036	1.0035401646
Constant			50.14348112
Product (index level)			76.67

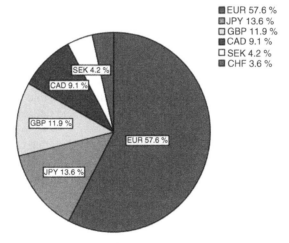

Figure 4.1   The dollar index.

Table 4.8   2- and 5-year nonparametric correlation between the euro and the rest of the dollar index component currencies. Notice the high correlation between the euro and the British pound, Swedish krona and Swiss franc. All rates are expressed in USD per currency.

	Correlations with the euro				
Years	JPY	GBP	CAD	SEK	CHF
2	0.039	0.974	0.659	0.985	0.915
5	−0.077	0.957	0.638	0.983	0.953

There's no doubt that the dollar index plays a dominant role in the financial markets and the dollar's daily changes have major effects on many other asset classes like commodities, precious metals, the bond and stock markets.

From the end of World War II until the early 1970s, the dollar was tied to other major currencies by the Bretton Woods fixed exchange rate agreement. After it became free-floating, the dollar went through a roller-coaster ride. It rose to an all-time high of 160 in 1985 but then retreated to almost where it started. At the beginning of 2002 it rose again to 120, making a 16-year high and more recently, in 2008, mainly because of the huge US trade deficit, it plummeted to an all-time low of 70.

The main fundamental factors affecting the dollar index are:

- the US trade deficit;
- US, Japanese, Canadian and European interest rates and bond yields;
- CPI inflation;
- quarterly gross national product (GDP);
- non farm payroll figures.

A quantitative statistical analysis of the relationship between the dollar index and the factors mentioned above would reveal the magnitude of their correlation with the dollar index and to what extent they might have an influence on the dollar's future value.

While data on tradeable instruments such as bond yields, the dollar, international bonds etc. are readily available, it is sometimes difficult to find appropriate fundamental data because they are often subject to revision and not always reported in a data-compatible format.

Table 4.9 lists some markets with readily-available data that correlate well with the dollar index and covers the 5-year period from January 2003 to December 2007 (in the second column) and the 10 years from January 1998 to December 2007 (in the third column). I included both a short and a long time span because, as it becomes apparent from Table 4.9, the correlations were not constant over time, usually strengthening during the most recent 5-year period. This was more pronounced in the case of the CRB index, crude oil and gold, mainly because investors turned to commodities as a hedge against the recent disorderly dollar decline.

The British pound, the euro and the yen had the highest negative correlation in both time spans, but this was expected as they are all components of the dollar index. The commodity that correlated best with the dollar index was gold ($r = -0.51$). Of course this is nothing new and it is normal for gold, which is denominated in dollars, to have a negative correlation with the dollar. Surprisingly, the dollar index correlated better with the Australian dollar, which is not a dollar index component, than with Gold.

Lastly, the dollar index did not correlate well with equity indices. The correlation with the S&P 500 reversed sign from weak positive to weak negative during the latest 5-year period. The equity index that correlated best with the dollar index was

Table 4.9 Correlation of monthly (21 day) percentage yields between the dollar index and related commodities. In the second column is the correlation using more recent data from 1 January 2003 to 31 December 2007 and the correlation using 10 years of data (from 1 January 1998 to 31 December 2007) in the third column.

Index/Commodity	Correlation Data – Years	
	5	10
OIX	−0.23	−0.13
Crude oil (NYMEX)	−0.26	−0.13
Natural gas	−0.14	−0.16
S&P 500	−0.17	0.01
Nikkei	0.12	0.13
Venture (Canada)	−0.36	−0.31
XAU	−0.36	−0.35
Silver	−0.33	−0.29
Gold (cash)	**−0.51**	**−0.49**
CRB index	−0.39	−0.32
Utility Index	−0.29	−0.11
Japanese Bonds	−0.10	−0.10
Bund	−0.15	−0.20
Bonds	−0.16	−0.23
10-yr Australian bond	−0.10	−0.25
10-yr Treasury yield	0.16	0.26
Interest rates (short)	0.14	0.18
Euro	**−0.98**	**−0.98**
AUD	**−0.66**	**−0.56**
GBP	**−0.84**	**−0.80**
YEN	**−0.65**	**−0.56**

Canada's Venture Index. This was no surprise as the Venture Exchange is heavily weighted with gold mining stocks.

Dollar index futures trade in the NYBOT (which has been recently acquired by the Intercontinental Exchange or ICE) under the symbol DX. The contract value is 1000 times the index and is currently trading at 73. Thus, if you sell one contract, you are basically shorting $73 000 against a basket of six foreign currencies.

4.9   THE XOI AND THE OIX

The continued surge in the price of oil confirms that oil supply is scarcely meeting demand. The excess demand is coming from China and India and will only get stronger. The question is not whether, but when, world crude productivity will start to decline, ushering in the permanent oil shock era. While global information for predicting this "event" is not so straightforward as the data M. King Hubbert used in creating his famous curve that predicted the US oil production peak, there are indications that most of the large exploration targets have been found, at the same time that the world's population is exploding.

On 26 February 2008 crude oil prices crossed the $100 barrier. High crude prices imply higher profitability for the oil industry which, in turn, will propel their stock prices even higher.

The AMEX oil index (XOI) and the CBOE oil index (OIX) are the most popular indices designed to measure the performance of the oil industry through changes in the prices of a cross section of widely-held corporations involved in the exploration, production, and development of petroleum.

The XOI was established with a benchmark value of 125 on 27 August 1984 and currently has 12 component companies, all involved in exploring, developing, producing, and refining petroleum. These range in size from the tiny $29 billion (market capitalization) Hess to the mighty $440 billion Exxon Mobil, the world's largest publicly-traded oil company.

Both indices are price weighted. Perhaps surprisingly, considering its use with the DJIA, price-weighted indices have major problems. In the XOI's case, the smaller and less-important companies now have far higher share prices than the big ones. This allows these smaller companies to unduly influence and distort index performance.

For example Apache, because of its rich $100 share price, comprises 11.7 % of the OIX by weight even though it is only a $33 billion company. Meanwhile, giant Exxon Mobil is weighted at 10 % of the XOI even though it is a massive $440 billion behemoth. The problem is that share prices are meaningless, and a company of any size can have whatever share price range it wants by splitting or reverse-splitting its stock.

An alternative and better way to weight an index, which is more common in newer indexes, is by market capitalization. This weighting solves the problem of a $1 move in a $10 stock having the same impact as an identical move in a $100 stock, despite the fact that the former situation represents a 10 % change, and the latter only a 1 % change. Not surprisingly, market cap weighted indexes are by far the most common. The classic example always provided for the market-weighted index style is the Standard & Poor's 500 index.

With the XOI's current price weighting, the bottom four components – which represent a hefty 23 % of the XOI's weight today – are a mere 9 % of its market capitalization!

Despite these problems, the XOI remains the most popular measure of the oil-stock sector today with the OIX a close second.

For comparison purposes, both the XOI and OIX components are listed in the same Table 4.10. As you can see their composition and weight are very similar. The

Table 4.10 Composition of the CBOE oil index (OIX) and Amex oil index (XOI) as of 2 February 2008. A blank cell indicates that the stock in that row is not included in the index.

Symbol	Name	Price 8/2/08	Market cap – billion	OIX weight	XOI weight
APA	Apache Corp	100.63	33.5	11.74 %	–
HES	Hess Corp	56.46	28.6	10.41 %	10.36 %
XOM	Exxon Mobil Corp	64.30	439.8	10.38 %	9.86 %
CVX	Chevron Corp	75.38	165.5	10.24 %	9.64 %
TOT	Total	79.26	158.3	9.64 %	8.30 %
RDS.A	Royal Dutch Shell	88.96	124.0	9.28 %	8.15 %
COP	Conocophillips	49.38	119.9	9.09 %	9.16 %
OXY	Occidental Petroleum	66.68	55.1	8.49 %	7.74 %
BP	British Petroleum	67.53	202.8	8.02 %	7.27 %
APC	Anadarko Petroleum	70.29	26.4	6.84 %	6.68 %
MRO	Marathon Oil Corp	81.71	35.0	5.87 %	5.34 %
REP	Repsol Ypf S.A	31.88	37.1	–	3.64 %
VLO	Valero Energy	59.06	32.1	–	6.75 %

main difference between them is that the Amex used Apache Corporation instead of CBOE's Repsol and Valero.

Table 4.11 lists some markets that correlate well with the Amex oil index. The data are composed of equity indices, commodities, currencies and interest rate-related markets. I statistically correlated these against the XOI on a same month basis, meaning there was no monthly offset between the XOI data series and the related markets. The highest correlation in both time spans was between the XOI and Canada's TSX index, but this was to be expected as the TSX is heavily weighted with oil exploration stocks. Surprisingly, Japanese bonds correlated considerably better with the XOI ($r = -0.31$) than US Treasury bonds ($r = -0.1$). Interest rates had virtually no correlation with the XOI.

As can be seen in Table 4.11 the correlations were not constant over time, sometimes strengthening from weak to medium or strong during the most recent 5-year period. This was more pronounced in the case of the dollar and dollar denominated commodities such as gold, crude oil, and the CRB index.

The XOI correlated better with the Australian dollar than the US dollar index and there was also strong positive correlation with the Australian All Ordinaries index. This was certainly a surprise since Australia is not a major oil-producing country.

Options on the OIX trade on the CBOE under the symbol OIX expiring every three months from the March quarterly cycle (March, June, September and December). Options on the XOI are also available from the AMEX.

Table 4.11   Correlation of monthly (21 day) percentage yields between the Amex oil index (XOI) and related indices. The correlation using more recent data from 1/1/2003 to 31/12/2007 is shown in the second column and the correlation using 10-year data (from 1/1/1998 to 31/12/2007) in the third column.

Index/commodity	Correlation Data–Years	
	5	10
OIX	0.99	0.99
Crude oil	**0.52**	0.42
Brent	0.49	0.43
Natural gas	0.3	0.31
S&P 500	0.48	**0.46**
TSX (Canada)	**0.74**	**0.47**
Venture (Canada)	0.49	**0.47**
Australia All Ordinaries	**0.54**	0.43
XAU	**0.54**	0.40
Gold	0.37	0.16
CRB index	**0.57**	0.44
Japanese bonds	−0.31	−0.31
Utility index	0.45	0.44
10 yr Treasury bond	−0.12	−0.1
10 yr Treasury yield	0.04	0.1
Dollar index	−0.21	−0.12
AUD	0.38	0.33
GBP	0.05	0.08
Yen	−0.06	0.05

4.10   THE CRB INDEX

The history of the CRB index dates back to 1957, when the Commodity Research Bureau constructed an index comprised of 28 commodities to track the performance of commodities as an asset class.

Since then, as commodity markets have evolved, the index has undergone periodic updates. Its name was changed to the Reuters CRB Index in 2001 and it was again renamed as the Reuters/Jefferies CRB Index (RJ/CRB) in July 2005 when it underwent its tenth and most recent revision, the collaborative effort of Reuters Plc. and Jefferies Financial Products, LLC.

The original CRB index included 28 commodities until the list was reduced to 21 in 1987, where it remained until a major revision in 1995 when it was further sliced down to 17 commodities. Of the 28 commodities included in the original CRB of 1957, foodstuffs such as rye, potatoes, onions and lard – that aren't really relevant to an evolving industrial economy – were gradually removed.

Table 4.12 Commodities included in the old and new CRB index and the Goldman Sachs Commodity Index (as of April 2007).

	Old CRB	New R/J CRB	GSCI
Crude oil	5.9 %	23.0 %	37.9 %
Brent	0.0 %	0.0 %	15.5 %
Heating oil	6.0 %	5.0 %	6.2 %
Unleaded gas	0.0 %	5.0 %	1.3 %
Natural gas	5.9 %	6.0 %	6.2 %
Gas/Oil	0.0 %	0.0 %	5.4 %
Corn	5.9 %	6.0 %	3.0 %
Wheat	5.9 %	1.0 %	5.9 %
Soybeans	5.9 %	6.0 %	2.1 %
Sugar	5.9 %	5.0 %	0.9 %
Cotton	5.9 %	5.0 %	0.8 %
Coffee	5.9 %	5.0 %	0.6 %
Cocoa	5.9 %	5.0 %	0.2 %
Orange juice	5.9 %	1.0 %	0.0 %
Cattle	5.9 %	6.0 %	2.8 %
Lean hogs	5.9 %	1.0 %	1.1 %
Gold	5.9 %	6.0 %	2.0 %
Silver	5.9 %	1.0 %	0.3 %
Aluminum	0.0 %	6.0 %	2.4 %
Copper	5.9 %	6.0 %	3.0 %
Nickel	0.0 %	1.0 %	0.9 %
Platinum	5.9 %	0.0 %	0.0 %
Lead	0.0 %	0.0 %	0.5 %
Zinc	0.0 %	0.0 %	0.7 %

During the latest revision in 2005 three new commodities were added (unleaded gas, aluminum and nickel) and an existing one (platinum) was eliminated for a net gain of two components. In addition, the CRB's traditional geometric averaging was also eliminated, in favor of a weighting arithmetic averaging which better tracks the true direction of commodities prices during today's volatile markets. By its very mathematical nature geometric averaging effectively continually rebalanced the index, decreasing exposure to rising commodities and increasing exposure to declining commodities.

To refresh the readers' mathematics, the formula for the geometric mean of a data set $[a_1, a_2, \ldots, a_n]$ is the n_{th} root of their product and it is useful for averaging quantities with the same or similar values in magnitude.

In the new CRB, crude oil has a weight of 23 times the weight of orange juice or hogs and 4.6 times the weight of sugar. You can see the composition of sub-sector weightings of the new RJ/CRB in Fig. 4.2 and the individual commodities in Table 4.12.

By diversifying into commodities, investors are better able to obtain desirable long-term results, while at the same time lowering the overall volatility of their portfolio.

The counter-cyclic nature of commodities to other financial assets such as equities makes commodities an ideal asset class to incorporate into a portfolio in order to achieve a more desirable return scenario. Attempting to find the right combination of contracts in obscure markets such as soybeans, pork bellies, cattle, and coffee would be difficult for a futures market professional and potentially disastrous for anyone else. Many mutual type commodity funds and money managers have surfaced, but most with unpredictable results and very few offering the true commodity portfolio necessary for proper asset diversification.

The Reuters/Jefferies CRB index has been recognized as the main barometer of commodity prices for many years and has been accepted globally as a standard for measuring the commodity futures price level.

To alleviate the need to choose individual commodities while facilitating the investment in a representative group, the New York Board of Trade (NYBOT) began offering futures contracts on the Reuters/Jefferies CRB index. The trading symbol is CR and the contract size is 200 times the index.

Buyers of the Reuters/Jefferies CRB index futures contract have direct participation in valuation changes of the component commodities (see Table 4.12 and also Figure 4.2). A "long" position provides opportunities for obtaining a hedge against inflation and dollar depreciation while at the same time reaping potentially extraordinary returns from commodity price appreciation.

4.11   THE GOLDMAN SACHS COMMODITY INDEX (GSCI)

The GSCI, created in 1991, currently includes 24 commodities and is designed to provide investors with a reliable and publicly available benchmark for investment performance in the commodity markets. Individual components qualify for inclusion in the GSCI on the basis of liquidity and are weighted by their respective world production quantities in the last five years of available data. A list of the components and their dollar weights, as of April 2007, is presented in Table 4.12.

The GSCI is heavily weighted in energy futures contracts, which constitute 72.5 % of the index compared with only 39 % for the Reuters/Jefferies CRB index, which was the main factor for the GSCI becoming the top-performing commodity benchmark in 2007. This, however, is not necessarily an advantage, as it limits the diversification into other commodities which is especially beneficial in periods of declining oil prices.

In Fig. 4.3 you can see a comparison between the Goldman Sachs commodity index (thick line), the RJ/CRB index (normal line) and crude oil futures (thin line). Notice how the Goldman Sachs commodity index closely follows crude oil prices.

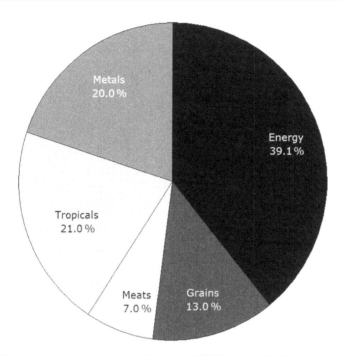

Figure 4.2   Sub-sector composition of the new RJ/CRB index. The Energy group includes crude oil, heating oil, unleaded gas and natural gas; the Grain group includes corn, wheat and soybeans; the Meat group includes live cattle and lean hogs; the Tropicals include sugar, cotton, coffee, cocoa and orange juice and lastly, the Metals group includes gold, silver, aluminium, copper and nickel.

Possible means of investing in the Goldman Sachs commodity index include the purchase of GSCI-related instruments, such as the GSCI futures contract traded on the Chicago Mercantile Exchange (CME).

In February 2007 the GSCI was acquired by Standard & Poor's and renamed the S&P GSCI.

4.12   THE XAU AND THE HUI

The Philadelphia Exchange (PHLX) Gold and Silver Sector (XAU) Index is a capitalization-weighted index composed of 16 companies involved in the gold and silver mining industry. The XAU was set to an initial value of 100 in January 1979. Options on the XAU trade under the same symbol in the Philadelphia Exchange.

The component companies and their weighing can be seen in Table 4.13.

Figure 4.3 Weekly chart of the S&P Goldman Sachs commodity index (thick bold line with the scale on the right), the RJ/CRB index (thin black line) and crude oil futures (thin grey line) from 2001 to February 2008. Notice how the Goldman Sachs commodity index closely follows crude oil prices.

Table 4.13 Composition of XAU index as of 8 February 2008.

Company name	Symbol	Weight
Barrick Gold Corp.	ABX	22.04 %
Agnico Eagle Mines Ltd.	AEM	4.39 %
AngloGold Ashanti Ltd.	AU	5.64 %
Yamana Gold, Inc.	AUY	5.15 %
Coeur d'Alene Mines Corp.	CDE	0.62 %
Freeport McMoran Copper	FCX	17.54 %
Gold Fields Ltd.	GFI	4.63 %
Goldcorp, Inc.	GG	13.00 %
Randgold Resources Ltd.	GOLD	1.74 %
Harmony Gold Mining Co.	HMY	2.10 %
Kinross Gold	KGC	6.64 %
Newmont Mining Corporation	NEM	11.97 %
Pan American Silver Corp.	PAAS	1.34 %
Royal Gold, Inc.	RGLD	0.44 %
Silver Wheaton, Inc.	SLW	1.70 %
Silver Standard Resources	SSRI	1.05 %

Table 4.14   Composition of HUI index as of 1/31/08.

Company name	Symbol	Weight
Barrick Gold	ABX	17.16 %
Newmont Mining	NEM	14.53 %
Goldcorp Inc.	GG	10.04 %
Yamana Gold	AUY	5.83 %
Randgold Resources Ads	GOLD	5.81 %
Agnico Eagle Mines	AEM	5.42 %
Kinross Gold	KGC	5.40 %
Golden Star Resources	GSS	4.95 %
Eldorado Gold Corp	EGO	4.89 %
Gold Fields Ltd. Adr	GFI	4.61 %
Harmony Gold Mining	HMY	4.38 %
Coeur d'Alene Mines	CDE	4.38 %
Hecla Mining	HL	4.32 %
Iamgoldcorp	IAG	4.22 %
Northgate Minerals	NXG	4.06 %

Another popular gold mining index is the AMEX's Gold BUGS index (HUI). BUGS is an acronym for Basket of Unhedged Gold Stocks. The index was introduced on 15 March 1996 with a starting value of 200.

The AMEX Gold BUGS index is comprised of 15 of the nation's largest "unhedged" gold mining stocks. It is a "modified equal-dollar weighted" index. As a result, most of the index's component stocks are equally weighted, yet the largest stocks still carry a greater weight than the smallest. The component companies and their weighing on the 31 January 2008 are depicted in Table 4.14.

The major difference between the two indices is that BUGS is made up exclusively of mining stocks that do not hedge their gold positions more than 18 months into the future. This makes the BUGS index much more profitable than the XAU when gold prices are rising, but can also compound its losses when gold declines.

4.13   THE VIX

The CBOE Volatility Index (VIX) is designed to reflect investors' consensus view of future (30-day) expected market volatility by averaging the weighted prices of out-of-the money options on the S&P 500 (SPX) index.

The name might be misleading as the VIX is not really a measure of market volatility but only of the price level of the SPX options, which is somewhat subjective and varies by opinions about the options that have nothing to do with volatility. The VIX also tells us something very important about the price of the options from which it is derived: It indicates whether the options are *expensive* or *cheap* relative to their historical prices. When the VIX is high, options are expensive, and when it is low, options are cheap. The option premium usually goes up when the market declines and it is usually a sign of fear.

I consider the VIX as a sentiment indicator because, unlike surveys and collections of information about bullishness or bearishness, it is an indicator based on traders using their capital during the course of the trading day willing to pay more for SPX put options if they perceive that a market correction is imminent. In that sense the VIX is the collective wisdom of the market at that instant.

There are three variations of volatility indexes: the VIX which tracks the S&P 500, the VXN which tracks the Nasdaq 100 and the VXD which tracks the Dow Jones Industrial Average.

The original VIX, introduced by the CBOE in 1993, measured the implied volatility or the amount that the OEX (S&P 100) options were selling above or below their fair value (as calculated by the Black-Scholes formula). The use of the Black-Scholes formula (which embodied a number of other factors like interest rates, time to expiration and historical volatility) tended to sometimes distort the expected volatility and so, in September 2003 the CBOE decided to change the calculation method. The new VIX used a newly-developed formula to derive expected volatility by averaging the weighted prices of the 30-day to expiration, out-of-the money puts and calls and was independent of the Black-Scholes option pricing model. The second noteworthy change was that the new VIX calculation used options on the S&P 500 index (SPX) rather than the S&P 100 (OEX).

For the sake of consistency the CBOE has created a historical record for the new VIX dating back to 1986 and continued the calculation of the original OEX VIX, but under the new ticker symbol "VXO".

Generally VIX values greater than 30 are associated with a large amount of volatility as a result of investor fear or uncertainty, while values below 20 generally correspond to less stressful, even complacent, times in the markets. Traders who want to trade the VIX directly can do so by purchasing futures or options on the VIX which trade actively on the CBOE. The contract size is $1000 the VIX and the symbol is VX.

Futures traders are most familiar with the fair value of stock index futures derived from the cost-of carry relationship between the futures and the underlying stock index. Since there is no carry between VIX and a position in VIX futures, the fair value of VIX futures cannot be derived by a similar relationship. Instead the fair value is derived by pricing the forward 30-day variance which underlies the settlement price of VIX futures. The fair value of VIX futures is the square root of this expected variance less an adjustment factor.

The VIX has ranged from a high of 48 in 1998 to a low of about 9 in 1993 (Fig. 4.4). The VIX generally declines during periods of orderly market advances and rises during periods of market declines. The steeper the decline, the greater the VIX.

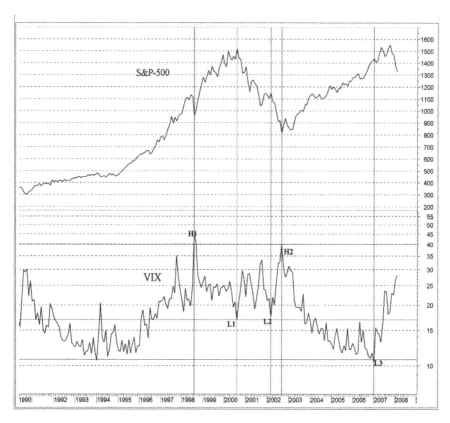

Figure 4.4 Monthly chart of the S&P 500 (top) and the VIX (bottom) from June 1990 to February 2008. Extreme tops in the VIX are marked H1 and H2 and extreme bottoms by L1, L2 and L3. Keep in mind that this is a line chart and consequently only closing prices are plotted, which are considerably higher or lower than the extreme intraday highs and lows respectively.

Certain levels of the VIX may predict turning points in the market. It is useful to examine selected periods and the relationship of the VIX and the market. For example, Figure 4.4 details some extremes in the VIX for the most recent 10-year period from 1998 to 2008.

Notice that the 2000 and 2002 bottoms in the VIX (marked L1 and L2 respectively in Fig. 4.4) coincide with tops in the S&P 500. The VIX usually forms extreme tops or bottoms at the same time as the S&P forms bottoms or tops but sometimes it may lead the S&P 500. Notice that in January 2007 the VIX declined as low as 10 (marked L3 in Figure 4.4) which preceded a major market decline by more than six months.

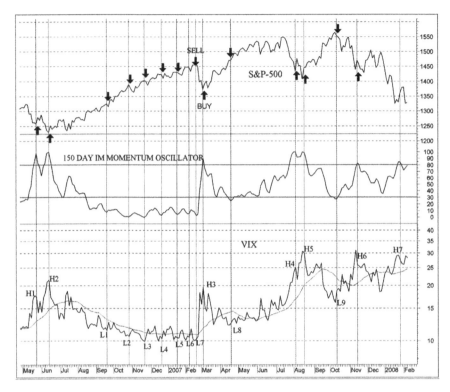

Figure 4.5 2-day chart of the S&P 500 (top) and the VIX (bottom) from May 2006 to February 2008. The 75 bar (150-day) intermarket oscillator is plotted in the middle chart. Extreme tops of the IM momentum oscillator (over 80) are marked H1–H7 and extreme bottoms (below 30) by L1–L9.

The absolute level of the extremes in the VIX is not very important and varies over time. The first two bottoms (L1 and L2) occurred with the VIX around 17, but during the third extreme bottom in 2007 the VIX declined as far as 10.

Tops in the VIX indicate market bottoms. The VIX rose above 40 in August 1998 (marked H1 in Figure 4.5) and in October 2002 (marked H2) which coincided with the end of the correction in 1998 and the end of the bear market in 2002 respectively.

To determine whether the VIX is useful in predicting short-term market tops or bottoms in real-time trading, let's examine the 2-day chart in Fig. 4.5. To help correctly identify the tops and bottoms in the VIX, I used the 150 day (75 bar in a 2-day chart) intermarket momentum oscillator, described fully in Chapter 9. The interpretation of this indicator is similar to the Williams' %R Oscillator. Buy signals were considered when the oscillator rose above a specific level (e.g. 80), formed a peak and subsequently reversed direction and fell below that level. The oscillator indicated a sell signal when it fell below a specific level (e.g. 30) and then rose above that level.

According to the interpretation above, the oscillator issued seven buy signals and nine sell signals during the period from May 2006 to February 2008. These are overlaid in the chart in Fig. 4.5. The signals marked H2, H3 and H5 correctly identified market bottoms while the other four buy signals were early by approximately two weeks on average. Only two signals (marked L7 and L9) correctly predicted market tops while the rest of the sell signals were premature. In these cases the time period that the VIX was early in predicting a market top ranged from two weeks to five months.

In view of the above we can conclude that the VIX, in spite of correctly predicting some market turning points, was early in predicting more than half of the market tops or bottoms. It is not, therefore, the "Holy Grail" that some people believe it is and should only be used together with other indicators for more accurate market timing.

5
The S&P 500

Interpretation is the revenge of the intellect upon art.

–Susan Sonntag

The calculation of the correlation coefficient between the index to be predicted and other related markets is the first step of a complete and thorough intermarket analysis. Of course, the final challenge comes from interpretation. Intermarket analysis relies on the premise that relationships in the past will be the same in the future so before making any conclusions it is always prudent to assess the stability of the correlation coefficient over time.

I chose to start this correlation analysis with a broad market index like the S&P 500 which is widely regarded as the best single gauge of the US equities market.

5.1   CORRELATION WITH INTERNATIONAL INDICES

The first step in a correlation or regression analysis is to decide whether you want to analyze the price on a daily, weekly, monthly or quarterly basis. Using long time scales has the added apparent theoretical benefit that averaging over long periods suppresses windowing errors and daily noise, revealing the underlying long term correlations. The choice of time periods is therefore very important and should depend on a trader's time horizon. This is illustrated in Tables 5.3 and 5.4 where the correlation rises dramatically when weekly returns replace daily data. As the time segment is reduced, noise becomes a bigger factor in the calculation and the correlation drops due to an abundance of change which is unfolding in the short term.

To better understand the evolution of correlations over time in Table 5.1 I have calculated price correlations between the S&P 500 and major world indices yearly from 1992 to 2007, in Table 5.2 up to 25 years long- and short-term nonparametric price correlations and in Table 5.3 nonparametric correlations between daily

Table 5.1 Yearly correlation between daily prices of the S&P and major world indices. Symbols: DJ-30 is the Dow Jones Industrials, RUT is the small cap Russell 2000 index, NDX is the Nasdaq 100, TSX is Canada's S&P TSX Composite Index and Euro Stoxx is the Dow Jones Euro Stoxx 50 Index which tracks the 50 most important stocks in the Euro zone. The 10th percentile row shows the yearly correlations below which certain percentages of cases fall. So for example, if the 10 % percentile of the correlation between the S&P 500 and the DJ-30 is 0.61, it means that the correlation was below 0.61 only 10 % of the time. The reverse is true for the 90th percentile row. Notice the significant improvement in correlation consistency during the latest 10-year period from 1998–2007 (bottom four rows).

Year	DJ-30	RUT	NDX	TSX	Euro Stoxx	DAX	CAC	FTSE	Nikkei	Hang Seng
2007	0.93	0.69	0.70	0.92	0.90	0.84	0.76	0.86	0.21	0.46
2006	0.97	0.85	0.75	0.81	0.94	0.95	0.92	0.87	0.52	0.90
2005	0.77	0.95	0.92	0.82	0.84	0.83	0.80	0.84	0.73	0.76
2004	0.84	0.96	0.94	0.86	0.87	0.91	0.83	0.76	0.02	0.75
2003	0.99	0.98	0.98	0.95	0.93	0.97	0.95	0.97	0.84	0.87
2002	0.98	0.96	0.85	0.98	0.98	0.96	0.98	0.98	0.76	0.85
2001	0.92	0.86	0.94	0.96	0.95	0.95	0.95	0.95	0.84	0.93
2000	0.59	0.46	0.67	0.57	0.59	0.50	0.61	0.64	0.35	0.59
1999	0.87	0.83	0.81	0.89	0.87	0.84	0.83	0.86	0.81	0.89
1998	0.92	0.28	0.80	0.38	0.66	0.61	0.76	0.69	−0.02	0.20
1997	0.97	0.93	0.91	0.94	NA	0.93	0.90	0.96	−0.22	−0.04
1996	0.99	0.73	0.97	0.97	NA	0.95	0.89	0.85	−0.09	0.93
1995	0.99	0.96	0.95	0.90	NA	0.78	0.02	0.98	0.23	0.92
1994	0.95	0.75	0.77	0.72	NA	0.04	0.34	0.68	−0.18	0.70
1993	0.93	0.92	0.73	0.84	NA	0.89	0.87	0.88	0.15	0.83
1992	0.24	0.49	0.52	−0.24	NA	−0.52	−0.34	0.45	−0.18	0.14

					1992–2007					
Average	**0.87**	0.79	**0.83**	0.77	NA	0.71	0.69	**0.82**	0.30	0.67
Median	**0.93**	**0.86**	0.83	**0.87**	NA	**0.87**	0.83	**0.86**	0.22	0.80
Std Dev	0.20	0.21	**0.13**	0.31	NA	0.41	0.37	**0.15**	0.40	0.31
Range	0.75	0.70	**0.46**	1.21	NA	1.49	1.32	**0.53**	1.06	0.97
10th Per	**0.49**	0.40	**0.52**	−0.24	NA	−0.52	−0.34	**0.45**	−0.22	−0.04
90th Per	**0.99**	**0.97**	**0.97**	**0.97**	NA	0.96	0.96	**0.98**	0.84	0.93

					1998–2007					
Average	**0.88**	0.78	**0.84**	0.81	**0.85**	0.84	0.84	0.84	0.50	0.72
Median	**0.92**	0.85	0.83	**0.87**	**0.89**	0.87	0.83	0.86	0.62	0.80
Std Dev	**0.12**	0.24	**0.11**	0.19	**0.13**	0.16	**0.12**	**0.12**	0.34	0.24
Range	0.40	0.70	**0.31**	0.60	**0.39**	0.47	**0.37**	**0.33**	0.86	0.73
10th Per	**0.61**	0.30	**0.67**	0.40	0.60	0.51	**0.62**	**0.65**	0.00	0.23
90th Per	**0.99**	**0.98**	**0.98**	**0.98**	**0.98**	0.97	**0.98**	**0.98**	0.84	0.93

Table 5.2 Long- and short-term Spearman's ρ nonparametric correlation between the S&P and major world indices. High correlations are in bold. Abbreviations: H = heteroscedasticity present (non homogeneous data), CL = curvilinear relationship, NL = non linear, NA = correlation coefficient not available because of insufficient data.

Years	DJ-30	RUT	NDX	TSX	Euro Stoxx	DAX	CAC	FTSE	Nikkei	Hang Seng
2	**0.98**	0.91	0.93	**0.96**	**0.98**	**0.97**	0.96	0.96	0.58	0.92
3	**0.98**	**0.97**	0.93	**0.98**	**0.99**	**0.98**	**0.98**	**0.98**	0.85	0.96
4	**0.97**	**0.99**	0.95	**0.99**	**0.99**	**0.99**	**0.98**	**0.98**	0.90	**0.98**
5	**0.98**	**0.99**	**0.97**	**0.99**	**0.99**	**0.99**	**0.99**	**0.99**	0.94 H	0.98 CL
10	0.88	0.57 H	0.93 CL	0.71 CL	0.89	0.89	0.91	0.90	0.81 NL	0.87 CL
15	0.96	0.87 H	0.98 CL	0.91 CL	NA	0.96	0.96	0.96	−0.3 NL	0.82 CL
20	**0.99**	NA	0.99 CL	0.94 CL	NA	NA	NA	**0.98**	NA	0.92 CL
25	**0.99**	NA	NA	0.94 CL	NA	NA	NA	NA	NA	NA

percentage returns of the S&P 500 and major world indices. The data used to derive the correlation coefficients are up to the end of 2007. You can find up-to-date values of nonparametric price correlations at http://www.csidata.com.

Care should be taken before using any of the numbers, especially the long-term price correlations in Table 5.2, as some of the relationships were not linear. I have marked these to indicate deviations from linearity, but in any case you should check a scatterplot or a chart of the related index before making a significant investment decision based on these numbers. For example, in Tables 5.1 and 5.2 the correlation coefficient between the S&P 500 and Russell 2000 in 2004 and 2005 is indicated higher than the corresponding correlation with the DJ-30. However, looking at the relevant scatterplots in Figs. 5.1 and 5.2, we can see that higher values of the Russell 2000 (Fig. 5.2, top right) are not distributed evenly around the linear regression line

Table 5.3 Long- and short-term Spearman's ρ nonparametric correlation between the S&P Daily % returns and major world indices. The 15-year correlation of the DJ Euro Stoxx 50 was not calculated as only nine years of data were available for this index.

Years	DJ-30	RUT	NDX	TSX	Euro Stoxx	DAX	CAC	FTSE	Nikkei	Hang Seng
2	**0.95**	**0.89**	**0.88**	0.65	0.48	0.49	0.51	0.50	0.12	0.13
4	**0.95**	0.84	**0.88**	0.62	0.44	0.43	0.43	0.42	0.11	0.10
5	**0.96**	0.84	**0.88**	0.62	0.46	0.48	0.45	0.42	0.11	0.10
10	0.93	0.81	0.84	0.65	0.44	0.49	0.44	0.42	0.13	0.13
15	0.92	0.77	0.80	0.60	NA	0.40	0.39	0.39	0.11	0.13
avg.	**0.94**	0.83	**0.86**	0.63	0.46	0.46	0.44	0.43	0.12	0.12

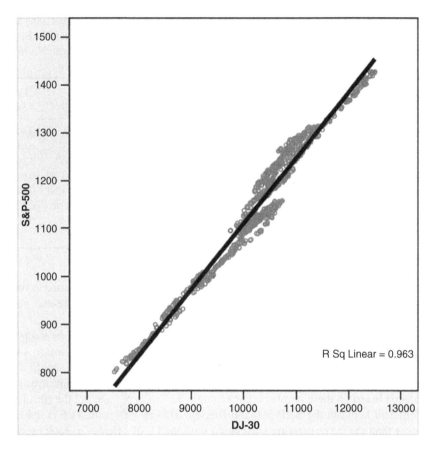

Figure 5.1 Scatterplot of 2-year closing prices of the S&P 500 vs. the Dow Jones Industrials. Although the homogeneity of variance around the regression line is not perfect, it is still better than the plot in Fig. 5.2.

and, as discussed in Chapter 2, this could distort the correlation coefficient between the two indices.

This is not usually a problem when transforming price data to differences or percentage yields. For example consider the scatterplots in Figs. 5.3 and 5.4 which are both between the S&P and the VIX. In Fig. 5.4 price data was converted to weekly yields.

As can be seen from Table 5.1 and also the graph in Fig. 1.4 (Chapter 1), the correlations are not constant over time, sometimes (although rarely) alternating from weak negative to strong positive.

In order to examine more closely the volatility of these correlations I have calculated at the bottom of Table 5.1 the average, median, standard deviation and the

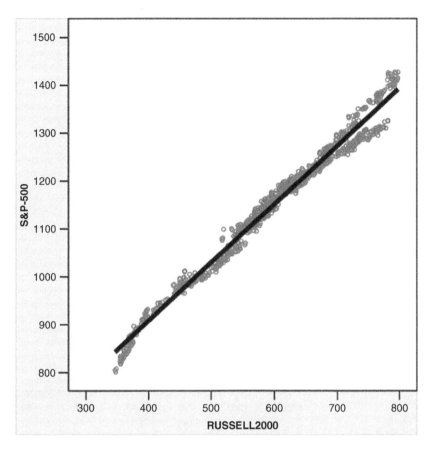

Figure 5.2 Scatterplot of 2-year closing prices of the S&P 500 vs. the Russell 2000 small cap index. Notice the increase in variance at the top right of the plot.

maximum range (highest minus lowest correlation value over each time span). The standard deviation, however, may not be the best measure of variance as most values were concentrated at the far right of the histogram (negative skew) and the correlation distribution deviated significantly from the normal Gaussian curve.

To deal with this problem I divided the yearly correlations in percentiles according to their level. So for example, if the 10 % percentile of the correlation between the S&P 500 and the DJ-30 is 0.61, it means that only 10 % of the yearly correlations were below 0.61. The correlation was more stable over time with high captalization indices like the DJ-30 and the FTSE. Small capitalization stocks, represented by the Russell 2000, had the most unstable relationship. In fact, correlation with European stocks was less volatile than with its US compatriot. Their correlation with the Euro Stoxx broke down during the most recent 10-year period only twice, in 2000 and 1998.

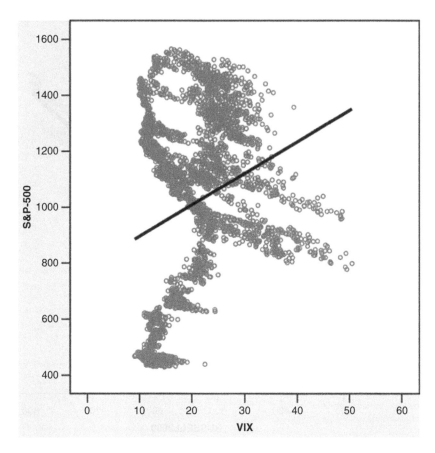

Figure 5.3   Scatterplot of the CBOE Volatility Index (VIX) vs. the S&P 500 over a 15-year period from 1993 to the end of 2007.

The correlation between the S&P 500 and other international and emerging market equities was highly erratic when considering yearly time segments, and over the 16-year study (Table 5.1), the relationship also varied substantially. This is because international relationships can change as the forces that drive earnings in Europe, Asia and elsewhere aren't identical to what is unfolding in Chicago and Silicon Valley. The correlation with British stocks was an exception because, although the correlation was not as strong as with the DJ-30, it was less volatile over time. The index with the weakest and most unstable correlation was the Nikkei 225 and this was evident in all time frames.

Rather than rely on historical correlations, a more comprehensive and dynamic approach is needed when making trading decisions. The number and frequency of these changes can complicate the design of intermarket trading systems as they rely

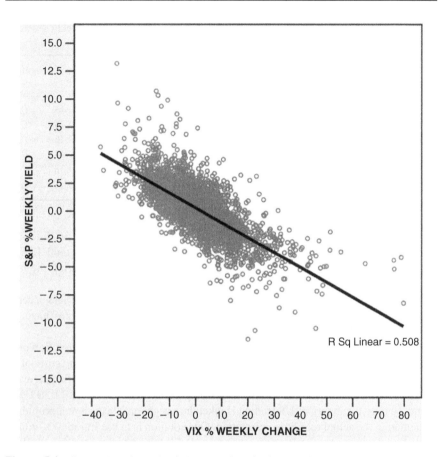

Figure 5.4 Scatterplot of weekly % changes of the CBOE Volatility Index (VIX) vs. weekly % returns of the S&P 500 over the 15-year period from 1993 to the end of 2007. The relationship has become approximately linear when taking percent yields.

on the principle that relationships in the past would be the same in the future. Markets may decouple and a strategy based on that assumption might produce considerable drawdown.

Taking into account the predicted future correlation rather than historical values could be advantageous in intermarket system design or long-term forecasting. One way of making a prediction of what the correlation is going to be in the future is to adjust the correlation coefficient, in order to take into account the most recent trend, by the trend or rate of change of the correlation during the most recent 5-year period.

The impact of globalization and free money flow across national borders can be seen in the rising correlations between the S&P 500 and international indices. The S&P 500 and Euro Stoxx 50 have been posting correlations in the range of 0.9 to

Table 5.4 Long- and short-term nonparametric correlation between S&P weekly % returns and major world indices.

Years	DJ-30	RUT	NDX	TSX	Euro Stoxx	DAX	CAC	FTSE	Nikkei	Hang Seng
2	**0.95**	**0.86**	0.84	0.69	0.77	0.76	0.78	0.74	0.46	0.49
4	**0.95**	**0.86**	0.85	0.67	0.75	0.73	0.73	0.67	0.44	0.46
5	**0.96**	**0.87**	**0.87**	0.69	0.75	0.72	0.74	0.68	0.46	0.47
10	0.92	0.82	0.84	0.74	0.74	0.73	0.73	0.70	0.43	0.50
15	0.92	0.79	0.79	0.70	NA	0.66	0.65	0.39	0.38	0.45
avg.	**0.94**	0.84	0.84	0.70	0.75	0.72	0.73	0.64	0.43	0.47

0.94 for the last two years (Table 5.1), up sharply from the 0.59 to 0.86 during the period from 1998 to 2000. Also the correlation of weekly yields with the FTSE has improved from 0.39 to 0.74 and with the DAX from 0.66 to 0.76 during the latest 2-year period (Table 5.4).

This trend is widely acknowledged for European indexes, but what is less accepted is that correlations between US and many other non-European indexes have also increased.

A comparison between Tables 5.2 and 5.3 reveals a significant deterioration of the correlation between the S&P and all non-US exchanges when comparing correlations between daily percentage yields instead of prices. This can be partly attributed (except for the TSX) to different time zones. Most European exchanges close at 11:30 US ET time, so only two hours of US trading is taken into account. This is a real problem in calculating the actual real-time correlation. One solution is to use Intraday 30-minute data and correlate the S&P change between 11:30 the previous day and 11:30 the next day but this will involve splitting a trading day in two. Obtaining 15 years of intraday data is also a problem. Another possible alternative is to compare the S&P with European index futures data as most of them close long after regular hours. Conveniently, the DAX and Euro Stoxx futures closing time happens to coincide with the US market closing time at 16:00 ET. Of course there is no overlap between the US and Asian markets so in order to predict Nikkei daily changes based on S&P changes the S&P has to be shifted one day in the past.

You should therefore take into consideration the trading hours of each index as non-US indices (except Canada's TSX and other American indices) trade during different time zones. The S&P is the last to close and therefore international indices can only be used to predict the S&P (short term) and not the other way around. For example, to derive the daily correlation between Japan's Nikkei and the S&P 500, the S&P 500 has to be shifted one day back in time as the current day's closing price is not known during Japanese trading hours. You can find trading hours for all the Exchanges in Chapter 4 (Table 4.1).

5.2 INTEREST RATES, COMMODITIES, FOREX AND THE VIX

The importance of changes in interest rates and their impact on equity markets has long been recognized by astute Wall Street analysts and technicians. Martin Zweig in his classic *Winning On Wall Street* provided a stock market timing model which is based on changes in the prime rate.

The old "Don't fight the Fed" maxim for years suggested that when the Fed starts lowering rates, it is time to start buying stocks. Conversely, when the Fed begins to raise rates, it is usually time to head for the exit. Unfortunately, investors who responded to this old canard and began buying stocks when the Federal Reserve Board started lowering rates were burned badly twice: once in 2001, and again in August 2007.

Over the past seven years we have been confronted with a reversal of the normal negative correlation between interest rates and share prices. This proves that a system relying on the historical correlation alone is not the best approach and a broader assessment of factors affecting the future relationship between stocks and interest rates is also required.

In the search for factors influencing price correlation, market corrections, uncertainties or perceived risks play a fundamental part, as Fig. 5.5 illustrates. The 1987 crash, the 1997 Asian financial crisis and the Long Term Capital Management crisis in conjunction with Russia's bond default triggered a sharp slide in stock prices and a subsequent rally in bonds, as investors fled to safety. This resulted in negative correlation between stocks and bonds (positive between stocks and bond yields).

An analysis of correlation at specific periods in the business cycle reveals a fundamental reason for the correlation reversal between stock prices and bond yields: The correlation with interest rates switches to positive during economic recessions. During the 1981–1982 recession bonds rallied, pushing yields lower, while stock prices declined. This pattern was repeated during the more recent recession in 2001–2003 (see Fig. 5.5).

Apart from the factors already discussed, inflation expectations or rising commodity prices can also induce a correlation reversal because rising inflation is negative for bonds and therefore positive for yields. Rising oil and agricultural commodity prices induced a correlation reversal again at the beginning of 2008 as illustrated in Fig. 5.5.

The fluctuation of correlations, however, is hardly limited to stocks and bonds. The correlation of weekly yields between the S&P 500 and the CRB index strengthened from near zero or a non-existent historical correlation to 0.15 as commodities became everyone's new favorite asset class.

The increase may not seem a lot but the question is whether the trend will continue. Factors that may have caused the correlation upturn may be the dollar's demise or even the money still rolling into commodities by way of the growing number of

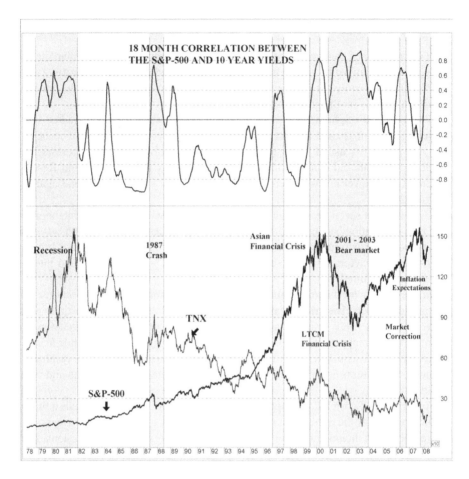

Figure 5.5 Weekly chart of the S&P 500 and 10-year treasury yields (TNX) from 1978 until May 2008. The top chart is the 18-month correlation between the S&P 500 and the TNX. Notice how the traditional long-term negative correlation turns positive in times of financial turmoil like the 1987 market crash, the 1997 Asian crisis and the Russian bond and subsequent Long Term Capital Management crisis (shaded in grey). Notice also how, at the beginning of 2000, the long-term correlation bias turned from negative to positive.

exchange-traded funds targeting this asset class. My opinion is that the correlation will revert to the mean as soon as the dollar index stabilizes and commodity prices return to their historical range.

The correlation of the S&P 500 with gold has also reversed from weak negative to moderate positive. If you are interested in gold a complete correlation analysis is included in Chapter 7 and a comparison of 14 intermarket systems in Chapter 11.

Table 5.5 Long- and short-term nonparametric correlation between the S&P, commodities, Forex and the VIX as of 31.12.2007. TNX is the CBOE 10-year Treasury Yield Index, XOI is the AMEX Oil Index, XAU is the Philadelphia Gold/Silver Stock Index, GOLD is the World Gold Index (XGLD), CRB is the Commodity Research Bureau Index and YEN is the JPY/USD exchange rate. Abbreviations: H = heteroscedasticity present (non homogeneous data), CL = curvilinear relationship, NL = non linear, NA = correlation coefficient not available because of insufficient data.

Years	VIX	TNX	XOI	Crude oil	XAU	GOLD	CRB	Dollar index	YEN
2	0.3 NL	−0.25 H	0.83	0.2 NL	0.4 H	0.73 H	−0.2 NL	−0.83	−0.3 H
5	−0.5 H	0.65 H	0.98 CL	0.88 NL	0.88	0.96 CL	0.81 H	−0.77 NL	0.3 H
10	−0.3 NL	0.5 NL	0.54 NL	0.37 NL	0.15 NL	0.12 NL	0.22 NL	−0.2 NL	0.3 NL
15	0.23 H	−0.4 NL	0.85 NL	0.61 NL	−0.2 NL	0.00	0.17 NL	0.09 H	−0.3 NL
20	NA	−0.8 NL	0.93 NL	0.53 NL	−0.3 NL	−0.3 NL	0.06	NA	NA
25	NA	−0.9 NL	NA	NA	NA	−0.3 NL	−0.06	NA	NA
30	NA	−0.8 NL	NA	NA	NA	−0.070	−0.09	NA	NA

Table 5.6 Nonparametric correlation between S&P and major commodity and financial weekly percentage returns.

Years	VIX	TNX	XOI	Crude oil	XAU	GOLD	CRB	Dollar index	YEN
2	**−0.81**	0.18	**0.56**	0.02	**0.47**	0.20	0.15	−0.17	−0.15
5	−0.75	0.20	0.51	−0.10	0.34	0.10	0.08	−0.08	−0.02
10	**−0.77**	0.19	0.44	0.03	0.15	0.02	0.07	0.06	−0.02
15	−0.70	0.02	0.46	0.01	0.12	−0.01	0.03	0.08	−0.04
avg.	**−0.76**	0.15	0.49	−0.01	0.27	0.08	0.08	−0.03	−0.06

The positive correlation between the S&P and oil for the last 20 years was also a surprise, although this was not consistent over time as their relationship deviated considerably from linearity. This was also the case with the majority of the correlations in Table 5.5 as the scatterplots revealed that most of them deviated from linearity or homogeneity. The correlation coefficients of weekly percentage returns, displayed in Table 5.6, however, were more reliable as none deviated excessively from the linearity assumption.

A comparison of the scatterplots of the CBOE Volatility Index vs. the S&P in Figs. 5.3 and 5.4 makes this more obvious.

Inconsistent or nonlinear relationships were also the reason that the high correlations depicted in Table 5.5 have faded away when taking weekly yields (in Table 5.6). A notable exception to the rule was the correlation between the S&P and the VIX which actually increased when using weekly yields.

Activities stemming from the "carry trade", which have emerged only recently, also managed to reverse the traditional weak positive correlation between the S&P and the yen to negative during the last three years (Table 5.5 and Fig. 5.6). You can find more information on the carry trade and the yen in Chapter 17.

The first step in running a correlation analysis is to decide on the best time interval for calculating price changes. To understand the basic financial factors behind a market's course over longer periods of time, more than 10 days of percentage returns should be used generally. On the other hand, weekly percentage yields are more suitable for shorter-term trading. The best time period for taking percentage differences can also vary from market to market. The objective is to take a variable that you're interested in (in this case the S&P 500) and see to what degree its changes can be explained by changes in some other potentially relevant variables for a range of different time spans.

Table 5.7 lists the correlation between the S&P and related markets using daily to quarterly percentage returns. As you can see, the correlation peaked at the three week interval for some markets (e.g. XOI), while a longer-term time span was more appropriate for calculating the correlation with other markets like interest rates (TNX). The VIX was an exception to the rule, as it actually correlated better with

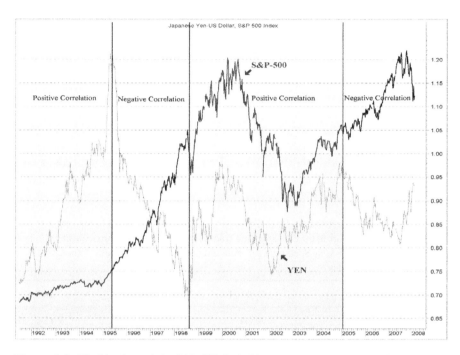

Figure 5.6 Weekly chart of the S&P 500 (in bold) and the Yen (Yen USD thin line) from 1992 until February 2008. Notice the alternating periods of positive (gray background) and negative (white background) correlation with the S&P 500 and how, in the beginning of 2005, the unwinding of the "carry trade" reversed the correlation from positive to negative.

Table 5.7 10-year correlation between the S&P and major commodity and financial indices using daily, weekly, 10 trading day (2-week), 15 trading day (3-week), monthly and quarterly returns for the 10-year period from the beginning of 1998 to the end of 2007.

Time segment	VIX	TNX	XOI	Oil	XAU	GOLD	CRB	Dollar Index	YEN
Daily	**−0.78**	0.23	**0.48**	−0.02	0.08	−0.04	0.04	0.14	−0.09
Weekly	**−0.75**	0.24	0.46	−0.01	0.14	0.00	0.06	0.08	−0.06
10 day	−0.74	0.26	0.46	−0.02	0.13	−0.02	0.03	0.08	−0.03
15 day	−0.74	0.24	**0.48**	−0.03	0.13	−0.02	0.02	0.06	−0.01
Monthly	−0.75	0.24	0.46	−0.03	0.13	−0.03	0.03	0.05	0.03
Quarterly	−0.70	**0.32**	0.37	−0.13	0.12	−0.01	−0.11	0.13	−0.02

the S&P 500 on a short-term basis (daily yields). This is probably because the VIX is a sentiment indicator and not a fundamental factor affecting changes in the S&P 500.

5.3   CORRELATION BETWEEN THE S&P 500 AND STOCKS

The 25 stocks with the best (positive) and the worst (negative) correlation with the S&P 500 are depicted in Tables 5.8 and 5.9 respectively, over a 5-year period until February 2007. Surprisingly, the five best correlated stocks are not S&P components but European stocks or ETFs. The 25 worst correlated stocks were mostly companies

Table 5.8   Nonparametric correlation between the S&P 500 and the 25 best correlated international stocks during the 5-year period from February 2002 to February 2007. Column 3 shows the 5-year Spearman's correlation coefficient and Column 4 shows the stock's underlying index.

Company Name	Symbol	Correlation	Index
Axa	AXA	0.986	CAC40
Netherlands Index ETF	EWN	0.98	AEX
Sage GRP	SGE.L	0.978	FTSE
Sweden Index ETF	EWD	0.977	OMXSPI
European Equity Fund	EEA	0.976	ESTX
Emerson Electric	EMR	0.975	S&P
Tri-Continental Corp.	TY	0.973	NA
Lincoln National Corp.	LNC	0.972	S&P
Exxon Mobil	XOM	0.967	S&P
United Technologies	UTX	0.961	S&P
Boeing Co.	BA	0.96	S&P
Altria Group	MO	0.959	S&P
Chevron Corp.	CVX	0.958	S&P
American Express	AXP	0.956	S&P
Pearson Plc	PSO	0.956	FTSE
Pepsico	PEP	0.955	S&P
BP Plc	BP	0.95	FTSE
Caterpillar Inc.	CAT	0.949	S&P
Public Service Enterprise	PEG	0.947	S&P
Alltel Corp.	AT	0.946	S&P
COGECO	CGO.TO	0.941	NA
Merril Lynch & Co.	MER	0.934	S&P
Dover Corp.	DOV	0.93	S&P
Citigroup	C	0.908	S&P
Procter & Gamble	PG	0.905	S&P

Table 5.9 Nonparametric correlation between the S&P 500 and the 25 worst correlated stocks. The 5-year Spearman's correlation coefficient is shown in Column 3 and the stock's underlying index in Column 4.

Company Name	Symbol	Correlation	Index
PRG-Schultz Int.	PRGX	−0.907	
Tenet Healthcare Corp.	THC	−0.864	S&P 500
European Diamonds Plc	EPD.L	−0.841	
Superior Industries Int.	SUP	−0.833	Russell 2000
Entercom Communications	ETM	−0.804	Russell 2000
Ramco Oil Services Plc	ROS.L	−0.8	
Farmer Bros Co.	FARM	−0.791	Russell 2000
Trimeris Inc.	TRMS	−0.791	Russell 2000
Fibernet Telecom Group	FTGX	−0.78	
Molins Plc	MLIN.L	−0.779	
Fifth Third Bancorp	FTB	−0.758	S&P 500
Libbey Inc.	LBY	−0.757	S&P 600
Blockbuster	BBI	−0.756	Russell 2000
Ninety Nine Only Stores	NDN	−0.751	Russell 2000
NTT Docomo ADS	DCM	−0.697	Nikkei
Enzon Pharmaceutical	ENZN	−0.696	Russell 2000
Fred's Inc.	FRED	−0.688	Russell 2000
Cray Inc.	CRAY	−0.686	Russell 2000
La-Z-Boy Inc.	LZB	−0.679	Russell 2000
Ballard Power Systems	BLDP	−0.678	TSX
Utstarcom Inc.	UTSI	−0.661	Russell 2000
Jardine Lloyd Thompson	JLT.L	−0.658	
GoAmerica Inc.	GOAM	−0.657	
Ariba Inc.	ARBA	−0.643	Russell 2000
Cabot Microelectronics Cp	CCMP	−0.639	Russell 2000

that did not follow the bullish trend during the period under study because of various company specific problems.

I wouldn't advise investing in these stocks as a means of diversification. On the other hand, some of them might recover and catch up with the S&P 500 provided that their problems are resolved.

6
European Indices

A little uncertainty is good for everything.

–Henry Kissinger

6.1   THE DAX

Trading in DAX futures has recently become very popular among US traders as it provides an additional liquid market to trade. The main advantages are currency diversification and a wider range of trading times. The German futures exchange (Eurex) is open 14 hours a day from 8:00 to 22:00 CET (02:00–16:00 US EST) and the longer trading times are convenient for both Australian and US-based traders. You can find an intermarket system for trading DAX futures in Chapter 13, but in order to make modifications or design your own system you will need a thorough understanding of its correlation with other international stock indices, currencies and commodities.

Correlations between the DAX and major international indices, forex and commodities are depicted in Table 6.1 and correlations with other European indices in Table 6.2. The DAX correlated best, with the Euro Stoxx 50. This was not surprising as both indices had a number of common component stocks. The second best correlation was with the French CAC 40 index, as both nations–whether they like it or not–are joined in the economic community. American indices had to be shifted back one day in time in order for the correlation values to have some predictive usefulness for the DAX, as all American exchanges closed $4^1/_2$ hours later. An alternative approach would be to correlate the DAX opening price with the previous day's closing price of the corresponding American index. This improves the correlation coefficient from 0.134 to 0.422 when comparing the last day's S&P 500 daily change with the DAX change between the current day's open and last day's close. Similar correlation analysis can be used to predict opening prices of lagging (in the time zone) international indices. For example the Nikkei opening price can be predicted based

Table 6.1 Nonparametric correlation between the DAX and major world indices for the 5-year period until 31 December 2006. The 5-year Spearman's price correlation coefficient is shown in column 3 and the correlation of daily and weekly yields (% changes) in column 4. All US indices were shifted one day back since the current day's closing price is not known at the time of the DAX close.

Index/Commodity	Daily prices	Yield %	
		Daily	Weekly
SP 500 (lag 1 day)	0.913	0.134	0.661
DJ-30 (lag 1 day)	0.884	0.125	0.652
NDX (lag 1 day)	0.847	0.167	0.614
TSX (lag 1 day)	0.881	0.097	0.505
Euro Stoxx 50	**0.992**	**0.878**	**0.928**
Stoxx 50	**0.971**	0.864	0.887
Tecdax	0.833	0.714	0.764
CAC 40	**0.995**	0.862	**0.904**
FTSE	**0.989**	0.724	0.767
Athens General	**0.980**	0.385	0.551
Utility index (lag 1 day)	0.912	0.085	0.242
Nikkei	0.900	0.231	0.535
Hang Seng	0.852	0.245	0.508
10 Yr tr. yld (lag 1 day)	0.715	0.062	0.375
Bund	0.372	−0.338	−0.377
Gold	0.660	−0.15	−0.113
Oil (Brent)	0.040	−0.039	−0.055
Euro	0.404	−0.21	−0.213
Dollar index (lag 1 day)	−0.25	0.080	0.170
Yen	0.030	0.082	0.074

on the last day's closing price of the S&P 500, or a European index opening can be predicted based on both the last day's closing price of the S&P and the current day's closing of Asian exchanges using a multiple regression model.

Notice that correlations between DAX and all other non equity index assets (below the Hang Seng in Table 6.1) broke down and even reversed sign when taking daily or weekly yields. This is because their relationship with the DAX was non linear thus invalidating the correlation analysis.

6.2 CORRELATION WITH STOCKS

In Table 6.3 you can see 15 US stocks (including foreign ADR) with the strongest correlation with the DAX over a 5-year period. An analysis by industry reveals that the DAX correlated best with interest rate sensitive groups like Utilities, Financials and Building Material stocks.

Table 6.2 Nonparametric correlation between the DAX and major European indices for the preceding 5 and 10 year period as of 31 May 2007.

Index	5 Year	10 Year
Euro Stoxx 50	**0.992**	**0.966**
Stoxx 50	0.971	0.944
CAC 40	**0.995**	0.94
Euronext 100	**0.996**	N/A
FTSE	0.99	0.925
SSMI (Swiss)	0.99	0.936
MIB-30 (Italian)	0.987	N/A
BEL-20 (Belgian)	0.986	0.734
Athens General	0.98	0.823
Irish Stock Index	0.987	N/A

Table 6.3 Nonparametric correlation between the DAX and the 15 best correlated US stocks (including ADRs) during the 5-year period from 1 June 2003 to 1 June 2007. The 5-year Spearman's correlation coefficient is shown in column 3 and the stock's industry group in column 4. As was expected, the DAX has the strongest correlation with European ADRs like Holland's Akzo and the Greek Telco OTE.

Company name	Symbol	Correlation	Industry
Akzo Nobel NV	AKZOY	0.985	Chemicals
Hellenic Telecomm	OTE	0.979	Telecomm
ING Group NV	ING	0.976	Financial
Orient Express	OEH	0.976	Lodging
Mexico Fund	MXF	0.976	Country fund
Chubb Corp.	CB	0.975	Financial
General Dynamics	GD	0.975	Defense
Cleco Corp.	CNL	0.975	Utilities
DPL	DPL	0.975	Utilities
Manitowoc	MTW	0.973	Farm Machinery
Be Aerospace	BEAV	0.973	Defense
Iconix Brand	ICON	0.972	Apparel
Laboratory Corp.	LH	0.972	Drugs
Nucor	NUE	0.972	Steel
Cemex	CX	0.971	Building materials

6.3 EUROPEAN FUTURES

European futures trade long after the closing of equity trading in the corresponding exchanges so a more realistic analysis (for trading purposes) would be to correlate European index futures with the corresponding US futures. A comparison of the daily

Table 6.4 Nonparametric correlation matrix between international futures for the 5-year period from 1 January 2002 to 31 December 2006. The FDAX is the DAX contract trading in the Eurex; the ES, YM, NQ and NKD are the S&P 500 e-mini, Dow, Nasdaq 100 and Nikkei contracts trading in the CME Globex; the ESTX is the Euro Stoxx 50 contract trading in the Eurex; the 6E is the Euro contract trading also in the Globex; the GC is the gold contract trading in the Comex; and the ZN is the 10-year Treasury note futures contract trading in the Globex.

Symbol index	FDAX DAX	ES SP 500	YM DJ-30	NQ Nasdaq	NKD Nikkei	FCE CAC 40	FESX Eurostx	6E Euro	GC Gold	ZN 10y TN
FDAX	1	**0.91**	0.89	0.85	0.90	**0.99**	**0.99**	0.41	0.66	−0.81
ES	**0.91**	1	**0.98**	**0.96**	0.92	0.93	0.88	0.68	0.86	−0.61
ER2	0.85	0.98	0.96	0.93	0.92	0.86	0.80	0.75	0.93	−0.53
YM	0.89	0.98	1	0.92	0.92	0.90	0.86	0.71	0.85	−0.60
NQ	0.85	0.96	0.92	1	0.85	0.86	0.82	0.63	0.81	−0.54
NKD	0.90	0.92	0.92	0.85	1	0.912	0.86	0.55	0.80	−0.69
FCE	0.99	0.93	0.90	0.86	0.91	1	0.99	0.44	0.69	−0.80
FESX	0.99	0.88	0.86	0.82	0.86	0.99	1	0.36	0.59	−0.82
EURO	0.41	0.68	0.71	0.63	0.55	0.44	0.36	1	0.82	−0.09
GC	0.66	0.86	0.85	0.81	0.80	0.69	0.59	0.82	1	−0.33
ZN	−0.81	−0.61	−0.60	−0.54	−0.69	−0.80	−0.82	−0.09	−0.33	1

yields in Tables 6.1 and 6.5 reveals a significant improvement of the correlations of daily changes which can only be attributed to the time lag factor between indices. This was most pronounced in the case of the DAX, whose correlation with the S&P improved dramatically from 0.13 (cash index) to 0.55 (futures). There was no

Table 6.5 Nonparametric correlation matrix of daily % changes between international index, currency and bond futures for the 5-year period from 1 January 2002 to 31 December 2006. Significant correlations are depicted in bold. The ZN is the 10-year Treasury note futures trading in the Globex.

Symbol index	FDAX DAX	ES SP 500	YM DJ-30	NQ Nasdaq	FCE CAC 40	FESX Eurostx	6E Euro	ZN TN
FDAX	1	0.55	0.52	0.49	**0.81**	**0.89**	−0.2	−0.29
ES	0.55	1	**0.82**	0.86	0.43	0.52	−0.1	−0.19
YM	0.52	**0.82**	1	0.67	0.41	0.50	−0.1	−0.16
NQ	0.49	**0.86**	0.67	1	0.37	0.45	−0.1	−0.21
FCE	**0.81**	0.43	0.41	0.37	1	**0.84**	−0.2	−0.23
FESX	**0.89**	0.52	0.50	0.45	**0.84**	1	−0.2	−0.26
EURO	−0.22	−0.12	−0.09	−0.14	−0.19	−0.22	1	0.33
ZN	−0.29	−0.19	−0.16	−0.21	−0.23	−0.26	0.33	1

significant difference, however, when comparing the direct price correlation between future and cash prices in Tables 6.1 and 6.4 as US cash indices were shifted back one day in time.

6.4 TIME FACTOR

It is obvious from Table 6.1 that the correlation of weekly percentage yields is stronger than the corresponding daily one. But why stop there? What about higher time increments? I have calculated in Table 6.6 Pearson's correlation of percentage

Table 6.6 Correlation variation between DAX and S&P futures (e-mini) for different time segment percentage yields for the 5-year period from 1 July 2002 to 30 June 2007. In the 3rd column is the correlation % change (improvement) from the previous time increment.

Days	Pearson's correlation	% change
1	0.617	
2	0.719	16.4
3	0.763	6.2
4	0.787	3.1
5	0.803	2.1
6	0.810	0.8
7	0.810	0.0
8	0.817	0.8
9	0.816	−0.1
10	0.824	1.1
11	0.825	0.1
12	0.822	−0.4
13	0.825	0.3
14	0.821	−0.4
15	0.822	0.1
16	0.824	0.2
17	0.823	0.0
18	0.824	0.1
19	0.823	0.0
20	0.825	0.2
25	0.831	0.8
30	0.847	1.9
35	0.853	0.7
40	0.863	1.3
45	0.872	0.9
50	0.876	0.5
75	0.890	1.6
100	0.893	0.3

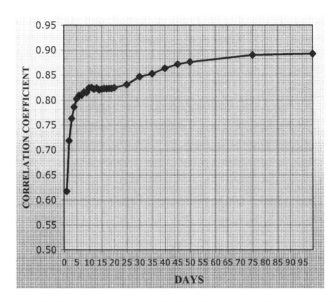

Figure 6.1 Graph of correlation variation for time intervals ranging from 1 to 100 days of percent yields between DAX and S&P futures (e-mini) for the 5-year period from 1 July 2002 to 30 June 2007.

yields for time intervals ranging from 1 to 100 days between DAX and S&P e-mini futures (ES). They are also plotted graphically in Fig. 6.1. A visual inspection of the graph reveals that the correlation improved exponentially for the first 5-day period, made a short-term peak at the 10-day increment and actually decreased slightly up to the 15-day time increment. It then started sloping up slightly to level off at 75 days. It is worthwhile noting that for longer than 10-day percentage differences, the correlation coefficient improved by only 8%. Therefore a time increment of five to ten days, when taking percentage differences, might be the optimum to use when designing short to medium term intermarket trading systems.

6.5 INTRADAY

The correlation of intraday percentage changes follows a similar pattern to the daily yields above.

In Table 6.7 I list Pearson's correlation for up to 1500 minutes (25 hours) of percentage yields between the DAX, Euro Stoxx 50 and S&P e-mini futures (ES). This was also plotted graphically in Fig. 6.2. The correlation between the DAX and

Table 6.7   Intraday correlation of 1 to 1500 minute (25 hour) percent changes
between the DAX , Euro Stoxx and S&P 500 futures for the 3-month period
from 1 January 2007 to 31 March 2007.

Minutes	Hours	ESTX	ES
5	0.08	0.877	0.724
10	0.17	**0.888**	0.741
15	0.25	0.891	0.754
20	0.33	0.893	0.763
25	0.42	0.895	0.768
30	0.50	0.897	0.774
35	0.58	0.899	0.780
40	0.67	0.900	0.782
45	0.75	0.901	0.787
50	0.83	0.902	0.789
55	0.92	0.904	0.793
60	1	0.905	0.797
65	1.08	0.906	0.802
70	1.17	0.907	0.807
75	1.25	**0.908**	0.810
80	1.33	0.908	0.812
85	1.42	0.908	0.813
90	1.50	0.909	0.814
95	1.58	0.909	0.815
100	1.67	0.908	0.816
125	2.08	0.910	0.823
150	2.50	0.910	0.830
200	3.33	0.913	0.836
250	4.17	0.915	0.842
375	6.25	0.916	0.850
500	8.33	0.918	0.862
750	12.50	0.925	0.884
1000	16.67	0.928	0.897
1250	20.83	0.928	0.900
1500	25	0.933	0.910

Euro Stoxx improved exponentially for the first 10-minute period, made a short-term
peak at the 75-minute increment, making only marginal improvements for the next
200 minutes.

The correlation between the DAX and S&P e-mini futures (ES), on the other hand,
made a short-term peak at the 75-minute ($1^1/_4$ hour) increment but continued rising
at a more moderate rate.

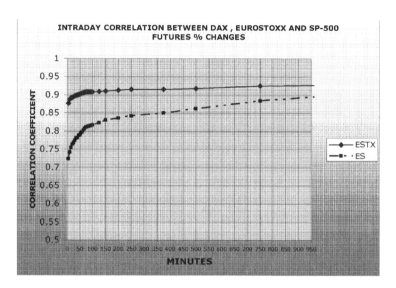

Figure 6.2 Graph of correlation between percent changes of DAX, Euro Stoxx (solid line) and e-mini S&P 500 futures (dashed line) for intraday time segments ranging from 5 to 1500 minutes (25 trading hours) for the 3-month period from 1 January 2007 to 31 March 2007. The correlation with Euro Stoxx futures flattens out after the first 75 minutes.

It is worthwhile noting that for longer than 10-minute percentage differences, the correlation coefficient between the DAX and Euro Stoxx futures improved by only 5 % but its correlation with the S&P e-mini improved substantially (23 %). It is therefore better to use longer time spans when designing short- to medium-term intermarket trading systems to trade the DAX based on its correlation with the S&P e-mini.

7
Gold

Good judgment is usually the result of experience and experience frequently is the result of bad judgment.

–Robert Lovell

In 1925, in a speech at the University of Cambridge, the English economist John Maynard Keynes called the Gold Standard "a barbaric relic" but even though the Gold Standard has since been abolished the "barbaric relic" has not lost its value. Federal Reserve Board chairman Alan Greenspan once wrote about gold: "This is the shabby secret of the welfare statistics' tirades against gold. Deficit spending is simply a scheme for the confiscation of wealth. Gold stands in the way of this insidious process. It stands as a protector of property rights . . .".

Gold topped $1000 an ounce in March 2008 as investors bid gold prices up amid worries about the falling dollar and the sub prime financial crisis. In fact, investors who bought gold in 2003 have more than tripled their initial investment, enjoying an annualized return of over 20 %.

One of the reasons gold has surged so much is that it's much easier to buy. For many years it was difficult for ordinary investors to trade gold. The minimum amount needed in order to buy gold bullion was $1 million. Buying gold coins or jewellery was also a problem because of the hassle of storing and reselling them. An alternative way to buy gold was to trade gold futures on the New York Commodities Exchange (COMEX). Most investors, however, do not have a futures account or prefer to trade only stocks because of the volatility and also the rollover costs. Investors can now buy shares of SPDR Gold Trust, an exchange-traded fund that can be bought and sold like any stock under the ticker symbol GLD. Each share represents one-tenth of an ounce of gold, and the shares are highly liquid.

In times of a financial crisis, rising inflation, or a weak dollar, gold does well but is it a good long-term investment? Gold peaked at about $840 an ounce in 1980 and was in a continuous decline until 2002. Anyone who invested in gold in 1988 would have made only 72 % on his initial investment and with inflation factored in would have made next to nothing over the 20 years from 1 January 1988 until the end of 2007. Meanwhile, a $1000 investment in the S&P 500 would have grown at a compound annual return of 10.6 % a year to $7500 in that time. Taking inflation into account the stock investor would still have made a 360 % profit and his initial $1000 investment would have grown to $4600 at an annualized rate of 7.4 % a year during the past 20 years. Investing in stocks generally does better against inflation over the long term because companies raise prices when inflation goes up. Growing productivity also helps stock prices keep ahead of inflation, which is not the case with gold.

Another reason for gold's mediocre long-term performance is the most fundamental concept of economics: supply and demand. Unlike other commodities which are used in industry and need to be continuously replenished, gold stays in the market.

7.1   CORRELATIONS WITH EQUITY AND COMMODITY ASSETS

Gold was traditionally uncorrelated with equities until a character change occurred in 2003. Gold started moving in the same direction with the S&P 500 and other international equity indices (see Fig. 7.1).

Before making any hasty conclusions, however, we should examine what the other asset classes were doing at the time. During that period the dollar was falling precipitously, inflation was rising and the rest of the commodities were also rising. I believe that the contemporaneous gold–equity appreciation only happened by chance and gold's gain had nothing to do with rising equity prices and more to do with the dollar's demise and the commodity-induced inflation.

Gold has been moving in lock step fashion with major averages until the summer of 2007 when fears of melt down in US financial markets triggered flight-to-safety demand for the yellow metal which decoupled from the S&P and moved to new highs in the following months.

In Tables 7.1 and 7.2 I list the correlation of weekly and two-week (10 working days) percent changes between gold and related equity indices, currencies and commodities. You can see that the correlation of weekly yields between gold and the S&P 500 changed from near zero to over 0.20 during the most recent 2-year period ending on 31 December 2007. For the reasons discussed above, I believe that this is only temporary and the correlation with equities will revert to the mean.

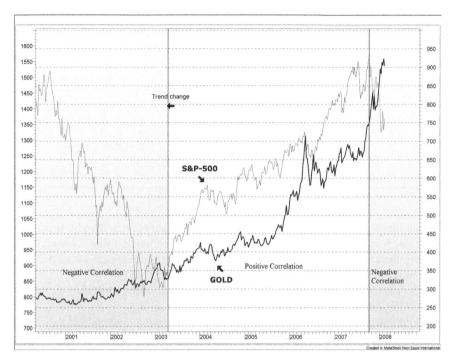

Figure 7.1 Weekly composite chart of the World Gold Index (thick black line with the scale on the right Y-axis) and the S&P 500 (thin grey line with the scale on the left Y-axis). Negative correlation is shaded in a gray background and positive with no background. Notice the correlation reversal in April 2003.

Table 7.1 Long- and short-term nonparametric correlation of weekly percentage changes between the World Gold Index and related commodity and financial indices up to 31 December 2007. TNX is the CBOE 10 Year Treasury Yield Index, XAU is the Philadelphia Gold/Silver Stock Index, CRB is the Commodity Research Bureau Index, Yen is the USD per yen exchange rate (JPY.USD) and TSX is the S&P Canada Composite Index.

Years	S&P 500	XAU	Silver	TSX	CRB	Dollar Index	Euro	Yen	TNX	Crude Oil
2	0.20	**0.78**	**0.82**	**0.46**	**0.63**	−0.55	**0.54**	0.24	0.03	**0.41**
5	0.10	**0.74**	**0.74**	0.31	0.55	−0.57	**0.54**	**0.32**	−0.08	0.23
10	0.02	**0.71**	0.66	0.18	0.45	−0.47	0.43	0.26	−0.10	0.17
15	0.00	**0.71**	0.66	0.18	0.43	−0.38	NA	0.23	−0.07	0.14

Table 7.2 Long- and short-term nonparametric correlation of 10-day percentage changes between the World Gold Index (gold spot) and related commodity and financial indices up to 31 December 2007. TNX is the CBOE 10 Year Treasury Yield Index, XAU is the Philadelphia Gold/Silver Stock Index, CRB is the Commodity Research Bureau Index, Yen is the USD per yen exchange rate (JPY.USD) and TSX is the S&P Canada Composite Index.

Years	S&P 500	XAU	Silver	TSX	CRB	Dollar Index	Euro	Yen	TNX	Crude Oil
2	0.16	**0.80**	**0.80**	**0.47**	**0.71**	−**0.63**	**0.61**	0.32	0.00	**0.51**
5	0.09	**0.74**	**0.71**	0.34	0.59	−**0.57**	0.53	**0.37**	−0.10	0.25
10	0.02	0.72	0.64	0.20	0.47	−0.49	0.47	0.25	−0.11	0.19
15	0.01	**0.73**	0.63	0.21	0.45	−0.39	NA	0.23	−0.09	0.15

But this is not the only change in gold's intermarket relations, and whether they will also revert to the mean is doubtful. A close inspection of Table 7.1 reveals that, during the last 5-year period since 2003, gold started moving closer to the entire commodity complex as represented by the CRB Index.

The traditional positive correlation between gold and silver has also recently increased significantly from 0.66 (strong) to 0.82 (very strong).

Gold and silver have always been positively correlated markets and their prices tend to move in the same direction. Their relationship, however, is not fundamental. The price of one does not move in a particular direction because the other market is moving the same way, as both markets are driven by the same fundamentals. This doesn't mean, however, that their relationship cannot be used in exploiting short-term market inefficiencies as the fundamental reasons (like the price of the US dollar) might not be reflected fully in the price of both at the same time.

Also, since gold is denominated in US dollars, it is reasonable to assume that it will be affected by the Federal Reserve monetary policy. In 2004 the Fed created excess liquidity. In the following 3-year period gold broke out from historical prices to new 10-year highs. After all, unlike paper money, gold cannot be printed. Long-term bullish factors for gold include explosive money supply growth, the US dollar, negative interest rates in the US, inflation and high commodity prices. Negative factors include Central Bank selling which can affect the yellow metal negatively in the short term.

Commodity prices may get seriously distorted by the underlying currency fluctuations and it pays to examine them with international eyes. Gold offers the best example in recent history.

To illustrate my point I have prepared two charts (Fig. 7.2). They are both of gold, the only difference being the currency gold is priced in. The first one (bold line) is in US dollars, and the other in euro. For the $3^1/_2$-year period from the beginning of 2002 and until about the middle of 2005 the first gold chart (in dollars) showed a strong up trend but this was not the case with the second chart (in euro)

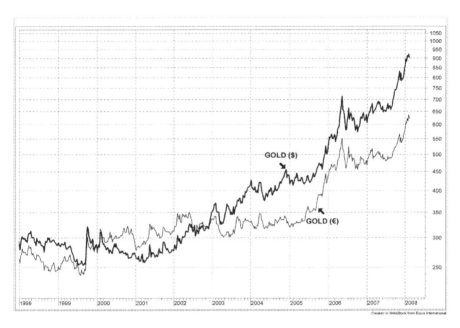

Figure 7.2 Weekly chart of gold spot prices in US dollars (thick bold line with the scale on the right Y-axis) and gold in euro (thin line with the scale again on the same axis). As you can see, European gold investors didn't profit from the 2002–2005 rally in gold.

which moved in a sideways range, finishing in April 2005 lower than it started in January 2002.

The gold's (in dollars) uptrend was caused by a bear market in the dollar, not a bull market in gold. During this period, the correct position for an international investor was a short dollar position, not a long gold position.

Gold is also tracking the crude oil market, for signals about futures inflation trends, and speculative sentiment towards the US dollar. Although its long-term correlation with crude oil futures is not as strong ($\rho = 0.41$ in Table 7.1) as it is with the CRB Index ($\rho = 0.63$), silver ($\rho = 0.82$) or the dollar index ($\rho = -0.55$), it can increase dramatically, in periods of rising volatility and sharp dollar declines (Fig. 7.3). During the preceding 3-year period there were four such incidents of market sentiment shift resulting in extremely close correlation between gold and crude oil (marked A, B, C and D in the chart in Fig. 7.3) which happened to coincide with the start of a sharp dollar decline. This is because, during periods of undisciplined dollar decline, their correlation with the dollar became the dominant price moving factor for both. Notice also that gold decoupled from oil two to three weeks before the dollar actually bottomed out as the market is always forward looking and discounted the end of the dollar's decline in advance.

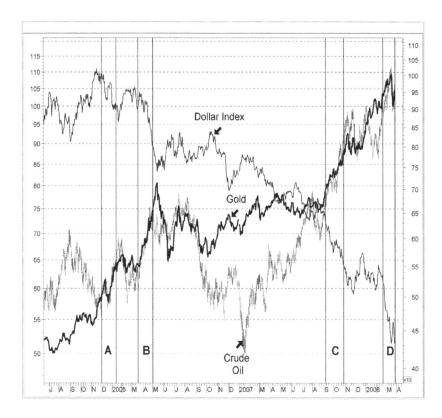

Figure 7.3 Daily composite chart of gold bullion spot prices (thick bold line with scale (divided by 10) on the right Y-axis), the dollar index (thin line) and NYMEX crude oil futures (grey price bars with the scale on the left Y-axis) from June 2005 to April 2008. Notice that in periods of sharp and uncontrollable dollar decline (bounded by vertical lines and marked A, B, C and D in the chart) the gold and oil charts coincide, indicating a market sentiment shift and resulting in a stronger correlation between the two commodities.

Finally don't forget that gold, like every other commodity, is subject to seasonal changes. Demand for gold is driven mainly by the jewellery industry. Gold prices usually spike up during the September through December period as jewellers stock up in gold prior to the year-end holiday shopping season.

Although seasonal patterns tend to recur each and every year in a more or less similar fashion, something that is more macro fundamental might override them. In the case of gold this factor was the dollar's weakness. In the bar chart in Fig. 7.4 you can see how gold's long-term (20 year) seasonality has been distorted by the recent (since 2002) bullish secular trend. Although the normal seasonal pattern is still there, the recent bullish trend that has been in place since 2002 pushed toward higher prices. As a result, the normal seasonal low is not as pronounced as it might

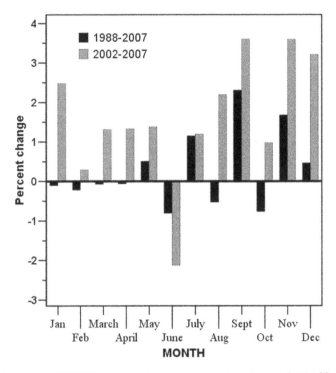

Figure 7.4 Average COMEX gold near-term contract percent changes for the 20-year period from 1988–2007 are shown in black, and for the most recent 6-year period from 2002–2007 in grey. Notice the seasonal strength in the September to December period when the jewellery industry is busy acquiring inventory for the holidays.

be otherwise. A secular bullish trend in energy and agricultural commodities has also caused anomalies in normal seasonal patterns, at least temporarily.

7.2   LEADING OR LAGGING?

It is very difficult to establish whether gold bullion prices are leading or lagging other related commodities by inspecting a composite chart visually (Figs. 7.5 and 7.6). Sometimes it leads, other times it lags, sometimes it moves coincidentally and at other times it does not respond at all to other correlated commodities. A rigorous mathematical analysis, however, reveals some repetitive persistency in gold's elusive maneuvers. This was contrived by calculating, in Table 7.3, lagging and leading correlations of weekly yields between gold and related commodities by shifting gold

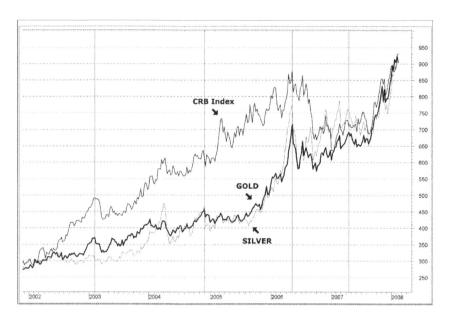

Figure 7.5 Weekly chart of the World Gold Index (in bold with the scale on the Y-axis), the World Silver Index (thin line in gray), and the CRB Index (normal line). Vertical lines were drawn at major peaks. No lead or lag is apparent from the charts as all three indices seem to peak at the same time.

Figure 7.6 Weekly chart of the World Gold Index (thick line in bold with the scale on the right Y-axis), the XAU Index (in gray), and the dollar index (normal line with the scale on the left Y-axis). Vertical solid lines were drawn at major peaks and dashed lines at major bottoms. No lead or lag is apparent from the charts as gold peaks at the same time that the dollar bottoms out and the XAU makes a top.

Table 7.3 Pearson's correlation coefficient of weekly percentage changes between the World Gold Index and the XAU, the dollar index, Canada's Venture Index and the Reuters/Jefferies Commodity Research Bureau Index (CRB). The correlations (except for the Venture Index) were calculated for the 15-year period from 1992–2006. Column 1 depicts the number of days that the gold data was shifted in time. A +1 day lag indicates that yesterday's gold weekly change was correlated with today's XAU, and dollar, CRB or Venture data and a lag of −1 indicates that tomorrow's gold weekly change was correlated with today's of the corresponding commodity. Therefore higher correlations with positive lags indicate a gold lead and higher correlations for negative lags indicate that gold lagged. Lag avg. (at the top of Column 1) is the weighted average of the lagging correlations and lead avg. is the time weighted average of the leading correlations.

Lag days	XAU	Dollar Index	Silver	Venture	CRB
lag avg.	0.291	−0.098	0.209	0.256	0.142
−10	−0.012	0.024	−0.033	−0.011	−0.018
−9	−0.002	0.026	−0.035	−0.003	−0.031
−8	0.018	0.028	−0.029	0.033	−0.028
−7	0.039	0.023	−0.017	0.077	−0.017
−6	0.055	0.015	−0.007	0.093	−0.010
−5	0.096	−0.003	0.021	0.134	0.014
−4	0.250	−0.067	0.158	0.235	0.103
−3	0.375	−0.126	0.275	0.320	0.189
−2	0.478	−0.191	0.381	0.384	0.261
−1	0.589	−0.249	0.495	0.474	0.344
0	0.679	−0.315	0.612	0.574	0.428
1	0.476	−0.233	0.454	0.417	0.330
2	0.328	−0.187	0.334	0.310	0.244
3	0.196	−0.129	0.218	0.222	0.161
4	0.058	−0.082	0.091	0.118	0.074
5	−0.070	−0.028	−0.026	0.027	−0.015
6	−0.066	−0.033	−0.036	0.013	−0.036
7	−0.068	−0.030	−0.040	0.015	−0.045
8	−0.068	−0.032	−0.042	0.009	−0.043
9	−0.070	−0.021	−0.040	−0.003	−0.047
10	−0.063	−0.013	−0.044	−0.013	−0.042
lead avg.	0.150	−0.113	0.167	0.179	0.120

yields from one to 10 days forward (positive values) and up to 10 days back in time (negative values). The leading/lagging correlations between gold and every other related commodity were then plotted individually in Figs. 7.7 to 7.11. For predictive purposes, we wish to detect which commodities have stronger leading correlations with gold. These relationships can then be used to predict the future course of events in trading systems or forecasting models.

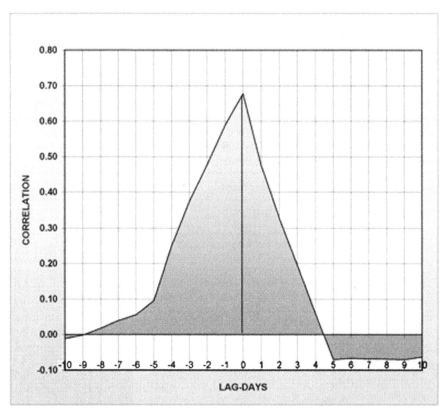

Figure 7.7 Correlation of weekly percentage changes between the World Gold Index and the XAU, for 1 to 10 day lag or lead. Higher correlations for negative values on the X-axis indicate that gold lags the XAU, and higher correlations for positive values on the X-axis that indicate that gold leads the XAU. In this case the gold correlations were higher for negative lag, indicating that it is lagging the XAU. The correlations were calculated for the 15-year period from 1992–2006.

The moment of truth has arrived for gold since the leading/lagging correlation analyses shed some light on the existence and nature of the predictive capability of related markets in forecasting the yellow metal's next move. Keep in mind that these indicate only the average short-term tendency and are not appropriate to use for longer-term trends. Important conclusions are summarized below.

- **The XAU** There was a strong positive contemporaneous (zero lag) correlation between the XAU and gold ($r = 0.68$ and $r = 0.62$ for weekly and daily yields

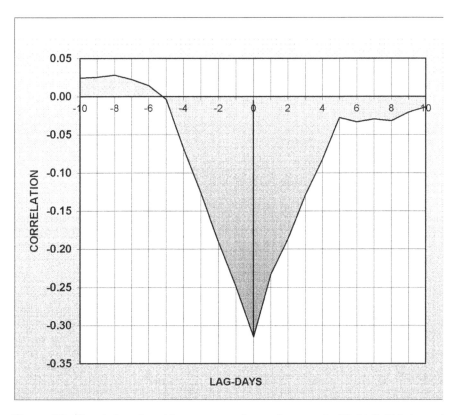

Figure 7.8 Correlation of weekly percentage changes between the World Gold Index and the dollar index, for 1 to 10 day lag or lead. Gold's initial lag reversed to a lead after the first couple of days. The correlations were calculated for the 15-year period from 1992–2006.

respectively). Based on the lag analysis, the XAU is leading gold for both weekly (Fig. 7.7) and daily yields (Table 7.4). The weekly yield weighted average of 10-day leading correlations was 0.29 compared with 0.15 for lagging correlations (Table 7.3). A longer-term lead of gold stocks over gold bullion was also noticed by John Murphy and mentioned in his book on intermarket analysis (see Bibliography).

• **The dollar index** had relatively weak coincident negative correlation when taking daily percent differences but this improved on raw price correlations (Table 7.5). It is reasonable to assume that, as gold is denominated in US dollars, it should lag the dollar. This was confirmed, however, for only the first two days of lag before gold took the lead. Notice the correlation actually turned positive for more than five days of lead (see Table 7.3 and Fig. 7.8).

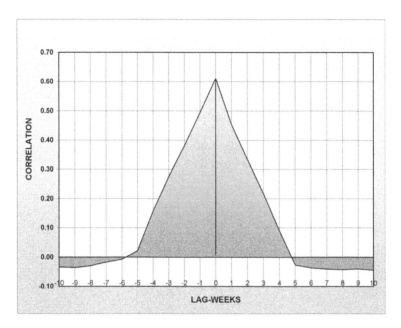

Figure 7.9 Correlation of weekly percentage changes between the World Gold Index and the World Silver Index (XSLV), for 1 to 10 day lag or lead. Silver correlated slightly better with leading (negative shift) gold values, suggesting that it is leading gold. The correlations were calculated for the 15-year period from 1992–2006.

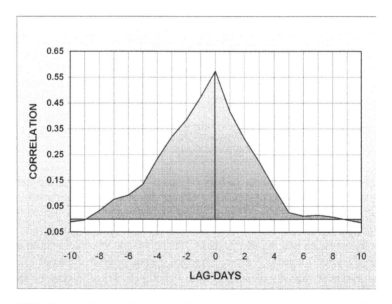

Figure 7.10 Pearson's correlation of weekly percentage changes between the World Gold Index and Canada's Venture Composite Index, for 1 to 10 day lag or lead. The Venture Index correlated slightly better with leading (negative values on the X-axis) gold prices suggesting that it is leading gold. Data for the Venture Index were available only for the 5-year period from 2002–2006.

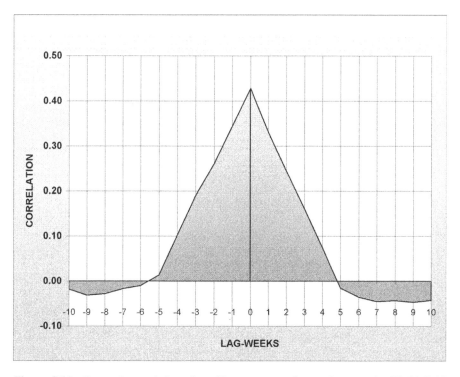

Figure 7.11 Pearson's correlation of weekly percentage changes between the World Gold Index and the Reuters/Jefferies CRB Index, for 1 to 10 day lag or lead. The CRB correlated slightly better with leading gold values, suggesting that it is leading gold. The correlations were calculated for the 15-year period from 1992–2006.

- **Silver** had the second best (after the XAU) correlation of weekly and daily yields. Silver moves more or less coincidentally with gold. A slight lead is barely evident in the graph in Fig. 7.9.
- **Canada's Venture Index** had the best coincident correlation based on raw prices ($r = 0.965$ in Table 7.5). The Venture Index is also leading gold prices (Fig. 7.10).
- **The CRB Index** had the worst positive coincident correlation for both weekly and daily yields. No significant lead or lag was apparent in Table 7.3 or Fig. 7.11.

We can therefore conclude, based on the correlation analysis above, that gold either lags or moves concurrently with other related commodities or indices. It is therefore better to use related markets in order to forecast gold rather than the other way around. The inferences drawn from this analysis are only useful for short-term predictions as the lag interval was limited to 10 days or less.

Table 7.4 Pearson's correlation coefficient of daily percent changes between the World Gold Index and the XAU, the dollar index, Canada's Venture Index and the Reuters/Jefferies Commodity Research Bureau Index (CRB). The correlations were calculated for the 15-year period from 1992–2006. Column 1 shows the number of days that the gold data was shifted in time. A lag of 1 day indicates that yesterday's gold daily change was correlated with today's XAU, Dollar, CRB or Venture prices. Therefore higher correlations with positive lags indicate a gold lead and higher correlations for negative lag indicate that gold lagged. Lag avg. is the time weighted average of the lagging (negative shift) correlations and lead avg. is the time weighted average of the leading (positive shift) correlations.

Lag days	XAU	Dollar Index	Silver	Venture	CRB
lag avg.	0.029	−0.005	0.007	0.033	0.008
−10	0.028	−0.009	0.025	0.031	0.000
−9	0.004	0.003	−0.008	−0.005	−0.013
−8	−0.006	0.001	−0.035	−0.004	−0.026
−7	0.015	0.019	0.013	0.030	0.015
−6	−0.013	0.014	−0.034	−0.007	−0.003
−5	0.033	−0.023	0.043	0.061	−0.002
−4	0.030	0.009	0.003	0.048	0.008
−3	0.028	0.002	0.010	0.059	0.021
−2	0.005	−0.010	0.012	0.014	−0.007
−1	0.092	−0.025	0.014	0.044	0.033
0	0.623	−0.313	0.619	0.572	0.409
1	−0.072	0.038	−0.064	0.009	−0.009
2	−0.029	−0.022	0.010	−0.017	0.013
3	0.001	0.006	0.003	0.030	0.001
4	0.005	−0.012	−0.002	0.010	0.002
5	0.004	−0.015	0.019	0.024	0.018
6	−0.034	−0.007	−0.032	−0.039	−0.034
7	−0.020	−0.001	−0.004	−0.003	−0.021
8	−0.017	−0.020	−0.028	−0.008	−0.004
9	−0.007	0.002	0.020	0.020	−0.006
10	0.006	−0.007	−0.002	0.014	0.012
lead avg.	−0.022	−0.001	−0.012	0.004	−0.002

7.3   WHICH TIME FRAME?

There are two problems when using raw price data to calculate statistical metrics such as correlation:

- Prices are not normally distributed.
- Relationships between markets are not linear.

Table 7.5 Pearson's correlation coefficient between the World Gold Index and the XAU, the dollar index, Canada's Venture Index and the Reuters/Jefferies Commodity Research Bureau Index (CRB).The correlations (except for Venture Index) were calculated for the 15-year period from 1992–2006. Column 1 shows the number of days that the gold data were shifted in time. A lag of 1 day indicates that yesterday's gold price was correlated with today's XAU, dollar index, CRB or Venture prices. Lag avg. is the time weighted average of the lagging correlations and lead avg. is the time weighted average of the leading correlations.

Lag days	XAU	Dollar Index	Silver	Venture	CRB
lag avg.	0.766	−0.633	0.822	0.908	0.846
−10	0.757	−0.626	0.807	0.892	0.843
−9	0.758	−0.627	0.809	0.894	0.842
−8	0.760	−0.628	0.811	0.897	0.843
−7	0.762	−0.629	0.814	0.899	0.844
−6	0.763	−0.631	0.817	0.902	0.845
−5	0.766	−0.631	0.820	0.911	0.846
−4	0.767	−0.632	0.822	0.910	0.846
−3	0.768	−0.634	0.824	0.910	0.847
−2	0.769	−0.635	0.826	0.911	0.847
−1	0.771	−0.637	0.829	0.916	0.848
0	0.790	−0.654	0.856	0.965	0.871
1	0.769	−0.638	0.829	0.916	0.846
2	0.767	−0.637	0.826	0.910	0.844
3	0.765	−0.636	0.825	0.909	0.842
4	0.763	−0.636	0.823	0.908	0.840
5	0.762	−0.636	0.822	0.910	0.839
6	0.760	−0.636	0.819	0.901	0.837
7	0.758	−0.635	0.816	0.897	0.835
8	0.756	−0.635	0.815	0.894	0.833
9	0.754	−0.634	0.813	0.892	0.831
10	0.753	−0.634	0.811	0.890	0.830
lead avg.	0.763	−0.636	0.823	0.907	0.840

Both problems are usually resolved when taking price differences or percent changes but what is the optimum time segment for calculating the difference?

In Table 7.6 I have calculated Pearson's correlation from 1 to 400 days percent changes between gold bullion, the XAU and the dollar index. This is also plotted graphically in Fig. 7.12.

The correlation variation in time is very similar for both the gold–XAU and the gold–dollar relationships. The gold–dollar correlation peaked for nine day changes,

Table 7.6 Pearson's correlation for different interval percent changes between gold
bullion, the XAU and the US dollar index based on 10-year data from 1 January 1997 to
21 December 2006. Columns 3 and 5 show the correlation % change from the previous time
increment.

Yield days	XAU	% Change	Dollar Index	% Change
1	0.626		−0.394	
2	0.652	4.2	−0.406	3.1
3	0.664	1.9	−0.418	2.8
4	0.670	0.9	−0.418	0.0
5	0.679	1.3	−0.422	1.0
6	0.688	1.3	−0.426	1.0
7	**0.691**	0.5	−0.427	0.3
8	0.693	0.2	−0.432	1.0
9	0.695	0.4	**−0.433**	0.4
10	0.696	0.1	−0.432	−0.2
11	**0.698**	0.2	−0.431	−0.4
12	0.698	0.0	−0.429	−0.4
13	0.697	−0.1	−0.429	0.1
14	0.693	−0.6	−0.428	−0.2
15	0.693	0.0	−0.427	−0.4
16	0.692	−0.2	−0.423	−0.9
17	0.691	−0.2	−0.422	−0.3
18	0.691	0.0	−0.423	0.2
19	0.692	0.2	−0.422	−0.1
20	0.696	0.6	−0.425	0.6
25	0.702	0.8	−0.440	3.6
30	0.711	1.4	−0.454	3.2
35	**0.720**	1.2	**−0.462**	1.7
40	0.724	0.6	−0.461	−0.2
45	0.725	0.1	−0.460	−0.1
50	0.725	−0.1	−0.455	−1.2
75	0.729	0.6	−0.437	−3.9
100	0.744	2.1	−0.432	−1.1
200	0.823	10.6	−0.450	4.1
300	0.873	6.0	−0.444	−1.4
400	0.886	1.5	−0.544	22.6

two days sooner than the gold–XAU. Both correlations then declined until the 20th
day. The similarity, however, ended there. The gold–XAU correlation kept rising
when taking longer time differences whereas the gold–dollar correlation peaked at
35 days.

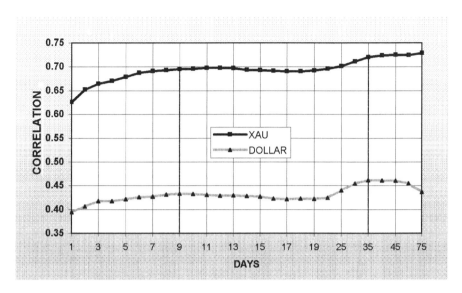

Figure 7.12 Graph of the correlation between gold bullion, the XAU (bold black line) and the dollar index (grey line) for variable time segment percent changes for the 10-year period from 1 January 1997 to 1 January 2007. The number of trading days used to calculate the percent changes is plotted in the X-axis and Pearson's correlation in the Y-axis.

In choosing the best time frame to use in a trading system or indicator, one's time horizon should also be taken into consideration. A time increment of nine days, when taking percentage differences, might be the best to use when designing short to medium term intermarket trading systems.

8
Intraday Correlations

Probable impossibilities are to be preferred to improbable possibilities.

—Aristotle

8.1 RELATIONSHIPS BETWEEN DIFFERENT TIME FRAMES

The analysis of correlations of weekly yields is not really very useful to day traders or short-term traders of stock index futures.

But what about intraday relationships?

In Table 8.1 you can see the correlation of percentage changes between the DAX, the Euro Stoxx 50 and the S&P 500 and the DOW e-mini futures for different time intervals ranging from five to 1500 minutes (25 hours). One trading day for the DAX and Euro Stoxx futures is 14 hours so the correlation study, although calculated over a three-month time span, involves only up to two days of percentage changes.

An empirical relationship between time (in minutes) and correlation, which is not so obvious from Table 8.1, unravels when the correlation is plotted vs. time in the graph in Fig. 8.1. You can see that the correlation increases exponentially up to a certain time increment (about 75 minutes) when it suddenly loses steam and starts to level out.

To assist traders I have derived the following empirical equations to convert correlations between different time frames.

For the DAX–Euro Stoxx relationship:

$$r_i = 0.87^*(T_i)^{.01} \tag{8.1}$$

and

$$r_i = r_j^*(Ti/Tj)^{.01} \tag{8.2}$$

Table 8.1   A total of 10 870 5-minute bars were used to calculate intraday correlation of percentage yields (changes) between the S&P 500 e-mini futures, the Euro Stoxx, the DAX and DOW e-mini futures for the 3-month period from 1 January 2007 to 31 March 2007. Significant correlations are depicted in bold.

Minutes	ESTX	DAX	YM
5	0.725	0.724	0.614
10	0.750	0.741	0.655
15	0.767	0.754	0.667
20	0.779	0.763	0.679
25	0.783	0.768	0.683
30	**0.788**	0.774	0.690
35	0.782	**0.780**	**0.694**
40	0.776	0.782	0.696
45	0.780	0.787	0.700
50	0.783	0.789	0.703
55	0.787	0.793	0.706
60	0.785	0.797	**0.707**
65	0.786	0.802	0.724
70	0.788	0.807	0.737
75	0.788	0.810	0.750
80	0.788	0.812	0.761
85	0.788	0.813	0.771
90	0.787	0.814	0.779
95	0.786	0.815	0.787
100	0.785	0.816	0.794
125	0.785	**0.823**	0.818
150	0.786	0.830	0.830
200	0.783	0.836	0.851
250	0.780	0.842	0.868
375	0.778	0.850	0.889
500	**0.786**	0.862	0.902
750	0.812	0.884	0.913
1000	0.830	0.897	**0.921**
1250	0.831	0.900	0.925
1500	**0.842**	**0.910**	0.928

and for the ES – DAX relationship:

$$r_i = 0.677^* T^{.04} \qquad (8.3)$$

and

$$r_i = r_j^*(Ti/Tj)^{.04} \qquad (8.4)$$

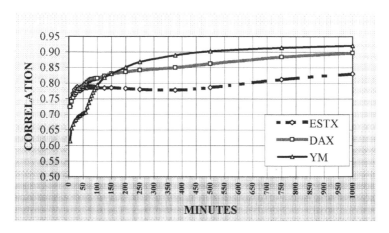

Figure 8.1 Intraday correlation of intraday percentage yields (changes) between the S&P 500 e-mini futures, the Euro Stoxx, the DAX and the DOW e-mini futures for the 3-month period from 1 January 2007 to 31 March 2007.

where r_i = Pearson's intraday correlation for time interval i; r_j = Pearson's intraday correlation for time interval j; T = time in minutes.

Equations 8.1–8.4 above are useful in calculating correlations and regression coefficients for all intraday time frames. For example we can use formula (8.3) to calculate an estimate of the 60-minute correlation between DAX and S&P e-mini futures:

$$r = 0.677^*60^{.04} = 0.797$$

Formula (8.4) can be used to convert correlations between intraday time frames. For example we know that the 15-minute correlation between the S&P e-mini and DAX futures is $r = 0.754$ and we want to know the corresponding 60-minute correlation coefficient. By substituting the 15-minute correlation in formula (8.4) we get:

$$r = 0.754^*(60/15)^{.04} = 0.797$$

8.2 INTERMARKET REGRESSION

The correlation coefficient calculated above can be used to forecast the expected change of one equity index future in terms of the other using the regression equation derived in Chapter 3. So for example:

- On 23 March 2007 and at 10:00 CET (02:00 US ET) the price of DAX futures was 6894.5 and the ES (S&P e-mini) was 1444.8.
- At 11:00 CET the DAX went up by 0.2 % to 6908 but the ES did not move at all.

- Using the regression equation we can calculate the expected change of the ES in terms of the DAX, based on historical data of 60-minute intervals as follows:

  In the case of highly correlated indices the regression line usually crosses through the origin so the constant can be ignored and the regression equation is reduced to:

$$ES = r^*sd(ES)/sd(DAX)^*DAX$$

  where: ES = S&P e-mini hourly % change; DAX = DAX futures hourly % change; sd = the standard deviation of hourly changes; r = Pearson's hourly correlation between the ES and the DAX. And the expected ES change based on historical correlations was:

$$ES = .797^*.185/.239^*.2 = .12\%.$$

There was therefore a divergence between e-mini and DAX futures, most probably due to the lateness of the hour (for US traders) and the e-mini needed to catch up. During the next two hours the ES outperformed the DAX by more than 0.16 %, thus nullifying the divergence.

8.3   WHICH TIME FRAME?

In order to choose the best time span for calculating percentage yields in a trading system or indicator, I have listed in Table 8.1 Pearson's correlation for up to 1500 minutes (25 hours) of percentage yields between the S&P e-mini, the Euro Stoxx 50 (ESTX), DAX and Dow e-mini futures. These were also plotted graphically in Fig. 8.1.

After carefully examining both the table and the graph the following conclusions can be drawn:

- Surprisingly, the S&P e-mini correlated better with the European futures than with its compatriot, the DOW e-mini, but only for shorter time segments up to 35 minutes of yields.
- Correlations with European futures peaked between 30 and 35-minute yields and this is probably the best value to use for short-term predictions based on Euro Stoxx futures.
- The S&P e-mini correlated better with the Euro Stoxx for very short yields (up to 35 minutes), with the DAX for medium (40 to 150 minute) yields and with DOW futures for longer term (over 150 minute or $2\frac{1}{2}$ hour) yields.
- The correlation between the S&P e-mini futures (ES) and the Euro Stoxx, after making a short-term top at the first 30-minute yield segment, went sideways for the next 470 minutes (8 hours) but started rising again sharply.
- On the other hand, after rising sharply for the first 35 minutes, the correlation between the S&P and the DAX continued rising at a more moderate rate.

- Similarly, the correlation between the S&P and DOW e-mini futures (YM), after making a short term plateau between the 35-minute and 60-minute increment, kept rising rather steeply until the end.
- The correlation coefficient between the S&P and Euro Stoxx futures improved by only 7 % for longer than 30-minute yields, whereas the correlation with the DOW improved by more than 30 %. It is therefore advantageous to use longer time frames when designing short-to-medium term intermarket trading systems to trade the S&P based on its correlation with the DOW.

Finally you should keep in mind that the values of the correlations in Table 8.1, although calculated from a big enough sample of 10 870 cases, are not written in stone but can vary considerably over time. For example, take a look at the chart of the S&P e-mini and Euro Stoxx 15-minute December 07 contracts. The correlation of 30-minute changes (in the top window) varies from a maximum of $r = 0.86$ on 19 September to a minimum of $r = 0.72$ on 9 October 2007. The corresponding average correlation calculated in Table 8.1 from a different sample from 1 January 2007 to 31 March 2007 was $r = 0.788$ (in bold) which is pretty close to the average in the chart in Fig. 8.2. In addition to the short-term variations mentioned above,

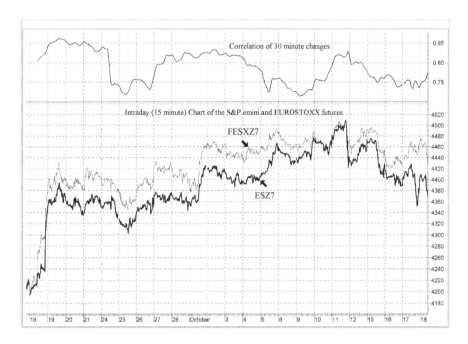

Figure 8.2 Intraday (15 minute) composite chart of the S&P e-mini (ESZ7), plotted with a thick bold line and the Euro Stoxx 50 (FESXZ7) December 2007 contracts from 18 September 2007 to 18 October 2007. The 10-day moving average of the correlation of the 30-minute changes is plotted in the top window.

the correlation can also digress from the mean during long time periods, caused by temporary decoupling of the underlying equity indices which is usually caused by a component stock specific problem not present in the other index.

8.4   LAGGING OR LEADING?

In practice, the main purpose of a predictive model is not to get the maximum explanatory value from a contemporaneous correlation analysis but to find a predictive market that shows changes and disparities between forecasted and observed values, warning of dangers and opportunities well ahead of time. In this context, we want the observed values to diverge from the statistically predicted values at times. This can only be accomplished by a leading/lagging correlation analysis which is simply a list of the correlations between values of a time series and other values of a related time series displaced at specified time intervals (lags).

Some problems arise in running a correlation analysis between US and European index futures, mainly because of the different time zones and trading hours. To deal with the time zone problem I had to convert all time zones to Central European time (CET) and in order to avoid division by zero errors in the correlation calculation (when one of the contracts was not trading), I deleted all US futures data when the European futures were closed (from 22:00 to 7:50 CET).

Although European index futures trade long after the underlying equity markets have closed, after 17:30 CET (when the European equity exchanges close) they move only on news from the other side of the Atlantic.

To deal with this problem and examine the effect of the US equity markets on European futures after the underlying main equity exchanges have closed or vice versa, I have divided the data into five separate groups according to the time of day. In the first group I have included only data until 14:30 CET (8:30 US EST). This is the time when European stock action and news are prevailing before the release of any important US economic news.

The second time segment was until US market open (15:30 CET or 9:30 US EST). The third group included only data until 17:30 CET (10:30 US EST) which is the closing time of most European stock exchanges. In the fourth group I have included all available data from 8:00 to 22:00 CET and, lastly, in the fifth group I have included only data after 15:30 CET (9:30 US EST). This is the time segment when the prevailing news that drives the markets originates mostly from the United States.

In addition, in order to determine which one was leading or lagging, the S&P e-mini was shifted both forward and backward in time.

Table 8.2 presents the leading, lagging and synchronous (coincident) correlations of 30-minute yields during the different time segments of the trading day between the S&P e-mini and Euro Stoxx futures, the DOW e-mini and the DAX, and in Table 8.3 you can see the intraday variability of the correlation between DAX and Euro Stoxx futures.

Table 8.2 Intraday correlation of 30-minute intraday yields (percentage changes) between S&P 500 e-mini futures, the Euro Stoxx, the DAX and DOW e-mini futures for specific time of day segments. Column 3 shows only data until 14:30 CET (Central European time) or 8:30 US EST, Column 4 shows only data until US market open (9:30 US EST), Column 5 shows only data until European close (17:30 CET) and Column 6 shows only data after US market open (9:30 US EST). The S&P data were shifted forward and back in time in order to calculate lagging and leading correlations.

30 min yields	lead/lag	<14:30	<15:30 US open	<17:30 EUR close	08:00–22:00 All day	>15:30
					TIME (CET)	
ESTX	synchronous	0.811	0.795	**0.781**	**0.788**	**0.815**
ESTX	lagging	0.663	0.65	0.632	0.652	**0.676**
ESTX	leading	0.668	0.655	0.634	0.649	0.665
YM	synchronous	0.606	0.596	0.680	0.690	**0.735**
YM	lagging	**0.512**	**0.503**	**0.569**	**0.583**	**0.615**
YM	leading	0.485	0.483	0.558	0.571	0.609
DAX	synchronous	**0.818**	**0.797**	0.776	0.774	0.798
DAX	lagging	**0.676**	**0.658**	**0.635**	**0.644**	**0.663**
DAX	leading	0.668	0.654	0.63	0.64	0.655

The following conclusions were drawn from the leading, lagging and synchronous time segmented correlations in Tables 8.2 and 8.3:

- The best synchronous correlation was between S&P e-mini and Euro Stoxx futures ($r = 0.788$ in bold in the Column-5 of Table 8.2 and $r = 0.815$ after 15:30 CET). The Euro stoxx was slightly leading the e-mini up to 15:30 CET but the lead

Table 8.3 Intraday correlation of 30-minute intraday yields (percentage changes) between the Euro Stoxx and DAX futures for specific time of day segments. In the first row only data until US market open (15:30 CET) were used, in the second row only data until European market close (17:30 CET) were used, and in the fourth row only data after US market open (9:30 US EST) were used. In order to calculate lagging and leading correlation the Euro Stoxx data were shifted forward and back in time.

	Time of day CET	synchronous	lagging	leading
		DAX		
<15:30	Before US open	0.857	**0.696**	0.687
<17:30	Before EUR close	0.883	**0.716**	0.707
10:00–22:00	All day	0.897	**0.740**	0.731
>15:30	After US open	0.948	0.789	0.781

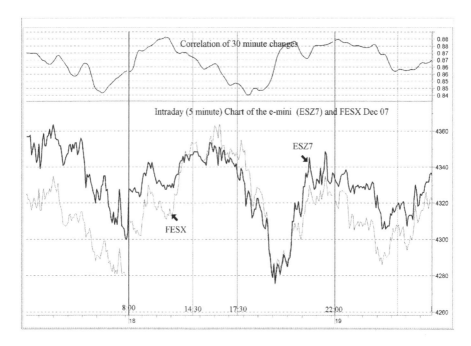

Figure 8.3 Intraday (5 minute) composite chart of the S&P e-mini (thick bold line) and Euro Stoxx 50 (thin line with the scale on the right Y-axis) contracts from 18–20 December 2007. The 5 bar moving average of the correlation of the 30-minute changes between the S&P e-mini and Euro Stoxx futures is also plotted in the top window. To illustrate the correlation variability during the trading day, vertical lines are drawn at the EUREX open (8:00 CET), at 14:30 CET (US pre-open), 17:30 CET (European equity close) and 22:00 CET (EUREX futures close). Euro Stoxx futures trade in the EUREX from 8:00 am CET to 22:00 CET. To avoid division by zero errors in the correlation calculation when the Euro Stoxx doesn't trade, non overlapping e-mini data (from 22:00 to 8:00 CET) were deleted.

reversed dramatically to a considerable lag (r lagging $= 0.676$ vs. r leading $= 0.665$) after the US market open. It is therefore better to avoid intermarket trading signals before 15:30 CET when designing an intermarket system to trade the Euro Stoxx based on its correlation with the S&P e-mini.

- The DAX futures lagged both the Euro Stoxx futures (Table 8.3) and the S&P e-mini (Table 8.2) for all time frames; a slight lag up to European close deteriorated significantly after 17:30 CET (European close). As the DAX correlated significantly better with Euro Stoxx futures than with the e-mini, it is better to use this relationship in designing an intermarket system to trade DAX futures, at least until US market open. After 15:30 both European futures lagged the US futures; therefore replacing the Euro Stoxx with the e-mini might have a lead time advantage, despite the lower correlation.

- Surprisingly, the DOW e-mini, despite the underlying index sharing all of its component stocks with the S&P 500, did not correlate with the S&P e-mini as well as Euro Stoxx futures. In addition, the DOW lagged the S&P e-mini during all time segments. It is therefore preferable to trade the DOW e-mini based on its correlation with the S&P e-mini and not the other way around.

The variability of the correlation during the trading day, presented in Table 8.2 in tabular form, can also be seen graphically in the chart in Fig. 8.3 where the correlation of 30-minute changes between the S&P e-mini and Euro Stoxx futures is plotted in the top window. For example, you can see that on 18 December 2007, the correlation rose to a maximum during the first time segment (before 14:30 CET) and then fell to an intraday low during the second and third time segments. It then rose again exactly to the level of the morning high during the end of the last time segment (after about 22:00 CET).

In designing intermarket systems to trade stock index futures, it is therefore better to use intermarket generated signals only when the underlying equity markets are closed and the leadership switches to related markets that are still open.

9
Intermarket Indicators

I'm a great believer in luck, and I find the harder I work, the more I have of it.
                                                                    –Thomas Jefferson

Classic technical analysis indicators, such as moving averages, only indicate the possible likelihood of the continuation of the current trend and they are certainly no guarantee of future direction, which can reverse on a dime.

The indicators presented in this chapter, unlike moving averages, will help you judge the direction of tomorrow's price, and possible trend reversals using intermarket correlations.

9.1   RELATIVE STRENGTH

Relative strength (RS) is a popular indicator which compares one security with another or with a benchmark index, for example a specific US stock with the S&P 500.

Relative strength in the stock market was popularized in the 1980s by William O'Niel in his classic *How to Make Money in Stocks*. O'Niel is also the founder of *Investor's Business Daily,* where he publishes the IBD® 100 stock list featuring companies that show superior earnings and strong price performance relative to the market average.

The relative strength is calculated by dividing the price of one security by the benchmark. The ratio is further smoothed by a moving average in order to eliminate the effect of erratic price movements or "noise" from daily price fluctuations.

When this ratio is rising, the numerator is outperforming the denominator and vice versa.

In Fig. 9.1 I use the ratio between the Gold ETF (GLD) and the dollar index (DXY). To remove daily noise the ratio is smoothed by its 3-day exponential moving

Figure 9.1 Composite chart of the Gold ETF (GLD) and the dollar index (DXY) for the 2-year period from July 2005 to July 2007. The 3-day moving average of the gold/dollar relative strength is depicted in the middle window and the 2000-day intermarket momentum oscillator (see Section 9.6) in the top window. Up and down arrows indicate sell and buy signals triggered by the oscillator crossing its 4-day moving average at overbought (over 80) and oversold (less than 50) levels respectively.

average (EMA). This is plotted in the middle window and, to avoid confusing it with Wilder's Relative Strength Index, I called it Intermarket Relative Strength. Classic technical analysis trendlines can be drawn by joining tops or bottoms. On 27 March 2006 the gold/dollar ratio broke the trendline drawn over the three previous peaks (the first, shorter trendline on the left of the chart in Fig. 9.1) and the price of the gold ETF surged 27 % from 55.7 to 71.1. Similarly, on 27 October 2006 the ratio broke its 5-month down trendline (second trendline in the middle) which indicated a trend reversal for gold.

The relative strength, however, cannot keep rising indefinitely, flagrantly violating long-term relationships. To determine overbought and oversold levels, I normalize it on a scale from 1 to 100 using the intermarket momentum oscillator (the formula is included in Section 9.6 below).

Values over a specific value (e.g. 80) indicate overbought levels and below another lower value (e.g. 50) oversold levels. In Fig. 9.1, I marked some possible buy and sell signals triggered by the oscillator crossing its 4-day moving average from below on oversold (less than 50) levels and crossing its moving average from above on overbought (over 80) levels respectively.

The relative strength between a stock and the appropriate index can also be used to evaluate one's stock portfolio. If the relative strength drops below its moving average while the price of the security is still rising, then it is time to consider heading for the exit while the stock is still strong.

This tactic can be combined with a moving average strategy to help you get out at a better price than if you were using a moving average of the price alone.

9.2 BOLLINGER BAND DIVERGENCE

This indicator was first introduced in my article "Detecting Breakouts" in *Technical Analysis of STOCKS & COMMODITIES* (see Bibliography) in order to calculate the divergence between price and money flow. It can also be used to calculate the divergence between a security and a related market. First the relative position of both securities in the Bollinger Bands is calculated and the divergence is derived by subtracting the relative position of the intermarket security from the base security. Indicator values vary from -100 to $+100$, values less than zero indicate negative divergence and over zero positive divergence. Buy signals are generated when the indicator reaches a peak above a certain level (usually 10 to 30) and subsequently declines. Similarly, sell signals are triggered when the indicator reaches a bottom below a certain level (usually -10 to -30) and rises.

The formula for the relative position of a security in the Bollinger Bands is derived as follows:

$$\text{SEC1BOL}=(\text{C-BollingerBBottom})/(\text{BollingerBTop-BollingerBBottom})$$
$$(9.1)$$

$$\text{but BollingerBandBottom}=\text{MA}-2\text{SD} \qquad (9.2)$$
$$\text{and BollingerBandTop}=\text{MA}+2\text{SD}. \qquad (9.3)$$

Substituting from (9.2) and (9.3) in (9.1) we get

$$\text{SEC1BOL}=(\text{C-MA}+2\text{SD})/4\text{SD}. \qquad (9.4)$$

The formula above will produce the relative position of a security in the Bollinger Bands. Values of 1 indicate that it has reached the top band and values of zero indicate that it has reached the bottom band. To eliminate negative values (when price falls below the bottom band) the final value is increased by one and the formula becomes:

$$\text{SEC1BOL}=1+(\text{C-MA}+2\text{SD})/4\text{SD} \qquad (9.5)$$

The divergence is then calculated by taking the 3-day exponential moving average percentage difference between the relative position of the related intermarket security and the security to be traded as follows:

$$DIVERGENCE=EMA(3)[(SEC2BOL-SEC1BOL)/SEC1BOL * 100] \qquad (9.6)$$

where SEC1BOL=Relative position of the base security in the Bollinger Bands; SEC2BOL=Relative position of the intermarket security in the Bollinger Bands; MA=Moving average; SD=Standard deviation; EMA=Exponential Moving Average.

There are some limitations with the underlying Bollinger Band theory that should be understood before applying it to trading:

- The formula involves the calculation of the standard deviation which makes the assumption of normality and it is therefore subject to error when the price distribution deviates significantly from normality.
- Because of scaling factors the formula doesn't work so well with negatively correlated markets.

You can find the MetaStock code for all intermarket indicators in Appendix A. There are two ways of entering data for the intermarket security (SEC2). The first method (used in the relative strength indicator) is by referencing the symbol and folder in the first line of the code. For example in the line

SEC2:=Security("C:\MetastockData\INTERMARKET\DXY0",C);

C:\Metastock Data\INTERMARKET is the folder in my hard drive where historical data for the dollar index is located; DXY0 is the symbol for the Dollar Index; and C indicates that I want to reference only the closing price.

An alternative method (used in the case of the Bollinger Band divergence indicator) is to drag and drop the indicator on the dollar index chart until it changes color to pink (the dollar index and not the indicator). This method cannot be used, however, when back-testing an indicator. An advantage of using the first method is that there is no need to have a chart of the intermarket security plotted in order to use the indicator. Tradestation users can only use the second method and a chart of the intermarket security should be always plotted together with the base security.

9.3   INTERMARKET DISPARITY

The disparity index was first introduced by Steve Nison in his book *Beyond Candlesticks: New Japanese Charting Techniques Revealed* (see Bibliography) and it has since been incorporated in the majority of popular technical analysis software.

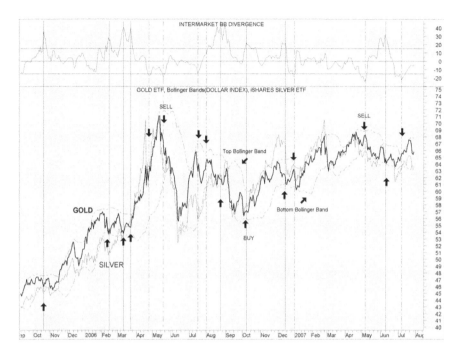

Figure 9.2 Composite chart of the gold (GLD) and silver (SLV) ETF. The 20-day intermarket Bollinger Band divergence indicator is depicted in the top window. Horizontal lines are drawn at the 15, 0 and −15 % divergence levels. Up arrows indicate buy signals triggered by Bollinger Band divergence peaks above the 15 % divergence level. Similarly, down arrows indicate sell signals triggered by Bollinger Band divergence troughs but only below the −15 % negative divergence level.

It is defined as the percentage difference or "disparity" of the latest close to a chosen moving average, and the formula is:

$$((Close - MA(Close, 30))/MA(Close, 30))^*100.$$

To calculate the intermarket disparity I subtract the disparity index of the base security from the disparity index of the intermarket security according to the following formula:

$$DS1=(SEC1-MA(SEC1))/MA(SEC1)^*100 \qquad (9.7)$$
$$DS2=(SEC2-MA(SEC2))/MA(SEC2)^*100 \qquad (9.8)$$
$$Intermarket\ Disparity\ (ID)=c^*DS2-DS1$$

where SEC1 = the base security (the security that you want to predict); SEC2 = the intermarket security. c has been introduced to take into account the sign of the correlation coefficient and can be either +1 in cases of positive correlation between

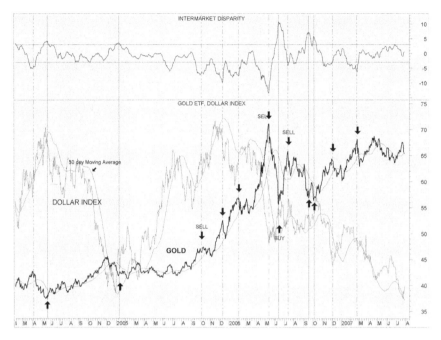

Figure 9.3 Composite chart of the gold ETF (GLD) and the dollar index (DXY). The 30-day intermarket disparity indicator is depicted in the top window. Buy signals are triggered by the intermarket disparity reaching a top and turning down on 3 % or greater positive divergence. Similarly sell signals are generated by the intermarket disparity reaching a bottom and turning up but only for divergence values below −3 % (negative divergence).

SEC1 and SEC2 or −1 in case of negatively correlated markets (like gold and the dollar index).

The interpretation is similar to the Bollinger Band indicator. Positive and negative values indicate positive and negative divergence respectively. A sell signal is generated when the divergence reaches a bottom and reverses below a certain negative level and a buy signal is generated when the indicator reaches a top and falls above a certain positive level. Unlike the Intermarket momentum oscillator (see Section 9.6 below), there are no upper or lower limits as these vary according to the securities being compared and their correlation.

A similar method was used by Murray Ruggiero in his book *Cybernetic Trading Strategies* (see Bibliography) to develop the mechanical trading signals based on intermarket divergence.

The difference between the two methods is that Ruggiero considers buy signals between positively correlated markets only when *DS1 <0 and DS2>0* and sell signals only when *DS1>0 and DS2<0* whereas the intermarket disparity indicator (ID) described above calculates the divergence precisely. It can issue buy signals when DS2-DS1 rises above a certain level even when both securities are above their moving average (both DS1 and DS2 are positive), which usually occurs when the disparity of the intermarket security (DS2) is considerably higher than DS1. Similarly Ruggiero's method issues buy signals between negatively correlated markets only when *DS1 <0 and DS2<0* and sell signals when *DS1>0 and DS2>0* whereas the ID indicator can issue buy signals even when both DS1 and DS2 are negative, which occurs only when the disparity of the intermarket security (DS2) is considerably lower than DS1.

9.4   INTERMARKET LRS DIVERGENCE

This indicator was first introduced in my article "Volume Flow Performance" in *Technical Analysis of STOCKS & COMMODITIES* (see Bibliography) in order to calculate the divergence money flow divergence between price and the volume flow indicator.

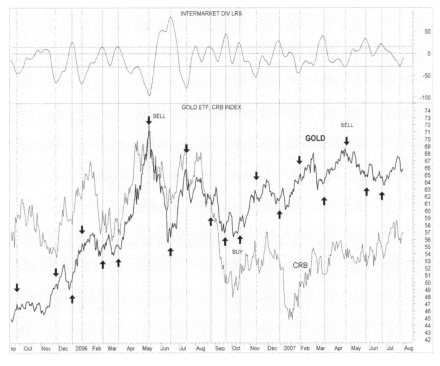

Figure 9.4   Composite chart of the gold ETF (GLD) and the CRB Index (CRB). The 15-day intermarket divergence LRS indicator is depicted in the top window. Buy signals are triggered by the intermarket LRS divergence reaching a top and turning down on positive divergence levels of 15 or greater. Similarly, sell signals are generated by the intermarket LRS divergence reaching a bottom and turning up, but only for divergence values below the −30 level (negative divergence).

It can also be used (with some modifications) to calculate the divergence of a security from its related intermarket. First the linear regression slope of both securities is calculated and the intermarket slope is then adjusted to take into account the difference in volatilities between the two securities. The divergence is then derived by subtracting the base security slope from the intermarket. Values below zero indicate negative divergence and values over the zero line positive divergence. Buy signals are generated when the indicator reaches a peak above a certain level (usually between 10 and 40) and subsequently declines. Similarly, sell signals are triggered when the indicator reaches a bottom below a certain level (usually from −10 to −40) and rises. Divergence levels vary according to the intermarket securities chosen for comparison.

9.5   INTERMARKET REGRESSION DIVERGENCE

The linear regression equation, derived in Chapter 3, is used to make a prediction of likely values of the dependent variable or the security to be predicted (gold in our examples), based on values of a correlated market. This method can only be used with price differences or yields as raw prices violate the two basic assumptions of regression: linearity and normality.

The regression line usually crosses through the origin and can be therefore ignored so the regression equation is reduced to:

$$Y(Pred) = r^* StDev(Y)/StDev(X)^* X \tag{9.9}$$

where r=Pearson's correlation between the related markets; Y=percentage yield of the security to be predicted (actual); Y(Pred)=predicted percentage yield; X=percentage yield of the intermarket security; StDev=standard deviation;

$$\text{and the divergence is } Y(Pred) - Y(actual). \tag{9.10}$$

Where a scatterplot reveals that the regression line does not cross the origin then we can add the Y-Intercept from formula (3.3) in Chapter 3 to formula (9.9) which becomes:

$$Y(Pred) = r^* StDev(Y)/StDev(X)^* X + MA(Y) - MA(X)^* r^* StDev(Y)/StDev(X).$$
$$\tag{9.11}$$

9.6   INTERMARKET MOMENTUM OSCILLATOR

A serious disadvantage in using all the above indicators is that extreme divergence levels vary according to the markets being analyzed. This is mainly because of price scaling differences between the base and intermarket security.

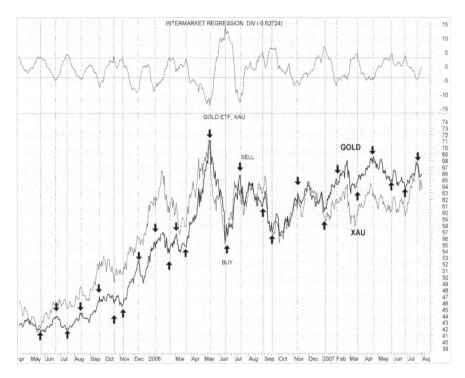

Figure 9.5 Composite chart of the gold ETF (GLD) and the XAU. The 300-day intermarket regression divergence indicator of the 15-day Gold-XAU yields is depicted in the top window. Buy signals are triggered by the intermarket regression divergence reaching a top and turning down on positive divergence levels of 3 or greater. Similarly, sell signals are generated by the intermarket regression divergence reaching a bottom and turning up but only for divergence values below the −4 level (negative divergence).

To automate the tedious work of identifying indicator extreme values, I use a simple momentum oscillator which I call the intermarket momentum oscillator. I use the following formula to calculate the new oscillator:

$$\text{Momentum} = \text{MA}, 3(\text{Indicator} - \text{Lowest}(\text{Indicator}, 200))^* 100/$$
$$(\text{MA}, 3(\text{Highest}(\text{Indicator}, 200) - \text{Lowest}(\text{Indicator}, 200))$$

where MA,3 = 3-day moving average; Highest and Lowest are the highest and lowest values of the indicator over the previous 200-day period.

The formula above will normalize the divergence on a scale from 1 to 100. Trading signal interpretation is similar to that of the stochastic oscillator:

- Buy when the oscillator falls below a specific level (e.g. 30) and then rises above that level, and sell when the oscillator rises above a specific level (e.g. 80) and then falls below that level.

- Buy when the oscillator falls below a specific level (e.g. 30) and then rises above a higher level (e.g. 40), and sell when the oscillator rises above a specific level (e.g. 90) and then falls below a lower level (e.g. 80).
- Buy when the oscillator rises above its signal line (moving average) and sell when it falls below the signal line.
- A combination of either one of the first two methods with the third.

An example of this oscillator applied on the intermarket relative strength is shown in Fig. 9.1. When the indicator is used to normalize divergence the buy and sell signals indicated above should be reversed as we want to buy at maximum positive divergence and sell at maximum negative divergence. Care should also be taken in interpreting indicator signals in trending markets. In this case the second method of interpretation would be more appropriate as the indicator can remain in the overbought area for a long period of time.

9.7   Z-SCORE DIVERGENCE

A comparison of two securities on the same chart is sometimes difficult and misleading because of price scaling differences. A convenient method of normalizing both prices on an equal scale is by converting the prices to their Z-scores. These are computed by subtracting the mean and dividing by the standard deviation according to the formula:

$$Z = (C - MA)/SD$$

Z-scores use the standard deviation as a unit of measure and indicate how many standard deviations the price falls above or below the mean. In order to eliminate decimal places and negative values it is sometimes convenient to transform them into a different scale with a mean of 50 (instead of 0) by adding 50 and multiplying by 10.

The Z-score divergence is computed by subtracting the Z-score of the base security from the intermarket and multiplying the result by their correlation coefficient. A visual inspection of the Z-scores and their differences can help you determine if you are positioned in the market in the correct direction and which one is leading or lagging.

An interesting chart is that of gold and the euro in Fig. 9.6. Although these markets have a fairly high degree of correlation, their relationship swings, with the euro switching position as follower and leader. Their spread is more accurate (because of scaling differences) when comparing the Z-scores (in the middle chart) rather than the prices themselves. Care should be taken when using this method for trading, because by using the standard deviation to convert prices to Z-scores we make the implicit assumption that the distribution of security prices is normal.

Figure 9.6 Composite chart of the gold ETF (GLD) (thick line with the scale on the right Y-axis) and the Euro (thin line on the left Y-axis). The 250-day (1 year) Z-scores of gold (thick line) and the Euro (thin line) are depicted in the upper window on the same scale. The Z-score illustrates more clearly the relation between gold and the Euro, especially in periods where both charts are very close in the bottom window.

Financial series, however, are rarely normally distributed. The Z-score will normalize prices regardless of statistical merit which is only absolutely correct in the case of perfectly normally distributed data. In the case of serious deviations from normality, unlikely events – such as the markets uncoupling even more – are more likely to occur than is the case in a normal distribution.

Nevertheless, the above limitations do not mitigate the usefulness of the Z-score indicator in comparing multiple related securities visually.

9.8   MULTIPLE INTERMARKET DIVERGENCE

All the indicators discussed above involve the comparison between two correlated markets. This concept can be extended to multiple markets where a prediction of the future direction of a security is extended to include multiple predictor markets.

This can be achieved by adding the divergences for each market after taking into account the redundant cross correlation between the predictor (independent) variables.

This can be achieved by weighing each predictor variable according to its part (or semi-partial) correlation coefficient with the dependent variable (the security to be predicted).

The part correlation coefficient represents the proportion of the variance of a predictor market (independent variable) that is not associated with any other predictors and is calculated by removing all variance which may be accounted for by the other independent variables. The remaining unique component of the independent variables is then correlated with the dependent variable. The computational formula for the part correlation coefficient is:

$$r_{y1(2)} = \frac{r_{y1} - r_{y2}r_{12}}{\sqrt{1 - r_{12}^2}} \tag{9.12}$$

$$r_{y2(1)} = \frac{r_{y2} - r_{y1}r_{12}}{\sqrt{1 - r_{12}^2}} \tag{9.13}$$

where: $r_{y1(2)}$ is the correlation between y (the dependent variable) and 1 (the first independent variable) with the influence of the second independent variable removed from variable 1.

$r_{y2(1)}$ is the correlation between y (the dependent variable) and 2 (the second independent variable) with the influence of the first independent variable removed from variable 2.

r_{y1} and r_{y2} are the correlations between the dependent variable y and the independent variables 1 and 2 respectively.

r_{12} is the correlation between the independent variables.

In the example in Fig. 9.7 the formula for the intermarket divergence LRS (top window) has been extended to include two predictor markets: silver and the dollar index by weighing each predictor variable according to its part correlation with the security to be predicted (gold). The complete double LRS divergence formula is included in Appendix A.

The linear regression slopes were compared over a 20-day interval. The time interval was used as a switch for increasing or decreasing the amount of trading signals. Decreasing the time segment produced more signals while increasing it reduced them.

Please note that because of gold's recent strength all examples presented in this chapter have a tendency to exaggerate negative divergence. To compensate for this divergence bias, asymmetrical divergence levels of $+15$ and -20 were chosen for the extreme positive and negative divergence levels respectively.

Figure 9.7 The 20-day double divergence between gold, the dollar index and the silver ETF is depicted in the top window. Extreme values of the divergence are indicated by the horizontal lines at +15 and −20.

9.9 MULTIPLE REGRESSION DIVERGENCE

In multiple regression, the goal is to predict the value of the dependent variable (the market to be predicted) from a set of k independent variables (related markets).

Multiple regression finds a set of partial regression coefficients b_k such that the dependent variable could be approximated as well as possible by a linear combination of the independent variables (with b_i etc. being the weight of the combination). Therefore, a predicted value, denoted Y, of the dependent variable is obtained from:

$$Y = a + b_1X_1 + b_2X_2 + \ldots . b_kX_k \qquad (9.14)$$

The coefficients of the multiple regression equation represent the amount by which the dependent variable (to be predicted) increases when one independent (predictor) variable is increased by one unit and all the other independent variables are held constant. They will therefore vary depending upon the other independent variables included in the regression equation.

Part correlation, discussed above, is also the basis of multiple regression.

The values of the regression coefficients are found using ordinary least squares. In this case it is more convenient to express the regression coefficients in matrix form. When more than two variables are involved, the formula becomes too long and cannot be programmed into MetaStock because of formula space limitations. They can, however, be calculated using any other programming language.

However, for a trader who is only interested in a few markets, there is an easier method. The linear regression coefficients can be calculated using any off-the-shelf statistical package and substituted in the MetaStock code. This method has the advantage of being able to select an effective set of predictor intermarket securities that will maximize the coefficient of determination, R squared.

The practical problem in multiple regression is one of identifying predictor variables that are highly correlated with the dependent variable but have low correlations among themselves.

There might be a tendency to continue including variables as long as there seems to be an increase in R squared. In practice, however, it is simply not feasible to find more than three predictor markets that are uncorrelated.

In choosing the best independent variables to include in the regression equation it is important to ensure that these are not too highly correlated with each other (i.e. Pearson's correlation should not exceed 0.80), because the regression may become unstable.

A counterintuitive point worth noting is that sometimes an independent variable that has zero or very low correlation with the dependent can lead to improvement in prediction if it is included in the regression equation. This is because it removes the irrelevant variance or "noise" that it shares with the other predictors but is not present in the dependent variable.

The gold example can be used again to illustrate some of these points.

The first step is to choose independent variables that are known to be related to gold and choose the best time increment to use when calculating percent changes.

The correlation analysis in Chapter 7 (Table 7.6) indicates that gold has the stronger correlation with the XAU and the dollar index when taking 9-day yields. This time segment was therefore used to construct the correlation matrix with related markets in Tables 9.1 and 9.2 using 15 and 10 years of data respectively. The correlation coefficients were similar in both tables, except for the correlation between the dollar index and gold which improved considerably (from −0.33 to −0.43) when using 10 years of data.

Considering that the dollar is a major fundamental factor affecting gold, I decided to use the shorter time period when calculating the regression equation coefficients.

We can now proceed with the regression analysis to predict gold in terms of the XAU, silver, the dollar, the CRB and the yen. These were chosen because they

Table 9.1 Correlation matrix of 9-day yields. The TNX is the CBOE 10-year Treasury yield index. Data for the most recent 15-year period were used to calculate the correlations. Only 10 years of data were available for the euro and therefore it was not included in the matrix.

	Gold	XAU	Silver	Dollar	CRB	Yen	TNX
			15 Year Correlation Matrix of 9-Day Yields				
Gold	1	**0.70**	**0.60**	−0.33	**0.43**	−0.19	−0.09
XAU	**0.70**	1	**0.54**	−0.22	0.42	−0.17	−0.05
Silver	**0.60**	**0.54**	1	−0.17	0.44	−0.11	0.02
Venture	**0.58**	**0.67**	**0.59**	−0.27	**0.47**	−0.24	0.08
Dollar	−0.33	−0.22	−0.17	1	−0.18	0.55	0.18
CRB	0.43	0.42	0.44	−0.18	1	−0.18	0.08
Yen	−0.19	−0.17	−0.11	**0.55**	−0.18	1	0.08
TNX	−0.09	−0.05	0.02	0.18	0.08	0.08	1

correlated well with gold but were not too highly related with each other. The euro was not included because of its high cross correlation with the dollar index ($r = -0.97$).

The first aspect to consider is how well the independent variables predicted the dependent variable, in this case gold. This is determined by the coefficient of determination, R squared. Model 3 (see Table 9.3) has an R^2 of 0.587 implying that 58.7 % of the variance in gold is explained by the predictor variables, the XAU, silver and the dollar.

Clearly the XAU is the largest contributor to the coefficient of determination, R^2 (Table 9.3). The first model (first line in Table 9.3) which consists of the XAU only has a coefficient of determination R^2 of 0.484, hence we can say that the contribution

Table 9.2 Pearson's 10-year correlation matrix of 9-day percentage yields. Data for the most recent 10-year period were used to calculate the correlations.

	Gold	XAU	Silver	Dollar	Euro	CRB	Yen	TNX
				10 Year Correlation Matrix of 9-Day Yields				
Gold	1	**0.70**	**0.58**	**−0.43**	0.40	**0.44**	−0.22	−0.09
XAU	0.70	1	**0.52**	−0.31	0.28	0.43	−0.19	−0.03
Silver	**0.58**	**0.52**	1	−0.26	0.23	0.43	−0.13	0.01
Venture	**0.58**	**0.67**	**0.59**	−0.27	0.23	0.47	−0.24	0.08
Dollar	−0.43	−0.31	−0.26	1	**−0.97**	−0.27	**0.54**	0.24
Euro	0.40	0.28	0.23	−0.97	1	0.21	−0.35	−0.24
CRB	0.44	0.43	0.43	−0.27	0.21	1	−0.25	0.10
Yen	−0.22	−0.19	−0.13	**0.54**	−0.35	−0.25	1	0.10
TNX	−0.09	−0.03	0.01	0.24	−0.24	0.10	0.10	1

Table 9.3 Model summary. The first model includes only the XAU. Silver, the dollar, the CRB and the yen are added one at a time in models 2, 3, 4 and 5 respectively. Adding the CRB and the yen make very little difference to the coefficient of determination R^2.

Model	R^2	R^2 change	R^2 % change	XAU	Silver	Dollar	CRB	Yen

Model	R^2	R^2 change	R^2 % change	Part correlations				
				XAU	Silver	Dollar	CRB	Yen
1	0.484	0.484	100	0.70				
2	0.549	0.065	13.4	0.46	0.26			
3	0.587	0.038	6.9	0.41	0.23	−0.20		
4	0.592	0.005	0.9	0.38	0.20	−0.19	0.07	
5	0.593	0.001	0.2	0.38	0.20	−0.18	0.07	0.03

of the XAU to R^2 was 0.484. When silver is added (in model 2) R^2 increases 13 % to 0.549 and the addition of the dollar index (model 3) adds a further 0.038 or 7 % to R^2. The CRB and the yen, in the fourth and fifth model respectively, contribute very little to R^2 and consequently add very little value to the predictive ability of the regression equation. This is also verified by their near zero part correlation coefficients (their correlation coefficient with gold after removing the effects of all other variables) depicted in the last two columns of Table 9.3.

The relative impact of each variable on gold is also of interest.

Each of the regression coefficients in Table 9.4 estimates the amount of change that occurs in the dependent variable (gold) for one unit change of the corresponding independent variable. We cannot say, however, that because the dollar index coefficient is larger than the corresponding coefficient for the XAU that the dollar is more important for predicting gold, as they use different scales of measurement. In order to make effective comparisons, all coefficients should be normalized. This is done by multiplying each variable by the ratio of its standard deviation to the standard deviation of the dependent variable (gold). The resultant normalized coefficients are then called standardized.

Table 9.4 Unstandardized regression coefficients.

Model	Constant	XAU	Silver	Dollar	CRB	Yen
1	0.121	0.31				
2	0.06	0.24	0.18			
3	0.071	0.216	0.166	−0.43		
4	0.068	0.207	0.153	−0.413	0.117	
5	0.066	0.207	0.151	−0.449	0.123	0.049

Regression coefficients

Table 9.5 Standardized regression coefficients. The yen produces the smallest regression coefficient (0.034).

		Standardized Regression Coefficients			
Model	XAU	Silver	Dollar	CRB	Yen
1	0.696				
2	0.540	0.299			
3	0.490	0.270	−0.208		
4	0.469	0.249	−0.199	0.080	
5	0.469	0.247	−0.216	0.085	0.034

Examining the standardized coefficients in Table 9.5 and their percentage weight in Table 9.6 we can see that when including all potential predictor markets (last line in Table 9.6) the XAU has the greatest impact on gold (45 %). The CRB, in spite of a moderate correlation with gold ($r = 0.44$), has a very low standardized coefficient (0.085) because of its high cross correlation with the XAU and silver.

In view of the above the CRB and the yen can be removed from the regression equation with very little loss to its predictive ability. Thus the equation reduces to:

$$G9 = 0.07 + 0.216^*X9 + 0.166^*S9\text{-}0.43^*D9 \qquad (9.15)$$

where the variables G9, X9, S9 and D9 are the 9-day percentage yields of gold, the XAU, silver and the dollar index respectively.

Thus we can calculate the divergence between the predicted (based on the related markets) and actual values of gold's 9-day yields using the above formula (9.15) by subtracting the second from the first.

The divergence was plotted in the top window of the chart in Fig. 9.8. Unlike conventional technical analysis indicators, all divergence indicators are leading price and it is therefore prudent to wait until the indicator forms a top or bottom and reverses direction before making any buy or sell decisions.

Table 9.6 Percentage weight of each variable in the model.

		% Weight			
Model	XAU	Silver	Dollar	CRB	Yen
2	64%	36%			
3	51%	28%	21%		
4	47%	25%	20%	8%	
5	45%	24%	21%	8%	3%

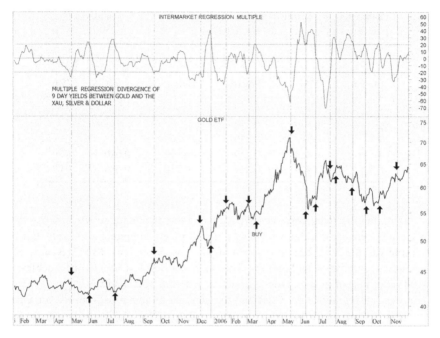

Figure 9.8 The multiple regression divergence between gold, the XAU, silver and the dollar index using 9-day percentage yields is depicted in the top window. Extreme divergences are indicated by the horizontal lines at +/−20 levels. Buy signals are triggered by the indicator forming a top above the extreme level and declining below 20, and sell signals are triggered by the indicator declining below −20, forming a bottom and rising above −20.

It would be interesting to see which of the indicators described above performs better in predicting gold. The winner will be revealed in Chapter 11, after some serious back-testing.

9.10   INTERMARKET MOVING AVERAGE

I have seen the intermarket moving average mentioned in a book on intermarket analysis but unfortunately the author did not provide the formula. To calculate the predicted moving average I use the multiple regression formula (equation 9.16) to predict gold prices based on their correlation with the XAU, the dollar and silver. The formula for this indicator is provided in Appendix A and the indicator is plotted in Fig. 9.9. Crossovers over the conventional (actual) moving average indicate that gold is undervalued and crossovers under the conventional moving average indicate that gold is overvalued relative to its related markets. Crossovers, however, cannot be used to generate buy and sell signals as gold can remain undervalued or overvalued for some time before following its peers.

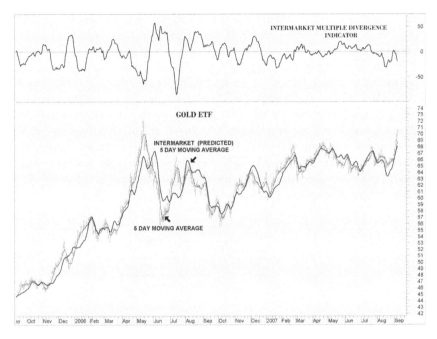

Figure 9.9   The intermarket (predicted) 5-day moving average (thick line) is plotted together with the classic 5-day moving average in the bottom window and the multiple divergence indicator in the top window. Notice that when the intermarket moving average crosses above the classic moving average the divergence (top window) turns positive.

This indicator, therefore, can only be used as a rough estimate of the price level relative to other correlated markets but can't be used in mechanical trading systems as these require precise and timely signals. It has not been included, therefore, in the comparison tests in Chapter 11.

9.11   CONGESTION INDEX

This indicator has nothing to do with intermarket trading but I thought that it would be a good idea to mention it in this chapter as it is used extensively with the trading systems in the second part of this book.

Market movements can be characterized by two distinct types or phases. In the first, the market shows trending movements which have a directional bias over a period of time. The second type of market behavior is periodic or cyclic motion, where the market shows no consistent directional bias and trades between two levels. This type of market results in the failure of trend-following indicators and the success of overbought/oversold oscillators.

Both phases of the market require the use of different types of indicator. Trending markets need trend-following indicators such as moving averages, moving average convergence/divergence (MACD), and so on. Trading range markets need oscillators such as the relative strength index (RSI) and stochastics, which use overbought and oversold levels.

The age-old problem for many trading systems is their inability to determine if a trending or trading range market is at hand. Trend-following indicators, such as the MACD or moving averages, tend to be whipsawed as markets enter a non-trending congestion phase. On the other hand, oscillators (which work well during trading range markets) are often too early to buy or sell in a trending market. Thus, identifying the market phase and selecting the appropriate indicators is critical to a system's success. The congestion index attempts to identify the market's character by dividing the actual percentage that the market has changed in the past x days by the extreme range according to the following formula:

$$CI = \frac{\dfrac{(C - C[X-1])}{C[X-1]} 100}{\dfrac{Highest(H, X) - Lowest(L, X)}{Lowest(L, X)}} \tag{9.16}$$

where C is the closing price; X is the time segment; and Highest and Lowest are the highest high and lowest low respectively for the chosen time period X.

To minimize daily noise the CI is further smoothed by a 3-day exponential moving average (see MetaStock formula in Appendix A).

The congestion index fluctuates between 100 and −100. The larger the absolute value, the less congested the current market. Readings between +20 and −20 indicate congestion or oscillating mode. Crossing over the 20 line from below indicates the start of a rising trend. Conversely, the start of a down turn is indicated by crossing under −20 from above.

The CI can also be used as an overbought/oversold oscillator. The indicator signals an exhaustion of the prevailing price trend and warns of an impending price reversal when it reaches an extreme reading either above 85 or below −85 and then reverses direction.

Unlike similar indicators, like the vertical horizontal filter (VHF) or Wilder's ADX, the congestion index is directional for the following reasons:

- It is self-contained in the sense that it eliminates the need for a second indicator to identify the trend direction.
- It is better in identifying trend reversals.
- It provides more accurate readings in cases of temporary pullbacks.
- The chart space is less congested.

In the example of the S&P 500 in Fig. 9.10, the CI was the first to identify a rising trend which started at the beginning of April 2007 and lasted until the end of May.

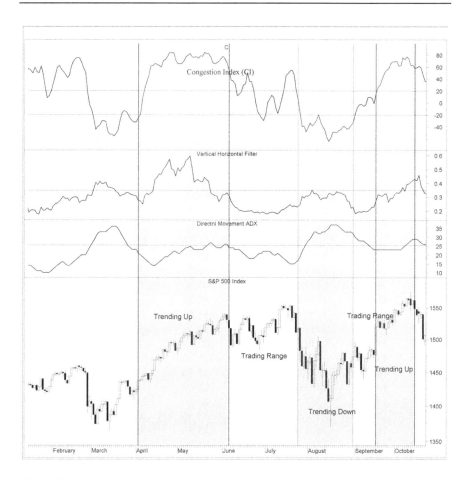

Figure 9.10 Chart of the S&P 500 from 1 February 2007 to 12 October 2007. The 3-day moving average of the 28-day CI is plotted in the top window, the 28-day vertical horizontal filter below and the 14-day ADX in the second from bottom window. CI detected both up trends (in gray) with virtually no lag.

On 5 April, the CI crossed over 20, decisively followed eight days later by the VHF crossing over 0.35 (the indicator's default value for a trend) on 16 April.

The ADX, on the other hand, missed the trend altogether. It was actually down at the beginning of the trend and started rising on 17 April, but by the time it crossed over 25 (indicating a trend) the trend was over.

But why the disparity between the indicators? The answer is in the calculation method. The VHF is calculated using the formula:

$$VHF = \frac{Highest(C, 28) - Lowest(C, 28)}{\sum ABS(C_i - C_{i-1})} \tag{9.17}$$

Table 9.7 Calculation of the VHF. Column B is the S&P 500 closing price, Column C shows the highest close of the last 28 days, Column D shows the lowest close of the last 28 days, Column E is their difference, Column F is the absolute value of the difference between consecutive daily closes, Column G is their sum for the last 28 days and Column H is the VHF.

A	B	C	D	E	F	G	H
Date	Close	Highest	Lowest	H-L	|(C-C[1])|	Σ	VHF
2/27/07	1399.04	1459.68	1399.04	60.64	50.3	190.96	0.318
2/28/07	1406.82	1459.68	1399.04	60.64	7.8	194.49	0.312
3/1/07	1403.17	1459.68	1399.04	60.64	3.6	194.01	0.313
3/2/07	1387.17	1459.68	1387.17	72.51	16.0	202.46	0.358
3/5/07	1374.12	1459.68	1374.12	85.56	13.1	210.47	0.407
3/6/07	1395.41	1459.68	1374.12	85.56	21.3	219.62	0.390
3/7/07	1391.97	1459.68	1374.12	85.56	3.4	206.83	0.414
3/8/07	1401.89	1459.68	1374.12	85.56	9.9	215.03	0.398
3/9/07	1402.85	1459.68	1374.12	85.56	1.0	214.43	0.399
3/12/07	1406.6	1459.68	1374.12	85.56	3.8	209.98	0.407
3/13/07	1377.95	1459.68	1374.12	85.56	28.6	229.21	0.373
3/14/07	1387.17	1459.68	1374.12	85.56	9.2	230.73	0.371
3/15/07	1392.28	1459.68	1374.12	85.56	5.1	233.39	0.367
3/16/07	1386.95	1459.68	1374.12	85.56	5.3	237.32	0.361
3/19/07	1402.06	1459.68	1374.12	85.56	15.1	251.42	0.340
3/20/07	1410.94	1459.68	1374.12	85.56	8.9	258.28	0.331
3/21/07	1435.04	1459.68	1374.12	85.56	24.1	280.67	0.305
3/22/07	1434.54	1459.68	1374.12	85.56	0.5	270.92	0.316
3/23/07	1436.11	1459.68	1374.12	85.56	1.6	267.8	0.319
3/26/07	1437.5	1459.68	1374.12	85.56	1.4	259.55	0.330
3/27/07	1428.61	1459.68	1374.12	85.56	8.9	256.15	0.334
3/28/07	1417.23	1459.68	1374.12	85.56	11.4	266.02	0.322
3/29/07	1422.53	1459.68	1374.12	85.56	5.3	270.05	0.317
3/30/07	1420.86	1457.63	1374.12	83.51	1.7	267.58	0.312
4/2/07	1424.55	1456.38	1374.12	82.26	3.7	269.22	0.306
4/3/07	1437.77	1451.19	1374.12	77.07	13.2	281.19	0.274
4/4/07	1439.37	1449.37	1374.12	75.25	1.6	277.6	0.271
4/5/07	1443.76	1443.76	1374.12	69.64	4.4	280.17	0.249

Column	Formula
C	= MAX(B9:B36)
D	= MIN(B9:B36)
E	= C36-D36
F	= ABS(B36-B35)
G	= SUM(F9:F36)
H	= E36/G36

Table 9.8 Example of calculating CI in Excel. The second, third and fourth columns are the S&P 500 high, low and closing prices respectively. Column E is the highest high of the last 28 days, Column F is the lowest low of the last 28 days, and Column G is the price percent change during the last 28 days. In column H is the percent daily price difference and in the last column is the CI.

A	B	C	D	E	F	G	H	I
Date	High	Low	Close	H H	L L	ROC	(HH-LL) /LL	CI
3/19/07	1403.2	1386.95	1402.06	1461.57	1363.98	−3.31	0.07	−46.23
3/20/07	1411.53	1400.7	1410.94	1461.57	1363.98	−2.58	0.07	−36.06
3/21/07	1437.77	1409.75	1435.04	1461.57	1363.98	−0.21	0.07	−2.94
3/22/07	1437.66	1429.88	1434.54	1461.57	1363.98	0.08	0.07	1.14
3/23/07	1438.89	1433.21	1436.11	1461.57	1363.98	−0.48	0.07	−6.68
3/26/07	1437.65	1423.28	1437.5	1461.57	1363.98	−1.22	0.07	−17.10
3/27/07	1437.49	1425.54	1428.61	1461.57	1363.98	−1.94	0.07	−27.06
3/28/07	1428.35	1414.07	1417.23	1461.57	1363.98	−2.63	0.07	−36.79
3/29/07	1426.24	1413.27	1422.53	1461.57	1363.98	−2.55	0.07	−35.57
3/30/07	1429.22	1408.9	1420.86	1461.57	1363.98	−2.52	0.07	−35.26
4/2/07	1425.49	1416.37	1424.55	1461.57	1363.98	−2.19	0.07	−30.55
4/3/07	1440.57	1424.27	1437.77	1456.95	1363.98	−0.92	0.07	−13.57
4/4/07	1440.16	1435.08	1439.37	1456.95	1363.98	−0.69	0.07	−10.12
4/5/07	1444.88	1436.67	1443.76	1449.25	1363.98	3.20	0.06	51.13

Column	Formula
E	= MAX(B22:B49)
F	= MIN(C22:C49)
G	= (D49-D22)/D22*100
H	= (E49-F49)/(F49+0.01)
I	= G49/H49

where Highest(C,28) is the highest close in the last 28 days; Lowest(C,28) is the lowest close in the last 28 days; and the denominator is the sum of the absolute value of the difference between consecutive daily closes for the last 28 days.

To help solve the mystery I calculated the 28 day readings, up to 5 April, for the VHF and CI indicators in the Excel sheets in Tables 9.7 and 9.8 respectively. Let's take a closer look what happened on 3 April (the first day of the breakout).

On that day the S&P was up 1 %, and as a result the denominator of formula (9.17) increased while the numerator decreased because the new 28-day high was lower than the previous one. As a result the VHF was down on the actual breakout and the start of the trend! On the other hand the CI shot up from −13 to 51 during the next two days, confirming decisively the start of a possible trend.

Part II

10
Trading System Design

Life can only be understood backwards but it must be lived forwards.
–Søren Kierkegaard

There are basically two ways to trade using technical analysis: discretionarily and systematically. Discretionary traders use technical indicators and their experience to make their trading decisions. System traders, on the other hand, rely on the trading signals automatically produced by computerized trading systems.

The disadvantages of discretionary trading are human emotions: fear and greed. When you are in a trade that seems to move against you, fear of loss and hope of recovery make it hard to cut your losses. Optimism keeps you in a losing trade, hoping that the price will eventually turn in your favor. On the other hand, when you are in a trade that starts to move to the upside, greed takes over and you take profits too early, missing the biggest part of the move.

Trading systems remove much of the emotion surrounding trading decisions, and can also save a lot of time.

But do they work?

Many people believe in the Efficient Market Hypothesis. The Efficient Market Hypothesis states that, at any given time, security prices fully reflect all available information. The implications of the Efficient Market Hypothesis are truly profound. But if markets are efficient and current prices fully reflect all information, then buying and selling securities in an attempt to outperform the market will effectively be a game of chance rather than skill.

This belief persists although it is rudimentary, false and intellectually dishonest. Researchers have uncovered stock market anomalies that seem to contradict the Efficient Market Hypothesis. One major criticism stems from the fact that market participants take into consideration other factors than just the price when they buy or sell an asset.

One such factor, not taken into account at all by the Efficient Market Hypothesis, is the concept of risk. Since different kinds of market players compute risk in different ways, it is perfectly possible that one participant views a certain stock price as a good buying opportunity, while another views the same price as a good selling opportunity. Another factor is different liquidity needs among traders. Some traders are gladly willing to pay a higher price just to make sure the trade is executed immediately while others may want to sell an asset in order to buy something else. Yet none of the traders above can be said to act irrationally. They simply have different needs for computing the value of different actions and states.

Another flaw in the Efficient Market Hypothesis is that prices tend to be slow to reflect all fundamental information. Without instantaneous adjustment, speculation based on the price trend may be profitable until all information is fully discounted and reflected in the price. Thus, the time lag can be exploited by technical systems in short-term speculation.

The search for anomalies is effectively the search for systems or patterns that can be used to outperform passive and/or buy and hold strategies.

Developing an effective trading system is by no means an easy task. It requires a solid understanding of the plethora of available parameters, the ability to make realistic assumptions and the time and dedication to develop the system. However, if developed and deployed properly, a trading system can yield many advantages. It can increase efficiency, free up time and, most importantly, increase your profits.

I have seen a lot of different approaches to designing trading systems and strategies. The most popular are trend and countertrend systems but other less common systems use breakout from consolidation, channel breakout or volatility concepts. Indicators and techniques that work for one trader do not necessarily work for others.

10.1   BACK-TESTING

Back-testing is a key component of effective trading-system development. It is accomplished by reconstructing, with historical data, trades that would have occurred in the past using rules defined by a given strategy. The results can be analyzed statistically and used to gauge the effectiveness of the strategy. Using this data, traders can optimize and improve their strategies, find any technical or theoretical flaws, and gain confidence in their strategy before applying it in real trading. The underlying theory is that any strategy that worked well in the past is likely to work well in the future and, conversely, any strategy that performed poorly in the past is likely to perform poorly in the future. Some of the advantages of back-testing a trading system are as follows:

• History repeats itself. Back-testing will reveal repeating patterns, disclosed by any number of indicators, oscillators or chart formations. Otherwise we would be shooting in the dark at every market turn.

- Traders have the confidence to rely on the systems.
- It provides an estimate of the probability and magnitude of the potential trade profits because the performance statistics can be reproduced by back-testing.

Since back-tests are always done with the benefit of hindsight, there are all kinds of ways to cheat on reported performance.

There are many factors traders pay attention to when they are back-testing trading strategies. Here is a list of the five most important things to remember.

Sample Size

For a strategy to have value it must be adaptable to many market types. To avoid unrealistic back-testing results that cannot be reproduced in actual trading it is essential that an adequate sample size must be measured both in number of trades and diversity of market trends. For example, if a strategy was only back-tested during the 2003–2007 bull market, it may not fare well in a bear market. It is often a good idea to back-test over a long time frame that encompasses several different types of market conditions.

Optimization

Trading system optimization is a controversial subject among analysts and traders. But what *is* optimization? When designing a technical trading system, the analyst must use an indicator or formula to produce trading signals.

All indicators, however, contain one or more variable parameters. A parameter can be set to one of several possible numeric values, which can greatly alter the behavior and performance of the indicator. The dilemma is what value to assign to each parameter. That is where optimization occurs. Optimization is the process of choosing the best parameter values for the indicator.

This is accomplished by having the software "try" a large number of different combinations of parameters or combination of indicators, until a set is found that gives the best result. The result could be net profits, percentage of profitable trades, minimum drawdown and so forth. An example of a trading system parameter is the length of a moving average used. It is very important to identify the ranges into which the values for parameters and criteria fall.

A thorough development of a trading system must involve the testing of thousands of parameter combinations to identify those that persist in producing profits, even though they are not necessarily the optimum. Thus, it is often better to pick up those parameters in the best ten percent of the parameters instead of the best based on stable neighbouring parameters.

Today's software for trading systems can take you down a dangerous path. A big profit, however, on an optimized test does not necessarily mean you have a good system. The danger with optimization is that what worked well in the past will almost certainly not perform as well in the future. Optimized variables can reflect irregularities in the data far more than any underlying logic of the market or the trading strategy.

Usually, such curve-fitting fails as soon as the parameters hit the real world with its random shocks, because the more control you take of the data by specifying indicators and their optimal parameters, the less substance is left in the data to provide predictive capacity. Statisticians call this a loss of degrees of freedom; traders call it curve-fitting.

Some analysts claim that if the data sample is large enough, then the curve-fitting captures most of the price dynamics and the future buy and sell signals will be just as good as the curve-fitted ones. These claims are generally accepted as being true because there is a lack of knowledge, but the truth is that they are based on nothing more than hope.

So how can we design trading models and avoid the illusion of optimization?

The usual way to validate an optimized trading system is to test the system on data it has never been tested on before — that is, test the system on some data set aside and not used when developing the model. This holdout data set is referred to as out-of-sample data. If the system performance holds up well on the out-of-sample data, we can be confident the system will perform as well in the future as it has in the past.

A more rigorous method of back-testing is that of walk forward testing. The concept is similar to out-of-sample testing but instead of optimizing on seven years of data and using the last three years for testing, a system is optimized on five years and then tested the next year. Once this test is completed, the whole time window is moved forward one year to include the year just tested and the system is then re-optimized. It is then tested again the next year. This process is repeated again and again, "walking forward" through the data series until all the data is exhausted. At the end, all tabulated one-year out-of-sample results are merged to create one large out-of-sample results segment and the system performance is evaluated based on the combined out-of-sample results.

The main advantage of using this method is that since market dynamics change slowly over time the optimum values based on the most recent five-year segment will be accurate in forecasting one year into the future before the model falls apart.

The time periods used in this example for optimization and walk forward testing are not set in stone. The selection of the optimization period depends on the available data and the time required to model the market dynamics. The walk forward period can be between 12–20 % of the optimization period.

Although computationally intensive, this is an excellent way to study and test a trading system. Even though optimization is occurring, in a sense all the trades are tested on what is essentially out-of-sample test data. In addition, the results will closely simulate the process that occurs during real trading, in which traders frequently re-optimize their systems to bring them up to date with fundamental or technical changes in the traded market or its intermarket relationships. Even though nothing can guarantee future results, this approach appears to be as close as we can practically come to estimating trading relationships during constantly changing market conditions.

Unfortunately, totally automated walk forward testing is not available in most popular off-the-shelf trading software and implementing it manually can be time consuming. There is, however, a Tradestation add-in that can be purchased separately. Walk forward testing is also available in Deepinsight Professional and TradersStudio.

A major drawback of out-of-sample testing is that to exhaustively determine the optimal indicator sets as well as their respective periods would require an inordinately large amount of data. If one uses this approach consistently, every piece of data must be thrown away after a single use in the testing phase. In addition to the cost of subscribing to data providers, some futures have only recently begun trading. If the amount of data you possess is limited, you may want to consider the following additional methods of reliability testing.

Cluster spotting and profit mapping: When optimizing a system, traders often save the parameter set which produces the highest level of profit. Once the system with the highest level of profit is identified, you should inspect the results of surrounding parameter values nearby to be sure it is not merely the result of a freak coincidence in the data. Optimal results which are surrounded by similar levels of profit are much more desirable. A better approach is to export the test results produced from each simulation to an Excel spreadsheet and plot a three-dimensional graph, with one parameter scaled along the X-axis, the second parameter scaled along the Y-axis and the profit as height along the Z-axis. Casually inspecting this graph, one can find the region where variations in both parameters have the smallest impact on profitability. Parameter sets in this range may be assumed to be more reliable than parameter sets which produce spikes of profits. This is because low parameter sensitivity in the past implies continued low sensitivity in the future, even though the parameter values producing maximum profits are outside this parameter range.

The process described above can be applied to a wide variety of trading systems as most of them are either already described by two parameters or can be altered to fit a two-parameter model by optimizing each rule or indicator separately.

Monte Carlo simulation: This technique is mainly used to obtain a more realistic figure for the drawdown statistic than the figure obtained by simulation testing and is performed by rearranging the trades randomly (hence the name).

To rearrange the trades, the Monte Carlo simulation uses a random number generator to select a random number between zero and one. This random number is then used to select a trade from the specified listing. The Monte Carlo simulation can reveal whether the account would have experienced a deeper drawdown and what the actual expected drawdown could be in real trading. If the Monte Carlo drawdown is significantly different to that obtained from the simulation model this can also indicate that the system has been overoptimized.

A limitation of this method is that the random number generator assumes that trade returns are independent of each other. It is therefore a good idea to check for autocorrelation of returns before running a Monte Carlo simulation.

Low number of inputs: By increasing the number of inputs to extremely high levels, you could design a system that fits almost perfectly around a price series. This system, however, will almost certainly fail when confronted with real time data that it has not seen before. It is therefore a good idea to keep the number of parameters in the model relatively low, because the larger the number of variables in the system, the easier it is to create an overoptimized system that will underperform in real time.

Diversification with intermarket indicators: Last but not least, the key to robust system development is to select non-correlated inputs that have predictive ability. Using a superfluous number of moving averages and oscillators that are derived from the same price series won't create a profitable trading strategy. In fact, it will most likely fail to work in real time. Rather than using standard, price derived indicators as your only input, try to ascertain what other markets are related to the market being traded and use the intermarket relationship as a filter or replacement of a redundant classic indicator. One interesting advantage of intermarket analysis is that it relies on at least two different data sources or price series. Most single market analysis tools are derived from the same price data. A price shock or bad data would affect all the indicators or tools based on those data. By using two different data sources, you can help to insulate yourself against such an event. The use of intermarket relationships in developing trading systems is explained extensively in the following chapters.

By using some of the above techniques, I am convinced that anyone can, at the very least, avoid trading with systems of absolutely no value. Considering the amount of money at stake in these highly leveraged and volatile markets, it's hard to believe anyone can justify trading a system without first performing some type of validation and reliability testing.

Markets: The choice of securities used in back-testing is also important. For example, if a broad market system is tested only on oil stocks, it may fail to do well in different sectors. As a general rule, if a strategy is targeted towards a specific sector, limit the stocks to that sector, but in all other cases, maintain a large universe for testing purposes.

Software inputs: Back-testing customization is extremely important. Many back-testing applications have input for commission amounts, round (or fractional) lot sizes, tick sizes, margin requirements, interest rates, slippage assumptions, position-sizing rules, same-bar exit rules, (trailing) stop settings and much more. To get the most accurate back-testing results, it is important to tune these settings to mimic your trading style and the broker that will be used when the system goes live.

Paper trading: The market is dynamic and strategies that performed well in the past fail to do well in the present because of changing market conditions. Be sure to paper trade a system to ensure that the strategy still applies in practice.

Data quality: Price data often contain errors, which can cause serious problems, Special care should be exercised when handling missing values as these are usually replaced by zeroes. Sometimes free internet data sources, such as Yahoo Finance, do not adjust stock prices for splits. The resulting gap will not only affect the system's profitability but will also bias the system to select the appropriate parameters to position itself on the right side of the market when the price jump (or split) occurred.

While easily spotted manually, data errors tend to corrupt a mechanical system if a price series is used for testing without careful data preprocessing and error checking. There is an option in Equis' Downloader to test the data for over 100 different error conditions. The most useful is testing for a large change in close (Error#1090).

Optimization Methods

Exhaustive search technique: The most common optimization method used by most commercial software (like MetaStock or Tradestation 2000) is the exhaustive search technique (also known as the brute force approach). Optimization is performed by testing every possible number of different combinations of parameters until a parameter set is found that produces the best performance of the system over some tradable price series.

This method is the preferred technique for solving problems in which all possible solutions can be tested within the available time because it is guaranteed to exhaust all the possibilities. The primary drawback to this approach is that it is highly labor-intensive and time-consuming, especially when there is a large number of parameters to be tested with wide test ranges.

The range and increments of values you specify will also affect the number of tests to be performed. The more values that must be tested, the more tests that must be run and the longer the optimization will take. To reduce the time required for testing, you can either reduce the number of parameters being tested or decrease the parameter range or reduce the number of inputs or indicators being optimized at the same time.

Monte Carlo method: A second optimization method is the "Monte Carlo" or stochastic tunneling approach. As the name suggests, this method selects different random parameter values and records the best-performing values for each optimization pass. It then narrows the range around the parameters, centering each parameter range on the previously detected best value. During each pass through the optimization, it gradually approaches toward the best solution. The Monte Carlo method will not always find the most profitable solution, but it performs better than the brute force approach when the search space is too large and the amount of time is limited. This approach is offered as an alternative to the brute force method by the Wealth-Lab Developer software.

Gradient descent method: A third optimization method is the gradient descent method, so named because it performs the optimization by trying to find the minimum of the error curve. This is achieved by calculating the direction of the error curve in which the trial solutions seem to produce better answers. This approach is faster than the other methods when the error curve is a smooth parabola, but there are problems when the error curve has local troughs as these may confuse the search and direct the gradient descent search away from the global minima of the error curve. A variation of this method, called the conjugate gradient descent, is used by some neural net software like Alyuda's Forecaster and NeuroIntelligence.

Genetic algorithm: A fourth optimization method is the genetic algorithm, so named because it simulates evolution. In a typical optimization problem there is a set of variables (called *individuals*) which controls the process. The genetic algorithm develops a fitness function to select the best individuals (survival of the fittest). These then undergo crossover and mutation to produce new individuals that are expected to be better solutions to the problem.

After the genetic algorithm mates fit individuals and mutates some, the population undergoes a generation change. The population will then consist of offspring, plus a few of the older individuals which the genetic algorithm allows to survive because they are the fittest individuals in the population, and the algorithm wants to keep them breeding. The newly formed combinations are then decoded and tested, and the genetic inheritance process continues for several generations until the time allotted for the search has expired or a satisfactory solution (algorithm) is found. During the mutation process the parameter variables are changed to optimize the model and minimize the error.

Genetic algorithms are a powerful tool for finding the best variables or combination of variables in designing a trading system or selecting and optimizing neural network parameters. They can also be used to select related markets or weighted composite indices in designing intermarket trading models.

This optimization method is popular with commercial neural net software (like NeuroShell Trader Professional, Tradecision, etc.) to identify the best inputs and optimize their parameters in designing a neural network or trading strategy. It is also used with some conventional trading software like TradersStudio with the Genetic Optimizer add-in. Unlike the brute force approach, the genetic algorithm will not identify the global optima that will maximize profitability. On the other hand, it is a much faster and more efficient technique as a near-optimum solution can be found in a fraction of the time required by the brute force approach. The genetic algorithm method is powerful enough to analyze hundreds of parameters within an acceptable timeframe, and the Genetic Optimizer settings add flexibility to this technique.

10.2   EVALUATING PROFITABILITY

Evaluating a trading system performance is not an easy task. Not only does a trader need to know the total profit but also how the system made the money. A system may be extremely profitable, but if it does not match the trading style or risk aversion of the trader using it, he will abandon it.

There are a number of statistical metrics that can be used to evaluate the efficacy of a trading system. Each has its advantages and disadvantages. The discussion of criteria selection begins with five core criteria, and develops a total of 13 evaluative concepts. These concepts are:

1 The percentage of profitable trades (P): This is the ratio of the profitable trades divided by the total trades and it is sometimes also called the *Probability of a Profitable Trade*. The main disadvantage of this criterion is that it tells us nothing about the magnitude of the profitable trades.

2 The profit factor (PF): This is the ratio of gross winnings to gross losses. Values above one indicate a profitable system.

3 Average profit/average loss (Rwl): This is the average winning trade divided by the average losing trade.

4 Total net profit: This is the total net profit that the system makes during the testing period. If this is a negative number, it indicates a loss. Commissions and interest earned when out of a trade are taken into account.

An important limitation of this metric is that because the total net profit shows only the bottom line result of trading a particular system, it doesn't reveal the path taken to attain that net profit. It does not show the losing trades and maximum equity drawdown experienced in the course of trading. There is another obvious problem when comparing trading systems over time periods of different lengths using only the total net profit criterion: more trades can occur over a longer period of time and thus higher net profits are possible.

5 The average profit per trade: This is the total net profit divided by the number of trades. This evaluation metric is appropriate for comparing performance over time periods of differing lengths. This criterion, however, is not perfect either, as a few large values that are well above or below the majority of the observed data can "pull" the average up or down, diminishing the usefulness of this metric in predicting the expected value.

6 Profitabilty: This metric was first introduced by Michael Harris in an article in *Technical Analysis of STOCKS & COMMODITIES* (see Bibliography) and combines both the percentage of profitable trades and the ratio of the average winning/losing trade into a single number according to the following formula:

$$Profitability = 10 \cdot \left(P - \frac{1}{1 + R_{wl}} \right)$$

where P = % winners; and R_{wl} = ratio of average winning trade to the average losing trade.

To eliminate decimal places and make the formula comparable with the profit factor I modified Harris's formula by multiplying the result by a factor of 10.

The interpretation of the results is as follows:

- the higher the value, the more profitable the system;
- values above 2 indicate a tradable system and above 4 a very good system;
- a negative value indicates that the trading system produced a net loss;
- profitability is always a little less optimistic than the profit factor.

An example of calculating all the metrics described above is included in the Excel spreadsheet in Table 10.1. The profitability of that particular system is depicted in row 55.

7 Profit/loss index: This is not a very popular metric but I decided to include it here as it is included in MetaStock's profit and loss report. MetaStock calculates the profit/loss index by combining the winning and losing trades into one value that ranges from -100 to $+100$.

8 Buy and hold profit: This is the profit resulting from a buy and hold strategy. A buy and hold strategy assumes that you buy on the first day of the test and hold the position until the end. The profit is calculated by using the price on the first and last days of the test, taking into account entry and exit commissions.

Most testing software use the stock price of the first date of the data loaded in the chart in calculating the buy and hold profit. This results in unrealistic comparison with the trading profit result, as the system test cannot produce signals before all indicators are calculated. This can make a big difference where indicators requiring a large amount of data are involved, like the regression divergence indicators (used in the next chapters) which require more than three years of data. In these cases, the buy and hold profit should be calculated manually from the date that your system started producing trades and not from the first day of the loaded data.

9 The buy/hold index: This is another metric reported only by MetaStock. This shows the percentage of the system's profit compared to a buy and hold strategy.

10 The luck coefficient: As the name suggests, this metric attempts to determine how "lucky" a system is by comparing the largest to the average trade. It is calculated according to the following formula:

$$LC = MAXW/AVGW$$

where MAXW = largest winning trade profit; AVGW = average winning trade profit.

11 Pessimistic rate of return (PRR): This metric effectively increases the number of losers in a system by the square root of total losers, and decreases the number of winners in a system by the square root of total winners. The result is then computed by multiplying the new number of winners by the average amount won, and dividing this by the new number of losers multiplied by the average amount lost.

The PRR is calculated according to the following formula, which is very similar to the one used for calculating the profit factor:

$$PRR = \frac{\left(\frac{W-\sqrt{W}}{N}\right) * AVGW}{\left(\frac{L-\sqrt{L}}{N}\right) * ABS(AVGL)}$$

where W = number of winning trades; L = number of losing trades; N = total number of trades; $AVGW$ = average winning trade profit; $AVGL$ = average losing trade profit. A value greater than 2 is good; a value greater than 2.5 is excellent.

For more information on this statistic see also Vince's *Portfolio Management Formulas: Mathematical Trading Methods for the Futures, Options and Stock Markets* (see Bibliography).

12 Efficiency: By comparing the entry and exit prices to the highs and lows of the move from entry to exit, you can get measures of how good your entry and exit technique is. Entry and exit efficiency is measured according to the following formula:

> For long trades: Entry Efficiency = (Highest Price − Entry Price)/
> (Highest Price − Lowest Price).
> For short trades: Entry Efficiency = (Entry Price − Lowest Price)/
> (Highest Price − Lowest Price).

Entry efficiency is therefore designed to measure how well a system enters into a trade, or how close the long entry was to the lowest point within the trading period and the reverse for a short signal.

Exit efficiency, on the other hand, measures how well a system exits a trade, and in the case of a long entry, how close an exit is to the highest point within the trading period range according to the following formula:

Exit Efficiency = (Exit Price − Lowest Price)/(Highest Price − Lowest Price)
    for long trades and
Exit Efficiency = (Highest Price − Exit Price)/(Highest Price − Lowest Price)
    for short trades.

Total efficiency is defined as the percentage of the realized profit in relation to the total profit potential during that trade according to the formula:

Total Efficiency = (Exit Price − Entry Price)/(Highest Price − Lowest Price)
    for long trades and for short trades:
Total Efficiency = (Entry Price − Exit Price)/(Highest Price − Lowest Price).

The total efficiency can also be expressed in terms of entry and exit efficiency:

Total Efficiency = Entry Efficiency + Exit Efficiency − 100.

As a general rule, entries and exits should capture 55 % or more of the high–low range, while overall efficiency should be more than 30 %. The average efficiency of a system is of course the average of all trade efficiencies.

13 The t-test: Statistical analysis can be used to evaluate the trade results and provide additional information and probability estimates. I haven't seen this method used very often, probably because it involves time-consuming calculations or because statistics is not a popular subject among traders. Statistics can also help the trader determine whether the performance of a system is due to chance, or if the trading model will hold in the future.

In this case a simple t-test is used to compare the mean of the simulated trade profit/loss results to some benchmark and to assess whether they are statistically different from each other. The statistical analysis involved makes certain assumptions about the trade sample and populations to which they belong, which may be violated when dealing with trading models. In any case it is a good idea to check the following assumptions:

• *Normality.* An important assumption in the t-test is that the underlying distribution of the data is normal. The distribution of profit/loss figures of a trading system may not be normal, especially if a stop-loss condition is used, as a lot of trades will cluster around the maximum loss. A visual inspection of the distribution of test results will often determine whether it conforms to the bell-shaped normal curve. More rigorous methods, such as the Kolmogorov-Smirnov normality test or Shapiro-Wilk's W-test can be used to determine whether the distribution is normal. In case of minor violations, the distribution can be modified by removing some outliers or transforming the data using a squashing function. The central limit theorem, which states that as the number of cases in the sample increases, the distribution of the sample mean approaches normality, can also come to the rescue in cases of large sample sizes.

- *Autocorrelation*. This violation is essentially one of serial dependence, which occurs when trade cases are not statistically independent of one another. This reduces the effective sample size. The extent of autocorrelation can be determined by computing the correlation between the profit and loss results with the same results shifted by n days in the past.
- *Sample size*. The system should produce more than 30 trades in order for the statistical results to be of any significance.

Some violations may be ignored, while others may be compensated for. Where there are more serious violations this test should be avoided.

To illustrate the use of the t-test in evaluating a system, I exported trade results from the SPY regression long-short test, presented in Chapter 12, into an Excel spreadsheet. The test data together with the t-test and an example of calculating some of the other test metrics described above is presented in Table 10.1.

Before performing a t-test comparison, the Kolmogorov-Smirnov normality test was used to check whether the distribution was normal. The test statistic was found to be 0.1 and the associated significance 0.2 which is greater than 0.05 (row 66), suggesting that the current distribution was not perfectly normal but not significantly different from a normal distribution. To check on the second assumption of autocorrelation, I copied the same results one row forward (from column C to column D) and calculated the correlation between columns C and D using Excel's CORREL function. In the current case, the autocorrelation was 0.28 (row 65), which suggests a weak correlation, but not as low as I would prefer.

The sample was not perfect but since none of the assumptions were violated we could proceed to calculate the t-test to compare the sample profitability against no profitability, by subtracting zero from the sample mean profit. To compare the mean against the benchmark, which in this case is the S&P 500 buy and hold performance, I subtracted the S&P performance from the mean. Next, I divided the resultant numbers by the estimated standard deviation to obtain the value of the t-statistic (in rows 59 and 61). Finally, I calculated the probability that I would get a t-statistic as large by chance alone by using the TDIST function included in Excel. This works out to be 0.02 % (in row 60). Since this figure is very small, it is highly unlikely that the results were profitable due to chance alone. When the system is compared to the S&P, however, the probability is 21.6 % (row 62) which suggests that if the system were tested on a number of different samples, about 22 % of the tests would not fare better than the S&P buy and hold method.

It should be clear by now that each criterion mentioned above has at least one drawback that keeps it from being the sole method by which to evaluate a trading system. In addition, drawdown or risk has to be considered separately as none of

Table 10.1   The profit/loss trade results for the SPY long-short system presented in Chapter 12 were used as an example of evaluating test results using a variety of statistical and empirical metrics.

A	B	C	D	E
2		Profit/loss	Profit/loss	Profit/loss
3	Date	per trade	(lag=1)	cumulative
4	31/01/96	−987.26		−987.3
5	15/03/96	366.25	−987.26	−621.0
6	21/08/97	−830	366.25	−1451.0
7	13/10/97	846.45	−830	−604.6
8	30/10/97	864.1	846.45	259.5
9	17/02/98	1668	864.1	1927.5
10	23/07/98	1134.73	1668	3062.3
11	10/11/98	572.49	1134.73	3634.8
12	26/05/99	764.07	572.49	4398.8
13	08/06/99	−638.64	764.07	3760.2
14	21/07/99	681.79	−638.64	4442.0
15	29/11/99	693.36	681.79	5135.3
16	29/03/00	1160.17	693.36	6295.5
17	26/06/00	−185.2	1160.17	6110.3
18	31/08/00	464.16	−185.2	6574.5
19	29/01/01	144.64	464.16	6719.1
20	09/03/01	19	144.64	6738.1
21	29/05/01	312.84	19	7051.0
22	26/09/01	2949.6	312.84	10000.6
23	04/12/01	2448.7	2949.6	12449.3
24	12/06/02	2076.7	2448.7	14526.0
25	25/10/02	147.56	2076.7	14673.5
26	27/03/03	258.46	147.56	14932.0
27	08/08/03	120.7	258.46	15052.7
28	06/10/03	−652.82	120.7	14399.9
29	26/03/04	554.36	−652.82	14954.2
30	29/04/04	−81.6	554.36	14872.6
31	16/09/04	−319.25	−81.6	14553.4
32	27/10/04	−84.08	−319.25	14469.3
33	22/11/04	1027.99	−84.08	15497.3
34	27/01/05	235.75	1027.99	15733.0
35	31/03/05	470.63	235.75	16203.7
36	22/06/05	1013.56	470.63	17217.2
37	29/09/05	224.62	1013.56	17441.8
38	29/11/05	1197.2	224.62	18639.0
39	05/01/06	−225.67	1197.2	18413.4
40	23/08/06	740.02	−225.67	19153.4
41	07/02/07	90.4	740.02	19243.8

(Continued)

Table 10.1   (*Continued*)

A	B	C	D	E
2		Profit/loss	Profit/loss	Profit/loss
3	Date	per trade	(lag=1)	cumulative
42	08/03/07	−156.8	90.4	19087.0
43	20/04/07	1121.68	−156.8	20208.7
44	17/09/07	97.92	1121.68	20306.6
45				
46		**FORMULA**		
47	Average profit /trade	495.3	=AVERAGE(C4:C44)	
48	Count	41	=COUNT(C4:C44)	
49	Winners	31	=COUNTIF(C4:C44,">0")	
50	Losers	10	=COUNTIF(C4:C44,"<0")	
51	Average Winner	789.3	=SUMIF(C4:C44,">0")/C49	
52	Average Loser	−416.1	=SUMIF(C4:C44,"<0")/C50	
53	% of profitable trades	75.6 %	=C49/C48	
54	Avg. Winners/Avg. Losers	1.90	=C51/ABS(C52)	
55	Profitability Rating	4.11	=10*(C53-1/(1+C51/ABS(C52)))	
56	Profit factor	5.88	=SUMIF(C4:C44,">0")/ ABS(SUMIF(C4:C44,"<0"))	
57	Standard Deviation	820.9	=STDEV(C4:C44)	
58	Standard Error of the mean	128.2	=C57/SQRT(C48)	
59	t-statistic return vs 0	3.9	=C47/(C57/SQRT(C48))	
60	Probability P/L>0	0.02 %	=TDIST(C59,C48,1)	
61	t-statistic return vs. S&P	0.8	=(C47-16138/C48)/ (C57/SQRT(C48))	
62	Probability >S&P	21.6 %	=TDIST(C61,C48,1)	
63	Coefficient of Variation	166 %	=C57/C47	
64	Max initial closed drawdown	−1451.0	=MIN(E4:E44)	
65	Autocorrelation (lag=1)	0.28	=CORREL(C4:C44,D4:D44)	
66	Kolmogorov-Smirnov test	0.099	Significance=0.2	

the profitability criteria take it into account. Therefore the evaluation of each system requires a subjective judgment on the part of the trader, based on his trading preferences, experience, and psychological profile.

Typically, a trader views a system as a "success" if it maximizes profit – subject to minimizing drawdown, minimizing exposure to the market and minimizing position risk – and provides a smooth equity curve. Additionally, trading systems can be compared on a statistical basis by performing the independent-measures single factor ANOVA procedure, which effectively quantifies between and within-group variations. ANOVA can be used to compare two or more samples of unequal sizes, although greatest accuracy is achieved with equal or approximately equal sample sizes. In cases of moderate departure from normality, ANOVA still provides a valid test, especially when the samples are relatively large.

10.3   DRAWDOWN AND OTHER RISK METRICS

The classical performance tests consider in detail the profitability of a technical trading system but fail to address its risk reduction properties. Increased risk must be compensated by incremental expected return and vice versa.

Drawdown is a very important statistic, since it represents your risk. But what do those drawdown figures represent? It is important to realize that there are different types of drawdown.

Maximum drawdown: Drawdowns are retracements in equity from previous equity highs in short, losing periods. Maximum drawdown is calculated by finding the highest peak in the equity curve and subtracting the subsequent lowest trough before the next higher peak in the equity curve.

There are two different ways to calculate maximum drawdown: open and closed trade. The maximum open trade drawdown occurs while the trade is open and the closed trade drawdown only represents the final actual realized loss when the trade is closed. This is typically the smallest drawdown and some system developers prefer to publish this one as it looks the best for marketing purposes. They argue that what matters most are realized closed profits and losses, and not what happens during a trade. I believe that this argument may have some value when it comes to reporting net profits but not in the case of drawdowns, because you will certainly experience larger drawdowns than shown by the maximum closed trade drawdown figures.

Maximum initial open drawdown: This is the maximum dollar "out of pocket" drawdown that you will first suffer before you finally start making profits.This drawdown is useful in evaluating the minimium account size required when testing trading systems on commodities and equity futures.

Total daily drawdown: This is the drawdown at market close and it is what will be reflected on the daily account balance on your statements that you get from your broker.

Maximum percentage drawdown: This is the maximum drawdown expressed as a percentage of the total equity which may not occur at the same point in time as the maximum dollar drawdown. For example, for a given equity curve you could have a situation where the maximum percentage drawdown of 50 % was caused when equity was reduced from a maximum of $10 000 to a minimum of $5000 (or a $5000 reduction in equity). Also from the same equity curve you could have a maximum peak-to-valley dollar drawdown of $400 000 when the equity was reduced from $1 000 000 to $600 000 even though the percentage reduction is only 40 %, less than the 50 % maximum peak-to-valley percentage drawdown caused when the equity was reduced from $10 000 to $5000.

Maximum position adverse excursion (MAE): This is defined as the most equity lost intraday by any single position.

Ideally we would like to have no drawdown in equity but in reality it cannot be avoided. There will be periods where traders experience a string of losses that outweigh any recent gains. The main implication of drawdown is the psychological effect it will have, as a large string of losses may cause the trader to abandon his trading system.

Finally, you should keep in mind that drawdown can sometimes be an unreliable figure. It should never be used on its own to compare two trading systems but always used in conjunction with profitability criteria.

MetaStock reports only the maximum initial drawdown which is usually lower than the maximum open drawdown but it is a helpful statistic as it will help determine the size of the account needed to begin trading the system.

In addition to drawdown, the following metrics use drawdown, time in the market or standard deviation to measure risk:

Risk/reward index: This index compares risk to reward and is defined as the ratio of the maximum open drawdown to the total net profits. MetaStock reports the reward/risk index by calculating the ratio of total net profits to maximum initial drawdown and normalizes it to a range of -100 to $+100$.

Risk adjusted return: A statistical method of comparing systems is to calculate the risk adjusted return. This is calculated by dividing the annualized rate of return on equity by the standard deviation of equity changes. The compounded rate of return is calculated according to the following formula:

Annual compounded rate of return = (ending equity − initial equity)$^{(1/n)}$ − 1

where n = test duration in years.

The standard deviation of equity changes is usually calculated monthly but can also be calculated annually depending on the time frame of the system to be analyzed.

This method involves time-consuming calculations. A quick method of obtaining the return/risk of different systems for comparison purposes is to divide the total profit by the standard deviation of profits. The test with the greatest return/risk ratio would be the best as long as the time period is the same.

RINA® index: Developed by RINA® Systems, this is a risk adjusted profitability metric. It is the ratio of the net profit divided by the product of the maximum open drawdown and percent of time in the market.

The number of consecutive losers: This is a test of how strong your stomach must be to trade the system. Before making any hasty conclusions, however, the dollar value of these strings of losses should be examined as well. A trading system may experience a long string of losses but actually lose very little money, compared to a short string of heavy losses.

Sharpe ratio: This is a measure of the mean excess return per unit of risk and describes how much excess return you are receiving for the extra volatility of trade results. It is calculated according to the following simple formula:

$$SR = (r - R)/\sigma$$

where r is the asset return; R is the return on a benchmark asset, such as the risk free rate of return of the US T-bill; and σ is the standard deviation of the excess return.

When calculating the Sharpe ratio it is important for all the variables to be calculated for the same time frame, e.g. if you are comparing annual returns the standard deviation should be annualized by multiplying by the square root of 365 divided by the time period (in days) used for the standard deviation calculation. Also all numbers (including the standard deviation) should be expressed in percentage terms.

The Sharpe ratio is used widely when evaluating mutual fund performance. These numbers are available for most mutual funds on the Morningstar web site at http://www.morningstar.com/ (subscription required). A Sharpe ratio of over 1.0 is good. Outstanding funds achieve something over 2.0.

A serious problem in using this metric is the assumption that asset returns are normally distributed which in reality is not always the case.

Sterling ratio method: Similar to the Sharpe method above, the Sterling ratio method measures risk adjusted return and is given by:

$$R(\%)/(D(\%) + 10\%)$$

where R = three-year average annual return; D = three-year average maximum annual drawdown.

Both the Sharpe and Sterling ratio methods compare variability of returns, as opposed to drawdown which measures losses.

The coefficient of variation of average profit: The coefficient of variation can be used instead of the average profit per trade in order to account for volatility of results. It is a useful statistic for comparing the degree of variation from one data series to another, even if the means are significantly different from each other.

This is calculated by dividing the standard deviation by the mean profit. It is often reported as a percentage (%) by multiplying by 100. The result is a unit-less, relative measure and risk adjusted comparisons can be made between different systems.

You should avoid using this metric when the mean profit value is near zero because the coefficient of variation becomes very sensitive to changes in the standard deviation, limiting its usefulness. A low positive value is the most desirable as this indicates a high profit with low variability.

The Calmar ratio: This is the average percentage yearly gain divided by the largest percentage drawdown.

The Ulcer Index: This risk metric is designed to measure only the negative return (drawdown) fluctuations and it is defined as the root mean square of equity drawdowns.

10.4   STOP-LOSS

A stop-loss order is used to liquidate a losing position upon the breach of a predefined maximum loss limit. When confronted with an equity drawdown on an active trade, a trader must choose between two conflicting actions: liquidating the trade in an attempt to conserve capital, or continuing with the hope of recouping losses on the drawdown.

The ideal stop is unique. Though no such ideal stop exists, a good idea is to place stops just outside the range of random price swings, not so close that it gets you out of a trade too soon but not so far away as to be meaningless. Your time horizon should also determine stop placement. Short-term traders looking for relatively small profits should use tight stops, while intermediate to long-term trend traders looking for big market moves should use loose stops placed far away from the current price in order to allow for random moves.

There are many types of stop loss conditions:

- *Initial stop-loss.* This is applied to the initial price when entering the trade. On entering a trade, the maximum loss, in points or percentage, that will be risked on the trade is determined. If the market moves against the position by this amount from the entry price, the stop is activated and the position is closed. One problem with this rule is that it doesn't account for volatility. With volatile stocks or futures, this range may be within the normal price action over a dull week.
- *Trailing stop-loss.* A trailing stop is designed to both limit loss and protect profit. The difference from the initial stop is that it applies to the highest price during the trade. If the market initially moves against the trader's position the stop is activated and in this case it is identical to the initial stop. If, on the other hand, the market initially moves in favor of the position, the stop is re-positioned x points or percentage from the current price.
- *Price level based stop.* This stop-loss is usually set at a price level of technical significance, i.e. a support or resistance. Stops are often placed near a significant

swing high or low in trending markets, while in trading markets, stops may be placed just above or below the current trading range.

- *Volatility stops.* Instead of defining the stop-loss in terms of a fixed percentage or dollar amount, a standard deviation or average true range threshold can be used to achieve a similar objective. This is my favorite as it seems a good compromise to the too tight or too loose dilemma.
- *Indicator based stop.* This is triggered by an indicator, the most popular being Wilder's parabolic stop and reverse (SAR) indicator. The term "parabolic" comes from the shape of the curve (resembling a parabola) created on the technical chart. The parabolic SAR is a trend-following indicator that is designed to create a trailing stop. It is primarily used in trending markets so the SAR is really inappropriate for range bound markets as it will whipsaw in and out of the market.
- *Time stop.* This is triggered after a predetermined period of time has elapsed.

There are a number of variants of the stops described above, and stops may also be set on combinations of the above.

Despite the many advantages of using them in your strategy, stop-losses are not a panacea. Here are some advantages and disadvantages of using stop-loss conditions:

- *Risk management.* The nature of the stop-loss order allows a certain degree of risk management, according to each trader's risk aversion, even though it might not improve overall profitability.
- *Catastrophic losses.* Stop-loss orders are essential to avoid catastrophic losses and reduce the risk of ruin.
- *Curve-fitting.* Stop-loss conditions can reduce the drawdown caused when trading in real time a bad or a curve-fitted system.
- *Psychological implications.* Stop-loss conditions contribute positively to a trader's emotional and psychological condition. By placing a simple stop-loss it is not necessary to agonize over unconscionably large equity drawdowns during the life of a trade.

And some disadvantages:

- A stop-loss could liquidate profitable trades prematurely.
- The nature of the stop-loss order does not allow the user to absolutely define the amount of risk. As stated in the risk disclosure statement issued by the Commodity Futures Trading Commission (CFTC): *Placing contingent orders, such as a "stop-loss" or "stop-limit" order will not necessarily limit your losses to the intended amounts, since market conditions may make it impossible to execute such orders.*
- A stop-loss might reduce the profitability of your system. Although stop-loss reduces the risk of a single large loss, it can generate a series of small losses, which in total can exceed the single loss. According to a study by William Chan published in the *Journal of the Market Technicians Association* (see Bibliography), after

back-testing fixed % and trailing % stop-loss conditions on both trend-following and mean-reversion trading strategies the author concluded that "The results from our tests indicate a significant negative correlation between the value added by applying these stop-loss rules and the profitability of the trading strategies tested. In other words, there was a tendency for these stop-loss mechanisms to *undermine the performance of the profitable trading strategies tested and improve that of the unprofitable ones in the test*"(my italics). Based on my experience in developing trading systems, I have also noticed that stop-loss conditions improve systems with poor exit conditions but tend almost always to degrade the profitability of a system with good and timely exit conditions. This is because an unrealized loss caused by an excessive price spike might be recouped by continuing with the trade instead of being converted into a realized loss on liquidation.

• The frustration involved in being stopped out of a position, only to have the market turn around, will prevent the trader from re-entering a good trade.

In conclusion I would have to agree that even though stops do not necessarily improve the final profitability of the results of a trading system they certainly contribute to a trader's peace of mind and prevent catastrophic losses in the case of unforeseen events. In a sense, stop-losses can be compared to premiums on an insurance policy and should be considered as an unavoidable cost of doing business.

10.5   PROFIT TARGETS

The use of profit targets is not uncommon, but in general they run contra to the popular principle "cut your losses short and let your profits run".

Profit targets effectively exit a trade once a predefined amount of profit has been achieved. Below are some variants of profit exits:

• *Percentage based*. This is the simplest method. The profit taking target is measured as a percentage of the initial price when entering the trade.
• *Double objectives*. This is similar to the first method with the difference that two profit targets are used, spaced further apart as profits get larger. Half of the initial position is liquidated upon reaching each target. This method has the advantage of increasing the chance of reaching at least one of the objectives while removing half the risk.
• *Price level based*. The target is usually set at a price level of technical significance, i.e. a support or resistance. In the case of technical systems based on pattern recognition the profit target is applied according to the specific formation. In the case of flag, pennant and rectangle formations I have derived statistically a formula to calculate the appropriate price target in my articles in the April 2005, May 2006 and June 2007 issues of *Technical Analysis of STOCKS & COMMODITIES*

(see Bibliography). You can also find the formula for calculating the price objective of rectangle formations in Appendix C.

- *Indicator based stop.* This is triggered by an indicator such as a stochastic reaching an overbought level in range bound markets.

10.6   MONEY MANAGEMENT

Money management concerns the actual size of the trade to be initiated, with consideration of account equity and potential for trade risk. It is extremely important for a trader to scale trading positions relative to available capital.

Effective money management is related to the risk of ruin, which can help determine the amount of capital needed to trade a given system. Effectively, the risk of ruin increases as the amount per position increases, and decreases as the probability of winning increases, or as the payoff ratio increases.

As every trade carries a potential for loss, there is a need to determine the maximum amount of capital to expose at each trade, given a finite capital base. There are a number of approaches in common usage. For example, the traditional Kelly system (see *Money Management Strategies for Futures Traders* by Balsara) evaluates the fraction of capital to expose, f, as the difference between the probable expected win and the amount expected to lose. Other methods include Vince's optimal f (see Bibliography). Monte-Carlo analysis can also be used to determine the optimal money management strategy by optimizing f according to the probability of success or failure.

10.7   NEURAL NETWORKS

Artificial neural networks are well suited in quantifying complex relationships between interrelated markets because they address the nonlinear nature of financial time series. The concept behind neural networks was originally brought forth almost 50 years ago and had its origin in studies of the mechanisms by which the brain learns. Neural network software is designed to mimic the working of the human brain when solving problems; they use information that the network has learned in solving problems with known outcomes, to solve similar problems with unknown outcomes.

Neural networks consist of highly complex nonlinear models that use various optimization techniques to find the model that most closely gives the output corresponding to the input. They select which of the inputs are relevant in predicting the answer and assign weighting factors to produce the correct forecast. The predicted output is based on the training, so it is critical that a relationship is present between the variables.

Neural network software are composed of three types of neuron layers: an input layer, one or more hidden layers, and an output layer. Transform functions serve as the connectors or neurons. During training, the transform functions establish the weights of the connections by seeking the optimum connective weightings that will result in a minimum of error between the network's prediction and the actual answer. Some modern commercial neural network software now actually have one layer for each hidden neuron, and the layers are added one by one as needed. They start training with an arbitrary set of starting weights and search for a set of weights that minimizes the network's errors. Training neural networks by minimizing the output error is conceptually similar to the least-squares technique used in statistical regression analysis where the formula for a line that best fits a collection of scattered points on a graph is found by minimizing the sum of the squared differences between the predicted and actual values.

Neural networks are primarily beneficial when the relationship between input and output data is not clearly understood, but a large number of sample sets of data are available. What distinguishes neural networks from artificial intelligence or standard programming practices? Neural networks are "trained with data" rather than programmed. This implies that neural networks improve with experience. The more data the network is trained with, the more reliable the answers will be.

Unlike conventional technical trading systems, neural network systems work well when technical and fundamental data are combined. It is sometimes difficult, however, to find appropriate fundamental data, which is often subject to revision and not always reported in a data-compatible format. Neural networks trained with fundamental data are more often used as longer-term screening strategies.

Fortunately you don't have to be a computer programmer in order to use neural networks as there is a wide selection of commercial neural network software, like NeuroShell Trader, Trading Solutions, Traders Studio with the Neural Studio & Kernel regression add-in, NeuralWorks Predict, Deep Insight, Tradecision, WealthLab Developer, etc. It is tempting to see techniques like neural networks as a panacea for predicting the market, but it is important to realize that these are simply a step in the correct direction to model the complex underlying mechanics of the financial markets.

There is general acceptance that neural networks are superior at modeling and predicting relationships within the financial market domain, due in part to their ability to model non-linear relationships in the noisy environment which the stock market represents. This praise may be premature in some areas such as trading and does not mean neural networks are the "Holy Grail".

The following is a list of limitations and criticisms of neural networks:

- A major limitation of neural networks that most traders or analysts are not aware of is *over-training* or *over-fitting*, which is analogous to curve-fitting in rule-based trading systems. As a neural net makes training runs through the data, if it can't minimize error level by learning real relationships between the input training data and the variable to be predicted, it will tend to find patterns that exist only by chance. This will result in an over-fitted model that will fail miserably when used in actual trading. There are no rigorous training methodologies that can avoid this problem entirely. Also, where there are multiple inputs, neural networks tend to find inputs which are important for making the prediction and weight unimportant ones near 0. This uses some of the power of the network and will also produce curve-fitted results because it produces a model which works well on the training data but performs poorly on out-of-sample test data.

- Another major problem encountered when working with neural networks is inter-pretability or their virtually non-existent explanatory capability. You can create a successful neural network without understanding how it works: the output would in all probability be completely valueless as a scientific resource. Generally, most researchers do not attempt to extract rules from their networks; rather they rely on statistical testing performed on out-of-sample results.

- There are obvious mismatches between the goals of neural networks and real traders. While neural networks are attempting to minimize forecast errors in train-ing, traders typically focus on maximizing profit and minimizing drawdown.

- Neural network systems tend to overtrade. For example, a neural network system based on rules similar to a conventional system could produce three to ten times the number of trades.

- An issue which can be confusing to new users of neural software is that it is very unlikely that you will get exactly the same results each time you train a network. This is counterintuitive and often leads to misconceptions among many traders who used conventional systems in the past. A conventional system, for example a moving average crossover system, uses a unique and specific relationship (between the two moving averages); all you have to worry about is getting accurate, precise data and then the system produces the appropriate unique signals. This is not the case, however, with neural systems because they start training with an arbitrary set of starting weights and therefore produce a different solution each time. This is a problem which cannot be overlooked, as it is often required to retrain the network up to 10 times in order for the solution to converge, meaning that all training outputs would have to be within a given tolerance limit of the correct answer. The resulting trained network would have deciphered the input conditions correctly and could then take new input data and presumably give good predictions every time. To deal with this issue, system developers started using the method of Kernel regression (see Chapter 3) as an alternative to neural networks as it always gives the same answers. Automation of the convergence process is also an alternative solution to the tedious training process.

- A neural network model can fall apart when confronted with market conditions that were not present during the training and optimization process. They therefore need to be retrained occasionally to take into account the new market dynamics.

- I have also heard criticisms citing the following conundrum: How can a technique which mirrors human intelligence be able to predict changes in the stock market when humans are remarkably poor at beating the market?

Despite these clear limitations, neural networks are still considered the tool of choice for investigating non-linear relationships amongst noisy and complex data sets. Of course neural networks are just tools in understanding one piece of the puzzle of the financial markets and their interrelationships and other pieces of the puzzle are still missing.

10.8   FUZZY LOGIC

Indicators are rarely definitively bullish or bearish, nor can they be considered to have precise values, such as true or false. More accurately, a technical indicator provides, as the name suggests, an indication of a situation, and not a black-or-white conclusion. Artificial intelligence developers decided to deal with this ambiguity by introducing the concept of fuzzy logic. Fuzzy logic uses propositional logic that is modified to allow the use of any value in the range of 0 to 1, rather than only the crisp values of 0 or 1.

The result is a value falling within the range of 0 to 1 considered partly true to the magnitude of that particular value. For example, can a stock's daily price change of 3 % be considered high while 2.9 % is not? A decision based on a crisp rule is difficult to develop, but by using fuzzy logic a rating or an indexed value from 0 to 1 can be applied. The resulting fuzzy logic should then be able to accommodate the vague linguistic terms closer to human judgment and intuition.

The following are a few of the advantages in incorporating fuzzy logic in your trading systems and indicators:

- *Simplicity of programming*. Fuzzy rules do not have to be as precise as traditional binary specifications. This will reduce the time spent in designing a trading system.
- *Familiarity*. Fuzzy systems can be used for developing systems that can be described with linguistic rules in which the experience of a trader can be incorporated in a natural way. Thus the behavior of the system would be more familiar for traders.
- *Speed*. Less time will be required to optimize the system.
- *Pattern recognition*. Experienced traders can recognize a formation or pattern on a chart but ask them to describe it precisely and you will get a different description from each. This makes pattern recognition an ambiguous task, more appropriate for fuzzy logic. By incorporating fuzzy indicators into your screening systems, you can scan for your favorite patterns or formations in multiple securities in a fraction of the time that you could do it manually.
- *Fundamental criteria* (for example William O'Niel's popular CANSLIM method) are relatively vague and the results depend on how one interprets them. In these cases, fuzzy logic could be used to transform ambiguous qualifiers, such as growth, leadership, supply and demand, etc., with crisp mathematical models for machine processing.

- *Errors.* Fuzzy logic is far more intuitive and closer to human judgment than binary logic and therefore more tolerant to bad data, outliers and other input data errors.

Fuzzy logic fits well to the perception of the traders. However, a trader sometimes adapts his strategies depending on market conditions, circumstances and other external stimuli. To add the necessary flexibility to your fuzzy system, a genetic algorithm can be used to optimize the internal fuzzy logic engine parameters to allow for a wider range of variations in order to take into account the ever-changing market conditions.

Despite the obvious advantages of using fuzzy logic, traders have been slow to embrace this new technology, and its use in the development of trading systems has been limited mainly to Wall Street professional consultants and academics. In fact, I don't know of any independent trader who uses fuzzy logic systems in trading. This may be because their implementation is not as straightforward as binary logic, or because of the high cost of purchasing artificial intelligence software or the complexity in using them. I have presented in this chapter three different artificial intelligence tools (neural networks, fuzzy logic and genetic algorithms) as well as traditional binary rule-based systems, but the focus each time has been only on a single method. This doesn't mean, however, that a combination of two or more different methods in a single strategy is not possible or without merit.

While an artificial intelligence system can be profitable, its use may be sub-optimal, in the sense that results may be constrained by the limitations of the technology. For example, while neural networks have the positive attributes of adaptation and learning, they have the negative attribute of a "black box" syndrome. By the same token, fuzzy logic has the advantage of approximate reasoning but the disadvantage that it lacks an effective learning capability. Merging these technologies provides an opportunity to capitalize on their strengths and compensate for their shortcomings. However, to design an effective hybrid system, the strengths and weaknesses of all component technologies must first be understood.

Commercial software vendors, eager to cash in on the new technologies, have already developed software that are capable of constructing a trading system which incorporates traditional as well as all the above artificial intelligence tools. The only obstacle in using them is the cost of the software and the time and skill required to learn to use the new software.

10.9 CONCLUSION

In approximately 500 BC, Confucius said, "Study the past if you want to divine the future." As far as I am concerned, this makes Confucius the first market technician. You should have learned by now, especially after reading the section on back-testing and the pitfalls of optimization, that there is no guarantee that a system, no matter how many hours you spent in back-testing it, is going to be profitable in the future.

For example, a change in market conditions or a price shock caused by an un-expected geopolitical event can devastate any system. In the world of trading there are no formulae that produce black and white results, and all rules must be based on partial knowledge. The paradox is that the market is a place where no transaction can be completed unless the opinions of the participants are diametrically opposed. You must therefore accept the fact that you are often going to be the participant who is wrong. You should accept losses with no remorse, no tears, no what-ifs, and no pointing fingers at others.

In order to survive, seek out strategies based on probabilities and focus on limiting your losses, money management and the mathematical principle of compounding.

The information on trading systems presented in this chapter is by no means exhaustive. I have included a number of books in the Bibliography, for the benefit of readers interested to learn more about the development of trading systems. I highly recommend Perry Kaufman's *Smarter Trading*, Chuck Lebeau and David Lucas' *Technical Trader's Guide to Computer Analysis of the Futures Markets*, and Murray Ruggiero's *Cybernetic Trading Strategies* which also includes chapters on intermarket trading systems.

Disclaimer

My editor has asked me to include the following disclaimer. Please read it carefully before proceeding with the trading systems in the next chapters

Hypothetical performance results have many inherent limitations, some of which are described below. No representation is being made that any account will or is likely to achieve profits or losses similar to those shown. In fact, there are frequently sharp differences between hypothetical performance results and the actual results subsequently achieved by any particular trading program.

Any performance results listed in the next chapters represent simulated computer results over past historical data, and not the results of an actual account. All opinions expressed anywhere in this book are only opinions of the author. The information contained here was gathered from sources deemed reliable; however, no claim is made as to its accuracy or content. Different testing platforms can produce slightly different results. My systems are only recommended for well capitalized and experienced traders.

11

A Comparison of Fourteen Technical Systems for Trading Gold

The market always does what it should do, but not always when.
                                                              –Joseph D. Goodman

I presented in Chapter 9 many different intermarket indicators that can be useful in developing trading systems. But which one has the best predictive capacity and which intermarket securities should one use for trading gold? Only testing can reveal the winner.

11.1   TEST SPECIFICATIONS

All single divergence indicators were tested using the Philadelphia Gold & Silver Mining Index (XAU) and the dollar index (DXY) separately in order to evaluate the best performing indicator and intermarket security at the same time. Double and multiple divergence indicators used the XAU–dollar index and XAU–silver–dollar index combinations respectively.

I used the gold ETF (GLD) instead of gold futures as not all investors or traders have a futures account. Unfortunately, the gold ETF started trading in the NYSE in November 2004. For this reason, for the time period that the GLD was not in existence (from January 1992 to November 2004) I used gold spot prices (after dividing them by 10) to create a "tradeable proxy". I then used MetaStock's downloader to join the proxy and actual GLD prices into one long continuous file of gold prices stretching from 1992 to 2007. Similarly, I joined the World Silver Index prices (after multiplying them by 10) with the SLV. Daily pricing data were obtained from Telechart after exporting them to MetaStock. The test results were compared with the buy and hold method (Table 11.1). All tests started with an initial equity of $100 000. In order to compare the systems with the buy and hold method, profits or losses were compounded to the initial equity.

Tests were carried out using MetaStock Professional 8.0 and test statistics are presented in Tables 11.1, 11.2 and 11.3. All orders were executed at next day's opening price at the market, and the commission charged was $10. Gold bullion

Table 11.1 Test results of some single intermarket systems from 1 December 1995 to 21 August 2007. All tests were profitable and outperformed the buy and hold method by a wide margin. The LRS system used the linear regression slope divergence method. The momentum oscillator was used to determine optimum divergence levels.

System	Buy & hold	Regression	Regression	LRS	LRS
Intermarket security		DXY	XAU	DXY	XAU
Total net profit	$67 509	$265 474	**$621 084**	$282 257	$244 097
Profit/loss %	68 %	265 %	**621 %**	282 %	244 %
Annual % gain/loss	5.8 %	23 %	**53 %**	24 %	21 %
Total no. of trades	1	27	**31**	21	16
Winning trades	1	16	**25**	19	13
Losing trades	0	11	6	**2**	**3**
Percent profitable	100 %	59 %	**81 %**	**90 %**	**81 %**
Avg. winning trade	$67 509	$14 306	**$20 410**	$10 135	$11 795
Avg. losing trade	0	−$7071	−$2941	−$2721	−**$1717**
Avg. win/avg. loss		2.02	**6.94**	3.73	**6.87**
Profitability coef.		2.62	**6.80**	6.93	6.85
Profit factor		2.94	**28.91**	35.39	29.76
Max drawdown	−$35 194	−$31 108	−$12 896	−$9 282	−$11 067
Risk/reward	52.1 %	11.7 %	**2.1 %**	**3.3 %**	**4.5 %**
Time in market	100.0 %	30.2 %	38.0 %	20.7 %	**24.0 %**
System Parameters					
Divergence days		400	400		
MA gold				30	40
MA intermarket				40	50
ROC – days		10	12		
IMO – days		200	200	200	200
IMO – buy		60	60	85	70
IMO – short		7	8	25	5
IMO – sell		15	15	25	15
IMO – cover		80	80	60	50
Time exit – bars		50	50	50	50

Table 11.2 Test results of some single intermarket systems from 1 December 1995 to 21 August 2007. All tests were profitable and outperformed the buy and hold method (in Table 11.1) by a wide margin. The XAU or the dollar index were used to calculate intermarket indicators. All systems used the momentum oscillator to determine optimum divergence levels.

System	BB	Disparity	Disparity	Z-score	Z-score
Intermarket security	XAU	XAU	DXY	DXY	XAU
Total net profit	$179 543	$290 447	$323 637	**$409 960**	$307 540
Profit/loss %	180 %	290 %	324 %	**410 %**	308 %
Annual % gain/loss	15 %	25 %	28 %	**35 %**	26 %
Total no. of trades	16	26	31	24	24
Winning trades	13	18	**23**	17	16
Losing trades	3	8	8	7	8
Percent profitable	81 %	69 %	**74 %**	**71 %**	67 %
Avg. winning trade	$8553	$11 080	$12 437	**$20 113**	$16 948
Avg. losing trade	−$5662	**−$1700**	−$6852	−$6807	−$6286
Avg. win/avg. loss	1.51	**6.52**	1.82	2.95	2.70
Profitability coef.	4.14	**5.59**	3.87	**4.55**	3.96
Profit factor	6.55	**14.66**	5.22	**7.18**	5.39
Max drawdown	**−$10 665**	−$35 424	−$26 844	−$30 650	−$26 863
Risk/reward	**5.9 %**	12.2 %	8.3 %	7.5 %	8.7 %
Time in market	**18.9 %**	26.7 %	24.1 %	38.4 %	28.9 %
			System Parameters		
Divergence days	100	15		500	100
MA gold	100	15	20		
MA intermarket	100	15	15		
IMO – days	200	200	200	200	200
IMO – buy	70	80	80	90	80
IMO – short	5	25	25	5	10
IMO – sell	30	30	30	50	50
IMO – cover	50	60	60	50	40
Time exit – bars	50	50	50	50	50

investors do not get any dividends or interest, so for a more realistic comparison with the buy and hold method, interest was credited at an average rate of 4 % when out of the market.

If you wish to replicate the tests, please keep in mind that for them to begin producing any signals the indicators used in each should be calculated first, and this requires a number of bars to be loaded. For example, the test using the regression divergence and the 200-day momentum oscillator will need 617 extra data bars to be loaded (11 for the ROC + 400 for the regression + 3 for the divergence EMA + 200

Table 11.3 Test results of the relative strength, LRS and multiple regression intermarket systems from 1 December 1995 to 21 August 2007. All tests were profitable and outperformed the buy and hold method by a wide margin. The XAU, the dollar index and silver were used to calculate intermarket divergence. The multiple divergence system outperformed all systems producing an astonishing profit of more than $1.2 million on a $100 000 initial equity.

System	RS (Diverg)	RS	LRS double	LRS double	Regresion multiple
Intermarket security	XAU	DXY	XAU - DXY	SLV - DXY	XAU - SLV - DXY
Total net profit	$267 542	$141 363	$370 418	$476 181	$1 263 992
Profit/loss %	268 %	141 %	370 %	476 %	1264 %
Annual % gain/loss	23 %	12 %	32 %	41 %	108 %
Total no. of trades	17	9	33	23	38
Winning trades	14	7	20	15	32
Losing trades	3	2	13	8	6
Percent profitable	82 %	78 %	61 %	65 %	84 %
Avg. winning trade	$14 487	$13 282	$17 460	$30 290	$36 601
Avg. losing trade	−$8410	−$6899	−$5702	−$6780	−$8064
Avg. win/avg. loss	1.72	1.93	3.06	4.47	4.54
Profitability coef.	4.56	4.36	3.60	4.69	6.62
Profit factor	8.04	6.74	4.71	8.38	24.21
Max drawdown	−$21 483	−$13 453	−$48 835	−$35 423	−$70 058
Risk/reward	8.0 %	9.5 %	13.2 %	7.6 %	5.5 %
Time in market	21.4 %	20.6 %	40.8 %	42.4 %	42.5 %

System Parameters					
Regression days		200			2500
MA gold			20	20	
MA intermarket SEC1			20	20	
MA intermarket SEC2			30	30	
ROC – days					11
IMO – days	300		300	200	300
IMO – buy	20		70	75	70
IMO – short	85		15	5	7
IMO – sell	35		10	7	14
IMO – cover	20		70	55	60
Time exit – bars	40	150	50	50	50

for the momentum oscillator + 3 for the momentum EMA) before the test can start producing trading signals.

This presents a problem when comparing the test results with the buy and hold method, because most trading simulation software use the stock price of the first date of the data loaded in the chart to calculate the buy and hold profit/loss. This will not make much of a difference where most normal indicators are concerned but will make a big difference when using intermarket indicators. To deal with this issue, I had to calculate the buy and hold profit manually using the date that the test could start producing trading signals. Thus the actual test period was from 11 December 1995 to 21 August 2007 but extra days were loaded to address the indicator lag issue.

Normally, when these type of systems are developed, two data sets should be used: one for optimization and the other for testing the optimized parameters on the new data. Since these tests were only carried out for comparison purposes, in order to simplify the process, optimization was carried out across the complete data set.

Another software issue that I encountered halfway through the test was that, for some reason, MetaStock did not execute certain trades. Instead it issued a rather cryptic "Cancelled – Open Cost" message, even though the account equity was more than enough to buy the shares. After contacting Equis technical support I found this was caused because I chose to execute orders with a one day delay. The program calculated the number of shares for the trade on the signal day and not the actual trade day. If the stock was up the next day, the number of shares calculated the previous day times the inflated price put it over the amount of equity available. To overcome this problem I had to increase the initial equity to \$111 111 and specify the default trade size to 90 % of the initial equity to (111 111 × 90 % = 100 000). This left ample margin for price increases on the next day. I hope Equis will modify the code on later versions to calculate the amount of shares on the actual trade and not the signal day.

11.2   TEST DESIGN

There are two types of trading system: trend-following and countertrend. These two strategies form the foundation on which all trading systems are built, and the markets provide the medium.

Basically, the goal with the countertrend system is to buy at the bottom and sell at the top, which is most often determined using oscillators. For example, a signal can be generated when the stochastic or other momentum oscillator begins to fade and falls below a certain level. Trend-following systems, on the other hand, rely on the hypothesis that the current trend is likely to continue in the future. Therefore they do not need to forecast the trend; instead they use trend-following indicators such as moving averages to determine only the direction of the trend. The main disadvantage of trend-following systems is that they do not work during sideways markets or choppy markets, i.e. 70 % of the time. On the other hand, the main disadvantage of countertrend systems is Newton's first law of inertia: A body in motion tends to stay in motion until it encounters an opposing force. Once a trend has been established, it has to overcome inertia forces, i.e. investors who missed the boat and are trying to get in late by buying the dips. This can cause contrarian indicators, like the Commodity Channel Index (CCI), the stochastics and other oscillators, to fail miserably.

The basic premise of the systems presented in this chapter, except for the relative strength (RS in Table 11.2) is divergence between gold and related intermarket securities and should be therefore classified in the countertrend category.

Divergence values vary from system to system. To avoid the computationally intensive process of determining the optimum divergence level for each system separately, the momentum oscillator (see Chapter 9) was used to identify extreme positive and negative divergence levels on a universal normalized scale from 0 to 100.

Because of the inertia effect mentioned above, divergence can keep rising without inducing a trend change. The following techniques had to be employed to deal with this very serious impediment, inherent in all countertrend systems:

- Wait for gold to respond to the divergence with the related market before triggering the buy signal. This was specified by the 5-day stochastic crossing over its 3-day moving average and the reverse for short sales.
- The momentum oscillator should change direction. This was specified by using the cross function available in MetaStock. Buy signals were generated when the momentum rose above a certain high value (usually 80) and then reversed direction crossing below this value from above.
- Asynchronous signals (lag) between the momentum oscillator and stochastics were dealt with by using MetaStock's useful alert function to extend the momentum signal for another three days.
- The most recent trend of the intermarket security (e.g. XAU) should lead gold. This was implemented by specifying that the rate of change of the intermarket security should be positive before issuing a divergence buy signal and the reverse for negative correlated markets (dollar index). This last condition was added later and seemed to improve results in cases of long-term divergence.
- The universal extreme value of the momentum oscillator was optimized in a range of ± 15 points above or below the default value (80 for oversold and 20 for overbought), to take into account incongruities between different systems and intermarket security combinations.
- To avoid the problem of whipsawing around the extreme levels, I used the 3-day exponential moving average of the momentum oscillator instead of the actual value of the oscillator itself.
- During protracted positive or negative divergences, the momentum oscillator might issue a false buy or short signal. To avoid taking action in such cases a minimum divergence level (usually zero) was required to verify the signal.

It is not all that important to close open trades at the exact bottom or top, so the second condition above wasn't implemented when closing long or covering short positions.

No stop-loss conditions or money management rules were used as the purpose of the tests was to compare the efficacy of the intermarket indicators. In practice, a stop-loss condition should always be used. Also, for comparison purposes, no other indicators were used except the intermarket indicators on test. This sometimes presented a problem in closing open trades and a time exit of 50 trading days (approximately two months) had to be used as certain intermarket indicators did not produce exit signals for prolonged periods of time.

Except for the general rules described above there were also some system specific rules which will be discussed next.

11.3   REGRESSION SYSTEMS

Intermarket regression was calculated according to formula (9.10) in Chapter 9 and results using the XAU and the dollar index are depicted in Table 11.1. The linear regression equation was constructed using the latest 400 trading days ($1\frac{1}{2}$ years) of data. The momentum oscillator period and rate of change were determined by optimization and the best parameter values on a profitability basis were 200 days for the momentum oscillator period and 10 days for the rate of change, which was in line with the results in Chapter 7 (Table 7.6). I used a period of 200 trading days for the momentum oscillator as shorter periods increased the total net profit by producing more trades – to the detriment, however, of profitability. As with any optimization, these values and their associated outcomes should be verified on an out-of-sample test because they are highly data dependent.

The dollar index test did not perform as well as the XAU on this particular test but this wasn't the case in the other tests. A disadvantage of all single regression tests is the relative low number of trades that they generate. On the other hand, their main advantage is that the regression system doesn't require any calculation or optimization of the regression coefficients as these are calculated automatically by the formula.

The multiple regression test, on the other hand, required the calculation of the regression coefficients before running the test. These could be calculated using a statistics program such as SPSS, but as they varied according to the amount of data included in the data set and the price yield interval, I decided to calculate a range of values using four different time frames and optimize them in the system test. The regression coefficient range of values is depicted in Table 11.4. After several optimization runs I concluded the following:

- The regression equation with the best coefficient of determination (R^2) did not necessarily produce the most profitable test results.
- The regression coefficient of the dollar index nearly doubled recently, from -0.3 to -0.6, indicating an intensification of the negative correlation between gold and the dollar. By the time this book is published, the negative correlation between gold and the dollar will most probably increase further, so it is a good idea to re-optimize this particular regression coefficient before using the system in real time.
- All regression coefficients in Table 11.4 produced profitable results so the final choice was only a matter of fine tuning.

Table 11.4 Variability of regression coefficients with time and rate of change interval. The coefficient of determination (R^2) for varying time frames is depicted in the last table.

	Regression coefficient – XAU			
Years	Rate of change – days			
	9	10	11	12
3	0.239	0.242	0.247	0.251
5	0.207	0.209	0.213	0.217
10	0.216	0.219	0.221	0.223
15	0.203	0.206	0.208	0.211

	Regression coefficient – SLV			
Years	Rate of change – days			
	9	10	11	12
3	0.201	0.201	0.192	0.19
5	0.21	0.21	0.203	0.202
10	0.166	0.164	0.161	0.163
15	0.175	0.174	0.173	0.173

	Regression coefficient – dollar Index			
Years	Rate of change – days			
	9	10	11	12
3	−0.574	−0.587	−0.604	−0.615
5	−0.538	−0.545	−0.545	−0.543
10	−0.433	−0.434	−0.434	−0.432
15	−0.292	−0.296	−0.298	−0.299

	R^2			
Years	Rate of change – days			
	9	10	11	12
3	0.736	**0.738**	0.733	0.732
5	0.679	0.68	0.676	0.675
10	0.588	0.587	0.588	0.587
15	0.582	0.583	0.583	0.584

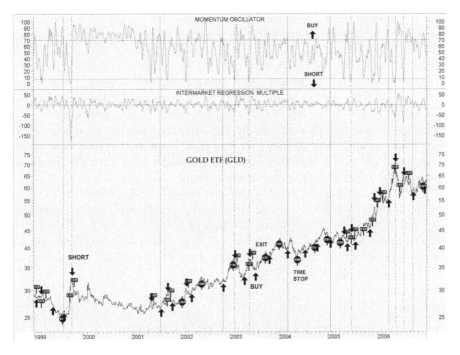

Figure 11.1   Chart of the gold ETF. Test signals generated by the multiple regression test (Table 11.3) are superimposed on the chart. The multiple regression indicator is depicted in the middle window and the 300-day momentum oscillator in the top window.

Thus by substituting the optimized parameters, the multiple regression equation was reduced to:

$$PG11 = 0.16 + 0.2X11 + .21S11 - 0.5D11 \qquad (11.1)$$

where PG11 is the predicted 11-day gold percentage change; X11, S11 and D11 are the 11-day percentage changes for the XAU, silver and the dollar index respectively.

Some buy and sell signals are shown in Fig. 11.1

11.4   RELATIVE STRENGTH (RS)

This was the only trend-following system and the obvious indicator to use in testing was the moving average. My first choice was the simplest trading rule ever: Buy when the RS line crosses over its moving average and sell when it crosses below the moving average. The only variable to optimize over the data was the moving average period. Unfortunately, test results were barely profitable and the system was abandoned. I then tried a more complicated system. The rules were as follows.

Buy when the RS line crosses over its linear regression line of six days ago. The system was optimized for the linear regression period. From the array of time periods used, the 200-day regression line was the most profitable for long entry and the 50-day for long exit. The code for the complete system is provided in Appendix A. This system was only profitable on the long side of the market, but produced very few trades making it suitable only for long-term investors. A countertrend system using the relative strength performed better for both long and short trades, producing more than double the trades of the previous system.

Buy signals of the countertrend system were issued when the momentum oscillator of the RS declined below 20 and then rose above 22 in the next four days. Similarly, sell short orders were triggered when the momentum oscillator of the RS rose above 85 and then crossed below 76 in the next four days. Please note that overbought and oversold levels of the RS indicator are exactly the opposite of all the other divergence indicators included in Chapter 9.

11.5   THE BOLLINGER BAND DIVERGENCE SYSTEM

The most robust set of parameters produced by optimization were 100 days for the Bollinger Band moving average and 70/5 for the momentum oscillator extreme levels.

This system did not produce many trades and, as a result, the total profit was less than other systems. Results of this test are shown in Table 11.2.

This system wasn't tested with the dollar index as it didn't perform well with negatively correlated markets.

11.6   THE Z-SCORE

I didn't expect a lot from this method because of the normality assumption violations discussed in Chapter 9, but decided to include it for comparison purposes.

The results (Table 11.2) were certainly a surprise, especially the dollar index test which outperformed all other single intermarket dollar index tests on a total net profit basis. It seems that although this method is statistically unsound, in practice normality was a good enough approximation to the price distribution for the system to produce profitable results.

The Z-score period was optimized for values between 100 and 600 in steps of 100. All values produced profitable results on both sides of the market. The best time increment, based on both performance and robustness was 500 days for the dollar index test and 100 days for the XAU.

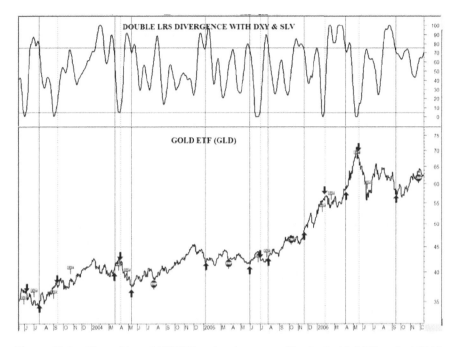

Figure 11.2   Chart of the gold ETF. Test signals generated by the double LRS method (Table 11.3) are superimposed on the chart. The double LRS indicator is depicted in the middle window and the 200-day momentum oscillator in the top window. Buy signals were generated when the momentum oscillator crossed below 75 from above and sell signals when it crossed over 5.

11.7   THE LINEAR REGRESSION SLOPE METHOD

This was tested extensively for both single divergence using the XAU and the dollar and also for double divergence using the XAU–dollar and silver–dollar pairs. This system performed very well.

   The best intermarket combination on a total net profit basis was the silver–dollar pair. There was no clear winner among the single divergence tests. The dollar index test performed better on a profit factor basis but the low turnover resulted in reduced total net profits. The results of the single and double divergence tests are shown in Tables 11.1 and 11.3 respectively and buy-sell signals of the double LRS divergence system with the dollar Index-Silver pair are depicted in the chart in Figure 11.2.

11.8   DISPARITY

The formula derived in Chapter 9 was used to calculate the disparity between gold and the XAU or the dollar index and extreme divergence levels were determined by the momentum oscillator. The moving average period for both gold and each intermarket security was optimized from five to 50 days in 5-day steps. The moving average period which produced the highest level of profit was 15 days for the gold–XAU pair and 20 days for the gold–dollar index.

The disparity system performed well on a profitability basis but suffered a comparatively larger drawdown.

11.9 DISCUSSION OF TEST RESULTS

Unfortunately, there exists no single metric to evaluate and compare different trading systems and assess what performance to expect in the future. Taking away all the details of a particular system, there are four statistics that enable you to assess a system. These are: the percentage of profitable trades; the average profit/loss ratio; the total net profit; and, last but not least; the drawdown or risk/reward ratio.

The percentage of profitable trades and the average profit/loss ratio can be combined in the profitability coefficient but there is also the drawdown and total profit to be considered.

Test results are shown in Tables 11.1, 11.2 and 11.3.

All tests were profitable and outperformed the buy and hold method considerably with less risk, being less than half of the time in the market.

The multiple regression test outperformed all other tests by a wide margin (Table 11.3), making an unbelievable profit of more than $1.2 million on a $100 000 initial equity, compared with a measly $67 000 profit of the buy and hold method.

It is, however, questionable whether the same performance can be reproduced in the future as it required optimization of the regression coefficients for that particular time frame. The single regression XAU system, on the other hand, required no optimization, as the regression coefficients were calculated automatically by the formula.

Based on profitability coefficient and risk/reward criteria, the single LRS system stood out. The relative strength system was untradeable in practice as it produced very few trades.

Generally more than 30 observations should be used in order to produce statistically significant results. The RS, Bollinger Band divergence, disparity and Z-score tests produced less trades during the test period. Intermarket trading systems, however, are at an infant stage and we should not just throw out these test results due to a lack of observations but use them as a stepping stone for further analysis in the future. For most trade system evaluations the number of observations should be an important factor; nevertheless, it should be understood that in divergence systems, a significant number of observations might be impossible to obtain.

A remedy for the low trade turnover would be a synthesis of intermarket with conventional technical analysis indicators. This was not implemented at this stage as the purpose of the tests was to assess the efficacy of the intermarket indicators on their own merit only.

In case anyone wishes to use any of the above systems I have to stress that these were not meant to be complete trading systems but were only designed in order to compare the efficacy of the intermarket indicators. The main problem is that they do not include proper exit conditions but rely solely on a fixed time exit or scarce divergence signals that might or might not materialize depending on the related market or the divergence level. This doesn't mean that they should be thrown away either, but rather should be used as a stepping stone in developing a complete system by being combined with classic technical analysis indicators or stop-loss conditions to anticipate any possible future market vicissitudes.

12
Trading the S&P 500 ETF and the e-mini

A stock market technician can apply all the technical indicators he wants to the stock market, but if he stops there, it's not going to work because the influences that affect the stock market are outside the market.

–John Murphy

The S&P 500 is the most unpredictable index to trade as it leads all other indices. Nevertheless, I did the best I could to select the most profitable intermarket securities and systems. The S&P 500 can be traded through its surrogate, the SPY ETF or e-mini futures. This chapter includes two systems. The first is a daily system for trading the SPY ETF, which requires holding the ETF for an average of 75 days. The second is an intraday system based on 15-minute data which takes advantage of the time difference between European and US markets. This one requires an average holding period of 10 hours and is most appropriate for short-term or day traders.

12.1 DAILY SYSTEM

In the past intermarket system developers relied (see *Cybernetic Trading Strategies* by M. Ruggiero) on the traditionally positive correlation between stocks and bonds to design intermarket systems to predict the S&P 500 based on T-bond futures. This rule has, however, been suspended in the past seven years by negative stock-bond correlation (see Section 5.2 and Fig. 5.5 in Chapter 5), which has necessitated a retreat to a more general position: The correlation can fluctuate because not everything that is good for bonds is also good for stocks. This rules out the use of bond or bond yields in predicting the S&P 500.

The next obvious candidates were European indices, but these did not perform so well on testing, despite high nominal correlations. I then tried various breadth indicators using the divergence systems presented in Chapter 11.

One of the best performing breadth indices was the percentage of stocks trading above their 40-day moving average. Every stock trading in the NYSE is represented in this indicator. Daily pricing data were obtained from Telechart (symbol: T2108). You can also calculate it yourself by running an exploration on all NYSE stocks, filtering out stocks, that are below their 40-day moving average. The result is then divided by the total number of NYSE stocks included in the exploration. Preferred shares should be excluded as they move more with interest rates than with the market.

Testing Procedure

I used the single regression divergence system (presented in Chapter 11) and optimized the trade parameters using actual data for the S&P 500 for the period from 1 January 1990 to 1 January 1997. The most robust set of parameters are included at the bottom of Table 12.1. The optimized parameters were then tested out-of-sample from 18 February 1997 to 26 September 2007 and the test results were compared with the profits earned from a buy and hold strategy covering the entire test period (Table 12.1). The simulation model was intended to replicate how traders actually use trading systems and therefore profits were not compounded, as this sometimes involved (during the latest phase of the test) holding large positions. Instead, an equal dollar amount of $20 000 per trade was specified.

All orders were executed at the opening price on the day following a system signal and execution costs were assumed to be $10. For simplicity's sake, dividends were not included in the calculation of both the buy and hold and system performance when in the market. All positions were closed on the last bar.

If you wish to replicate the tests, please keep in mind that for the test to begin producing signals, the regression indicator should first be calculated and this requires at least 477 bars to be loaded.

The divergence model did not perform very well on the short side of the market and it was abandoned in favor of a different approach, which initiated short positions when the intermarket security (percentage of stocks above their 40-day moving average) reached an extreme point and reversed direction. Results for the divergence long only and the long–short system are summarized separately on Table 12.1.

The criteria used to generate buy and sell signals can be summarized as follows.

Buy: A long position was initiated when the regression divergence reached an extreme value and reversed direction.

The intermarket momentum oscillator was used to help detect divergence extreme values of the regression divergence indicator and, more precisely, buy signals were issued when the 40-day intermarket momentum crossed under 80 from above. To

Table 12.1 Test results of the daily SPY systems from 18 February 1997 to 17 September 2007. Both tests were profitable and outperformed the buy and hold method by a wide margin and considerably less risk. Both systems used the regression divergence method for long trades. The second system used a different method to trade on the short side as well. The momentum oscillator was used to determine optimum divergence levels.

Test	Buy & hold	Regression	Regression hybrid
Periodicity	Daily	Daily	Daily
Long/short	Long	Long	Long–Short
Security on test	SPY	SPY	SPY
Intermarket security		T2108	T2108
Transaction cost per trade	$20 000	$20 000	$20 000
Total net profit	$16 138	$32 931	$37 850
Profit/loss %	81 %	165 %	189 %
Annual percent gain/loss	8 %	16 %	18 %
Total number of trades	1	22	41
Winning trades	1	19	31
Losing trades	0	3	10
Percent profitable	100 %	86 %	76 %
Gross profit	$16 138	$17 660	$24 467
Gross loss	$0	−$586	−$4161
Avg. winning trade	$16 138	$929	$789
Avg. losing trade		−$195	−$416
Ratio avg. win/avg. loss		4.76	1.90
Profitability coefficient		6.90	4.11
Profit factor		30.1	5.9
Max. drawdown	−$19 178	−$4070	−$4054
Max. % drawdown	−96 %	−7 %	−6 %
Max. trade loss	$0	−$319	−$977
Max. consecutive losses	0	2	3
Risk/reward	119 %	12 %	11 %
Reference bars needed	0	477	477
Start date/test	2/18/97	2/18/97	2/18/97
End date	9/17/07	9/17/07	9/17/07
Test period (years)	10.6	10.6	10.6
Average trade length in days	3863	61	45
Trades/year	0.1	2.1	4
Time in market	100 %	35 %	48 %
Stock price at start of test	81.88	81.88	81.88
Stock price at end of test	148.1	148.1	148.1
System Parameters			
ROC days		20	20
Momentum oscillator – bars		40	40
Momentum oscillator – buy		80	80
Momentum osc. (long exit)		15	15
Time exit-bars		100	100

exclude cases where both the base and the intermarket security were in decline, the following conditions were also required: The stochastic should be above its moving average and the 2-day rate of change of the intermarket security should be positive.

Sell: The long position was liquidated on the exact opposite to the buy conditions above. A sell signal was generated when the intermarket momentum oscillator reached an extreme reading below 15 and reversed direction, subsequently crossing over 15.

Sell short: A contrarian interpretation of the breadth indicator was used to initiate short positions when the percentage of stocks above their 40-day moving average reached an extreme value above 72 % and then reversed and crossed below its 15-day exponential moving average. To deal with whipsaw problems, the breadth indicator should have also crossed below 65 % in the next nine days or earlier. During extremely bullish periods, as in 2003 or 2006, the indicator had a tendency to remain in overbought territory for extended periods. To exclude premature signals, the short order was not executed unless the S&P 500 crossed below its 15-day exponential average as well.

Buy to cover: The exact opposite of the short sale condition was not sufficient to cover all short positions in a timely fashion, as this breadth indicator did not always reach extreme low values before the market reversed and the emerging rally wiped out all profits from the short sale. There was therefore a need for more complex criteria in order to include the situations when the indicator did not perform as expected. Thus the short positions were closed when the breadth indicator reached an extreme reading below 25 and then rose above 30 or the S&P 500 crossed over its 5-day moving average on oversold breadth indicator readings (below 40).

A stop loss was also added to cover all other situations not included in the above.

Evaluation of Results

The results for both tests are summarized in Table 12.1. I have marked in the accompanying chart in Fig. 12.1 when each buy/sell signal occurred but only (because of space limitations) for the time sub-period from September to December 2006.

In the period tested, the results were very impressive. The buy and hold strategy would have shown a profit of $16 000 compared to $33 000 for the long-only and $38 000 for the long–short model.

The long-only divergence system won 86 % of the time with a profit factor of 30 but, most notably, this was achieved with substantial risk reduction. The maximum drawdown was only $4000 or 7 % of equity, an amount most traders would be comfortable with. Not so comfortable was a drawdown of $19 000 or nearly 96 % of their initial equity, which the buy and hold investors lost during the 2001–2002 traumatic bear market.

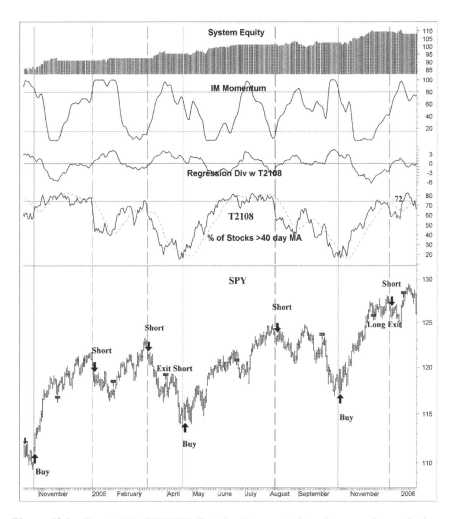

Figure 12.1   Chart of the SPY ETF. Test signals generated by the regression method are superimposed on the chart. The system equity line is plotted in the top window and below the 40-day momentum oscillator and the corresponding intermarket regression divergence indicator. The intermarket security used by the regression indicator is the NYSE % of stocks above their 40-day MA and is depicted, together with its 15-day moving average, in the third window. Buy signals are generated by the momentum oscillator crossing under 75 from above and sell signals when it crosses over 15. Short signals are triggered when the intermarket breadth indicator rises above 72 and then falls under 60.

One of the major benefits from transaction timing is obtained by avoiding the price declines that occur during bear markets and this was true for the current systems tested.

Both systems initiated only two trades during the 2001–2002 bear market. The first one was marginally profitable. The second, in March 2000, was initiated after a premature divergence signal, but managed to show a modest profit at close even though it resulted in the test's maximum open drawdown.

The major problem with intermarket divergence systems is that they do not produce a lot of trades. This is because these systems take advantage of temporary market inefficiencies to generate signals. These inefficiencies do not occur very often and, as a result, all divergence systems produce very few signals. The current system was no exception. The long-only divergence model produced only 22 trades during the 10-year test duration. The short–long system improved on the trade turnover by adding another 19 trades on the short side of the market. Short trades did not perform as well, but this was no surprise as the S&P advanced 8 % per year on average during the test period.

Considering the fact that 87 % of professional money managers haven't beaten the stock market average 10-year performance, I feel that a mechanical trading system that for the past 10 years has at least doubled the market's annualized returns is very worth considering.

12.2 E-MINI INTRADAY SYSTEM

This system took advantage of the time difference between US and European exchanges to trade the S&P 500 e-mini before the US market opened, and it is based on the divergence between the e-mini and the Dow Jones EuroStoxx 50 futures.

I used the following method for creating continuous contracts: The most dominant or current contract was used until the next one became dominant. A problem arising from the use of dominant contracts is that the price difference between the old dominant contract and new dominant contract at the time of roll-over may be large enough to create a discontinuous break in the price series, thus a false signal. This can be taken care of by adding the price difference at roll-over to the older contract. The current trading simulation involved joining the March and June contracts of the e-mini and EuroStoxx contracts.

Several other assumptions underlie the trading model.

The default trade size was five contracts per trade (or approximately $20 000 at the time of the first trade). The initial and maintenance margins were assumed to be 5.5 % and 4.4 % of contract value respectively and 50 % of total funds were allocated to the initial trading capital and the other 50 % was held back for potential margin calls. Returns were calculated as a percent of initial trading capital and compared to the buy and hold method which involved buying and holding five contracts for the duration of the test. No interest was credited to the account when out of the market as this was assumed to cancel out additional slippage and skid costs.

I used for this test the LRS single divergence system (presented in Chapter 11) and optimized the trade parameters using 15-minute intraday data of the December 2007 e-mini futures contract (ESZ7). The optimal parameters are included at the bottom of Table 12.2.

Table 12.2   Test results of the intraday S&P e-mini intermarket LRS system from 16 January 2007 to 14 June 2007. The intermarket security used for the LRS divergence comparison was EuroStoxx 50 Futures (FESX). The test outperformed the buy and hold method by a wide margin and considerably less risk. The 250-bar momentum oscillator was used to determine extreme divergence levels.

Test	Buy & hold	LRS
Periodicity	15 minute	15 minute
Security on test	ES	ES
Intermarket security		FESX
Number of shares/contracts	5	5
Transaction cost per trade	$20 000	$20 000
Total net profit	$18 890	$59 147
Profit/loss %	94 %	296 %
Annual percent gain/loss	231 %	724 %
Total number of trades	1	72
Winning trades	1	50
Losing trades	0	22
Percent profitable	100 %	69 %
Gross profit	$18 890	$75 300
Gross loss	$0	−$16 153
Avg. winning trade	$18 890	$1506
Avg. losing trade		−$734
Ratio avg. win/avg. loss		2.05
Profitability coefficient		3.67
Profit factor		4.7
Max. drawdown	−$47 625	−$5024
Max. % drawdown	−238 %	−10 %
Max. trade loss	$0	−$3149
Max. consecutive losses	0	3
Risk/reward	252 %	8 %
Reference bars needed		510
Start date/test	1/16/07	1/16/07
End date	6/14/07	6/14/07
Test period (years)	0.41	0.41
Average trade length – days	149	0.44
Trades/year	1	176
Time in market	100 %	21 %
Price at start of test	1441	1441
Price at end of test	1516.75	1516.75

System Parameters	
LRS – bars	9
Momentum oscillator – bars	250
Momentum oscillator – buy	70
Momentum osc. (long exit)	15
Time exit – bars	50

I then tested the system out-of-sample on e-mini continuous data from 16 January 2007 to 14 June 2007. An extra 500 bars (10 days) had to be loaded for the system to start producing trades. The data were downloaded from interactive brokers using Metaserver RT (www.traderssoft.com).

The S&P leads all other markets and therefore it is the most difficult market to predict, at least using intermarket indicators. The only time that the S&P doesn't lead other international markets is when the US equity markets are closed. Thus trades were taken only from 1:00 am EST (9:00 am CET), when European futures start trading, until 9:30 am EST (15:30 CET), when US markets open for trading.

Because of the reduced trading hours and also the reasons mentioned in Section 12.1 above, the divergence model produced only about 20 trades for the whole five month duration of the simulation. These were too few for a statistically valid conclusion. To increase the number of trades (and profits) I added conventional technical analysis indicators to the model. The problem with conventional indicators is that some indicators, like moving averages, only work in trending market conditions and others only in oscillating markets. To determine the appropriate market phase I used the Congestion Index (CI) presented in Chapter 9.

To refresh your memory here is a brief review. This function compares the percentage that the market wandered to the actual percentage the market rose during the last 15-bar period.

The less the absolute value of the indicator, the more congested the market.

This strategy was more complicated to program, as it included three different criteria for initiating positions. The final system was able to switch gears and trade in three modes: divergence, trending and congestion.

More precisely the criteria for initiating positions were as follows.

Long Entry

Divergence conditions: No divergence signals were allowed after 10:00 US EST for the reasons mentioned above. For the divergence signal to initiate a long entry the following four conditions were employed:

- The divergence between the 9 bar (135 minute) linear regression slope of the ES e-mini and ESTX futures should be positive.
- The intermarket momentum indicator was used to help detect divergence extreme values of the divergence indicator. Long trades were initiated when the 250 bar (5-day) intermarket momentum oscillator rose over 70 and reversed direction.
- It's not unusual for high divergence readings to register for a long time before the tradeable starts responding. Therefore it was desirable that the e-mini should also confirm the reversal. This was ensured by specifying that the 5-bar stochastic should be above its 4 bar moving average and the CI rose above the previous bar reading.

- An additional condition requiring that the rate of change of the 5-bar intermarket security (ESTX) should be positive was added to eliminate divergence signals when both the intermarket security and the base security were declining.

Congestion conditions: The 15-bar CI was used to diagnose the market character. This condition generated signals if the absolute value of the CI was less than 20 and the following conditions were true.

- The lowest value of the 15 bar stochastic was below 30 and the stochastic crossed above its 4 bar moving average.
- The price rate of change for both the e-mini and the intermarket security was 0.1 % or higher.

Trending conditions: The CI was again used to identify the market phase. Signals were generated only if the CI rose above 20. To ensure that no trades were initiated in extremely overbought situations when the trending phase was about to end, no signals were allowed if the CI was above 85. The most popular technical trending indicators, the Moving Average Convergence Divergence (MACD) and the moving average, were used to initiate conditions and, more precisely, a buy signal was issued when:

- the MACD was above its 9-bar exponential moving average and at the same time the price was also above the 40-bar moving average;
- the 9-bar rate of change of the intermarket security was above 0.4 % (double that of the e-mini). Also the divergence momentum was above 50 (the mid point of its range).

Long Exit

Always remember that it is the exit technique that determines the success of the entry signal. Timely sell conditions are more difficult to implement using divergence conditions alone as they tend to initiate sell signals prematurely. The divergence conditions described above were used in the opposite fashion and the Congestion Index was again used to identify the market phase and liquidate the position using the appropriate trending or non-trending indicator. An extra condition was introduced to avoid trend reversals. This condition liquidated the position if the CI rose above 85 and then fell, during the next three 15-minute bars, below 60.

All trading methods will occasionally fail, especially intraday systems, as breaking adverse economic news can have unexpected results and price shocks. Therefore some form of protection should be put in place to cut losses short and let profits run. Traders use a number of different methods to calculate stop-loss conditions: standard deviation, average true range, percentages, support violation, etc. The stop-loss that I chose to use here liquidated long positions if the closing price fell below 1.6 times the average true range of the last eight bars. This last condition reduced losses and drawdown but at the expense of decreasing the percentage of profitable trades.

Short

The exact opposite of the long entry conditions described above were used to initiate short positions. The congestion condition exploited declines from overbought situations and the trend condition initiated short positions during a decline when the MACD crossed under its exponential moving average, and at the same time the price was under its 40-day moving average and the CI below −20.

Buy to Cover

A strategy similar, but opposite, to the long exit strategy was used to cover short positions. A volatility stop-loss was also used to cut losses in cases of unexpected reversals when the price crossed over the lowest value of the last four bars plus 1.6 times the average true range of the last eight bars.

Evaluation of Results

The results of the intraday trading simulation using a 5-month test period are shown in Table 12.2 and test signals from 17 May 2007 to 1 June 2007 are superimposed in the chart in Fig. 12.2. The returns using this approach as compared to buy and hold are impressive. The model made over $59 000, three times the amount made by the buy and hold investor and it was profitable on both the long and short side of the market.

The stop-loss condition reduced the drawdown dramatically to only $5000 or 10 % of equity compared to a $47 000 or 240 % of equity suffered by the buy and hold method. This also helped keep the reserve capital required for margin calls very low.

The amalgamation of the three different conditions enhanced returns over the single divergence method. It was difficult, however, to determine which specific condition contributed more to the overall profitability because the MetaStock system tester does not provide this information.

In this case, the application of the stop-loss condition improved total profits from $50 700 (no stop-loss) to $59 200 by reducing the size of some individual losses. However, it had the adverse effect of decreasing the frequency of winning trades slightly from 71 % to 69.4 %. Although massaging the results with a stop-loss condition does not necessarily add validity to the system, it does contribute to a trader's peace of mind.

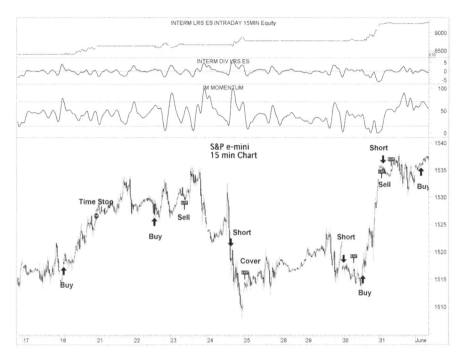

Figure 12.2 Intraday 15-minute chart of the S&P 500 e-mini (ES) from 17 May 2007 to 1 June 2007. Test signals generated by the intraday system are superimposed on the chart. The equity line is plotted in the top window (the right-hand scale should be multiplied by 10), the single intermarket LRS divergence indicator is depicted in the second window and the corresponding 250-bar momentum oscillator in the third window. The intermarket security used for the LRS indicator was EuroStoxx 50 Futures (FESX).

One of the major benefits of short-term intraday trading is the ability to exit or even reverse the trade in the event of an unexpected and inevitable price reversal, a situation that occurs very often because of breaking economic news. On the other hand, intraday trading requires the trader's constant attention and can only be implemented by professional or full-time traders unless an automated trading platform is being employed.

If you want to use the system in real time trading you should keep in mind there can be sharp differences between hypothetical performance and real trading results as trading systems are prepared and optimized with the benefit of hindsight. Regardless of the hours spent in back-testing and optimizing systems on historical data, the future cannot be optimized.

13
Trading DAX Futures

There are two times in a man's life when he should not speculate: when he can't afford it and when he can.

–Mark Twain

In Chapter 6 we discussed the relationship between the DAX and major international indices and commodities. I will now use a related index with the highest correlation with the DAX in order to develop an intermarket divergence system to trade DAX futures.

A close inspection of Tables 6.1 and 6.2 reveal that either the CAC 40 or the EuroStoxx 50 would be a good choice. The correlation between the DAX and the CAC was slightly better on absolute price basis but the EuroStoxx, on the other hand, was a little better when taking daily and weekly yields. This was also the case between the corresponding index futures.

The dilemma was resolved by testing. Both the profit factor and total profits suggested that the CAC 40 was more effective in predicting the DAX. It seems that the traditional historical antipathy between the German and the French people does not extend into their markets as, whether they like it or not, their economies are linked together in the European Union.

Another factor that influenced my decision to select the CAC is the fact that the EuroStoxx shared no less than 13 common component stocks with the DAX, which can reduce its predictive correlation.

The same problem inherent in all divergence models (discussed in the previous chapter) was also encountered here, as the system generated only 22 signals during the 4-year testing period. A classic moving average crossover system was also included for the benefit of active traders. The system was profitable but was not able to outperform the buy and hold method. By using intermarket conditions, however, I was able to improve on the system's performance, filtering out a large number of unprofitable trades.

Finally, for the benefit of investors who prefer not to trade futures, I also include an intermarket system to trade the 10 stocks that weight the most, on a percentage basis, on the DAX index.

13.1 INTERMARKET DIVERGENCE SYSTEM

The disparity indicator, explained in Chapter 9, was used to generate buy and sell signals. To refresh your memory, this indicator compares the disparity (which is defined as the distance of the current price from its moving average) between a security (in this case DAX futures) and the corresponding intermarket (CAC 40 futures).

Divergence indicators are usually premature in generating sell short signals, especially in up-trending markets which was the case for the DAX during the test period. This condition was therefore only used to trade on the long side of the market. Instead, classic technical analysis conditions were used to generate short sales.

Setting up the Tests

You cannot, of course, trade the DAX directly so I had to use DAX futures (FDAX) for my trading simulation model. A major problem that I encountered during the testing procedure was that Reuters Datalink provided only three years of historical data for DAX futures, which were not enough for both in-sample and out-of-sample testing. To deal with this issue I used the index itself for the design and optimization of the trade parameters, keeping the meager futures data for testing. To minimize the curve-fitting effect, I divided the data into three segments. The first dataset was used to develop the rules and optimize system parameters. The second segment was used to test the optimized parameters during the development process, and the third out-of-sample segment was used to evaluate the results. Although the out-of-sample segment was from 13 March 2003 to 11 November 2007, the system started producing trades on 19 January 2004 as it required 210 bars in order to calculate all the indicators involved. Several assumptions underlie the trading model. The default trade size was one contract per trade and, to avoid margin calls and the associated problems mentioned in the previous chapter, the test was conducted in points and converted to Euro at €25 per DAX point. Long and short signals were executed next day at the open and no interest was credited to the account when out of the market as this was assumed to cancel out additional slippage and skid costs. The commission of 0.08 points (€2), which is the commission charged by discount brokers, was deducted from each trade. Returns were calculated as a percent of the account required to trade each system and compared to the buy and hold method which involved buying and holding one DAX contract for the duration of the test. The compound formula was used to annualize percentage returns and for simplicity's sake rollover costs were ignored.

The amount of the account required was the greater of the initial margin of €18 253 required to trade DAX futures (at the time of writing) or the maintenance margin

(€14 603) plus the initial drawdown. The percent standard deviation of change in equity was calculated by dividing the monthly change in equity in points by the price of the DAX futures contract also in points, and the risk adjusted return was calculated by dividing the annualized return by the percent standard deviation of the change in equity.

Tradesim version 4.22 was used to simulate trading a portfolio of the following 10 stocks that had more than 70 % weight on the DAX: E.ON, Siemens, Allianz, Deutsche Bank, Daimler Chrysler, Deutsche Telekom, BASF, SAP, RWE, and Bayer.

The same conditions used in the DAX futures system were also used to trade these stocks but only on the long side of the market. The initial trading capital was €28 000 (which is the same as the account size required to buy and hold one DAX futures contract), and the margin was specified at 50 %. The trade amount was €20 000 per stock and the profits were compounded (only for the stock test). Commission of €10 per stock was deducted from each trade. The time exit was 50 trading days for the stock test and 80 trading days for the futures test.

Long and short conditions were optimized separately. Although trading only one side of the market can bias the results; had I optimized both sides concurrently, a fair percentage of the positions wouldn't have been realized because of an active position in the opposite direction. To construct the buy and sell conditions I tested a number of criteria individually and then I began to combine them, identifying parameter combinations and conditions that persisted in producing profits, even though they were not necessarily the optimum. The disparity indicator wasn't used to generate short trades as it did not perform well on testing. To trade on the short side of the market traditional indicators were used instead, and included the stochastic or the MACD which switched according to the appropriate market condition (congestion or trending).

The system was defined as follows:

Buy condition 1: Buy next day at the open if the 10-day disparity divergence rises above 2 and the 200-day divergence momentum oscillator crosses above 65 and reverses direction while at the same time the CAC 40 is trending up during the preceding 6-day period, the DAX closes higher than yesterday and the stochastic is higher than its 4-day moving average. The third criterion was added in order to exclude high divergence signals when both indices were declining and the fourth condition ensured that the DAX started responding. This condition was optimized for the moving average period used in the disparity indicator.

Buy condition 2: I added a second condition in an effort to increase the turnover, as the divergence criteria described above produced only about 10 long trades during the 4-year test duration. This condition incorporated three indicators: the first two were used as market phase filters and the third as the trigger. Buy signals were only generated when the DAX was in trading range and the stochastic indicator rose above 30 and above its 4-day moving average. I used the 35-day congestion index (CI) and the 20-day linear regression slope (LRS) to identify the market phase and the trend strength. The filter's logic is straightforward: If the more recent slope is less than 0.2 % per day and the price is in the lower 35 % of its 35-day trading range, then the market is in a trading range. Again this condition was tested and optimized individually with satisfactory results. The linear regression slope period was optimized from 15 to 35 in steps of five days. The value that produced the most profits in both in-sample segments was 20 days and this was used for the out-of-sample test.

I spent a lot of time searching for the best exit conditions as timely exit criteria are essential to a profitable system. I found that no single condition produced the "Holy Grail", but a combination of the following five criteria resulted in the best exit strategy.

Sell condition 1: This was the exact opposite of the first buy condition. The value of the divergence momentum oscillator was optimized from 5 to 25 in steps of five. The first three values (5 and 10) were the best and the lowest value was chosen for the out-of-sample test.

Sell condition 2: All bullish trends eventually end. The CI indicator was utilized to identify the trend's conclusion. Long positions were liquidated when the CI declined more than 40 points and the price rate of change declined during the last three days, while the disparity with the CAC 40 was negative.

Sell condition 3: The condition was added in order to close long positions in a downtrend. A moving average crossover condition was used to identify the downtrend and a sell signal was triggered when the MACD crossed below its 7-day moving average and the disparity with the CAC 40 was negative. Both moving averages were optimized and the most robust set of parameters were found to be 10 and 150 for the short and long period respectively.

This condition did not do any good to the out-of-sample results as the DAX was in an uptrend during most of the test duration, but it helped terminate trades in adverse market conditions for both in-sample tests.

Sell condition 4: An additional intermarket condition was added to close long positions in short term downtrends when the negative divergence between the DAX and the CAC 40 fell below -1 but only when both declined more than 0.5 % during the last two days. This condition was more effective when the DAX declined more than the CAC 40.

I spent a lot of time trying to find effective short-sale conditions as the DAX was in a steep uptrend during 90 % of the first in-sample test duration. Finally I came up with the following conditions. No less than four conditions were needed in order to close short positions in time before the uptrend resumed.

Short condition 1: The logic behind this condition was very similar to the second condition used to close long positions described above. In this case the MACD was also used to confirm the trend reversal. More specifically, a short sale was triggered when the CI dropped by more than 50 points, the MACD was below its trigger (its 7-day exponential moving average) and the DAX was in a downtrend during the last 20 days (specified by a negative linear regression slope).

Short condition 2: This was the exact opposite of the second buy condition and incorporated a filter to identify a trading range and a trigger to issue the signal. Short sales were initiated only in a trading range and were triggered when the 25-day stochastic rose above 85 and than fell below 70 while the 5-day stochastic was below its 4-day moving average. The CI and the linear regression slope were again used to identify the market phase.

Cover condition 1: This was similar to the positive divergence condition used to produce long signals above except that the rate of change was not included in this case.

Cover condition 2: The idea of including this condition was to close short positions on the conclusion or reversal of the downtrend. A buy to cover signal was triggered when the CI rose by more than 40 points.

Cover condition 3: This was the opposite of the third sell condition above and closed short positions when the MACD crossed above its trigger but only when the 10-day moving average was below the 150-day moving average (i.e. the DAX was in a downtrend). This did not improve the out-of-sample test results, as the DAX was almost always in an uptrend during the test duration (from 2004 to 2007) but it did make a difference during the in-sample testing.

Cover condition 4: The second buy condition was also repeated here to close short conditions when the stochastic was oversold in a range bound market.

Evaluation of Results

The test results of the intermarket disparity divergence system are summarized in Table 13.1. For comparison purposes, the buy and hold method returns for both time segments are also included in the first and third columns. The test results of the out-of-sample test on DAX futures for the period from 18 March 2003 to 2 November 2007 are depicted in the second column and the test results on the DAX index for the period from 5 January 1999 to 2 November 2007 were also included in the fourth column in order to evaluate the system performance in both bullish and bearish market conditions.

Table 13.1   The test results of DAX futures and the DAX Index disparity tests are depicted in Columns 2 and 4 respectively. All tests were profitable and outperformed the buy and hold method by a wide margin despite the DAX's steep uptrend during the first test period. The DAX futures test was performed on a shorter duration sample (from 19 January 2004 to 2 November 2007) as not enough historical data were available.

Test	Buy & Hold	Disparity	Buy & Hold	Disparity
Security on test	FDAX	FDAX	DAX Index	DAX Index
Intermarket security		FCE		CAC 40
Account size required	€27 893	€18 611	€91 104	€18 255
Total net profit	€93 096	€122 350	€65 411	€163 907
Profit/loss %	334 %	657 %	72 %	898 %
Annualized % gain/loss	47 %	71 %	6 %	30 %
Annual % profit/loss	88 %	174 %	1	102 %
Total number of trades	1	22	1	49
Winning trades	1	17	0	33
Losing trades	0	5	100 %	16
Percent profitable	100 %	77.3 %	€65 411	67.3 %
Gross profit	€93 096	€130 757	€0	€254 893
Gross loss	€0	−€8408	€65 411	−€90 986
Avg. winning trade	€93 096	€7692	€0	€7724
Avg. losing trade		−€1682	€65 411	−€5687
Ratio avg. win/avg. loss		4.57		1.36
Profitability coefficient		5.93		2.49
Profit factor		15.55		2.80
Max. drawdown	−€24 913	−$12 708	−€148 685	−$29 486
Max. % drawdown	−89.3 %	−15.8 %	−74.0 %	−42.2 %
Max. initial drawdown	−€13 288	−€4006	−€76 501	€0
Max. consecutive losses	0	2	0	3
Risk/reward	26.8 %	10.4 %	227.3 %	18.0 %
% standard deviation of equity	3.86 %	2.85 %	6.7 %	4.1 %
Risk adj. annualized return	12 %	25 %	0.9 %	7.2 %
Sharpe ratio	11.1	23.2	0.3	6.1
Start date/test	1/19/04	1/19/04	1/5/99	1/5/99
End date	11/2/07	11/2/07	11/2/07	11/2/07
Test period (years)	3.8	3.8	8.8	8.8
Test period (days)	1383	1383	3223	3223
Total trade length (days)	1383	998	3223	1707
Out of market (days)	0	385	0	1516
Average trade length – days	1383	45	3223	35
Average trade length – bars	948	32	2210	25
Trades/year	0.3	5.8	0.1	5.5
Time in the market	100.0 %	72.2 %	100.0 %	53.0 %

(Continued)

Table 13.1   *(Continued)*

	System Parameters			
Disparity bars		10		10
Momentum oscillator – bars		200		200
Momentum oscillator – buy		65		65
Momentum oscillator – exit		5		5
Time exit-bars	948	80	2210	80
Divergence buy		0		0
Divergence sell		0		0
ROC bars		6		6

As usual, the divergence system generated only few signals. Because the period of the first test was on the whole bullish, selectivity worked to our advantage. Fewer and longer trades produced a higher annualized rate of return and profit factor. In the mixed market conditions of the second test (from 1999–2007), the elaborate sell conditions were triggered sooner, reducing the average holding period of each trade from 32 to 25 trading days.

During the period from January 2004 until October 2007 covered in the first test, except for a brief time in the beginning and at the end, the DAX was in an almost 45 degree uptrend. Even though it is very difficult to beat the buy and hold method under such a bullish market, the system managed to outperform it by riding the better part of the trend and selling short to capture small profits during the inevitable minor corrections or the initial sideways market.

During the course of the four-year simulation, the system made €122 000 with only 22 trades, which were roughly 77 % accurate. The profit factor was 15.5 and the maximum drawdown was €12 700 or 16 % of equity, which occurred on 14 March 2007, mainly due to a premature long signal. This particular trade, however, produced a modest profit at close, even though it resulted in the test's maximum open drawdown. The buy and hold investor, on the other hand, suffered a traumatic €25 000 drawdown during the June 2006 correction, which wiped out almost all (90 %) of his equity.

The risk-adjusted annualized return was 25 %, more than double that of the buy and hold method. The initial drawdown was only €4000, requiring a much smaller account to trade this system, compared with the €13 300 required by the buy and hold method. All metrics indicated that the system outperformed the buy and hold method by a ratio of more than 2:1.

You should always keep in mind, however, that "a rising tide floats all boats" and investigate whether outstanding profits are due to sheer genius on your part or to overriding market conditions that make it difficult to lose. A robust trading model should be able to take advantage of rich periods, and at least survive lean periods with a minimum of loss. To investigate whether the system performed well under diverse

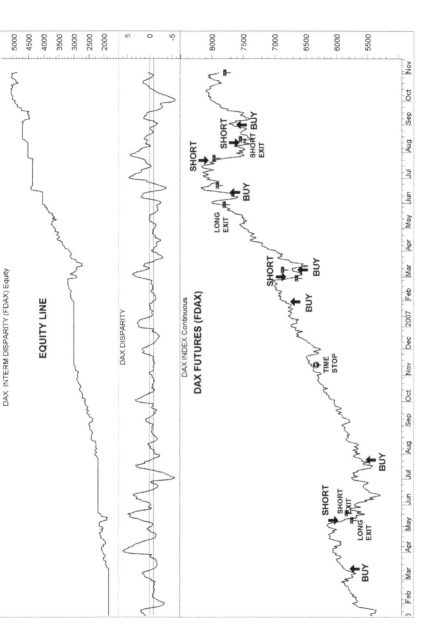

Figure 13.1 Chart of the continuous DAX futures contract (FDAX) from February 2006 until November 2007. Buy and sell signals are superimposed on the chart. The disparity test equity line is plotted in the top window and the intermarket disparity indicator below. The intermarket security used was CAC 40 futures (FCE).

market conditions, I tested the same system for the January 1999 to October 2007 period, which included the 2003–2007 bull market and the devastating 2000–2003 bear market.

The test results are presented in the last column of Table 13.1 and the corresponding buy and hold results in the fourth column. The system couldn't repeat the outstanding results of the first test but managed to produce 2.5 times the buy and hold profits with 13 % of the risk. It initiated 13 long trades during the bear market, of which five were profitable, and managed to get out with modest losses from all the rest except one. The maximum drawdown happened on 3 April 2001, because of three consecutive losses.

The buy and hold investor, on the other hand, suffered a catastrophic loss of €150 000 during the 2002–2003 bear market which wiped out his initial equity and all his profits. As a consequence, the account size required to buy and hold one DAX contract for the entire test duration increased dramatically to €91 000, or five times the amount required to trade the system. The risk-adjusted return of buying and holding the DAX was only 0.9 % or one-eighth the return of the disparity system.

The same system was then tested on 10 DAX component stocks that between them account for 70 % of the index. Test results are summarized in the last column of Table 13.2. The system generated 116 trades which were 65 % accurate on average. It made a total of €108 000 during the four-year duration and the maximum drawdown occurred in August 2007 during a generous correction of the DAX. As can be seen in Figure 13.2, this event coincided with the system's worst monthly profit.

The system did beat the buy and hold method but lagged significantly behind the test on DAX futures. This was mainly because it traded only the long side of the market on a system optimized to trade both long and short. This is confirmed by looking at the equity line of the futures system which actually made money during the summer of the 2007 correction by selling short immediately after the start of the decline.

The spectacular returns of the first test, however, are not likely to be repeated in the future, as (at the time of writing) it looks like the current bull market is about to end. For any given system, different price histories will bring forth a different range of possible outcomes. This is clear by the completely different results produced by the same system but on different time frames (Columns 3 and 5 in Table 13.1). It would be reasonable, however, to expect the system to produce similar results to the second test, as the test sample incorporated both bullish and bearish market conditions. Even so, both results are compelling enough to merit attention.

13.2 MOVING AVERAGE CROSSOVER SYSTEM

I include this system in order to demonstrate how you can enhance the accuracy and profitability of the results using intermarket criteria as a filter. I used the moving

Table 13.2 The test results of moving average crossover and the intermarket enhanced test on DAX futures are depicted in Columns 3 and 4 respectively. The intermarket filter helped in outperforming the buy and hold method by a wide margin despite the DAX's steep uptrend during the test period. In the last column, test results of the disparity system on 10 DAX components stocks are depicted. In this case only long signals were considered.

Test	Buy & hold	MA Cross	MA Cross intermarket	Disparity
Security on test	FDAX	FDAX	FDAX	10 Stocks
Intermarket security		None	FESX	FCE
Account required	€27 893	€26 444	€22 697	€28 000
Total net profit	€93 096	€58 946	€94 759	€108 100
Annualized % gain/loss	47 %	36 %	54 %	49.34 %
Total number of trades	1	51	26	116
Winning trades	1	26	14	75
Losing trades	0	25	12	41
Percent profitable	100 %	51.0 %	53.8 %	64.7 %
Gross profit	€93 096	€122 659	€124 582	€172 516
Gross loss	€0	−€63 713	−€29 823	−€64 416
Avg. profit/trade	€93 096	€1156	€3645	€932
Ratio avg. win/avg. loss		1.85	3.58	1.46
Profitability coefficient		1.59	3.20	2.41
Profit factor		1.93	4.18	2.68
Max. drawdown	−€24 913	−$14 618	−€19 254	−€15 507
Max. initial drawdown	−€13 288	−€11 839	−€8092	€0
Max. consecutive losses	0	6	4	7
Standard deviation % of equity	3.86 %	3.3 %	3.3 %	7.8 %
Risk adjusted annualized return	12 %	11.0 %	16.3 %	6.3 %
Start date/test	1-19-04	1-19-04	1-19-04	11-24-03
End date	11-2-07	11-2-07	11-2-07	11-2-07
Test period (years)	3.8	3.8	3.8	3.9
Test period (days)	1383	1383	1383	1439
Total trade length (days)	1383	1156	1094	1439
Out of market (days)	0	227	289	0
Average trade length – days	1383	23	42	29
Total trade length – bars	948	809	766	1007
Average trade length – bars	948	16	29	20
Trades/year	0.3	13.5	6.9	29.4
Time in market	100.0 %	83.6 %	79.1 %	100.0 %
Time exit – bars	948	60	60	50

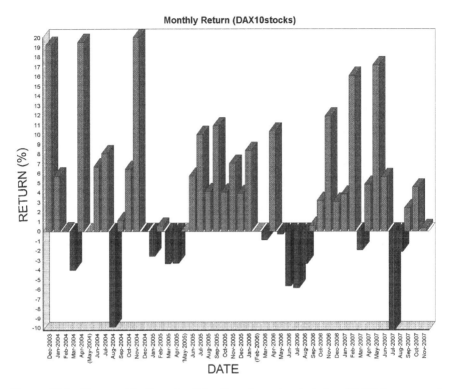

Figure 13.2 The monthly % profit of the disparity system tested on 10 DAX component stocks. The worst monthly return was in July 2007 during the summer 2007 correction.

average crossover, a popular and widely used trend-following method, to construct a system to trade DAX futures. The system was then enhanced using intermarket criteria and their performance is compared in Table 13.2.

Test Procedure and System Design

A dual moving average crossover system generates a buy signal when the shorter of two moving averages exceeds the longer one; a sell signal is generated when the shorter moving average falls below the longer moving average.

The short and long moving average period was optimized using data for the DAX index for the period from 1993 to 2003 and the system was then tested out-of-sample for the period from 19 January 2004 to 2 November 2007 on continuous DAX futures data obtained from Reuters Datalink.

To avoid false signals associated with a congested market, the CI indicator was again used to detect the prevailing market trend. If the absolute value of the 40-day

CI was above 30, it was assumed that a trend was developing and the moving average condition was used for long and short signals. If the absolute value of the CI was under 30 then the stochastic indicator was used to trigger buy and sell short orders to take advantage of oscillations associated with a range bound market.

The best parameter set that managed to produce profits for long signals, in both out-of-sample and in-sample testing, was 15 days for the fast moving average and 20 days for the slow average. In the case of short sale signals, these values were 10 days and 20 days for the fast and slow moving average periods respectively. The moving average optimization, however, apart from producing the best parameters, also created a problem. The slow moving average was in fact not slow at all, and therefore it did not take into account the longer-term trends; as a result, some short sales that were initiated in bullish markets produced losses. To deal with short signals in a rising market, a second slower moving average condition was introduced that blocked any short sale signals when the 2-day was above the 150-day moving average. This extra condition helped improve the overall performance on the short side of the market. The best parameters for the stochastic (used only in a congested market) were to buy when the 5-day stochastic crossed above its 4-day moving average and at the same time the 40-day stochastic was below 30. Similarly, short sales were initiated when the 5-day stochastic crossed below its 4-day moving average and at the same time the 40-day stochastic rose above 70.

Long positions were liquidated when either of the following conditions were true: The CI dropped by 40 points or more during the last three days, or the 40-day stochastic rose above 85 and then dropped below 75 but only when the CI was below 20 (in a congested market).

Short positions were covered when: The CI rose by 40 points or more during the last three days or the MACD crossed its 7-day exponential moving average and the price also rose above the 7-day moving average.

As you can see, the performance of the classic moving average system (summarized in the third column of Table 13.2) is nothing to write home about. It did not manage to outperform the buy and hold strategy during the out-of-sample bullish test period, but it outperformed it in both in-sample tests during mixed market conditions.

The disparity indicator was then used in order to filter out some signals that resulted in unprofitable trades. This time I used the Euro Stoxx 50 Index (STOXX50E) for in-sample testing and Euro Stoxx futures (FESX) for the out-of-sample test. Thus the disparity indicator was used to filter out long trades when the disparity divergence between the DAX and Euro Stoxx was negative. The opposite was added to the sell conditions, in order to exclude some premature exit signals and prolong the holding period in the case of positive disparity. Both short conditions were also enhanced by adding, this time not one but two, extra intermarket conditions. Thus a short signal wasn't executed unless both the disparity was negative and the intermarket security declined as well.

Evaluation of Results

The net effect of enhancing the system with the intermarket conditions is summarized in the fourth column of Table 13.2. The additional complexity of adding the intermarket signals reduced the number of trades by half to an average of one trade every two months. What was lost through fewer positions, however, was more than made up by tripling the stake per trade.

Market conditions were very favorable for the buy and hold investor as the DAX was in an almost continuous uptrend during the test period. Nevertheless, the intermarket enhancement did help to outperform the buy and hold method by 4 percentage points on a risk-adjusted return basis but only marginally on a total profit basis.

In conclusion I am convinced that although the enhanced moving average crossover system did not improve substantially on the buy-and-hold profitability, it does add strength to the case for incorporating intermarket conditions that work in synergy with the conventional component parts of the system.

14

A Comparison of a Neural Network and a Conventional System for Trading FTSE Futures

To conquer fear is the beginning of wisdom.

–Bertrand Russell

The Financial Times Stock Exchange FTSE 100 index is the last of the trilogy of our equity index trading systems.

FTSE futures are traded on the Euronext LIFFE CONNECT electronic trading system from 9:00 am to 10:00 pm Central European Time under the symbol Z (IB platform). The Z futures market has a daily trading volume of approximately 100 000 contracts and a daily price range of approximately 100 points. The contract value is £10 per FTSE point and the overnight maintenance margin was £3000 at the time of writing. Either each broker or the exchange can change margins periodically according to market volatility.

Neural network-based systems have generated a great deal of interest lately but are they as effective as the software vendors claim? I decided to investigate. In the first part of this chapter I will present a conventional rule-based system using the multiple regression model which produced the best results in trading gold (see Chapter 11). I used NeuroShell Trader Professional to construct a neural network model using, for comparison purposes, the same intermarket relationships with the conventional multiple regression system. The software's built-in genetic algorithm was then used to select the best inputs and optimize the parameters. The neural system is presented in the second part of this chapter and the code and detailed step-by-step procedure are set out in Appendix C.

14.1   CORRELATION WITH INTERNATIONAL INDICES

In order to select the best correlated indices to use in the multiple regression model, a correlation matrix of 10-day (two week) percentage returns of major equity, currency and interest rate indices was calculated (Table 14.1).

The best and most obvious correlation of the FTSE, which stems from the UK's membership of the European Union and its geographical position, was with the corresponding European indices but because of the high multicollinearity between them, only one can be included in the regression model. The best choices seemed to be either the Euro Stoxx 50 ($r = 0.85$) or the French CAC 40 ($r = 0.83$) but it was a close call. The dilemma was resolved by testing, and the CAC 40 was the finalist as it produced slightly better results on preliminary testing. The FTSE did not seem to respond, at least short term, to interest rates or interest rate changes as its correlation with short sterling rates was virtually zero.

With financials and oil and gas stocks making up almost 45 % of the index, the next obvious candidates to include in the regression model were the bank and oil sector indices. I chose the American S&P Bank Index (BIX) and the Amex Oil Index (XOI) instead of the corresponding European sector indices, because of their lower cross correlation with the CAC 40 index.

Thus the final multiple regression equation used in the model consisted of three independent variables and had the following form:

$$FTSE = -0.11 + 0.551 * CAC + 0.097 * BIX + 0.116 * XOI \qquad (14.1)$$

Table 14.1   Pearson's correlation of two-week (10 trading day) percentage returns between the FTSE and other related markets. The ESTX is the Dow Jones Euro Stoxx 50 index, the BIX is the S&P Bank index, the XOI is the Amex oil index, the GBP is the USD per British pound sterling rate and the FSS is the three-month short sterling interest rate futures.

				Correlation of 10-day returns				
	FTSE	S&P	ESTX	DAX	CAC	BIX	XOI	GBP	FSS
FTSE	1.00	0.76	0.85	0.78	0.83	0.53	0.43	−0.29	0.01
S&P	0.76	1.00	0.78	0.77	0.76	0.72	0.45	−0.12	−0.03
ESTX	0.85	0.78	1.00	0.93	0.96	0.50	0.35	−0.26	−0.09
DAX	0.78	0.77	0.93	1.00	0.89	0.51	0.32	−0.22	−0.11
CAC	0.83	0.76	0.96	0.89	1.00	0.50	0.35	−0.25	−0.10
BIX	0.53	0.72	0.50	0.51	0.50	1.00	0.28	−0.09	0.03
XOI	0.43	0.45	0.35	0.32	0.35	0.28	1.00	0.05	−0.01
GBP	−0.29	−0.12	−0.26	−0.22	−0.25	−0.09	0.05	1.00	−0.12
FSS	0.01	−0.03	−0.09	−0.11	−0.10	0.03	−0.01	−0.12	1.00

where FTSE is the predicted 10-day percentage return of the FTSE index; CAC is the actual 10-day percentage return of the CAC 40 index (FCHI); BIX is the actual 10-day percentage return of the S&P bank index (BIX); XOI is the actual 10-day percentage return of the Amex oil index.

14.2   SETTING UP THE TESTS

For a strategy to have value it must be adaptable to changing market conditions so I divided the available data into two segments. I then used the first segment to develop and optimize the regression model and the second segment of data to test it. There is no best way to divide the data into testing and out-of-sample segments. However, the out-of-sample segment must be long enough and different enough to be able to make a judgment on whether the model is valid and can be used later in actual trading without unpleasant surprises. In this case, the development period was from 1991 to 1999, and the out-of-sample period from 2 February 2000 to 19 December 2007. The out-of-sample period, which included a complete market cycle, was different enough from the in-sample period and long enough in duration to judge the model's usefulness. You should keep in mind that you will need to load an extra 210 bars in order to take into account the time lag in calculating all indicators involved.

A problem was again encountered with the historical data: The available data for FTSE and CAC 40 futures were not enough for both in- and out-of-sample testing. Another problem was that FTSE futures closed earlier than CAC 40 futures (the exchange only recently extended the trading time until 21:00 GMT). For the reasons mentioned above I decided to use the actual index prices for developing and testing the model.

You cannot, of course, trade the index directly and therefore realtime trading results may differ from the simulated ones presented below.

Several assumptions underlie the trading model. The default trade size was one contract per trade, and to avoid margin calls and the associated problems, the test was conducted in points and converted to British pounds at £10 per FTSE point. Long and short signals were executed the same day at the close and no interest was credited to the account when out of the market as this was assumed to cancel out additional slippage, skid and contract rollover costs.

The commission charged by discount brokers of 0.17 points (£1.7) was deducted from each trade. Returns were calculated as a percent of the account size required to trade each system over the back-test period and compared to the buy and hold method which involved buying and holding one FTSE contract for the duration of the test. Rollover costs involved in the buy and hold contract were ignored. The compound formula was used to annualize percentage returns.

The required account size was the greater of the initial margin required to trade the FTSE futures (£3750) or the maintenance margin (£3000) plus the initial drawdown.

The percent standard deviation of change in equity was calculated by dividing the monthly change in equity in points by the value of the FTSE index also in points and the risk-adjusted return was calculated by dividing the annualized return by the percent standard deviation of the change in equity.

14.3 SUMMARY OF CONDITIONS

Intermarket divergence systems usually generate few signals and this was the case with the FTSE system as it produced only 22 signals on aggregate during the eight-year test duration. To increase turnover I added a second condition which took advantage of temporary pullbacks during strong trends but only on positive intermarket divergence. This extra condition generated another seven long trades, thus increasing the number of trades to a sufficient number for a valid statistical evaluation of the system.

The system can be summarized as follows:

Buy condition 1 (intermarket): The most powerful use of the intermarket momentum oscillator (IMO) is registered when the indicator reaches an extreme reading (usually above 50) and reverses direction. This signals an exhaustion of the downtrend and warns of an impending price reversal. Thus a buy signal was generated if the 200 bar IMO crossed under 50 from above.

To eliminate premature signals, I used the 10-day stochastic and the 5-day exponential moving average to confirm the price reversal as follows: The system executed the IMO buy signals only if the FTSE crossed over its 5-day moving average and the stochastic indicator had crossed over 20 during the last three days prior to the divergence signal day.

Buy condition 2 (pullbacks): I used Bollinger Bands to identify temporary pullbacks as follows: A buy signal was generated if the FTSE declined below the lower band during the last three days and the IMO was over 50.

To ensure that this was a temporary correction and not a long-term bear market decline, buy signals were only taken if the FTSE was up by more than 2.4 % (0.03 % per day on average (specified by the linear regression slope) during the last 80 days.

Sell conditions: This was the exact opposite of the first buy condition. The position was liquidated when the IMO reached an extreme low value, reversed and crossed over 30. Once again the 10-day stochastic and the 10-day moving average were used as confirming indicators and sell signals were only taken if the FTSE crossed below its 10-day moving average and the stochastic crossed below 80.

Short conditions: These were very similar to the sell conditions described above, with the addition of an extra confirming requirement that the 10-day stochastic should be below its 4-day moving average before executing the signal.

Buy to cover: This was similar to the first buy condition described above.

14.4   EVALUATION OF RESULTS

The results for both tests are summarized in Table 14.2. I have also marked in the accompanying chart in Fig. 14.1 when each buy and sell signal was triggered but only (because of space limitations) from October 2005 to December 2007.

In the period tested, the results were very impressive. During the course of the eight-year simulation, which included the devastating 2001–2002 bear market, the system made more than £50 000 with only 29 trades, which were roughly 83 % accurate. It managed to produce a profit factor as high as 9.9 while holding the maximum drawdown to £6000 or 12 % of equity, which occurred on 24 April 2003, mainly due to an unpropitious short trade during the sharp recovery from the preceding bear market downtrend.

The risk and return statistics were also impressive. The monthly standard deviation of equity was only 3 % during the 8-year test duration which produced an 11 % risk adjusted return and a more than adequate Sharpe ratio of 9.4. The buy and hold investor, on the other hand, suffered a rather traumatic £35 600 drawdown during the 2002–2003 bear market which, because of the margin calls, expanded the account size required to hold one FTSE contract dramatically, from the initial minimum amount of £3000 to the ponderous sum of £38 600.

The severity of the drawdowns should have wiped out any buy and hold investors long before they could have enjoyed the profits from the ensuing 2003–2007 bull market. The intermarket system, however, managed to keep drawdown relatively low by avoiding long trades during the intervening bear market.

A perfect trading system is, however, impossible (is a perfect market possible?), and the current intermarket system is certainly no different. I identified the following flaws after inspecting carefully the trade signals on the chart.

The timing of the exits was not the best or most efficient. Some signals fired prematurely during extended up-trends but were late to materialize when needed most.

In addition a couple of winning trades suffered large adverse price movements (adverse excursions) between 180 to 250 FTSE points before becoming profitable. This was because of premature entry signals which are very common with countertrend divergence indicators.

This suggests that although the model was robust and maintained a more than acceptable balance between risk and reward, the timing of the entry and exit signals can be further improved by adding more conventional technical analysis rules and indicators.

Table 14.2   Profit/loss report. Out-of-sample test results of the FTSE multiple regression system based on its long-term relationship with the French CAC 40, the Amex oil index (XOI) and the S&P bank index (BIX).

Test	Buy & hold	Regression
Security on test Intermarket security	FTSE	FTSE CAC, XOI, BIX
Account required	£38 613	£6105
Total net profit	−£67	£50 256
Profit/loss %	−0.2 %	823 %
Annualized % gain/loss	0.0 %	33 %
Total number of trades	1	29
Winning trades	0	24
Losing trades	1	5
Percent profitable	0 %	82.8 %
Gross profit	£0.00	£55 905
Gross loss	−£67	−£5649
Avg. winning trade		£2329
Avg. losing trade	−£67	−£1130
Ratio avg. win/avg. loss		2.06
Profitability coefficient		5.01
Profit factor		9.90
Max. drawdown	−£35 611	−£6015
Date of max drawdown	3-12-03	4-24-03
Max. % drawdown	−92.2 %	−12.4 %
Max. initial drawdown	−€35 611	−£3104
Max. consecutive losses	1	2
Risk/reward	−52 835 %	12.0 %
Standard deviation % of equity	4.22 %	3.00 %
Risk adjusted annualized return	0.0 %	11 %
Sharpe ratio	−1.1	9.4
Reference bars needed		210
Start date/test	2-1-00	2-1-00
End date	12-19-07	12-19-07
Test period (years)	7.9	7.9
Total trade length (days)	2878	1912
Out of market (days)	0	966
Average trade length – days	2878	66
Trades/year	0.1	3.7
Time in market	100.0 %	66.4 %
System Parameters		
Rate of change – bars		10
Momentum oscillator – bars		200
Momentum oscillator – buy		50
Momentum oscillator – sell		30
Time exit – bars		100

Figure 14.1 Chart of the FTSE from October 2005 to December 2007. Test signals generated by the multiple regression method are superimposed on the chart. The 200-day divergence momentum oscillator is plotted in the top window.

There is a limit to the performance that can be achieved using a single indicator and many traders overlook the fact that using a diverse set of indicators, developed specifically to work together, can add value and increase profitability.

As I have mentioned in previous chapters, the underlying dynamics of the market can change over time. The regression coefficients used by the current system were the best at the time of writing this chapter (December 2007). The markets, however, don't stand still once a system is defined and by the time that this book is published, it is possible that some adjustments might be necessary.

14.5 A NEURAL NETWORK SYSTEM FOR TRADING THE FTSE

The real power of a neural net is in its ability to move a large amount of data and model relationships, if any, between the input and output. The output, of course, will depend on the input and a relationship between the security to be predicted and the input data series should exist in the first place. You should therefore include only those systems that you are sure have a relationship with the market to be predicted (in this case, the FTSE). In fact, one of the most powerful and easiest approaches for building a neural network system is using inputs from an existing profitable, rule-based system. This way, the neural system will try to improve results on known existing relationships instead of searching on red herring relationships that may not exist. In developing

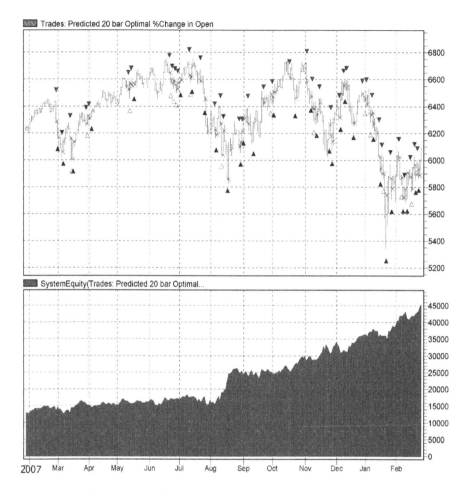

Figure 14.2 Chart of the FTSE from February 2007 to February 2008. Test signals generated by the ROC neural net system are superimposed on the chart. The equity line is plotted in the bottom window. The solid up arrows denote long entry, the solid down arrows short entry and the hollow up arrows denote covering of short position. New long/short signals closed any open short/long positions.

a neural network to trade the FTSE, I tried the same related markets (the CAC 40, BIX and XOI) used by the conventional multiple regression system described above. I then combined the outputs from the neural system with conventional indicators to develop a hybrid strategy.

A problem encountered in developing the neural system was that, unlike conventional rule-based optimizers, the generic algorithm used by the neural network to select and optimize the inputs is intolerant of even moderately correlated inputs. When I tried to input all three related markets (the CAC 40, the BIX and the XOI), the algorithm used either the last two (the BIX and the XOI) or only the CAC, completely ignoring the others despite a moderate correlation ($r = 0.5$) between the CAC and the BIX and a rather weak ($r = 0.38$) correlation between the CAC and the XOI. I had to deal with this by developing another primary neural network strategy and feeding the outputs from the first tests back into the primary network strategy.

Over-fitting is probably the most dangerous illusion a developer can encounter because it leads to false predictions that are based on isolated occurrences within the analyzed data set, and not genuine persisting relationships. An over-fitted model can be produced by including too many inputs or hidden neurons. This increases the capacity of the network which often leads to memorization instead of a genuine learning progress. To mitigate the effects of over-fitting I reduced the maximum number of hidden neurons from the program's default 10 to 7.

Another common problem with neural network systems is that they tend to trade too often or too sporadically. In NeuroShell this can be adjusted by increasing the desired shortest or longest average trade span (on the optimization tab). You can also adjust the number of trades indirectly by changing the training objective, for example from "maximize net profit" to "maximize return on trades".

A technical support representative suggested that yet another way to deal with the problem of overtrading is to increase commission costs. This will penalize bad trades more and cause the system to avoid them. The profit calculations, however, will be incorrect but these can be adjusted by adding back the excess commissions.

Test Procedure

The appropriate data sets for the FTSE, the CAC 40, the XOI and the BIX were loaded on a NeuroShell chart page.

I chose to select manually the data set sizes used for training, testing and out-of-sample testing, although it is now possible to optimize these as well (using the Adaptive Turboprop 2 add-on).

As a general rule, the data reserved for training the model should include enough varying market conditions to allow the generation of rules that can cope with likely scenarios, rather than just what has happened most recently. But if the time period is too long or too old then the rules will be affected by outdated relationships and the trading results will suffer. Perhaps a good rule of thumb is to allocate approximately 80 % of the available data for the training and testing subsets and to use the rest for out-of-sample confidence testing.

The available data was divided into three datasets. The neural net was trained on data spanning from 27 April 1993 to 31 December 2002. The second dataset, from 1 January 2003 to 31 December 2004 was used for testing during training or "paper trading" and the last one for out-of-sample testing.

The genetic algorithm optimized the model's parameters on the training sample, but the testing sample was also used during the optimization process in order to try each new optimal solution. The testing sample is not therefore a true out-of-sample data set and an additional three years, spanning from 1 January 2005 to 27 February 2008, were reserved to see how the final model fared on data that it had never seen before.

Having established the testing samples, we can now proceed in specifying the following: Input data preprocessing, the prediction output, the size and structure of the neural system, and the trading details (commission, margin, etc.).

Inputs

Of course, the key to a successful neural network model is in choosing the best inputs. Having established the most appropriate intermarket securities in the first part of this chapter, the next and most arduous task was deciding on the best preprocessing method.

An initial consideration of the inputs to the neural network concerns whether to use raw data (e.g. direct prices of the target and intermarket securities), or preprocessed data (e.g. price differences). This step is extremely important, since neural systems train much better on relative numbers such as differences, oscillators, momentum and ratios, which provide the relevant relationships explicitly rather than forcing the system to discover them. The more pertinent the data that you provide to the network, the better it will train and it is therefore important to select the training data carefully and preprocess them before training.

But which is the best transformation to use?

The hardest task was in deciding whether to use raw data, preprocessed data of the intermarket securities, or spreads between the FTSE and its related markets. As there are no standard rules available for determining the appropriate preprocessing method, I decided to use a brute force trial and error method and train a large number of neural nets with different inputs, discarding the preprocessing methods of the models which performed the worst.

Simple preprocessing included taking percentage differences of the price data, simple and exponential moving averages and the stochastic and disparity indicators. More elaborate preprocessing consisted of taking spreads between the target market (in this case the FTSE) and its related markets. This involved taking differences of the percentage price differences, and the disparities. I used nine different preprocessing transformations on aggregate, including the raw price inputs, but because of space limitations I chose to present only the best three in Table 14.3. These were the percentage changes of the intermarket securities (ROC), the relative percentage changes or spread between the FTSE and the intermarket securities and finally the relative disparities (the distances from their moving average) between the FTSE and the intermarket indices.

Table 14.3 Out-of-sample profit/loss report. Out-of-sample test results of three intermarket neural network systems on the FTSE based on its relationship with the French CAC 40, the Amex Oil Index (XOI) and the S&P Bank Index (BIX). The first test (ROC) was based on the % rate of change of the intermarket securities, the second on the relative % rate of change between the FTSE and the intermarket securities and the third on the relative disparity indicator. The last three rows indicate the genetic algorithm optimized contribution of each intermarket security on the system. The objective used to optimize the network structure was return on trades. The maximum open trade drawdown is the difference between the entry price and the worst price during any trade multiplied by the point value.

Test	Buy & hold	ROC	ROC (relative)	Disparity
Intermarket security		BIX, XOI	BIX	CAC
Account required	£3750	£3750	£3750	£3750
Total net profit	£12 292	£47 247	£32 503	£32 910
Return on account %	338 %	1575 %	1083 %	924 %
Return on trades %	25.4 %	1574 %	1083 %	1097 %
Annual return on trades %	8.1 %	500 %	344 %	348 %
Total number of trades	1	102	89	100
Winning trades	1	67	62	64
Losing trades	0	35	27	36
Percent profitable	100 %	65.7 %	69.7 %	64.0 %
Gross profit	£12 293	£69 176	£47 442	£49 370
Gross loss	£0	£21 929	£14 939	£16 460
Avg. winning trade	£12 293	£1032	£765	£771
Avg. losing trade		£627	−£553	−£457
Avg. win/avg. loss		1.65	1.38	1.69
Profitability coefficient		2.79	2.77	2.68
Profit factor		3.15	3.18	3.00
Max. drawdown	−£11 458	−£6304	−£5428	−£3375
Max. open drawdown	−€816	−£3471	−£4014	−£3271
Max. initial drawdown	−€635	£0	£0	−£561
Max. consecutive losses	0	3	4	3
Risk/reward	93 %	13 %	17 %	10 %
Start date/test	01/04/05	01/04/05	01/04/05	01/04/05
Output end date	02/27/08	02/27/08	02/27/08	02/27/08
Test period (years)	3.15	3.15	3.15	3.15
Test duration – bars	797	797	797	797
Avg. trade length – bars	797	8	5	4
Trades/year	0.3	32.4	28.3	31.8
Beginning price	4847.0	4847.0	4847.0	4847.0
Ending price	6076.5	6076.5	6076.5	6076.5
System Parameters				
% change – days in the future		20	15	15
Hidden neurons		7	7	7
Input Contributions				
BIX		69 %	100 %	0
CAC		0	0	100 %
XOI		31 %	0 %	0 %

The out-of-sample and paper trading performance of all three systems are compared in Tables 14.3 and 14.4. Trading signals and a graph of the system equity for the first (ROC) out-of-sample test are also presented in the chart in Figure 14.2. A review of their comparative performance suggests that the simple price percentage difference transformation may be the best to use as it beat all others on profitability metrics, in both out-of-sample and in-sample tests. You should not, however, throw out the disparity transformation as it had significantly lower drawdown during the out-of-sample test.

The option of full optimization was used, which means that the genetic algorithm could optimize parameters but also discard any unnecessary inputs. It is interesting to note that in the second and third tests, which were fed with more elaborately preprocessed inputs, the genetic algorithm used only one intermarket security in constructing the final model, whereas it used both the BIX and the XOI in the case of the simpler price rate of change (ROC) preprocessing method. In order to compare the conventional system, which used all three intermarket securities in predicting the FTSE, with the current neural model, I had to construct a fourth strategy which used the outputs of the first three neural prediction models as inputs. Full optimization was used again to select the best inputs and optimize the predicted thresholds. The result was a strategy that used inputs from the first (ROC) and the third systems (disparity) but excluded all inputs from the second system (relative ROC). The disparity inputs were only used for covering short positions.

The combined system (Table 14.5) did not manage, however, to improve on the ROC model by much on a profitability basis but reduced the drawdown considerably.

The same conventional indicators that were used in the MetaStock system described in the first part of this chapter were then added to the combined strategy to produce a hybrid system.

A moving average and a stochastic crossover were used to confirm neural inter-market signals and filter out any untimely entries. A full description of each model and the rules and indicators used is included in Appendix B.

Only the indicator parameters and the neural prediction thresholds were optimized this time. The additional indicators reduced the number of trades considerably but they must have filtered out some profitable trades as well, because the overall performance of the hybrid system was degraded (Table 14.5), although the average profit per trade was actually higher.

On enabling the genetic algorithm's full optimization option the system reverted to the combined model, discarding all additional conventional indicators. This suggested that the choice of indicators was not the best as they conflicted with the internal unknown neural network rules. A major drawback of neural networks is that a trader cannot see the rules that lead to the predictions. This makes the task of adding more rules a laborious and time-consuming process as the system developer has no other choice but to rely on a trial and error process. An alternative method is to extract the network rules using sensitivity analysis. This can be accomplished by adjusting the level of inputs and recording the change in the outputs. The data can then be used to

Table 14.4   Profit/loss report. Testing sample results of the same intermarket neural network systems presented in Table 14.3. This sample (from 1 February 2003 to 31 December 2004) was used to evaluate the optimized parameters derived from the training process. The last six rows depict the contribution of the intermarket securities on each system and the parameters of the rate of change and disparity inputs as optimized by the genetic algorithm.

Test	Buy & hold	ROC	ROC (relative)	Disparity
Intermarket security		BIX, XOI	BIX	CAC
Account required	£10 225	£4 218	£8207	£5051
Total net profit	£8045	£27 416	£17 053	£21 363
Return on account %	79 %	650 %	208 %	423 %
Return on trades %	20.1 %	914 %	568 %	712 %
Annual return on trades %	10.0 %	457 %	284 %	356 %
Total number of trades	1	78	62	81
Winning trades	1	52	43	56
Losing trades	0	26	19	25
Percent profitable	100 %	66.7 %	69.4 %	69.1 %
Gross profit	£8045	£36 747	£26 265	£29 308
Gross loss	£0	−£9331	−£9212	−£7945
Avg. winning trade	£8045	£707	£611	£523
Avg. losing trade		£359	−£485	−£318
Avg. win/avg. loss		1.97	1.26	1.65
Profitability coefficient		3.30	2.51	3.14
Profit factor		3.94	2.85	3.69
Max. drawdown	−€7225	−£2889	−£6097	−£2476
Max. open drawdown	−€4495	−£2170	−£6097	−£1435
Max. initial drawdown	−€7225	−£1218	−£5207	−£2051
Max. consecutive losses	0	4	3	5
Risk/reward	90 %	11 %	36 %	12 %
Start date/test	1/2/03	1/2/03	1/2/03	1/2/03
Output end date	12/31/04	12/31/04	12/31/04	12/31/04
Test period (years)	2.00	2.00	2.00	2.00
Test duration – bars	504	504	504	504
Avg. trade length – bars	504	7	6	4
Trades/year	0.5	39.1	31.0	40.6
Beginning price	4009.5	4009.5	4009.5	4009.5
Ending price	4814.3	4814.3	4814.3	4814.3
System Parameters				
% change – days in the future		20	15	15
Hidden neurons		7	7	7
Input Contributions				
BIX		69 %	100 %	0
CAC		0	0	100 %
XOI		31 %	0	0
ROC – Period		1	2	
ROC – Period		4		
MA periods				6

Table 14.5 Combined neural and hybrid system profit/loss report. Out-of-sample test results of two intermarket combined strategies tested on the FTSE from 4 January 2005 to 27 February 2008. The first strategy (Combined) used the outputs of the three neural network tests described in Table 14.3, whereas the second strategy was a hybrid neural and conventional rule-based system. The last four rows indicate the best threshold parameters as optimized by the genetic algorithm.

Test	Buy & hold	Combined neural	Hybrid
Intermarket security		BIX, XOI, CAC	BIX, XOI, CAC
Account required	£3750	£3750	£3750
Total net profit	£12 293	£53 164	£23 703
Return on account %	328 %	1418 %	632 %
Return on trades %	25.4 %	1510 %	790 %
Annual return on trades %	8.1 %	480 %	251 %
Total number of trades	1	176	63
Winning trades	1	110	36
Losing trades	0	66	27
Percent profitable	100 %	62.5 %	57.1 %
Gross profit	£12 293	£85 491	£44 943
Gross loss	£0	£32 327	£21 240
Avg. winning trade	£12 293	£777	£1248
Avg. losing trade		−£490	−£787
Avg. win/avg. loss		1.59	1.59
Profitability coefficient		2.38	1.85
Profit factor		2.64	2.12
Max. drawdown	−£11 458	−£4641	−£8064
Max. open drawdown	−€816	−£3471	−£3858
Max. initial drawdown	−€635	£0	−£572
Max. consecutive losses	0	5	3
Risk/reward	93 %	9 %	34 %
Start date/test	01/04/05	01/04/05	01/04/05
Output end date	02/27/08	02/27/08	02/27/08
Test period (years)	3.15	3.15	3.15
Test duration – bars	797	797	797
Avg. trade length – bars	797	5	11
Trades/year	0.3	56	20
Beginning price	4847.0	4847.0	4847.0
Ending price	6076.5	6076.5	6076.5
Thresholds			
Enter long (ROC)		0.41	0.14
Sell (ROC)		−0.21	−0.41
Short (ROC)		−0.02	0
Cover (Disparity)		0.00	0

develop approximate rules. Unfortunately, this is also time-consuming as the number of different input level combinations to be tested is very large.

Outputs

While it may seem appropriate to attempt to predict the price sometime in the future, this is a particularly difficult task because price changes do not tend to be smooth. Predicting price direction appears easier and is more likely to be successful. Using this approach, however, a different problem comes up: a high degree of directional accuracy may not translate to high returns after costs if the movement in the forecast direction is small and therefore the strength of the move in that direction has to be predicted as well. NeuroShell offer a number of choices and the one which best combined both strength and directional prediction seemed to be the 20-day optimal percent change in the close. This, according to the NeuroShell help file, "in contrast to simply predicting the change, the optimal change will try to predict the optimal closing price change to the next peak/valley within the specified number of bars into the future".

Trading Specifications

The default trade size was one contract per trade, the point value was set at £10 per FTSE point and the required initial margin to £3750. Long and short signals were executed next day at the open and no interest was credited to the account when out of the market as this was assumed to cancel out additional slippage, skid and contract rollover costs.

Returns were calculated as a percent of the account required to trade each system and compared to the buy and hold method which involved buying and holding one FTSE contract for the duration of the test. Rollover costs were ignored. NeuroShell calculated also the return on trades which is achieved by taking the cumulative sum of all returns for each trade. For long trades, this is calculated according to the following formula:

$$\text{Return} = 100 * (\text{exit price} - \text{entry price} - \text{commissions})/$$
$$(\text{entry price} + \text{commissions}).$$

The maximum open drawdown was calculated by subtracting the worst intraday price during any trade from the entry price and multiplying by the point value. The initial drawdown was the maximum amount that the equity curve dipped below zero before the system started making profits.

There are two ways of calculating the required account size. If you assume that profits are withdrawn from the account each time that a position is closed, then the account size is determined by the margin plus the maximum drawdown of the worst trade. Alternatively, assuming that profits are compounded to the available account funds, the required account size should be calculated by adding the initial drawdown to the required margin. Most software (including NeuroShell) use the first method for calculating the required account size. Maybe this is a more realistic representation of how traders utilize their available funds but since I used the second method for all previous tests in this book, for the sake of consistency I decided to continue using it for the current tests as well.

The risk/reward was calculated by dividing the maximum drawdown by the total net profit. Obviously the less the risk/reward ratio, the better the system. NeuroShell also offered a choice of specifying the desired longest and shortest average trade span. These are useful in adjusting the number of trades, as a longer time span will involve less trades. These settings, however, are not absolute commands to the optimizer; they are more like requests, which the optimizer will try to honor if it can, without sacrificing too much of the objective (profit, etc.). In this case, despite setting the minimum average trade span to seven bars, the last system was short of this target by three bars, producing an average trade span of only four bars.

Network Architecture

After the input and output selection is complete, the training process can be initiated. There are basically three parameters to specify in order to control the size and structure of the model:

The number of hidden neurons: Older artificial neural networks were composed of three types of neuron layers: an input layer, one or more hidden layers, and an output layer. They used any number of neurons to connect adjoining layers which had to be specified by the developer. Most modern ones actually have one layer for each hidden neuron but the number of hidden neurons (and the associated layers) still has to be specified by the developer. This is not an easy task as there are no standard rules available for determining the appropriate number of hidden neurons. Ruggiero (see Bibliography) suggests starting with the same number of hidden neurons as the number of inputs and then retraining each model 10 times, adding nodes until results begin to converge.

In NeuroShell Trader there is no option to specify the number of initial hidden neurons. The software actually chooses the correct number of neurons automatically by starting with zero hidden neurons (which is equivalent to linear regression) and adding nodes one by one as needed. There is an option, however, to specify the maximum number of hidden neurons. In the current analysis, in order to avoid over-fitting, I limited the number of hidden neurons to seven.

Training objective: There are obvious mismatches between the goals of neural networks and real traders. While neural networks are attempting to minimize forecast errors in training, typically traders focus on trying to maximize profits. While these are both valid goals, a trader's definition of "success" is different yet again. One trader may seek to maximize profit while another risk-adverse trader may prefer to minimize drawdown.

The training objective is vital in neural network systems as it is used for the optimization of the network structure. Choosing different objectives could result in significantly different results. NeuroShell gives you a choice of 25 different target objectives, which include academic (for example the option to minimize forecast error) and trading (to maximize profits or minimize drawdown) objectives.

After some experimentation I chose to maximize return on trades, as this objective produced stable systems with good overall profit/loss statistics, moderate drawdown and a reasonable number of trades. Of course it is important to use the same objective for all tests, otherwise any comparisons will be meaningless.

Evaluation of Results

The current analysis was mainly intended to compare neural network with conventional rule based technical analysis systems. Because of the sampling restrictions explained above, the neural net out-of-sample segment was considerably shorter than the corresponding period used to test the conventional system. For obvious reasons, in a situation where time periods of different lengths are being compared, the total net profit criterion is misleading and therefore the comparison should be limited to other profitability criteria which are independent of the back-test sample length. The drawdown figures were also not comparable because the neural shorter out-of-sample segment did not include the 2002–2003 bear market.

Another important factor to take into account is the different optimization methods used by the software. MetaStock uses the brute force approach while NeuroShell uses a genetic algorithm (for a full description and advantages or disadvantages of both methods please see Chapter 10). In addition, I used the genetic algorithm's option to optimize the input contribution, a feature not available from MetaStock. This option was disabled in the case of the last (hybrid) strategy.

Before proceeding with analyzing the results I should make it clear that it is very unlikely that you will get exactly the same results with the ones presented here in Tables 14.3–14.5. This is because neural networks start training with an arbitrary set of starting weights which results in a slightly different solution each time that the network is trained.

Despite the shorter sample, none of the neural network systems managed to beat the multiple regression system (see Tables 14.2, 14.3 and 14.5). A major disadvantage of the conventional system, however, was the low turnover (about four trades per year) which makes it suitable only for patient traders or long-term investors.

During my research into intermarket neural network systems I noticed that they tend to trade much more often than the corresponding conventional divergence systems. This is a significant advantage because filtering a conventional system leads to even fewer trades which makes them unsuitable for short-term traders. In addition, more trades can be translated to higher profits and return on account. This was certainly true with the current neural systems which produced no less than 30 trades per year on average, enough to satisfy most active traders.

Curve-fitting is probably the most dangerous snare a trader can walk into but, fortunately, the consistent performance between the testing and out-of-sample results (in Tables 14.3 and 14.4) suggested this was not the case.

In fact the only significant difference between the out-of-sample data (Table 14.3) and the testing data (Table 14.4) was the magnitude of the profits. The out-of-sample produced a higher overall net profit mainly because of the longer segment period but also because of higher price levels of the FTSE during the test.

When judging the system's worth, it is important to compare it to the buy and hold strategy. All neural net systems succeeded in beating the buy and hold method by a wide margin and considerably lower risk. In addition, they avoided the huge £11 500 drawdown which hit the buy and hold investor during the steep correction in January 2008. Although the neural systems avoided the sharp plunges in the market and associated catastrophic losses they can, similarly to conventional systems, fail as well, so it is always a good idea to include a stop-loss condition. Stop-loss conditions were not included in the current study as they would have distorted results by improving the bad systems and making any comparison irrelevant.

14.6 CONCLUSION

While there is no assurance that neural networks can beat a typical rule-based system on a profit/trade basis they can most certainly beat it on a total net profit basis. A major disadvantage of conventional systems is the low number of trades. This is not, however, the case with neural network systems which can produce five to ten times as many trades which are usually associated with higher profits.

In constructing a viable neural system all we would have to worry about is providing the most appropriate inputs and then let the neural net train to arrive at the best model. Of course our inputs cannot include the universe of factors that explain stock index fluctuations because no formula or model exists that can predict accurately all the supply-and-demand dynamics that affect stock index prices. Fortunately, we don't need a perfect trading system but only a profitable one. Instead of perfection, we should aim to construct a viable system that can produce reasonable profits while avoiding large drawdowns that can wipe out all profits and lead to margin calls.

Neural network models are excellent at deciphering hidden patterns and relationships in market data as they have the capability to model the ambiguity and identify the nonlinear characteristics of financial time series which do not easily succumb to analysis by the classic statistical techniques. This is not to say that they can't be analyzed by conventional methods but neural networks simply make a better job of analyzing nonparametric price series without making any unrealistic assumptions. This does not imply, however, that neural networks are the "Holy Grail" that traders have been looking for. A major drawback is their virtually non-existent explanatory capability which makes it impossible to see the rules that led to the predictions. As my research has revealed, this makes it difficult to incorporate additional classic technical conditions or risk management considerations into a neural network-based trading system as they may degrade the system's performance by conflicting with its unknown internal neural-based rules.

I believe my findings may have also a practical significance in deciding on the appropriate data preprocessing techniques, in order to exploit more efficiently the hidden intermarket relationships.

Finally, you should keep in mind that the world does not stand still once a model is defined; network models age in the same way as conventional rule-based models and you should always keep one step ahead by re-training your system on more recent data.

15
The Use of Intermarket Systems in Trading Stocks

Successful strategies in trading often require doing what most people find distinctly uncomfortable.

–Jack Schwager

If you own shares of Archer Daniels Midlands (ADM), have you ever thought of following corn futures? What is the possible impact of a steep drop of the price of copper on the Phelps Dodge stock? It may be worth your effort to analyze such correlations.

Intermarket analysis can be a valuable tool when you trade individual or groups of stocks. This can be accomplished by comparing commodity-related stocks with the corresponding commodity or index. Since many stock groups have strong correlation with commodity markets, it also makes sense to analyze this relationship.

Some classic examples include the relationship between energy stocks and the price of crude oil, the correlation between gold miners and gold bullion or the impact of interest rate changes on financial stocks.

The systems presented in this chapter for trading oil and gold stocks are examples of using the correlation between a stock and a related commodity to develop a trading system.

15.1 TESTING METHOD

The correlation matrix between sector indices and related commodities is presented in Table 15.1. The best correlated commodity was used to construct an

Table 15.1   Correlation matrix (using 15-year data) of 10-day % yields.

	S&P 500	XOI	XAU	UTY	CRB Index	Gold	Crude Oil	Natural Gas
S&P	1	0.47	0.13	0.34	0.06	−0.02	−0.02	0.02
XOI	**0.47**	1	0.30	0.34	0.39	0.14	**0.41**	0.26
XAU	0.13	0.30	1	0.11	0.44	**0.70**	0.19	0.11
UTY	0.34	0.34	0.11	1	0.04	0.04	−0.03	0.10
CRB	0.06	0.39	0.44	0.04	1	0.45	0.54	0.35
Gold	−0.02	0.14	0.70	0.04	0.45	1	0.14	0.08
Oil	−0.02	0.41	0.19	−0.03	0.54	0.14	1	0.28
Gas	0.02	0.26	0.11	0.10	0.35	0.08	0.28	1

intermarket trading system based on the divergence of each stock from the corresponding commodity.

My research has shown that using the relative strength between a stock and its corresponding index (e.g. between an oil stock and the XOI) as a filter to exclude weak stocks can improve performance.

A correlation between two related markets, however, doesn't always mean that one market can always be used to predict the other. To deal with this issue I used Pearson's correlation between the stock and its corresponding index as a filter to exclude stocks during periods that they decoupled from the corresponding index. This new condition improved performance and decreased drawdown as it filtered out signals on stocks with specific problems having nothing to do with their industry group.

All tests started with an initial equity of $100 000 and 10 % of total capital was allocated per trade. In order to compare them with the buy and hold method, profits or losses were compounded to the initial equity. No buying on margin was used for either system.

Portfolio test simulations were carried out using Tradesim Enterprise Edition version 4.2.2 (a MetaStock plug-in). The most useful test statistics are presented in Table 15.2. All orders were executed at next day's opening price at the market, and the commission charged was $10. No interest was credited when out of the market. The minimum trade size was specified at $3000 and any position was limited to 15 % of traded volume.

If you wish to replicate the tests, please keep in mind that for the test to begin producing signals, the indicators used in each should first be calculated and this requires a number of bars to be loaded.

The buy and hold profit was calculated by buying equal dollar amount of all stocks in the corresponding index (e.g. all 12 constituents of the XOI index in the case of the oil stocks system) on the date of the first portfolio trade and selling them on the last day of the test.

Table 15.2   Profit/loss report of the intermarket oil stock system. In the first column is the profit of buying and holding all XOI components for the entire test duration. In the second column are profit statistics using 10 % of capital per trade and in the last column using a fixed $10 000 capital per trade. Comparison with the buy and hold is only meaningful using the first method, as the second method used only one tenth of the initial buy-and-hold capital.

System	Buy & hold	Oil stocks (% of equity)	Oil stocks (equal dollar)
Intermarket security		Crude oil	Crude oil
Number of stocks		244	244
Initial equity	$100 000	$100 000	$100 000
Capital/trade	$100 000	10 %	$10 000
Total net profit	$354 347	$1 618 573	$295 982
Profit/loss %	354 %	1619 %	296 %
Annual percent gain/loss	30 %	135 %	25 %
Total number of trades	1	347	320
Winning trades	1	251	231
Losing trades	0	96	89
Percent profitable	100 %	72.3 %	72.2 %
Avg. winning trade	$354 347	$8353	$1677
Avg. losing trade	$0	−$4980	−$1026
Ratio avg. win/avg. loss		1.68	1.63
Profitability coefficient		3.49	3.42
Profit factor		4.40	4.24
Drawdown %	−6.0 %	−5.4 %	−5.5 %
Risk/reward	18.7 %	3.5 %	3.9 %
Start date/test	8/1/95	8/1/95	8/1/95
End date	8/1/07	8/1/07	8/1/07
Test period (years)	12.0	12.0	12.0
Trades/year	0.1	29	27
System Parameters			
Correlation days		300	300
LRS oil stocks		20	20
LRS intermarket SEC1		25	25
LRS intermarket SEC2		25	25
IMO – days		200	200
IMO – buy		70	70
IMO – sell		7	7
Time exit–bars		100	100

15.2   A SYSTEM FOR TRADING OIL STOCKS

The portfolio model consisted of 244 oil and gas stocks, trading in the three major US exchanges, the NYSE, AMEX and Nasdaq, and was tested in the preceding

EQUITY

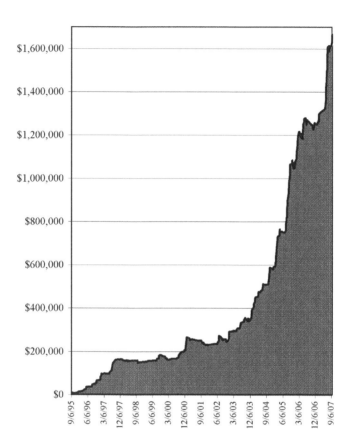

Figure 15.1   Oil stock system closed trade equity line.

12-year period from 8 August 2005 to 8 August 2007. The portfolio embraced oil and gas stocks across all sub industry groups, including drilling and exploration, major integrated oil and gas, pipelines, independent oil and gas, equipment and services and oil and gas ETFs.

Penny stocks were excluded as a first run revealed that these did not move in tandem with the rest of the group, mainly because of their own stock-specific financial problems.

Only long positions were considered as shorting individual stocks is not always possible. It depends on the broker's ability to borrow the stock but, even if this was possible, I wouldn't advise it as you can find yourself in a very dangerous predicament in case of a takeover or a surge in oil prices because of an unexpected geopolitical event.

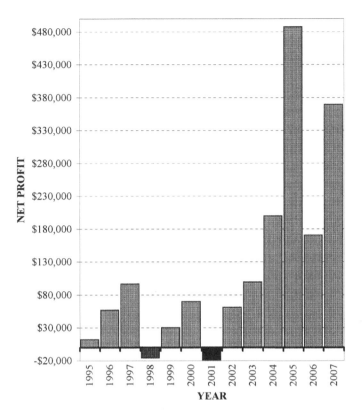

Figure 15.2 Graphical representation of yearly profits (oil stock system). The best year was in 2005 when the system made more than $480 000 and the worst year was in 2001 when it lost $19 000. The distribution presented above shows significant positive skewness. This suggests that most of the profits were made during the later part of the test during the recent run in crude oil prices.

Before proceeding with the test design the correlation matrix between 10-day yields of the Amex Oil Index (XOI) and related commodities and stock indices (depicted in Table 15.1) was calculated for the preceding 15-year period. Because of high cross correlation between stock indices, only one stock index should be included in the model. It is reasonable to include a broad stock index like the S&P 500 since, as the name suggests, oil stocks are stocks and not commodities, and are inevitably influenced by the general direction of the market and the economy as well as the price of oil itself. In fact the XOI correlated better with the S&P 500 ($r = 0.47$) than with crude oil futures ($r = 0.41$ in Table 15.1).

My final selection of related markets included NYMEX crude oil futures and the S&P 500. High correlation with the market to be predicted is not the only criterion in choosing the best model but low cross correlation between predictor variables is

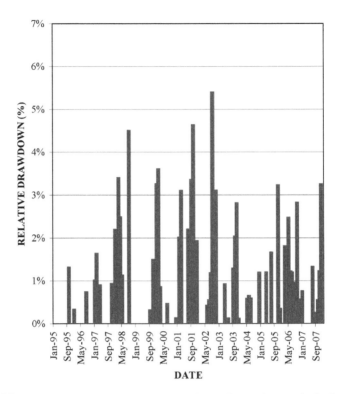

Figure 15.3 The percent drawdown is on the vertical axis and time on the horizontal axis. The drawdown was quite low and it only exceeded 4 % of equity three times during the 12-year period: Once in September of 1998, once in October 2001, and the last time in September of 2002.

also important. In this case there was no correlation between crude oil and the S&P 500 ($r = -0.02$).

This system was based on the successful double linear regression (LRS) slope indicator used in Chapter 11 to trade gold. Preliminary testing showed that this system produced more profits with less drawdown. The linear regression length was optimized and the most robust parameter set was 35 days for both intermarket securities and 10 days for the stocks. The following additional entry conditions improved on the model's performance:

- The 50-day moving average of the relative strength between the stock and the XOI was required to be above the corresponding 200-day moving average. This condition was introduced in order to eliminate weak stocks with temporary stock specific problems. This additional condition not only improved the profit factor but also helped reduce drawdown.

Figure 15.4 Graphical representation of percent winning trades (top) and percent losing trades (bottom). After some initial volatility the winning percentage settled around 72 % and the losing percentage around 28 %. The initial volatility can be attributed to the reduced number of oil stocks trading in 1995–1996.

- Pearson's correlation was used as a filter to exclude stocks that temporarily decoupled from the group. The requirement was that Pearson's correlation between the stock and XOI should be 0.5 or more.
- A money flow condition was added to the entry conditions, which helped to reduce drawdown by excluding stocks in a downtrend. The Volume Flow Indicator (VFI), first introduced in my June 2004 article in *Technical Analysis of STOCKS & COMMODITIES* was used.

The following conditions improved on the timeliness of exits:

- Divergence based exit signals were triggered only when the 15-day stochastic was below its five-day moving average

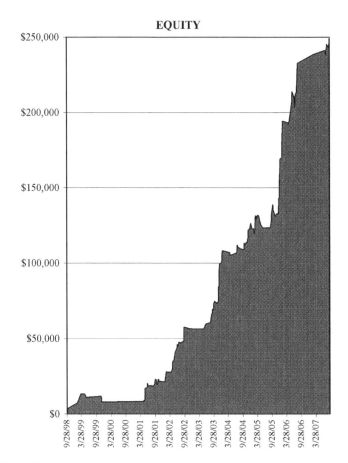

Figure 15.5   Closed trade equity (gold stock system).

- A money flow to sell when the VFI crossed below its 100-day moving average and the Finite Volume Element (FVE) indicator crossed below the zero line was added. This last condition helped to reduce maximum drawdown from 7.1 % to 5.4 % of equity.

15.3   EVALUATION OF THE OIL STOCK MODEL

When specifying the test parameters in a portfolio test of a basket of stocks, the first thing that you have to decide is the capital per trade. Different amounts or different methods (fixed or compounding) can produce very different results. I used a fixed percentage (10 % of equity) capital per trade in the first simulation but as this method

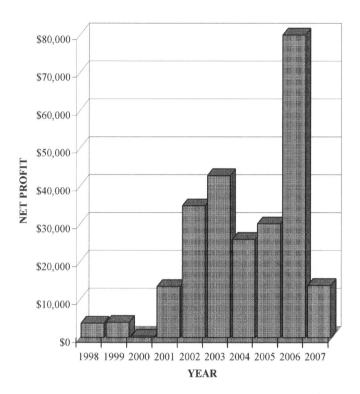

Figure 15.6 Graphical representation of yearly profits (gold stock system). The most profitable year was 2006 when the system made nearly $80 000 and the worst in 2000 when it barely broke even.

involved (during the latest phase of the test) holding large positions in each stock I decided to include a second simulation with a fixed dollar amount of $10 000 per trade.

The results of the first method are depicted in the second column of Table 15.2. I also included a graphical presentation of the equity line, the yearly profits, the drawdown and the percentage of profitable trades in Figures 15.1, 15.2, 15.3 and 15.4 respectively. The system outperformed the buy and hold method by a wide margin and producing more than $1.6 million of net profits in the 12-year period of the test.

The average drawdown (Fig. 15.3) was quite low and it only exceeded 4 % of equity three times during the 12-year period: Once in September 1998, when the XOI dropped more than 17 % and twice during the devastating bear market of 2001–2002.

It would be difficult to realize the same amount of total profits by fixing the capital per trade to $10 000. Although most profitability metrics (profit factor, win/loss ratio, etc.) were not affected, the total net profit dropped rather dramatically but so did the

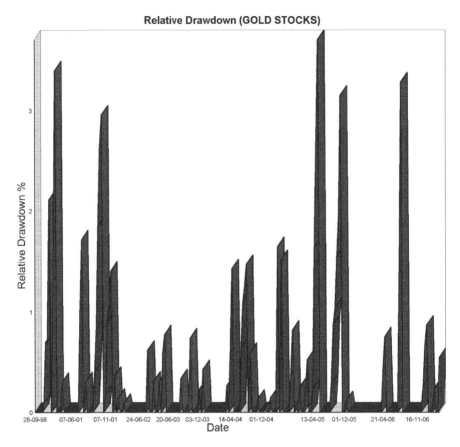

Figure 15.7 The percent drawdown is on the vertical axis and time is on the horizontal axis. The drawdown was quite low and it only exceeded 3.5 % of equity two times during the 9-year period: Once in December of 2000, and once in June 2005.

maximum drawdown. This method is not comparable with the buy and hold method as only a small percentage of equity was invested at any time.

15.4   TRADING GOLD STOCKS

This system exploited the strong correlation between gold mining stocks and gold bullion prices.

A problem in testing this system is that only a few gold mining stocks trade in the major US exchanges. After excluding all industrial metal and silver miners, the portfolio on test consisted of only 55 gold producers. Some of these stocks started trading fairly recently so a shorter testing period (from 11 September 1998 to 11 September 2007) than the one used in the oil stock system was used.

For the same reasons mentioned in the previous test, only long positions were considered.

Table 15.3 Profit/loss report of the intermarket gold stock system. In the first column is the profit of buying and holding all XAU components for the entire test duration. In the second column are profit statistics using 10 % of capital per trade and in the last column using a fixed $10 000 capital per trade. Comparison with the buy and hold is only meaningful using the first method, as the second method started with only one tenth the capital used by the buy-and-hold method.

System	Buy & hold	Gold stocks (% of equity)	Gold stocks (equal dollar)
Intermarket security		Gold (spot)	Gold (spot)
Number of stocks	16	55	55
Initial equity	$100 000	$100 000	$100 000
Capital/trade	$100 000	10 %	$10 000
Total net profit	$122 267	$243 105	$123 770
Profit/loss %	122 %	243 %	124 %
Annual percent gain/loss	14 %	27 %	14 %
Total number of trades	1	222	220
Winning trades	1	151	147
Losing trades	0	71	73
Percent profitable	100 %	68.0 %	66.8 %
Avg. winning trade	$122 267	$2107	$1117
Avg. losing trade	$0	−$1058	−$554
Ratio avg. win/avg. loss		1.99	2.02
Profitability coefficient		3.46	3.37
Profit factor		4.24	4.06
Drawdown %	−40.4 %	−3.7 %	−3.1 %
Date of max drawdown	11/17/00	6/7/05	11/30/99
Risk/reward	41.9 %	4.2 %	3.0 %
Start date/test	9/11/98	9/11/98	9/11/98
End date	9/10/07	9/10/07	9/10/07
Test period (years)	9.0	9.0	9.0
Trades/year	0.1	24.7	24.4
System Parameters			
Correlation days		500	500
IMO – days		200	200
IMO – buy		70	70
IMO – sell		7	7
Time exit – bars		80	80

The system was based on the regression divergence model discussed in Chapter 11 as it performed slightly better than the LRS method on preliminary testing. The double LRS method, used for trading oil stocks, could not be used as there was only a single intermarket security (gold) for calculating the divergence.

There were no variables to optimize, except for the momentum oscillator entry threshold. All additional entry conditions, used for the oil stock test above, were tested and included in the current system as they improved on the test performance.

Comparison test results for percent of equity and equal dollar capital per trade are shown in Table 15.3, the equity line, the yearly profits and the drawdown in Figures 15.5, 15.6 and 15.7 respectively.

Based on profit factor, profitability, and win/loss ratio criteria this system performed slightly better than the oil stock system. However, the total net profit was considerably less, mainly because the portfolio of the available gold stocks on test contained only 55 stocks, a quarter of the stocks contained in the corresponding oil stock portfolio. One way to increase total dollar profit is to enlarge the portfolio by adding Australian, British and Canadian gold miners. This should not be a problem as it is now possible, with certain online brokers like interactive Brokers, Internaxx, Etrade or SaxoBank, to trade international stocks using a single account.

The drawdown was considerably less than the oil stock system, exceeding 3 % of equity only three times during the nine-year test: Once in December 2000 (-3.4% of equity), during the end of gold's precipitous long-term decline, once in 2005 (-3.7% of equity) because of a short-term correction and once in 2006 (-3.3% of equity).

15.5 CONCLUSION

While the scope of this book is to demonstrate the efficacy of intermarket analysis when applied to market averages, the systems presented above demonstrate that it can be applied in a similar manner and just as profitably to stock trading. The examples presented in this chapter are by no means exhaustive of intermarket stock trading systems and the basic method can be used for trading stocks belonging in various other sectors, as long as the sector index data are readily available.

16
A Relative Strength Asset Allocation Trading System

The market can remain irrational longer than you can remain solvent.

–John Maynard Keynes

In the first chapter I presented a static asset allocation investment strategy where international stocks, commodities, bonds and forex were used to decrease the overall volatility of a properly structured portfolio while maintaining return characteristics. Diversification obviously reduces risk, and asset allocation analysis is important because it enables us to assign a value to the expected risk.

The main weakness of the static model, however, is that it relies on historical returns to calculate the risk-adjusted return of the portfolio asset allocation. Rather than rely on historical returns, a more comprehensive and dynamic approach is needed when making trading decisions. This criticism is generally valid as historical returns are very unlikely to be repeated in the future.

Take, for example, the performance of the stock market from 2000 to 2007. An investor who bought an S&P index fund in 2000 hasn't made any money, whereas another investor who bought the same index fund in 2003 has had a 70% return on his investment. In addition, historical returns are not the only variables that can change over time because, as I have demonstrated in Chapter 5, correlations between asset classes can also change. For example, the correlation between stocks and bonds has been highly unstable during the last four years, with the correlation coefficient alternating from positive to negative.

Thus developing timing strategies to dynamically allocate portfolio assets among a choice of investments can greatly enhance portfolio performance with no additional risk. Even during the strongest bull markets, not every investment rises at the same rate or at the same time. In addition, only a few investments, such as money market, precious metals, bonds, or certain commodities are less likely to lose money in a down market.

The goal of this study was to compare the performance of the static buy and hold with a dynamic asset allocation method. The search was on for the timing tool that would trigger the move to the strongest asset classes or sectors that would systematically keep the assets moving into the right instrument in approximately the right time frame. The positive benefits of this investment approach are obvious. A minor problem, however, is that it crosses regulatory boundaries as multiple accounts are needed to trade domestic and international stocks, futures and forex. Fortunately, it is now possible to do this with certain international brokers like Interactive Brokers, Saxobank or Internaxx.

The current method is based on the relative strength between an investment and a benchmark which, for the purposes of this study, was the S&P 500.

16.1   TESTING PROCEDURE

The test period covered was from 16 July 1999 to 27 November 2007, which covered a complete market cycle that included a bull and a bear market.

The system was tested on two different portfolios. The securities tested in the first simulation are depicted in Table 16.1 and include a wide variety of investments from all asset classes. They include one commodity index future (the GSCI), 13 international stock indices, four interest rate futures, four currencies and 15 commodity futures: four metal, two energy and nine agricultural contracts. The available data for international index futures did not cover the entire test period so I had to use data for the indices themselves. Of course the indices themselves cannot be traded but were, for testing purposes, a good enough approximation. The proliferation of exchange traded funds (ETF) gives traders a chance to profit from moves in commodities without the risk of leveraged futures contracts.

In the second simulation, for the benefit of investors who prefer to trade only stocks, I tested a wide variety of ETFs which included six commodity funds, 44 international country funds, 63 US sector funds, six bond funds, and four currency ETFs (see Table 16.2).

The test results were compared with returns of buying and holding a static diversified portfolio consisting of the SPY ETF (40 %), an emerging market ETF (5 %), a European equity ETF (5 %), bonds (10 %), the commodities included in the CRB Index (30 %) and the euro (10 %). The diversified portfolio composition and returns are depicted in Table 16.3. Although returns would have been better had I used the Goldman Sachs Commodity Index (GSCI) instead of the CRB Index, I preferred to use the latter as it was not so heavily weighted in energy (for the composition of the GSCI and CRB see also Chapter 4). In order to demonstrate the advantages of diversification, the results were also compared with buying and holding only the S&P 500 for the entire test duration.

Table 16.1 Futures, currencies, US sector and international indices included in the first test are depicted in the second column and the Reuters Datalink symbols in the last column. Reuters forex symbols are different from other vendors and usually they have the =suffix or the =R suffix (indicates Reuters platform data). Reuters also uses the @: prefix to indicate futures contracts and the c1 suffix to indicate continuous contracts which are created by merging different current month contracts on expiration.

A/A	Security Name	Symbol (Reuters)
1	Australia All Ordinaries	.AORD
2	Brazil Bovespa Index	.BVSP
3	BSE SENSEX (India)	.BSESN
4	CAC 40 Index	.FCHI
5	Dow Jones Euro Stoxx 50	.STOXX50E
6	Germany DAX	.GDAXI
7	Greece General Share	.ATG
8	Hong Kong Hang Seng	.HSI
9	Korea KOSPI	.KS11
10	Mexico IPC	.MXX
11	Moscow Times Index	.MTMS
12	Nikkei 225 Index	.N225
13	United Kingdom FTSE 100	.FTSE
14	Amex Pharmateutical Index	.DRG
15	Utility Index	.UTY
16	Australian Dollar	AUD=
17	British Pound	GBP=
18	Canadian Dollar-US Dollar	CADUSD=R
19	Japanese Yen-US Dollar	JPYUSD=R
20	Swiss Franc	RD-CHF=
21	Euro	RD-EUR=
22	Gold (cash)	XAU=
23	GOLDMAN SACHS COMMODITY INDEX	@:GIc1
24	COPPER HG ELECTRONIC	@:1HGc1
25	ALUMINUM COMEX COMPOSITE	@:ALc1
26	LIGHT CRUDE COMPOSITE	@:CLc1
27	NATURAL GAS COMPOSITE	@:NGc1
28	COTTON NO 2	@:CTc1
29	ORANGE JUICE	@:OJc1
30	SUGAR 11	@:SBc1
31	SOYBEANS COMPOSITE	@:Sc1
32	SOYBEAN OIL E-CBOT	@:ZLc1
33	WHEAT COMPOSITE	@:Wc1
34	CORN E-CBOT	@:ZCc1

(Continued)

Table 16.1 *(Continued)*

A/A	Security Name	Symbol (Reuters)
35	COFFEE C	@:KCc1
36	LIVE CATTLE	@:LCc1
37	100 OZ GOLD COMPOSITE	@:GCc1
38	MINI SILVER E-CBOT	@:ZZc1
39	3MTH EURO DOLLAR COMPOSITE	@:EDc1
40	US 10YR T-NOTES PIT COMPOSITE	@:TYc1
41	10YR BOND	@:CGBc1
42	5YR T-NOTE E-CBOT	@:ZFc1

The initial account size was $500 000 and an equal dollar amount of $30 000 per trade was specified for both simulations. Although investors typically trade futures on low margins, no margin leverage was used in the first trading simulation model as this would have distorted the equal allocation percentages. In actual trading the use of margin would increase the percentage return on account and percent drawdown but it wouldn't affect the other performance metrics.

All orders were executed at the opening price on the day following a system signal and execution costs were assumed to be $10. For simplicity's sake dividends were not included when in the market. It was assumed that the cumulative profits were held in an interest bearing account when out of the market and all open positions were closed on the last bar.

To develop and optimize the system rules and parameters, I used a portfolio of securities and similar indices not included in the samples on test, identifying parameter combinations and conditions that persisted in producing profits for the majority of the securities on test, even though they were not necessarily the optimum. The initial system consisted of a simple moving average crossover of the relative strength indicator, buy signals were generated when the relative strength crossed over its trigger and sell signals when it crossed under. This system, however, despite optimizing for both moving averages – the relative strength smoothing average and the trigger – produced less than satisfactory results. On plotting the signals on the chart it was evident that the system failed for the following reasons:

- sometimes in bear markets securities were selected just because they were stronger than the benchmark (the S&P 500) even though they were also in a downtrend. Most of these trades inevitably resulted in losses;
- whipsaw around the moving average;
- late signals which were triggered at the top or during highly overbought conditions.

To deal with these problems I decided to add the following additional conditions:

- The 25-day exponential moving average should be pointing up, to ensure that the security was in an uptrend.

- To avoid the problem of whipsawing the relative strength should also be pointing up.
- The stochastic indicator was used to filter out buy signals in overextended markets.
- The correlation coefficient was used to filter out securities that were highly correlated with the S&P 500 during bear markets as they did, sooner or later, follow the leader down.

Table 16.2 The exchange traded funds (ETF) included in the second test are depicted in the second column and their symbols in the last column.

A/A	Security Name	Symbol
1	Mexico Equity & Income	MXE
2	Chile Fund Inc.	CH
3	Morgan Stan Dw Eastern Europe	RNE
4	Templeton Russia & East Europe	TRF
5	Spdr Index Dj Stoxx 50 Fd	FEU
6	Malaysia Fund Inc.	MAY
7	Aberdeen Australia Equity Fd	IAF
8	Western Asset Emerging markets	EDF
9	Emerging Market Telecom Fd	ETF
10	Singapore Fd Inc.	SGF
11	Taiwan Greater China Fund	TFC
12	Indonesia Fund	IF
13	The Central Europe and Russia	CEE
14	Turkish Invest Fund	TKF
15	Templeton Emerging Markets Fund	EMF
16	iShares MSCI Italy	EWI
17	Thai Fund Inc.	TTF
18	China Fund Inc.	CHN
19	Japan Smaller Capitalization	JOF
20	iShares MSCI Switzerland	EWL
21	Templeton Dragon	TDF
22	iShares MSCI South Africa	EZA
23	iShares MSCI France	EWQ
24	iShares MSCI Sweden	EWD
25	BLDRS Emerging Markets 50 ADR Fd	ADRE
26	India Fund	IFN
27	Asia Pacific Fund	APB
28	iShares S&P Europe 350	IEV
29	iShares MSCI Germany	EWG
30	iShares MSCI Spain	EWP
31	iShares S&P Latin America 40	ILF
32	iShares MSCI United Kingdom	EWU
33	iShares MSCI Australia	EWA

(Continued)

Table 16.2   *(Continued)*

A/A	Security Name	Symbol
34	iShares MSCI South korea	EWY
35	iShares MSCI Malaysia	EWM
36	iShares FTSE/Xinhua China 25 Index	FXI
37	iShares MSCI EAFE	EFA
38	iShares MSCI Hong Kong	EWH
39	iShares MSCI Taiwan	EWT
40	iShares MSCI Brazil	EWZ
41	iShares MSCI Japan	EWJ
42	iShares MSCI Singapore	EWS
43	iShares MSCI Mexico	EWW
44	iShares MSCI Cananada	EWC
45	iShares DJ Consumer Services Fund	IYC
46	iShares DJ Financial services Fund	IYG
47	iShares DJ Consumer Goods Sector	IYK
48	iShares S&P SmalCap 600	IJR
49	iShares S&P SmalCap 600 Value	IJS
50	iShares S&P SmalCap 600 Growth	IJT
51	iShares S&P MidCap 400 Growth	IJK
52	iShares S&P 500/Barra Value	IVE
53	iShares S&P 500/Barra Growth	IVW
54	iShares Russell 1000 Value	IWD
55	iShares Russell 1000 Growth	IWF
56	iShares Russell 2000	IWM
57	iShares DJ Industrial Sector	IYJ
58	iShares DJ Healthcare Sector	IYH
59	iShares DJ US Energy Fund	IYE
60	iShares DJ US Basic Materials	IYM
61	iShares DJ Technology Sector	IYW
62	iShares DJ Telecommunications	IYZ
63	iShares DJ Trasportation Average	IYT
64	iShares Nasdaq Biotechnology	IBB
65	iShares DJ Dividend Index Fund	DVY
66	iShares DJ US Real Estate	IYR
67	iShares DJ Utilities Index Fund	IDU
68	iShares S&P Global Utilities	JXI
69	HOLDRS Utilities	UTH
70	HOLDRS Telecom ETF	TTH
71	HOLDRS Biotech ETF	BBH
72	HOLDRS Software	SWH
73	HOLDRS Pharmaceutical	PPH
74	HOLDRS Regional Bank ETF	RKH
75	HOLDRS Retail ETF	RTH
76	HOLDRS Oil Service ETF	OIH

Table 16.2   *(Continued)*

A/A	Security Name	Symbol
77	HOLDRS Semiconductor	SMH
78	HOLDRS Wireless	WMH
79	HOLDRS B2B Internet ETF	BHH
80	HOLDRS Internet Architecture ETF	IAH
81	HOLDRS Internet Infrastructure ETF	IIH
82	HOLDRS Internet ETF	HHH
83	HOLDRS Broadband ETF	BDH
84	iPath S&P Goldman sachs Crude Oil	OIL
85	PowerShares DB Commodity ETF	DBC
86	iShares G. Sachs Natural resources	IGE
87	iShares Silver Trust ETF	SLV
88	SPDR Gold Shares	GLD
89	PowerShares DB Agriculture Fund	DBA
90	ProShares UltraShort Real estate	SRS
91	ProShares UltraShort Financials	SKF
92	ProShares UltraShort Dow	DXD
93	ProShares UltraShort Russell 2000	TWM
94	ProShares UltraShort S&P500	SDS
95	SPDRs Select Sector Health care	XLV
96	SPDRs Select r Consumer Staple	XLP
97	SPDRs Select Discretionary	XLY
98	SPDRs Select Sector Technology	XLK
99	SPDR S&P Homebuilders ETF	XHB
100	SPDRs Select Sector Utilities	XLU
101	SPDRs Select Sector Industrials	XLI
102	SPDRs Select Sector Materials ETF	XLB
103	SPDRs Select Sector Energy	XLE
104	SPDRs Select Sector Financials	XLF
105	SPDRs S&P 500 Trust ETF	SPY
106	PowerShares QQQ Trust	QQQQ
107	PowerShares Dynamic Retail Portfolio	PMR
108	DIAMONDS Trust ETF	DIA
109	Flaherty & Crumrine Preferred Inc	PFO
110	Morgan Stan Emerging market Debt	MSD
111	Dreyfus Stra Mun Bond Fd	DSM
112	iShares Lehman 7–10Year T-Bond	IEF
113	iShares Lehman 20+ Year T-Bond	TLT
114	Aberdeen Asia-Pacific Income Fd	FAX
115	PowerShares US Dollar Bearish Fd	UDN
116	Rydex CurrencyShares Australian $	FXA
117	Rydex CurrencyShares Euro	FXE
118	Rydex CurrencyShares Yen	FXY

Table 16.3 Composition and performance of the static diversified portfolio from 16 July 1999 to 29 November 2007. Its performance was compared with the dynamic asset allocation system in Table 16.4.

Asset	Symbol	Allocation	Profit/Loss
SPDRs S&P ETF	SPY	40 %	$(5100)
Asia Pacific Fund	APB	5 %	$49 547
S&P Europe 350	IEV	5 %	$13 753
Bonds		10 %	$15 826
Euro	EUR	10 %	$32 413
Commodities	CRB	30 %	$83 095
Total		100 %	$189 534

Thus the final system was defined as follows.

Buy Conditions

The relative strength indicator was smoothed with a 150-day moving average. The period was rather long, but nevertheless it was the most consistent in producing profitable signals for the majority of the securities on test.

A buy signal was generated if the relative strength crossed above its 120-day moving average and at the same time the following conditions were also true:

- The 2-day rate of change of the 25-day exponential moving average was positive.
- The 20-day linear regression slope of the relative strength was positive.
- The correlation coefficient between the security and the S&P was less than 0.5.
- The 100-day stochastic indicator was less than 80.
- The 25-day moving average of the volume flow indicator was positive.

This last money flow condition was introduced to ensure that the money was flowing in and not out of the security. This indicator was tested in my July 2004 article "Volume Flow Performance" (see Bibliography) with more than satisfactory results.

There was a problem, however, with this indicator, as Reuters provided no volume data for the indices. Volume data for the futures contracts were also unreliable as they were split in different calendar or size (mini or full size) contracts. The volume flow indicator was therefore used only in the second (ETF) test. In the first test this was substituted by a different condition that did not require any volume data. The additional condition alleviated the whipsaw problem even further by executing long signals only when the relative strength made a new 250-day high.

Sell Conditions

A sell signal was generated if the relative strength crossed below its 90-day moving average and at the same time, in order to exclude false whipsaw signals, its 3-day rate of change was less than −0.5 %. An additional money flow condition was added, but only in the second test, where volume data were available.

16.2 DISCUSSION OF RESULTS

The test results of the relative strength system are summarized in Table 16.4, the equity line in Figure 16.3, and the monthly profits of the ETF system is depicted in

Table 16.4 Test results of the relative strength system for the period from 28 August 2000 to 27 November 2007. Column 2 is the return of buying and holding the SPY ETF, in Column 3 is the performance of buying and holding a strategically diversified static portfolio, in Column 4 is the test results of the relative strength test on a futures and international index selection and in column 5 test results on an ETF portfolio. All tests were profitable and outperformed both benchmarks by a wide margin.

Test	Buy & hold	Buy & hold	Test I	Test II
Securities on test	SPY	Static Portfolio	Futures	ETF
Intermarket security			S&P 500	S&P 500
Capital/trade	$500 000	$500 000	$30 000	$30 000
Total capital	$500 000	$500 000	$500 000	$500 000
Total profit	($15 074)	$189 534	$480 641	$600 797
Profit/loss %	−3.0 %	37.9 %	76 %	120 %
Annualized % gain/loss	−0.4 %	4.5 %	8.1 %	11 %
Total number of trades	1	6	50	139
Winning trades	1	5	37	83
Losing trades	0	1	13	56
Percent profitable	100 %	83 %	74.0 %	59.7 %
Gross profit	−$15 074	$194 634	$420 908	$594 362
Gross loss	$0	−$5100	−$40 267	−$98 565
Avg. winning trade	$0	€38 927	$11 376	$7161
Avg. losing trade	(€15 074)	−$5100	−$3097	−$1760
Avg. win/avg. loss			3.67	4.07
Profitability coefficient			5.26	4.00
Profit factor			10.45	6.03
Max. drawdown	−$246 058	−$42 066	−$22 801	−$42 916
Date of max drawdown	10-11-02	07-24-02	5-5-03	12-5-02
Max. % drawdown	−49.2 %	−8.4 %	−4.6 %	−8.6 %
Max. losing trade	−€15074	−€5100	−$7419	−$7260
Max. consecutive losses			5	8
Std deviation of equity	4.46 %	3.93 %	1.78 %	2.58 %
Risk-adjusted return	−0.1 %	1.2 %	4.6 %	4.5 %
Sharpe ratio	−1.0	0.1	2.3	2.9
Avg. trade length – days	2649.0	2649.0	495	218
Trades/year	0.1	0.8	7.0	19.2

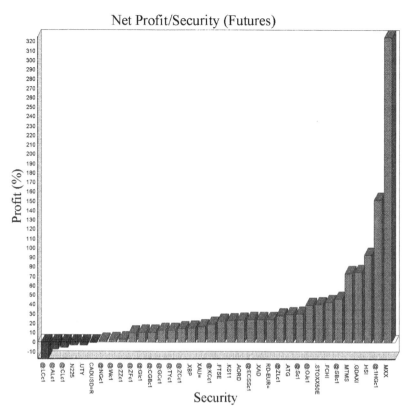

Figure 16.1 Security profit distribution of the first relative strength test on futures. The most profitable trades involved the Mexico IPC Index and copper futures which soared 325 % and 150 % respectively. The worst trade involved cattle futures which lost 17 %.

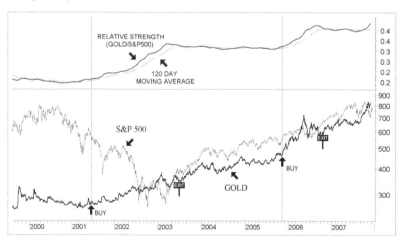

Figure 16.2 Composite chart of gold (cash prices) in bold and the S&P 500 from May 2000 until November 2007. The 150-day relative strength with its 120-day moving average (dotted line) is plotted in the top window. Buy and sell signals are superimposed on the chart. The last trade was never closed.

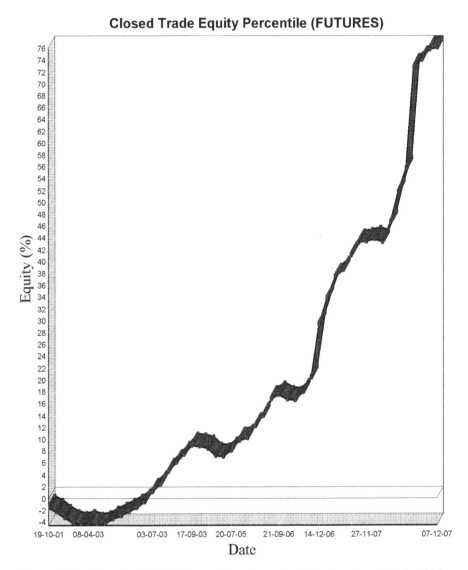

Figure 16.3 Closed equity (%). The worst drawdown of –4.6 % of equity occurred on 5 May 2003 and was mainly due to losses from the Australian All Ordinaries Index and Aluminum futures.

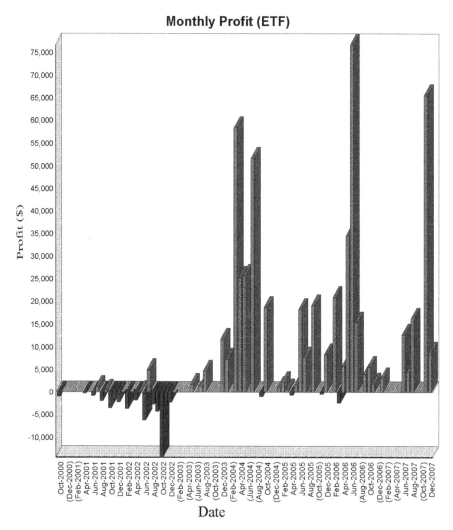

Figure 16.4 Monthly profit distribution of the relative strength ETF system (Test II). The system did not start making any money until the end of 2003, mainly because it was too heavily weighted in stock sector ETF. The worst drawdown of −8.6 % of equity occurred on 5 December 2002 and was mainly due to losses from the energy sector ETF (IYE), the health care sector ETF (XLV) and the Templeton Dragon Fund (TDF). The best performing ETF was the iShares Latin America 40 (ILF).

Figure 16.4. You can also see in Figure 16.2 typical buy and sell signals generated by the system, in this particular case for the Gold futures contract. For comparison purposes, the buy and hold method returns for both a 100 % US equity and a static diversified portfolio are also included in the second and third columns. The returns using the dynamic as compared to the buy and hold or static approach are impressive. The futures portfolio made over $480 000 compared to a $15 000 loss suffered by the investor who bought and held the S&P ETF during the 7-year test duration.

Furthermore, the dynamic asset allocation model added value over the static diversified portfolio with a reasonable turnover of six to seven trades per year. Over the 7-year period, examined within the confines of this test, the dynamic strategy increased the average diversified static portfolio yearly annualized return by 660 basis points, from 4.5 % to 11 % per year, and increased the Sharpe ratio by 2.80 points. None of the systems made any money during the 2000–2002 bear market but, unlike the S&P, they managed to get through with minimal losses. The futures portfolio (Test I) which had the least exposure to equities, suffered the lowest drawdown and had the highest risk-adjusted return. The best performing commodities were copper futures (HG) and No. 11 sugar futures (SB) and the best performing equity indices were the Mexico IPC Index (MXX), the Hang Seng (HSI) and the Russian Moscow Times Index (MTMS). The worst performers were live cattle (LC), aluminum futures (AL) and the Nikkei 225 Index. These are depicted graphically in Figure 16.1.

The ETF portfolio, on the other hand, had heavy exposure to equities and as a consequence suffered a rather heavy drawdown during the 2001–2002 bear market. The maximum drawdown of $42 000 or 8.6 % of equity occurred in December 2002. This was, however, small change compared to the devastating $246 000 (or 50 % of equity) drawdown suffered by the investor who bought and held an S&P index fund.

The best performing ETFs were the iShares S&P Latin America 40 Index fund (ILF), the iShares MSCI Singapore Index Fund (EWS) and the Goldman Sachs Natural Resources Fund (IGE). The worst performing ETFs were the Asia Pacific Fund, the iShares MSCI Switzerland Index Fund (EWL) and the SPDRs Select Sector Health Care Fund (XLV).

By looking at the buy and sell signals on the chart and examining some of the worst losers a common pattern emerged:

- The majority of the losing trades occurred in 2002, during the last phase of the bear market.
- Some of the worst performing ETFs involved defensive sectors like health or energy which outperformed the S&P 500 during the initial bear market phase but failed to follow through and reversed during the last and final part of the bear market.

In an effort to alleviate some of the losses, I tried adding a stop-loss condition but decided to abandon it as it stopped out too many profitable trades as well, reducing considerably the overall system profitability.

16.3   CONCLUSION

The current system may not enter or exit a trade at the exact bottom or top but it *will* systematically keep your assets moving into the right instrument in approximately the right time frame. Investment survival depends on an investor's ability to adapt to the market and this can only be achieved by a dynamic asset allocation model.

In the current system, because of the limitations of the programming language, only binary asset selection has been employed but nonetheless results were impressive. A selection process which would combine several assets at once would of course be preferable. This could be implemented by starting out with a diversified portfolio similar to the one described in Table 16.3, and revising the portfolio composition monthly, replacing the weaker assets or sectors with the stronger ones.

One of the most significant disadvantages of using the relative strength method in trading is probably the fact that the indicator always produces signals, even in declining markets. In other words, in a bear market, the danger exists that in a selection decision based on relative strength alone, preference will be given to the defensive assets that decline less, but end up losing money none the less. This presents a challenge to the reader for possible improvements which could be implemented by combining the current system with a classic technical system; the relative strength indicator adding value by filtering out trades involving weaker asset classes.

17
Forex Trading Using Intermarket Analysis

Human decisions affecting the future, whether personal, or political or economic, cannot depend on strict mathematical expectation, since the basis for making such calculations does not exist.

–John Maynard Keynes

17.1 THE FOREX MARKET

The foreign exchange market, commonly referred to as the "forex" or "FX" market, is the largest and most liquid market in the world as the 3.3 trillion USD daily turnover dwarfs the combined turnover of all the world's stock and bond markets. Banks, import/export companies and multinationals, as well as hedge funds and other large institutions trade trillions of dollars on the forex market every day. Because of their superior liquidity, forex markets are less prone to manipulation by even the largest players, although the central banks intervene from time to time to affect the price movements of their respective currencies. Such interventions, however, can only influence currency values for short periods as market trends tend to move currencies against the central bank. One example is the Bank of Japan intervening in order to push down the value of the yen in order to promote exports.

Some countries, such as China, manage the exchange rates of their currency. In this chapter I will focus on countries with floating exchange rates.

Forex is an exchange where one country's currency is exchanged for another's through a "floating" exchange rate system. A trade is executed with the simultaneous buying of one currency while selling the other.

Although the FX market is not centralized on an exchange, two electronic brokers – EBS and Reuters – dominate the interbank market. The Electronic Broking Service

(EBS) partnership was set up in 1990 to challenge the monopoly that the Reuters' electronic system enjoyed. It is owned by a consortium of 16 banks including Citibank, Chase Manhattan, Credit Suisse First Boston, JP Morgan and UBS. The system connects all member banks to each other so they can buy or sell currency. This was one of the first electronic exchanges and that is why the FX market has been slow, compared with equity markets, to develop internet-based trading. A new generation of web-based products using internet technology is trying to give electronic access to a wider range of participants, including corporate treasury departments, hedge funds, and even independent forex traders. Among these new systems are Irish e-commerce firm Cognotec, Seattle-based Financial Market Solutions (FMS), and New York's MatchbookFX. In addition, some banks already have or are developing web-based systems of their own to trade with clients. But most bankers concede that the next stage will be a system that connects not only clients and banks, but banks and other banks. The system that achieves enough critical mass to become indispensable could quickly turn into the industry standard, sidelining other competing systems.

The forex market is open 24 hours a day, every working day. It begins trading on Sunday at 5pm US EST in Wellington, New Zealand and follows the sun to Sydney, Tokyo, Seoul, Hong Kong, Singapore, Bombay, Dubai, Moscow, Athens, Frankfurt, Geneva, Paris, London, New York, Chicago, Los Angeles and Honolulu before starting again. Markets stay open 24 hours during that period and therefore gaps are never seen on daily charts, because the close of previous day is the open of the next.

While it is possible to trade a variety of international currencies, seven are by far the most popular, providing six currency pairs with the US dollar acting as the benchmark in each. The currencies are the euro, the US dollar, the yen, the British pound, the Swiss franc, the Canadian dollar and the Australian dollar and their market share is:

- The euro (EUR/USD)   28 %
- The yen (USD/JPY)   7 %
- The British pound (GBP/USD)   14 %
- The Australian dollar (AUD/USD)   5 %
- The Swiss franc (USD/CHF)   4 %
- The Canadian dollar (USD/CAD)   4 %

Pairings with the US dollar are known as "majors" and non-US dollar pairings are known as "crosses". For example, a popular cross is the GBP/EUR or the EUR/JPY. Cross pairs can be derived from the majors; for example, the EUR/JPY is the EUR/USD divided by the USD/JPY. Exchange rates must be consistent across all currencies, or else it will be possible to make riskless profits by arbitrage trading cross against major pairs.

The main trading systems used in forex are those that follow trends (a popular maxim in the market is "the trend is your friend"), or systems that buy or sell on breakouts. This is because economic indicators often cause large price movements that tend to last for prolonged periods of time.

Advantages in Forex Trading

Apart from the superior market liquidity, which helps ensure price stability, forex trading has the following advantages over equity trading:

- *No commissions*: There are no commissions in forex trading, only the point spread. The spread is not fixed but can vary according to the broker, the currency pair, liquidity and volatility and it is usually 1–4 points or pips (see also about hidden commissions below).
- *Increased leverage*: The margin required by most forex brokers is only 1–2 %, compared to a 50 % margin required for equity markets and 5–15 % for futures.
- *Leveraged carry interest*: When you're long a currency pair, your account is credited with the interest of the first currency and debited with the interest of the second currency. For example, if you're long the USD/JPY, you earn $9.17 interest per day on each contract of 100 000 units, even if you've only put in $2000 as your 2 % margin.
- *Continuous trading* makes it possible to respond to breaking news immediately, day or night.
- *Liquidity* and *24-hour trading* contributes to less slippage and more efficient execution of stop loss or limit orders.
- There is *less random noise* (that is, volatility) in the forex markets, and trends are generally of a long-term nature.
- You can *diversify* your portfolio with foreign currencies. This is particularly effective in declining stock markets, just where it is needed most.
- Currencies tend to follow fairly *strict rules*, and are therefore more predictable using technical indicators than equity markets.

Of course nothing is perfect, especially in the financial markets, and forex trading can have some major problems:

- *Commissions*: When choosing a broker, it is essential to do your homework. Most brokers advertise "commission free" but is it really? How do brokers make money to cover their platform costs? In practice, brokers conceal points to the price spread in lieu of commissions. The interbank spreads are usually 1–2 pips but brokers usually widen them by 1 or more pips. For example, assuming that the interbank or real quote in the yen (USD/JPY) is 104.89/104.90 (bid/ask), the broker's platform will show 104.87/104.92. If a trader buys $1 000 000 at 104.92, the broker will debit his client's account with 104 920 000 yen whereas he would have to pay only 104 900 000 to his bank in order to cover the trade. The 20 000 yen ($190) is the hidden commission that the trader has to pay twice (once for opening and once for closing his position).
- *Leverage*, as long as it is used properly, is a great tool. There are many brokers today that offer 100 to 1 (1 % margin) and even 200 to 1 leverage. That means

that you could open an account with $10 000 and control $2 000 000. This can be disastrous, especially when the market moves against you. For example, if you are long the USD/JPY and the yen goes up by more than 0.5 % then your entire equity will be wiped out. This is not something that happens only rarely, as there is a 20 % chance that the yen will go up by more than half a percent in a day and a 6 % chance that it will go up by more than one percent based on 15 years of historical data.

- *Data*: Developing a mechanical trading system to trade forex requires back-testing. And back-testing requires high quality historical price data. There are serious problems with the consistency and accuracy of data obtained from different providers which is surprising considering the size and liquidity of the foreign exchange market. In the forex market, unlike the future and stock markets, there is no central exchange to speak of and consequently no "official" historical data exist as such. Various forex data vendors combine data collected from a number of banks. Some of them filter the data in order to remove outliers and low volume trades. As a result historical data can vary according to the number of banks being used to compile the data and the filtering method used. Another issue affecting mainly the consistency of the opening and closing prices is the time zone in which the data provider is located, as every source reports the open or close at different times, which of course would give different prices. Yet another issue causing disparities in the daily extreme prices is the way that banks determine the high and low. A bank will call a high or low depending on how much volume went through at that rate. For example, let's suppose that the USD/JPY fell to a 103.55 intraday low but only $2 million went through at that rate. Some banks will call that the official low whereas other banks will ignore it and report a higher low of 103.60 that was traded on higher volume. This is not a problem if large amounts are traded, but can be confusing to small traders who can sometimes find that their trade went through at a price below the official low or above the official high of the day. Depending upon the time frame and trading frequency, this disparity can be highly significant and can create serious problems in back-testing mechanical systems if the trading model is developed and tested on a different data set from the one upon which it will actually be traded. For a realistic mechanical system you will need to use the same data provider as your broker, otherwise you may find that your actual trading performance differs considerably from the system's predicted results.

- *Carry trades* are popular in the FX market as they guarantee traders extra return on their medium or longer term positions. If you are a long-term trader, however, it is essential to choose the right broker, because you may find you are paying instead of receiving the carry interest as some FX brokers pay less than market rates on long balances and charge considerably more on short cash balances. In addition, they apply a tier method when calculating interest to long cash balances (similar to the insurance deductibles). Let's consider the following example which simulates a real trade using a popular broker. You entered a long position to buy $100 000 and sell 10 400 000 yen on 23 May 2008 intending to take advantage of the near zero interest rates in the yen. This particular broker credits long US dollar balances over $10 000 with the Fed Funds overnight rate less 0.5 % (which comes to $2.05 - 0.50 = 1.55\%$) and debits short yen balances with JPY Libor minus 1.5 % (which is $0.56 - 1.5 = -2.06\%$). Supposing that you reversed the trade in a year and assuming, for the sake of simplicity, that the USD/JPY rate has not changed then your carry trade interest would consist of the interest received on the long USD position (which would be ($100 000 - $10 000)*1.55 % = $1395) minus the interest that your broker would have charged you on the short yen position (10 400 000*2.06 %/104 = $2060). When you close the trade you would be surprised to find out that instead of receiving the interest spread of $1490 (100 000*1.49 %) you had to pay $665. Your broker pocketed the whole amount of the carry interest from his bank plus $665 from you which comes to a total of $2155 without even taking any currency risks at all! This is on top of the point spread that he made on each trade.

17.2   FOREX FUNDAMENTALS

When it comes to trading, like anything else, you have to have a very good handle not only on technicals but also fundamentals. Luckily, unlike with stocks, in forex there are only few economies to look at.

Currency prices are affected by a variety of economic and political conditions, the most important of which are interest rates and, to a lesser degree, inflation and political stability.

One of the main driving forces behind foreign exchange trends is the interest rate spread between the currencies in the pair to be traded. Although such interest rate differentials may not appear very large, they are of great significance in a highly leveraged position. Generally, economic strength and political stability during the business cycle can lead to higher interest rates and thus a higher currency.

However, it is by no means a certainty that the currency with the higher interest rate will be stronger. If the reason for the high interest rate is runaway inflation or excessive government budget deficits, it may undermine confidence in the currency and override the benefits perceived from the high interest rate. Moreover, high interest rates can be a disadvantage to a nation in the long term, because they make it more difficult to compete with countries enjoying lower rates.

On the other hand economic weakness can lead to lower interest rates as central banks attempt to improve conditions. Because this process often involves increasing the money supply, a country's currency usually falls in value as a response.

In addition, the following economic reports, statistics or news can also affect currency exchange rates:

- *Trade balance*: This is a measure of the difference between imports and exports of tangible goods and services. Typically, a nation that runs a substantial trade deficit has a weak currency due to the continued commercial selling of the currency. However, this can be offset by financial investment flows for extended periods of time. The United States has been running a substantial trade deficit in recent years and changes in this figure can affect the US dollar significantly. US trade figures are released monthly.

- *FOMC meetings*: The Federal Open Market Committee holds eight regularly scheduled meetings per year. At these meetings, the Committee reviews economic and financial conditions and determines the appropriate stance of monetary policy by adjusting the overnight discount rate (which is the interest rate charged to borrow directly from the Federal Reserve Bank to meet regulator reserve requirements). The Fed may also attempt to change the federal funds rate (the interest rate that banks charge other banks to lend their surplus balances at the Federal Reserve) through the use of open market operations like purchasing and selling government securities. With this mechanism, the FOMC attempts to affect price levels in order to keep inflation within the target range while maintaining stable economic growth and employment. Changes in rates affect interest rates for consumer loans, mortgages, bonds, and the exchange rate of the US dollar. Increases in rates or even expectations of increases tend to cause the dollar to appreciate, while rate decreases cause the currency to depreciate. Almost as important as what the Fed does with interest rates is the statement that they release which can sometimes reveal what they might do in the future.

- *ECB rate announcements*: The European Central Bank rate announcements are usually well anticipated and the actual decision does not tend to impact the market a lot. The ECB President's press conference, however, is more important because it can provide a clue on the likelihood of further rate changes. Often, the language used in the press conference holds important signals on how the ECB feels about inflation and the economy.

- *BOE rate decision*: The main task of the Bank of England's Monetary Policy Committee is to set the monetary stance by fixing the overnight borrowing rate, which is crucial in determining short-term rates. The Bank of England Monetary Policy Committee also issues a statement with every rate decision. When it comes to interest rates, the future direction of rates is generally far more important than its current rate and because the decision itself is normally highly anticipated, the wording of the BOE statement is usually even more important than the actual interest rate level.

- *Consumer Price Index (CPI)*: This is a measure of the average level of prices of a fixed basket of goods and services purchased by consumers. The monthly reported changes in CPI are widely followed as an inflation indicator. Rising consumer price inflation is normally associated with the expectation of higher short-term interest rates and may therefore be supportive for a currency, although significant inflationary pressure will often lead to an undermining of the long-term confidence in the currency involved.

- *Producer Price Index (PPI)*: This is a measure of the average level of prices of a fixed basket of goods received in primary markets by producers. The monthly

PPI figures exclude food and energy and can therefore obscure the more important consumer inflation trend.

- *Quarterly GDP figures*: This is the broadest measure of aggregate economic activity available. A high GDP figure is often associated with the expectations of higher interest rates, which is frequently positive, at least in the short term, for the currency involved.
- *Housing starts*: High construction activity is usually associated with increased economic activity and can therefore be supportive of the involved currency. Housing starts are one of the earliest indicators of the housing market, only trailing building permits in timeliness.
- *Building permits*: This figure is used as the earliest indicator for developments in the housing market as issuing a building permit is the first step in the construction process. An increase in building permits implies an increase in investment and general optimism about the economy.
- *US non-farm payrolls*: Monthly changes in payroll employment reflect the net number of new jobs created or lost during the month. Large increases in payroll employment are seen as signs of strong economic activity that could eventually lead to higher interest rates that are supportive of the currency, at least in the short term. This report is released on the first Friday of each month and tends to move markets.
- *Durable goods orders*: This is a measure of the new orders placed with domestic manufacturers for immediate and future delivery of factory hard goods. Monthly percent changes reflect the rate of change of such orders. Durable goods orders are measured in nominal terms and can therefore be misleading as they include the effects of inflation. The PPI growth rate must be subtracted in order to obtain the inflation-adjusted durable goods orders. Rising durable goods orders are again associated with stronger economic activity.
- *Michigan sentiment figures in the US, the German business climate or IFO index, and the Tankan quarterly survey in Japan*: The University of Michigan Confidence Survey is considered one of the foremost indicators of US consumer sentiment. It assesses consumer confidence regarding personal finances, business conditions and purchasing power based on hundreds of telephone surveys. This number is released monthly and tends to move markets as it is a leading indicator of an economic downturn. The IFO index is equally important as Germany is responsible for approximately a quarter of the total Euro-zone GDP and it is therefore viewed as a significant economic health indicator for the Euro-zone as a whole. The Tankan Survey is released quarterly by Japan's central bank, and measures business confidence in Japan. The report is based on a survey sent out to corporations and it covers business conditions, supply and demand conditions, sales and profits, capital expenditure, employment, etc. The results can provide some insight into upcoming monetary policy and interest rates and are used to formulate monetary policy.
- *Political events* such as G7 meetings.
- *News*: National elections and the war in Iraq are examples of events that have affected currency values.

In simple terminology, news drives the market; whether that news is economic or political makes no difference. However, you should keep in mind that it is easy to blame an obvious news event because the market tends to build up a vulnerability and then wait for any reasonably appropriate event as a catalyst to extenuate the built up tension.

17.3   THE CARRY TRADE

Few people can resist the lure of free money and hence the popularity of cross-currency carry trades. In a currency carry trade, the speculator borrows money in a low-interest rate currency and buys higher-yielding assets in a different currency. Today, the low-rate currency is usually the Japanese yen; higher yielding assets are bonds, currencies like the Australian dollar, the New Zealand dollar or the British pound but sometimes more volatile assets such as emerging market equities. The biggest risk is generally that the exchange rate moves against you – the higher-interest rate currency rapidly devalues, reducing the value of your assets relative to your borrowing. Also, these transactions are generally done with a lot of leverage, so a small movement in exchange rates can result in huge losses unless hedged appropriately. A popular hedging method is buying a three-month forward option on the yen at the Chicago Mercantile Exchange.

While the yen-carry trade can be profitable, there's no such thing as a free lunch. Playing the wide spread between the cost of money in Japan and other higher-interest rate markets in the end may turn out to be a fool's game.

The following is an example of a scenario for disaster: As we head into the economic slowdown, speculators who borrow in yen to invest in risky cyclical assets will cut their losses, bail out and buy yen to repay debt. A rising yen would put interest rate carry trades positions under water, causing them to sell off and head back into the yen, and so on in a vicious circle.

17.4   TRADING THE JAPANESE YEN

The yen is the third most widely traded currency in the world, after the US dollar and the euro, and is traded worldwide by banks, corporations, institutions, hedge funds, speculators and commercial hedgers. Because of the big interest rate differential with the other currencies, the yen is also very popular among the "big boys" because of the "leveraged carry interest" mentioned above.

The yen is traded 24 hours a day in the forex interbank markets but yen futures can also be traded on the Chicago Mercantile Exchange (CME), the New York Board of Trade (NYBOT) or the CME GLOBEX system electronically. Yen futures trade on the CME from 9:30 to 14:00 under the symbol JY, and from 8:30 to 16:00 on the GLOBEX under the symbol 6J. The lowest increment (pip) is 0.000001 and the contract size is ¥12 500 000. For the benefit of small traders, the GLOBEX has recently introduced the e-mini (symbol J7) which is half (¥6 250 000) the full-sized contract. On the NYBOT the symbols are YY and SN for the full sized and e-mini contracts respectively.

Since 1999 (except for a brief weakness in 2002) the yen has been moving in a sideways range, between 102 and 125, with the natural equilibrium at around 115. However, it broke out in March with the dollar sinking to as low as 96 yen to the dollar as liquidity was withdrawn by carry traders, despite interventions by the Bank of Japan.

The Japanese government would love a weak yen, perhaps as low as 125 yen to the dollar, to help promote exports, making them more competitive with cheaper exports from China. On the other hand, if the US deficit continues to expand, the dollar/yen will get weaker, not because the Japanese economy is doing better but because the US deficit is getting fatter.

Speculators and commercial hedgers who trade currency futures often use technical analysis to determine trading signals. Most of these indicators (for example moving averages) exploit price trends, while others exploit price volatility.

I'll have to admit that trying to trade classic moving average crossover entries in the traditional sense has never worked for me. Such a simple approach works great in trending markets but will slaughter your account in sideways markets. Admittedly, the methods I use to trade with today have a few more components than two moving averages on a chart, and almost always include intermarket indicators.

The yen, like the dollar and the euro, correlates better with interest rates and recently (because of the "carry trade") with equity indices rather than commodity prices (as is the case with the Australian or Canadian dollar).

In Table 17.1 you can see the correlation between 1–20 day percent changes of the yen and the S&P 500, the Nikkei 225, the euro, the dollar index, the 10-year Treasury yield (TNX) and Japanese Government Bond futures (JGB) using up to 11 years of variable time spans.

It is clear from Table 17.1 that, mainly because of the "carry trade" the absolute correlation with all related markets (except perhaps the dollar index), has been increasing at a steady pace when using more recent data for the correlation calculations and this is more pronounced in the case of equity indices. For example, the correlation of daily changes between the yen and the S&P 500 has increased from nearly zero to a negative correlation of −0.373 during the last two years. Similarly, the correlation of daily changes between the yen and the 10-year Treasury yield (TNX) also increased significantly from nearly zero to a moderately strong value of −0.49. The strengthening in the trend of the negative correlation between the yen and the Nikkei 225 is more evident when using 10 or more days of price differences.

The highest and diachronically persistent correlation was with the dollar index and the TNX and they were both used to develop a trading system using the regression divergence indicator and the disparity indicator.

Table 17.1 Pearson's correlation of daily and 1–20 day (4 week) percentage changes between the yen (YEN/USD) and related forex, interest rates and equity indices using 2–11 year of data from 1 January 1997 to 31 December 2007. In the first column is the number of years of data used. The TNX is the 10-year Treasury yield, and the JP Bond is the 10-year Japanese Government bond futures (JGB). Unfortunately, data for the Japanese Bond has been available only since 14 March 2005. Notice the increasing trend of negative correlations between the yen and equity indices as the older data are discarded. The yen is expressed in dollars per yen (for example 0.0096154) and not in the usual yen per USD (for example 104).

Years	S&P 500	Nikkei 225	Euro	Dollar Index	TNX	JP Bond
			Correlation of daily % changes			
11	−0.09	0.048	0.342	−0.507	−0.083	n/a
6	−0.145	−0.02	0.478	−0.59	−0.29	n/a
3	−0.243	−0.113	0.417	−0.53	−0.377	0.027
2	**−0.373**	−0.125	0.36	−0.487	−0.493	0.029
			Correlation of weekly % changes			
11	−0.028	0.068	0.345	−0.534	−0.05	n/a
6	−0.085	−0.091	0.5	−0.62	−0.275	n/a
3	−0.167	−0.263	0.5	−0.598	−0.383	0.147
2	−0.259	−0.3	0.456	−0.559	−0.488	0.183
			Correlation of 10 day % changes			
11	0.014	−0.022	0.352	−0.541	−0.11	n/a
6	−0.076	−0.09	0.54	−0.65	−0.285	n/a
3	−0.24	−0.343	0.547	−0.637	−0.43	0.238
2	−0.312	−0.393	0.535	−0.615	−0.55	0.335
			Correlation of 15 day % changes			
11	0.011	−0.036	0.37	−0.556	−0.182	n/a
6	−0.07	−0.09	0.56	−0.67	−0.28	n/a
3	−0.298	−0.39	0.6	−0.685	−0.447	0.29
2	**−0.397**	**−0.457**	**0.581**	**−0.653**	**−0.56**	0.377
			Correlation of 20 day % changes			
11	0.046	0.06	0.375	−0.554	−0.186	n/a
6	−0.065	−0.09	0.574	−0.675	−0.27	n/a
3	−0.33	−0.4	0.61	**−0.684**	−0.47	0.37
2	−0.45	**−0.48**	0.56	−0.63	−0.56	**0.44**

The fact that the yen is already a minor (13.6 %) component of the dollar index doesn't seem to have serious repercussions on the correlation values as the strong correlation between the yen and the euro (which is the major component of the dollar index) indicates. Nevertheless, just to make sure, I created a pseudo dollar index using the formula 4.2 (explained in Chapter 4), taking into account all other currency components except the yen, and calculated the correlation of 15-day percent changes between the yen and the pseudo dollar index over a six-year span. The result was an 11 basis point reduction in correlation from -0.67 to -0.56 which still beats all others.

The S&P 500 was also used, but only as a confirmation of the dollar index divergence signal and not to generate autonomous signals. This last condition wasn't verified by back-testing as the correlation between the yen and the S&P 500, stemming from the "carry trade", is something that emerged recently. To deal with this problem I used the TNX as an alternative confirmation when back-testing the system using older data. Thus the system could switch to TNX if the condition was not verified by the S&P 500.

The same problem inherent in all divergence models (discussed in the previous chapter) was also encountered here, as the system generated only 28 trades during the seven-year out-of-sample testing period. To increase the turnover I added a volatility breakout component which increased the number of trades to 39, sufficient for a statistical evaluation of the system.

To develop the volatility component I used the SD*ADX indicator, introduced in my article "Las Vegas or Los Nasdaq" first published in the January 2005 issue of *STOCKS & COMMODITIES* (see Bibliography). This indicator is calculated by multiplying Wilder's ADX by the standard deviation and dividing by the moving average. The SD*ADX indicator was used to detect low volatility periods which, just like the calm before a storm, usually precede violent breakouts.

Low volatility periods can also be detected by a contraction of the Bollinger Bands or low values of the ADX indicator, but my research has shown that the SD*ADX indicator, which combines both methods, is superior to both when used alone.

Testing Procedure

In order to develop the system I divided the available data into two segments. I then used the first segment to test different rules and optimize the indicator parameters and the second segment of data to test and evaluate the results. No optimization, except for the S&P 500 condition, was carried out in the second phase of testing.

Several assumptions underlie the trading model.

The default trade size was one round lot of $100 000 per trade. Long and short signals were executed the same day at the close. This doesn't present problems in real-time trading since forex markets are open 24 hours and a trade can be executed virtually seconds after the close indicated by the data.

When the system was long the USD, the interest difference between the dollar and the yen, currently at $4.15 - 0.80 = 3.35\%$ was credited to the account and when short the 3.35 % interest was debited to the account.

The commission of 1.5 pip (or $100\,000*0.015/115 = \$13$), was deducted from exit trades. Returns were calculated as a percent of account required to trade each system and compared to the buy and hold method which involved buying \$100 000 and selling yen for the duration of the test. The compound formula was used to annualize percentage returns.

The amount of the account required was the 2 % margin required by major forex brokers plus the initial drawdown. The percent standard deviation of change in equity was calculated monthly and the risk-adjusted return was calculated by dividing the annualized return by the percent standard deviation of the change in equity.

Three different indicators were used to define the intermarket rules: According to Table 17.1 the yen correlated best with the dollar index for 15–20 day percentage changes. On testing, the 15-day segment produced slightly more profitable results and this value was substituted in the regression divergence indicator. The intermarket momentum oscillator (IMO) was again used to identify extreme divergence levels. The 10-day disparity indicator was used to quantify divergence between the yen and the TNX, as this indicator performed better than the regression method on testing. The one-day rate of change of the S&P 500 was also used to confirm signals. I could not back-test this last condition effectively, as there was no correlation between the yen and the S&P 500 before 2006, but since their relationship (because of the "carry trade"), has recently changed dramatically, the system should be reevaluated and perhaps the S&P 500 may play a more dominant role in the future.

The combined intermarket regression-disparity-volatility system was defined as follows:

Buy condition 1 (intermarket): A buy signal was generated if the 200 bar IMO of the 15-day YEN-DXY regression divergence rose over 70 and declined by more than 4 points during the next four days. To eliminate premature signals, I used the 10-day moving average to confirm the price reversal as follows. The system executed the IMO buy signals only if the 2-day moving average of the yen crossed over its 10-day moving average and the yen rose intraday (closed above the open). To further eliminate false signals during periods that the yen decoupled from the dollar index, I used a second intermarket condition which required a positive YEN-TNX disparity or the S&P 500 rising more than 2 %.

Buy condition 2 (intermarket): A buy signal was generated if the 10-day disparity divergence rose above 4 and reversed direction but only during short-term oversold conditions defined by the 5-day stochastic crossing over 20 from below.

Buy condition 3 (volatility): The SD*ADX indicator was used to detect extremely low volatility and the Bollinger Bands to detect breakouts. This condition tended to produce some unprofitable trades so the signals were filtered using an intermarket condition. Thus a buy signal was generated if the SD*ADX dropped below 0.11 and the yen subsequently crossed over the Bollinger Band top during the next three days, but only if the disparity with the TNX was positive or the Dollar Index was above its 20-day moving average.

The opposite of the first two conditions, with the addition of a trailing stop loss, was used to liquidate the trades as follows:

Sell condition 1 (trailing stop loss): Any open trades were stopped out if the yen crossed below the lower 10-day Bollinger Band.

Sell condition 2 (intermarket): The position was liquidated if the IMO dropped below 30 and then reversed while the MACD was below its signal line.

Sell condition 3 (intermarket): The position was liquidated when the disparity dropped below −4 and reversed direction but only when the yen was in a short-term overbought state specified by the five-day stochastic crossing below 80.

Sell short: The exact opposite of the first three buy conditions was used to generate short signals.

Buy to cover: Once again, the exact opposite of the sell conditions described above were used except that an extra requirement was added for the dollar index to be above its 20-day moving average or the yen above its 10-day moving average as the system tended to close short positions rather prematurely.

Please keep in mind that the conditions described above can only be used to trade the USD/YEN pair which is positively correlated with the dollar index, the TNX and the S&P 500. To trade the YEN/USD pair or Japanese yen futures, which are negatively correlated with the dollar index, the TNX and the S&P 500, the system should be modified as follows.

A minus sign should be added to the disparity formula to take into account the negative correlation. Also the disparity extreme values used to signal trades by the first system will have to be adjusted to take into account the reverse sign of the correlation between the YEN/USD and the TNX. This is because the disparity between negatively correlated markets is less (in absolute values) than the corresponding disparity between positively correlated markets. Another thing to change is the inequality sign in all references to the S&P and the DXY moving average. Therefore the inequality sign in the buy conditions should be reversed from > to < and the opposite in the sell or short conditions. Luckily there is no need to adjust the regression divergence indicator as the formula detects the correlation sign and adjusts automatically.

I did limited testing of the reverse system on JY futures and the system performed as expected, reversing the signals produced by the USD/YEN system. I have not presented the results as Reuters did not provide enough data to cover the entire testing period chosen for the USD/YEN test. The code is, however, included in Appendix A.

Evaluation of Results

The results for both tests are summarized in Table 17.2. I have also marked in the accompanying chart in Figure 17.1 when each buy/sell signal occurred but only (because of space limitations) from January to December 2007. The net profit is shown on the sixth row and the total profit (including the interest income resulting from the interest rate spread between the two currencies) is shown on the next row. Buying and holding $100 000 (and selling yen) produced a small loss but this was offset by the considerable "carry interest" difference of $20 700 credited to the account during the seven-year period. The results of the initial pure intermarket system are shown in the third column and the combined system profit/loss statistics in the last column.

In the period tested, the results of the combined system were very impressive. During the course of the seven-year simulation, the system made more than $70 000 with only 39 trades, which were roughly 72 % accurate. The profit factor, which is defined as gross profits divided by gross losses, was 7.8. A profit factor above 4 is considered excellent.

The system sustained a maximum drawdown of $5900 or 5.9 % of equity, which occurred on 30 July 2001, mainly due to a trade initiated by an unpropitious regression divergence buy signal during the yen's temporary decoupling from the dollar index, which was not closed in time to limit the loss.

If you achieve a higher return with a lower standard deviation than buy and hold, that is your first piece of evidence that you are achieving a greater return with less risk and that your returns are more likely to be stable over any given period. In this case, the standard deviation of 1.4 % was 1.2 percentage points lower than that of buy and hold and the risk-adjusted return was 42 % compared with a 1 % loss of the buy and hold.

In addition, the buy and hold investor suffered a precipitous $29 000 or 29 % of equity drawdown and a rather steep initial drawdown of $11 184, increased the account required to buy the USD/YEN, because of the margin calls, from the initial minimum requirement of 2 % or $2000 to $13 184.

Certain drawbacks of a strategy, which are not readily apparent from the profit-loss statistics, can only be diagnosed by heeding the signals of a trading system once they are in place. After inspecting carefully the trade signals on the chart, I identified the following weaknesses.

The timing of the exits was not always the best as they were sometimes late and other times too early to close out trades. This occurred more often on signals produced by the first system which relied solely on intermarket conditions to enter and exit trades. This is because intermarket generated signals can fail, where there is a temporary decoupling of the base security from its related intermarket.

Table 17.2   Profit/loss report. In Column 3 you can see the test results of the pure intermarket regression test and Column 4 the volatility enhanced results. All tests were profitable and outperformed the buy and hold or short and hold strategies.

Test	Buy & hold	Intermarket	Intermarket + Volatility
Security on test	USD/YEN	USD/YEN	USD/YEN
Intermarket security		DXY, TNX, SPX	DXY, TNX, SPX
Trading amount	$100 000	$100 000	$100 000
Account required	$13 184	$5216	$3058
Total net profit	−$2726	$37 456	$72 585
Total profit (incl. interest)	$20 715	$35 735	$71 152
Profit/loss %	157.0 %	718 %	2374 %
Annualized % gain/loss	14 %	35 %	58 %
Total number of trades	1	28	39
Winning trades	0	20	28
Losing trades	1	8	11
Percent profitable	0 %	71.4 %	71.8 %
Gross profit	0	$42 189	$83 214
Gross loss	−$2726	−$4733	−$10 629
Avg. winning trade		$2109	$2972
Avg. losing trade		−$592	−$966
Ratio avg. win/avg. loss		3.57	3.08
Profitability coefficient		4.95	4.73
Profit factor		8.91	7.83
Max. drawdown	−$29 270	−$4199	−$5914
Max. initial drawdown	−$11 184	−$3216	−$1058
Max. loss	−€29 270	−$1397	−$2518
Max. consecutive losses	1	3	2
Standard deviation % of equity	2.54 %	1.55 %	1.37 %
Risk adjusted annualized return	−1 %	23 %	42 %
Sharpe ratio	−3.1	19.7	39.2
Reference bars needed		418	418
Start date/loaded data	03-05-99	03-05-99	03-05-99
Start date/test	02-01-01	02-01-01	02-01-01
End date	31-12-07	31-12-07	31-12-07
Test period (years)	7.0	7.0	7.0
Test period (days)	2554	2554	2554
Total trade length (days)	2554	971	1875
Out of market (days)	0	1583	679
Average trade length – days	2554	35	48
Time in market	100.0 %	38.0 %	73.4 %

Table 17.2   (*continued*)

System Parameters		
Disparity bars	10	10
Rate of change – bars	15	15
Momentum oscillator – bars	200	200
Momentum oscillator – buy	70	70
Momentum oscillator – (long exit)	30	30
Disparity buy	4	4
Disparity sell	−4	−4

Figure 17.1   Chart of the Japanese yen (USD/YEN) from January to December 2007. Test signals generated by the regression method are superimposed on the chart. The 10-day disparity with the TNX (10-year Treasury yield) is plotted in the top window, and below is the intermarket momentum oscillator of the regression between the yen and the dollar index. The 15-day standard deviation*ADX product is also plotted above the yen chart.

Adding the volatility trailing stop loss condition in the second (combined) test, did improve on the results by eliminating large drawdowns but failed to close trades in cases of small and gradual adverse movements. More stringent exit rules, however, failed to improve on profitability as they tended to close out trades far short of their maximum profit potential.

Premature entry signals, however, did not affect the bottom line, as trades triggered by early signals usually ended up profitable.

Although I was not entirely satisfied with all entry and exit conditions the model was robust and maintained a more than acceptable balance between risk and reward. The timing of the entry and exit signals, however, can be improved further by combining conventional technical analysis with intermarket rules and indicators, thus filtering unprofitable or untimely signals.

17.5   THE EURO

The euro is the single currency currently shared by 15 of the European Union's member states (Belgium, Germany, Greece, Spain, France, Ireland, Italy, Luxembourg, Netherlands, Austria, Portugal, Finland, Slovenia, Cyprus and Malta).

When the euro was first launched in 1999, it became the new official currency of 11 member states, replacing the old national currencies – such as the Deutschmark and the French franc – in two stages. It was first used as a virtual currency for cashless payments and accounting purposes, while the old currencies continued to be used for cash payments. It appeared in physical form, as banknotes and coins, for the first time on 1 January 2002.

The euro is not the currency of all EU Member States. Two countries (Denmark and the United Kingdom) agreed an 'opt-out' clause in the Treaty exempting them from participation, while the remainder (many of the newest EU members plus Sweden), have yet to meet the conditions for adopting the single currency. Nevertheless the euro is the single currency for more than 320 million Europeans. Including areas using currencies pegged to the euro, it directly affects close to 500 million people worldwide. The name – the euro – was chosen at the European Council meeting in Madrid in 1995 and the euro symbol – € – was inspired by the Greek letter epsilon (ϵ). It also stands for the first letter of the word "Europe" in the Greek alphabet, while the two parallel horizontal lines crossing through the symbol signify stability.

When the euro came into being, monetary policy became the responsibility of the independent European Central Bank (ECB), which was created for that purpose. Fiscal policy (tax and spending) remains in the hands of individual national governments – though they undertake to adhere to commonly agreed rules on public finances known as the Stability and Growth Pact.

The euro's miserable debut on 1 January 1999 had developed into a stunning bull market by 2004. Since breaking out in the spring of 2002, the euro has enjoyed a strong, vigorous bull market over the past six years, which can be mainly attributed to

Table 17.3 Pearson's correlation of 15-day (three week) percent changes between the euro (EUR/USD) and related commodity and forex markets using 2–9 years of data from the euro's launch on 1 January 1999 to 31 December 2007. In the first column is the number of years of data used. The TNX is the 10-year Treasury yield, and the Bund is the 10-year German Bund futures (GBL).

Correlation of 15 day % changes between the euro and related markets

Data Years	Euro Stoxx	TNX	10-year bund	Gold	CRB	GBP	AUSD	Yen/USD
9	−0.23	−0.26	0.22	0.43	0.26	0.73	0.52	0.37
5	−0.16	−0.28	0.27	0.51	0.37	0.76	0.62	0.52
3	−0.01	−0.10	−0.03	0.52	0.48	0.77	0.57	0.58
2	0.01	−0.27	0.17	0.61	0.57	0.77	0.59	0.58

the weakness of the dollar and the US twin deficit rather than strength in the Euroland economy.

When currency guru George Soros was asked about the weakness in the US dollar in June 2002, he predicted that the greenback could drop as much as 30 % before the move was over. The dollar has dropped by more than 50 % since, from 0.94 dollars to the euro to 1.47 by the end of 2007 and there are no indications that the move is over.

But how can the euro be predicted using intermarket relationships?

To quantify its correlation with related markets I compiled three tables. In Table 17.3 you can see how the correlation of three week percent changes between the euro and European stock indices, US and European interest rates, commodities and other currencies evolved during the nine years of its existence. In Table 17.4 you can see how different percent changes can affect the correlation, and in Table 17.5 you can see how well a related market's weekly percentage price change can predict next week's change of the euro.

The most important conclusions drawn from these tables are summarized below:

- The relation with the Euro Stoxx 50 index has recently deteriorated from a negative correlation of −0.23 to nearly zero during the last two years from 2005 to 2007 (Table 17.3). Unlike correlation with other indices, the correlation with Euro Stoxx is stronger when taking 10-day price differences (Table 17.4), suggesting a short-term relationship. Also a slight lead of the euro is evident from Table 17.5.
- The euro correlates better with US rather than European interest rates, especially in the longer term (more than three months).
- The correlation with gold and the CRB has been trending up when using more recent data (Tables 17.3 and 17.4), and it is stronger for short to medium percent changes (two to three weeks). The euro lags both the CRB and gold slightly (Table 17.5).

Table 17.4 Pearson's correlation of different percentage changes between the euro and related commodity and forex markets using five years of data from 1 January 2003 to 31 December 2007. In the first column is the number of trading days used to calculate the percentage differences, which varied from 1 to 126 days (six months). Weekends and holidays were not included.

5 year correlation of % changes between the euro and related markets								
% change – days	Euro Stoxx	TNX	10-year bund	Gold	CRB	GBP	AUSD	Yen/USD
1	−0.20	−0.32	0.31	0.52	0.26	0.69	0.57	0.46
5	−0.19	−0.27	0.23	0.53	0.35	0.73	0.61	0.47
10	−0.2	−0.28	0.24	0.52	0.36	0.75	0.61	0.50
15	−0.16	−0.28	0.27	0.51	0.37	0.76	0.62	0.52
21	−0.13	−0.27	0.27	0.50	0.38	0.78	0.63	0.54
63	−0.06	−0.32	0.21	0.47	0.27	0.79	0.80	0.69
126	−0.05	−0.32	0.16	0.3	0.16	0.75	0.79	0.74

- The correlation between the euro and the British pound, stemming from Britain's membership of the European Union, is the strongest of the group. The relationship is strong for both short and long term time segments and constant through the years. A lead of the euro is clearly evident from Table 17.5. This indicates that it is better to use the euro to predict the British pound and not the other way around.
- There is also strong correlation with the Australian dollar. This is more pronounced for longer term percent change intervals (more than three months). Also it is evident from Table 17.5 that the euro leads the Australian dollar.
- The relation with the yen has also been increasing recently (Table 17.3). It is evident from Table 17.4 that the correlation is stronger when taking three or more months of percentage changes.
- The euro seems to lead all other currencies.

17.6 TRADING THE EURO

A trend-following strategy seemed the most appropriate to use in order to take advantage of the euro's strong trends.

The classic method involved a plain moving average but trades were not initiated according to the usual rules of price crossing over the moving average but only when the moving average turned up by a certain minimum amount or filter. This filter adjusted itself according to volatility. To accomplish this, the filter was defined as 0.7 standard deviations of the moving average daily changes. A second filter was also employed to filter out signals in trendless periods and eliminate false signals when prices were moving sideways.

Table 17.5 Pearson's correlation coefficient of weekly percentage changes between the euro and Euro Stoxx 50, 10-year Treasury yield (TNX), 10-year Bund futures (GBL), gold (cash), the Commodity Research Bureau Index (CRB), the British pound (GBP/USD), the Australian dollar (AUS/USD) and the yen (JPY/USD). The correlations were calculated using data for the five-year period from 2003–2007. The first column depicts the number of days that the euro data were shifted in time. A 1-day lag indicates that yesterday's euro weekly change was correlated with today's Euro Stoxx, TNX, or CRB data and a lag of −1 indicates that tomorrow's weekly change was correlated with today's weekly change of the corresponding commodity. Therefore higher correlations with positive lags indicate a euro lead and higher correlations for negative lag indicate that the euro lagged. The avg row is the average of lagging or leading correlations.

Predictive correlation of weekly % changes between the euro and related markets

Lag days	Euro Stoxx	TNX	10-year bund	Gold	CRB	GBP	AUSD	Yen/USD	
−5	0.01	−0.04	0.03	0.02	0.02	−0.03	0.01	0	
−4	−0.02	−0.08	0.05	0.13	0.08	0.09	0.12	−0.07	Euro lags
−3	−0.04	−0.1	0.08	0.21	0.15	0.22	0.22	−0.15	
−2	−0.10	−0.15	0.12	**0.30**	0.21	0.37	0.34	−0.23	
−1	−0.12	−0.2	0.16	0.39	0.28	0.51	0.45	−0.33	
avg.	−0.05	−0.11	0.09	0.21	0.15	0.23	0.23	−0.16	
0	−0.19	−0.27	0.23	0.53	0.35	0.73	0.61	−0.47	
1	−0.16	−0.19	0.17	0.39	0.28	**0.58**	**0.48**	**−0.4**	
2	−0.14	**−0.27**	0.10	0.28	0.2	**0.47**	0.38	−0.3	
3	−0.10	−0.1	0.07	0.17	0.12	0.34	0.24	−0.25	Euro leads
4	−0.06	−0.07	0.04	0.07	0.04	0.27	0.13	−0.16	
5	−0.02	−0.03	0.03	−0.05	−0.03	0.10	0.00	−0.05	
avg.	−0.10	−0.13	0.08	0.17	0.12	0.35	0.25	−0.23	

A popular indicator used to quantify the trend is Wilder's ADX. This was my first choice but it did not perform as expected on testing, as it was too slow to indicate a trend change, giving up a substantial portion of profits during the early part of the trend. I then tested the Congestion Index (CI), first introduced in Chapter 9, which performed considerably better than the ADX, as it was quicker to indicate the beginning of a trend.

The system was then enhanced using a simple intermarket rule, filtering out trades when the euro was moving against two of its intermarket peers: 10-year US bond yields (TNX) and commodities (the CRB index).

This simple intermarket rule improved the results by a wide margin, nearly doubling the profit factor of the system.

The problem in back-testing intermarket rules, encountered in the yen test, was also present here as the correlation with the CRB index was not constant during the optimization and out-of-sample testing periods and almost doubled, from 0.26 to 0.57, during the most recent out-of-sample test.

As a result, the older (in-sample) test did not perform as well as the most recent out-of-sample test. By the time this book is published correlations with the CRB index might once again change and the reader should reevaluate the results and reoptimize the CRB moving average parameters if necessary, as soon as more data become available. Correlations with the TNX, except for a brief period in the beginning of 2005, were more or less stable through the euro's nine-year life span.

The system can be summarized as follows. Buy when

$$MA - \text{lowest } (MA,3) > 0.7^*\text{filter} \tag{17.1}$$

$$\text{And ABS (CI)} < 40 \text{ and CI-lowest (CI,3)} > 3 \tag{17.2}$$

$$\text{And CRB} > MA \text{ (CRB,35) and TNX} < MA(TNX,5) \tag{17.3}$$

where MA is the 10-day moving simple average; the filter is the 20-day standard deviation of daily moving average changes; MA(CRB,35) is the 35-day moving average of the CRB index; and MA(TNX,5) is the five-day moving average of the TNX.

The first condition was triggered only when the moving average exceeded its three-day lowest value (rather than the current day's value) by an amount greater than the filter in order to take into account small gradual movements which would not exceed the filter in a single day but would be significant when added over a three-day span.

The same conditions in reverse were used to sell short.

$$MA\text{-Highest}(MA) < 0.7^*\text{filter} \tag{17.4}$$

$$\text{And ABS (CI)} < 40 \text{ and CI-highest (CI, 3)} < -3 \tag{17.5}$$

$$\text{And CRB} < MA \text{ (CRB,35) and TNX} > MA(TNX,5) \tag{17.6}$$

The moving average is not the best indicator to use for exits as it lags price, giving up a considerable amount of profits. Using the reverse rules for liquidating trades gave up a substantial amount of profits as the signals were sometimes late to close a position and other times did not materialize at all.

I spent a lot of time testing various exit conditions and finally decided to use Wilder's Parabolic Stop and Reverse (SAR) formula. By increasing the acceleration factor from the default value of 20 % to 40 % Wilder's stop-loss formula produced timely exits with minimum profit loss and reasonable drawdown.

For the benefit of readers not familiar with the parabolic I thought that a brief description would be useful. The Parabolic Stop and Reverse was introduced by J Welles Wilder in his 1978 book, *New Concepts in Technical Trading Systems* (see Bibliography) and is a trailing stop designed to address the problem of lagging exit signals in trend-following systems. The parabolic formula solves the price lag problem by tightening stops at an accelerating rate. The price must continue to move in the direction of the trend, otherwise the trade is stopped out. The trailing stop moves with the trend, accelerating closer to price action as time passes, giving a parabolic look to the indicator path, and hence its name.

The Parabolic is calculated according to the following formula:

$$SAR = AF \times (EP - SAR(-1)) + SAR(-1)$$

where $SAR(-1)$ is yesterday's SAR; AF is the acceleration factor; and EP is the extreme high or low point of the previous day.

Wilder used an initial value of 0.02 (20 %) as the accelerating factor (AF). The AF was then increased by 0.02 each time a new extreme point was made and up to maximum value of 0.2. These are the default values used by most software but can be adjusted by the user. Changing the AF will tighten the stops, thus making the system faster but more sensitive to noise. The choice for the AF should reflect the price characteristics of the base security being analyzed, and the strategy and personal preferences of the trader using the indicator.

In the euro's case a slightly faster AF of 0.04 combined with a maximum value of 0.10 was found to produce more timely exits. Long positions were liquidated when

$$\text{Closing Price} < \text{SAR } (0.04, 0.1) \tag{17.7}$$

$$\text{And Closing Price} > \text{SAR } (0.04, 0.1) \tag{17.8}$$

for short exits.

Even though my original intention was to use the parabolic only for exit signals, it had to be added to the entry and short conditions as well, otherwise a long or short entry was stopped out the same day if the price was below the SAR, thus distorting the number of trades and probability of win statistics.

Testing Procedure

The total time span of the available data for the euro was from 1 January 1998 to 21 January 2008 divided into one testing and one out-of-sample segment. The first segment, the testing and development period, was from 1 January 1998 to 21 January 2003 and the period from 22 January 2003 to 21 January 2008 was reserved for out-of-sample testing. Keep in mind that for the test to start producing trades, an extra 47 days had to be loaded which were required for the calculation of the CI indicator and its moving average.

The default trade size was one round lot of 100 000 units (or €100 000) per trade. Long and short signals were executed the same day at the close. When the system was long the euro, the interest difference between euro and the USD, currently at $3.75 - 4.30 = -0.55\%$ was debited to the account and when short the interest was credited to the account. The average during the test period interest difference of 2 % was subtracted from the buy and hold profits.

A commission of 1 pip (or $100\,000*0.0001 = €10$), which is the commission charged currently by Oanda, was deducted from each trade. Returns were calculated as a percent of the account required to trade each system and compared to the buy and hold method which involved buying €100 000 and selling the corresponding amount of dollars for the duration of the test. The compound formula was used to annualize percentage returns.

The amount of the account required was the 2 % minimum margin required by the NFA and US based forex brokers, plus the initial drawdown. The percent standard deviation of change in equity was calculated monthly and the risk-adjusted return was calculated by dividing the annualized return by the monthly percent standard deviation of the change in equity.

17.7   EVALUATION OF RESULTS

The current system is a perfect example of how to use intermarket conditions to improve on classic technical analysis indicators.

The results of both tests are summarized in Table 17.6. I have also marked in the accompanying chart in Figure 17.2 when each buy/sell signal occurred but only (because of space limitations) from November 2006 to January 2008. The net profit is shown on the sixth row and the total profit (including the interest difference between the two currencies) on the next row. The results of the buy and hold strategy are in the second column, the classic moving average system results are shown in the third column and the intermarket enhanced combined system profit/loss statistics are in the last column.

Buying and holding €100 000 (and selling dollars) produced a considerable profit but this was offset by the "carry interest" difference of $−€10\,000$ during the five-year period as the average US dollar interest rate was 2 % more than the euro's during the test period.

In the period tested, the results of the intermarket enhanced system were very impressive. During the course of the five-year simulation, the system made more than €45 000 with only 38 trades, which were roughly 58 % accurate. The profit factor was 4.1 and the maximum drawdown was only €7950 or 8 % of equity, which occurred on 24 February 2004 mainly due to an untimely short signal which was not closed in time to limit the losses.

The risk and return statistics are also shown in Table 17.6. The monthly standard deviation of equity was only 1.64 % during the test duration which produced a 48 % risk-adjusted annualized return and a more than adequate Sharpe ratio of 45. The buy and hold investor, on the other hand, suffered a peak to valley maximum drawdown of €20 000 and a €2580 initial drawdown which, because of the margin calls, increased the account required to buy the EUR/USD from the initial minimum amount of 2 %

Table 17.6 Profit/loss report. You can see in Column 3 the test results of the classic moving average test and Column 4 the intermarket enhanced results. The intermarket enhanced test outperformed the classic moving average considerably.

Test	Buy & hold	MA	MA & Intermarket
Security on test	EUR/USD	EUR/USD	EUR/USD
Intermarket security			CRB, TNX
Number of units	€100 000	€100 000	€100 000
Account required	€4580	€3460	€2660
Total net profit	€37 090	€28 910	€45 750
Total profit (incl. interest)	€27 093	$27 893	$44 678
Profit/loss %	592 %	806.2 %	1679.6 %
Annualized % gain/loss	56 %	55 %	78 %
Total number of trades	1	62	38
Winning trades	1	28	22
Losing trades	0	34	16
Percent profitable	100 %	45 %	58 %
Gross profit	€37 090	€70 250	€60 620
Gross loss		−€41 340	−€14 870
Avg. winning trade	€37 090	€2509	€2755
Avg. losing trade		−€1216	−€929
Ratio avg. win/avg. loss		2.06	2.96
Profitability coefficient		1.25	3.27
Profit factor		1.70	4.08
Max. drawdown	−€19 930	−€11 900	−€7950
Date of max drawdown	11-16-05	10-10-05	02-24-04
Max. % drawdown	−19.9 %	−11.9 %	−8.0 %
Max. initial drawdown	−€2580	−€1460	−€660
Date of max initial drawdown	3-21-03	5-15-03	5-15-03
Max. loss		−€3300	−€2980
Max. consecutive losses		6	4
Risk/reward	53.7 %	41.2 %	17.4 %
Standard deviation % of equity	2.48 %	2.03 %	1.64 %
Risk-adjusted annualized return	22 %	27 %	48 %
Sharpe ratio	20.6	25.1	44.8
Reference bars needed	47	47	47
start date/loaded data	11-17-02	11-17-02	11-17-02
Start date/test	1-22-03	1-22-03	1-22-03
End date	1-21-08	1-21-08	1-21-08
Test period (years)	5.0	5.0	5.0
Test period (days)	1825	1824	1824
Total trade length (days)	1825	1089	779
Out of market (days)	0	735	1045
Average trade length – days	1825	18	21
Trades/year	0.2	12.4	7.6
Time in market	100.0 %	59.7 %	42.7 %

Table 17.6 (*continued*)

Test	Buy & hold	MA	MA & Intermarket
		System Parameters	
MA – bars		10	10
CI – bars		40	40
MA CRB			35
MA TNX			5

or $2000 to $4580. There is no doubt that the system's relatively low drawdown can be attributed to the parabolic trailing stop. The parabolic, however, is no panacea. Although it solves the lag problem of trend-following systems by trailing stops closer to price, it still suffers when the market turns choppy. Although the parabolic was only used to close trades initiated by trending signals, it was sometimes late to materialize, especially in sideways markets.

The classic moving average test, although profitable, did not manage to outperform the buy and hold method on a net profit basis but it did produce slightly higher profits and risk-adjusted return when the interest rate differential was subtracted from both results. This test was only included here to demonstrate the dramatic improvement that can be accomplished by adding a couple of intermarket rules to your trading system.

The inferences drawn from the tests presented above is that while intermarket relationships can be a stand-alone method for trading, you can also incorporate them by any means in a trend-following discipline such as a moving average system to improve, sometimes dramatically, the system profitability.

17.8   THE AUSTRALIAN DOLLAR

The Australian (or Aussie) dollar is the fifth most actively traded currency in the foreign exchange markets, trailing behind the United States dollar, Japanese yen, euro, and British pound and it accounts for approximately 5.5 % of worldwide foreign exchange transactions.

The Aussie dollar along with the Canadian dollar, the New Zealand dollar and the South African rand is regarded as a "commodity currency", owing to the sizable role of commodity production in the Australian economy. It was first introduced in 1966 when it replaced the Australian pound and introduced a decimal system to the nation. In September 1974, Australia replaced the peg to the US dollar in favor of a peg to a basket of currencies, and in December 1983 the Australian dollar was allowed to float, controlled mainly by the forces of supply and demand.

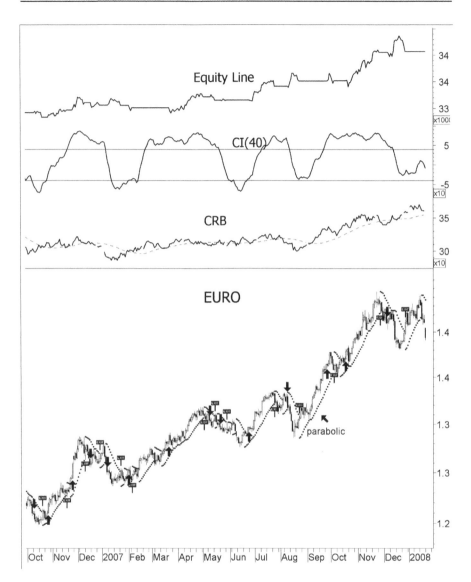

Figure 17.2   Chart of the euro (EUR/USD) from October 2006 to January 2008. Test signals generated by the intermarket MA system are superimposed on the chart. The equity line is plotted in the top window, the 40-day CI indicator below and the CRB index in the third from the top window.

Figure 17.3 Weekly composite chart of the Australian dollar (in bold) and gold bullion (thin line) from 1998 until March 2008. The Australian dollar decoupled briefly from gold in 2005, thus correcting from the 2003–2004 excesses.

The Australian dollar had been in a long-term bear market, trading as low as 47 cents to the dollar until a double bottom reversal in 2001. Since then, economic growth in China and the secular bull market in commodities have helped propel it by more than 100 %. The Aussie dollar is popular amongst currency traders because of its high yield (currently at 7.4 %) and the government's limited intervention in the FX market. Additionally, the $AUD, because of its strong correlation with gold (see Figure 17.3) and other commodities, offers diversification in a foreign currency portfolio.

The Aussie dollar appreciated by more than 70 % against the Japanese yen, to 107 yen per A$ from its low of 62 yen in September 2002. Japanese banks and traders played the "currency carry" game, borrowing yen in Tokyo at zero percent, and buying Aussie dollars which were invested in short-term deposits yielding 7 % or more. Besides the higher yield on the carry trade they also enjoyed a significant currency gain until the summer of 2007 when the start of the bear market in equities triggered an unwinding of the carry trade and an appreciation of the yen from the all-time high of 107 yen to the A$ to a low of 88 in March of 2008 (see Figure 17.4).

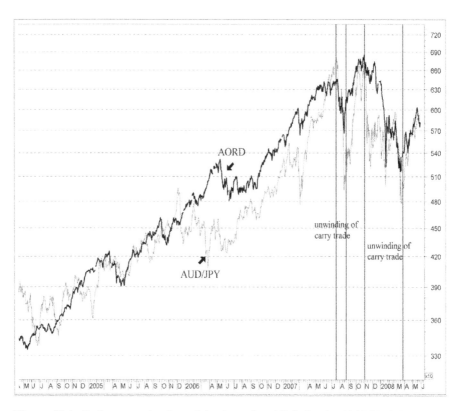

Figure 17.4 Daily composite chart of the Australian All Ordinaries (AORD) (in bold) and the AUD/JPY exchange rate (thin line) from September 2005 until May 2008. Notice the high correlation of the AUD/JPY stemming from the yen carry trade.

Most interesting is the interplay of capital flows versus trade flows in currency markets. The Australian dollar, despite a long string of trade deficits, appreciated sharply against the Japanese yen, which enjoyed a significant trade surplus with Australia. In this case the interest rate difference was wide enough to propel a massive flow into the Australian dollar. But Japan is Australia's largest export market and the overvalued Aussie dollar has hurt businesses outside of the resource sector, thus dichotomizing the Australian economy into two sections. The resources boom extended employment and housing in the resource rich regions such as Western Australia, Queensland, and some parts of South Australia, while there was stagnation in the industrial capitals of Sydney and Melbourne where the unemployment rate was much higher.

Despite its booming commodity exports, Australia is importing more goods from abroad than it exports, resulting in a current account deficit of 7 % of GDP in 2007.

Table 17.7   Pearson's correlation matrix of weekly percent changes between the Australian dollar (AUD/USD) and other major currencies using 10 years of data from 1 January 1998 to 31 December 2007. In the third column is the Canadian dollar (CAD/USD) rate, in the sixth column is the dollar index and in the last column is the yen (YEN/USD) rate.

	AUD	CAD	Euro	GBP	Dollar	Yen
AUD	1	**0.50**	0.49	0.44	**−0.53**	0.29
CAD	0.50	1	0.32	0.27	−0.40	0.16
Euro	0.49	0.32	1	0.68	−0.97	0.32
GBP	0.44	0.27	0.68	1	−0.73	0.29
Dollar	−0.53	−0.40	−0.97	−0.73	1	−0.52
Yen	0.29	0.16	0.32	0.29	−0.52	1

The high deficit forces the central bank to keep high interest rates in order to attract foreign lenders and carry traders.

The direction of commodity and gold prices and their impact on trade flows, interest rate differentials with the US, Japan and other countries, commodity prices and the AUD/JPY carry trade, are all key variables moving the Aussie dollar.

I have calculated in Tables 17.7–17.10 the correlation of weekly and monthly changes between the Australian dollar and related commodities, currencies and equity indices. A large part of both the Australian and Canadian exports consists of basic materials and this is reflected in their currencies. The Aussie dollar had the strongest correlation with the Canadian dollar ($r = 0.61$ in Table 17.9). It is also interesting

Table 17.8   Pearson's correlation matrix of weekly percent changes between the Australian dollar (AUD/USD) and other related commodity and equity indices. The correlations were calculated using 10 years of data from 1 January 1998 to 31 December 2007. In the fourth column is COMEX copper futures, in the sixth column is the Canadian Venture Composite index, in the seventh column is the Australian All Ordinaries index and in the last column is Canada's TSX Composite index. Notice that the Australian dollar correlates better with Canadian rather than with Australian equity indices.

	CRB	Gold	XAU	HG	VX	AORD	TSX
AUD	0.35	0.46	**0.47**	0.31	**0.48**	0.24	0.27
CRB	1	0.46	0.44	0.38	0.50	0.15	0.27
Gold	0.46	1	0.69	0.30	0.57	0.14	0.19
XAU	0.44	0.69	1	0.31	0.67	0.26	0.33
HG	0.38	0.30	0.31	1	0.44	0.24	0.29
VX	0.50	0.57	0.67	0.44	1	0.53	0.61
AORD	0.15	0.14	0.26	0.24	0.53	1	0.58
TSX	0.27	0.19	0.33	0.29	0.61	0.58	1

Table 17.9   Pearson's correlation matrix of monthly percent changes between the Australian dollar (AUD/USD) and other major currencies using 10 years of data from 1 January 1998 to 31 December 2007. In the third column is the Canadian dollar (CAD/USD) rate and in the last column is the yen (YEN/USD) rate. Notice the high correlation between the AUD and the CAD.

	AUD	CAD	Euro	GBP	Dollar	Yen
AUD	1	**0.61**	0.54	0.46	**−0.55**	0.31
CAD	0.61	1	0.36	0.29	−0.41	0.16
Euro	0.54	0.36	1	0.75	−0.98	0.39
GBP	0.46	0.29	0.75	1	−0.78	0.34
Dollar	−0.55	−0.41	−0.98	−0.78	1	−0.55
Yen	0.31	0.16	0.39	0.34	−0.55	1

to note that the correlation is stronger with Canadian equity indices. Its correlation with the Canadian Venture index is 0.53 and with the TSX index it is 0.39 whereas the correlation with the Australian All Ordinaries index is only 0.34 (Table 17.10). This is not the case, however, with the AUD/JPY rate, whose higher correlation with Australian equities (see Figure 17.4) reflects the influence of the yen carry trade as traders borrow yen at near zero rates and invest them in the Australian stock market.

A strong long-term relationship between the Australian dollar and gold is evident from the chart in Figure 17.3. While this relationship broke down briefly in 2005, the correlation was restored in the first quarter of 2006. It is also evident that the price of gold is leading the Aussie dollar at bottoms but seems to lag slightly at tops. Gold

Table 17.10   Pearson's correlation matrix of monthly percent changes between the Australian dollar and the CRB Index, gold bullion (cash), the XAU, COMEX copper futures, Canada's Venture Index, Australia's All Ordinaries and Canada's TSX index. Data from 1 January 1998 to 31 December 2007 were used to calculate the correlations. Notice that the Australian dollar correlates better with the XAU ($r = 0.47$) than with the price of gold ($r = 0.41$).

	CRB	Gold	XAU	HG	VX	AORD	TSX
AUD	0.38	0.41	**0.47**	0.38	**0.53**	0.34	0.39
CRB	1	0.49	0.50	0.40	0.51	0.16	0.29
Gold	0.49	1	0.70	0.33	0.58	0.14	0.17
XAU	0.50	0.70	1	0.34	0.69	0.31	0.30
HG	0.40	0.33	0.34	1	0.44	0.26	0.29
VX	0.51	0.58	0.69	0.44	1	0.56	0.68
AORD	0.16	0.14	0.31	0.26	0.56	1	0.68
TSX	0.29	0.17	0.30	0.29	0.66	0.69	1

Table 17.11 The value of Australian exports of mineral commodities in Australian dollars and as percentage of total exports during 2006–07. Coal includes both thermal (A\$ 6762) and metallurgical coal (A\$ 15035). Source: Australian Bureau of Agricultural and Resource Economics.

Mineral	A\$	Percent
Coal	21797	20.5 %
Iron & steel	17262	16.2 %
Oil and gas	15676	14.7 %
Gold	10320	9.7 %
Nickel	8377	7.9 %
Copper	6520	6.1 %
Alumina	6224	5.8 %
Aluminum	5648	5.3 %
Other minerals	4972	4.7 %
Zinc	4306	4.0 %
Lead	1579	1.5 %
Titanium minerals	1176	1.1 %
Diamonds & gems	774	0.7 %
Uranium	660	0.6 %
Manganese	482	0.5 %
Zircon	478	0.4 %
Silver	221	0.2 %
Total	106 472	100 %

bottomed out in February 2001, six months before the Aussie dollar, after it broke out from a double bottom formation. By the time that the price of gold touched a new high on 17 March 2008, bursting through the psychological barrier of $1000 an ounce on the spot market, the Australian dollar had already peaked, twelve days earlier.

Currency traders should therefore be quick on their feet and sell quickly when the gold market looks overextended and due for a correction, as the Aussie can move 1–2 % in a single day at the first sign of trouble.

Beyond its relationship to gold, the Australian dollar correlates well with the whole commodity complex, as commodity exports accounted for 63 % of the country's exports in 2007.

As you can see from Table 17.11, coal is Australia's biggest export accounting for 20 % of total exports. In addition, Australia is the world's biggest exporter of metallurgical coal, the type used by steelmakers. According to the Australian Bureau of Agricultural and Resource Economics, Australia exported 120 million tons of metallurgical coal in 2007, which accounted for a whopping 57 % of total world exports. Australia is the world's fourth largest producer of gold bullion, behind

China, South Africa and the United States and despite the strong correlation with the Australian dollar ($r = 0.46$), gold accounts for only 9.7 % of total exports.

Disclaimer: The analysis presented in this chapter is based upon data gathered from various sources believed to be reliable. However, no guarantee is made by Markos Katsanos as to the reliability and accuracy of the data.

All statements and expressions are the opinion of the author and are not meant to be investment advice or solicitation or recommendation to establish market positions. Readers are strongly advised to conduct thorough research relevant to trading decisions and verify facts from various independent sources.

18
Conclusion

I returned and saw under the sun, that the race is not to the swift, nor the battle
to the strong, nor yet riches to men of understanding, nor yet favor to men of
skill; but time and chance happeneth to them all.

–Ecclesiastes (King James Bible)

Traditional boundaries of the various marketplaces are coming down everywhere and the interbreeding is almost out of control. In order to prevent the process of aging, it is important to focus on the changing environment and reassess your trading systems and methodology.

There is clear and incontrovertible evidence that the markets are linked to each other. Monitoring these relationships and incorporating them in your trading models can give you a trading advantage. Intermarket correlations, however, change over time and you must periodically subject your trading system to a testing regime that will permit your system to profitably mimic the unknown economic laws that cause these changes.

Although technical intermarket analysis considers only the action of the markets and is not based on any economic theory, the statistical evidence and test results presented in this book and elsewhere, have convinced me that it is a viable technique.

Contrary to popular belief by the non-believers, statistics don't lie. They can be distorted, bent, misused, and even misinterpreted but unless they are materially altered, which of course removes them from the category of statistics, they tell their own true story in a very clear and understandable way.

The test data presented in this book showed significantly superior returns of inter-market transaction timing models compared to a buy and hold policy.

The paradox of investing is that since stocks have a long-term upward bias, increasing your holding period increases the probability of profit. The mantra of mutual fund managers don't lose sleep over large drawdowns, as long as they don't underper-form the S&P 500 and are more concerned about missing the next upside rather than losing billions during a bear market. However buy and hold investors who embrace this philosophy make unrealistic assumptions about their tolerance for pain and loss, because a small correction – and not even a primary bear market – may wipe them out financially.

In addition, the approach of most investors is to have no risk management at all and it becomes obvious too late that this is extremely dangerous. Transaction timing is of course one, but not the only, strategy for reducing portfolio risk.

Diversification provides substantial risk reduction if the components of a portfolio are uncorrelated. The benefits of diversification are well known; most investment managers extend their operations by including bonds and cash in a stock portfolio already expanded across many industry groups. Less well known is the fact that commodity futures are an attractive diversification candidate. While it would be unrealistic to expect the spectacular returns of the past few years most of the non industrial commodities have weak to non existent correlation with equities and can effectively decrease the overall volatility of a properly structured portfolio while maintaining or improving return characteristics.

In addition, individual commodities tend to be uncorrelated which will reduce portfolio risk even more.

Another overlooked asset class which should be included in one's portfolio is foreign currencies or forex. Banks and other institutions already use the forex markets in order to hedge foreign exposure but this is not so widely used by individual investors. An example would make this easier to understand.

Consider a European investor who invested in the S&P 500. In 2007 he would have made a 3.5 % profit in dollar terms but on converting his account to his local currency he would be looking at a 7 % loss. Hedging the currency exposure would require only 2 % margin (or $2000) on a $100 000 account which would have resulted in repatriation of all profits unimpaired. A US investor, on the other hand, by selling the dollar short (or buying euros) would have increased his paltry 3.5 % to a respectable 14 % return on account. These dramatic differences are due to the weak dollar and international investors should always take into account the direction of the currency markets.

A combination of market timing and asset diversification (discussed in Chapter 16) is an alternative approach to a static diversification allocation. The return/risk characteristics could be increased even more by utilizing classical market timing to shift capital among several asset classes, depending on relative performance.

It is beginning to appear that technical analysis is becoming too popular as computer models proliferate and stress short-term results. You should remember that classic technical analysis indicators such as moving averages are lagging indicators calculated from past data and are limited in assessing the current trend. Regardless of the hours spent in back-testing, there is a limit beyond which a system based on a lagging indicator can be improved any more. Thus the addition of leading indicators that anticipate reversals in trend direction is essential and beneficial to the system's performance. These can only be implemented by taking into consideration directional movements of correlated markets.

Although the performance results that appear in this book may create the impression that all market turns can be identified by intermarket divergence indicators, this is not always the case. No market timing technique or indicator is infallible. Just about the time you become convinced that one is, and you are comfortable with its application and performance results, it will invariably fail. Intermarket divergence indicators are no exception and they usually fail in periods of temporary decoupling between traditionally correlated markets.

Having a good exit strategy, therefore, should be an essential part of your trading system. Then, like the pilot getting ready to bail out from his falling aircraft, the only challenge left is in summoning the courage to push the mouse button (or call your broker).

It should be noted that while the scope of this book was to demonstrate the efficacy of intermarket analysis when applied to market averages or financial futures, the same methods can also be applied in a similar manner to stock trading. Since many stock groups are hooked to commodity markets, it also makes sense to use these relationships to enhance your stock trading system.

The inferences drawn from the tests presented in this book are by no means exhaustive. They are presented as a challenge to the serious trader to stimulate his reevaluation of intermarket techniques as a working tool and to introduce a testing framework which amalgamates both intermarket and classic technical analysis indicators.

Anyone who has become even semi-scholarly about the market knows that there are no mathematical formulas that produce black or white results, or reliable and immutable intermarket relationships that can predict every market quirk but you should instead seek out strategies based on probabilities.

You should not aspire for a perfect system but must completely accept the fact that occasionally your system is going to be wrong.

Fortunately, you don't need a perfect trading system, for trading profits anyway. Instead of perfection you should aim to construct a viable system that can produce reasonable profits, while avoiding large drawdowns that can wipe you out of the game.

Finally, I cannot stress enough that effective money management is essential for long-term survival. Most traders approach a trading decision considering only the expected gain but they overlook what is far more important: the potential loss. The objective of any money management system is to cut losses short and let profits run. Avoiding losses is far more important to long-term performance than making big profits because of one basic mathematical principle: It takes a far greater percentage gain to make up for a given percentage loss.

Appendix A
MetaStock Code and Test Specifications

A.1 METASTOCK CODE FOR THE INDICATORS DESCRIBED IN CHAPTER 9

(Copyright Markos Katsanos 2008)

Intermarket Relative Strength Indicator

To create this indicator click on the indicator builder $f_{(x)}$, click on new and then copy the following code in the formula box.

You will also need to change the first line of the code to point to the appropriate folder in your hard drive where data for the dollar index are located.

```
SEC2:=Security("C:\Metastock Data\INTERMARKET\DXY0",C);
D1:=Input("MA DAYS",1,300,3);
RS:=Mov((C/SEC2),3,E);
RS
```

Intermarket Bollinger Band Divergence

The indicator should be applied on the plot of the related intermarket security.

```
D1:=Input("PERIOD FOR BB",5,1000,40);
D2:=Input("PERIOD FOR BB INTERMARKET ",5,1000,40);
sec1BOL:=1+((C- Mov(C,D1,S)+2*Stdev(C,D1))/(4*Stdev(C,D1)));
sec2BOL:=1+(INDICATOR-
```

```
Mov(INDICATOR,D2,S)+2*Stdev(INDICATOR,
  D2))/(4*Stdev(INDICATOR,D2));
DIVERG1:=(sec2BOL-sec1BOL)/SEC1BOL*100;
diverg:=Mov(diverg1,3,E);DIVERG
```

Intermarket Disparity

You will also need to change the first line of the code to point to the appropriate
folder in your hard drive where data for the dollar index are located.

```
SEC2:=Security("C:\Metastock Data\METAS\DXY0",C);
D1:=Input("MA PERIOD BASE SECURITY",5,200,30);
D2:=Input("MA PERIOD INTERMARKET SECURITY",5,200,30);
D3:=Input(" FOR +VE CORRELATION +1, FOR -VE -1",-1,1,-1);
DIS1:=((C - Mov(C,D1,S)) / Mov(C,D1,S)) * 100;
DIS2:=((SEC2 - Mov(SEC2,D2,S)) / Mov(SEC2,D2,S)) * 100;
DIV1:=(D3*DIS2-DIS1);
DIVERG:=Mov(DIV1,3,E);DIVERG
```

Intermarket LRS Divergence

The indicator should be applied on the plot of the related intermarket security.

```
D1:=Input("DAYS FOR DIVERG",1,200,15);
D2:=Input("DIVERG POSITIVE +1,-VE-1",-1,1,1);
D3:=D2*Stdev(C,200)/Stdev(P,200);
LRSI:=LinRegSlope(P,D1)/Abs(Ref(P,-D1+1))*100;
LRS:=LinRegSlope(C,D1)/Abs(Ref(C,-D1+1))*100;
DIVERG:=(D3*LRSI-LRS)*100;
Mov(DIVERG,3,E)
```

The formula above should only be used when comparing securities at similar price
levels. When applied to compute the divergence between a high and a low priced
security (e.g. Gold and Silver futures) then both prices should be normalized or the
third line of the code should be modified to adjust for the price level as follows:

```
D3:=D2*Stdev(C,200)/Stdev(P,200)*Mov(P,200,S)/Mov(S,200,S);
```

Intermarket Regression Divergence Indicator

In the first line of the code, SEC2 should be the symbol of the appropriate intermarket
security and its correct folder in your hard drive.

```
SEC2:=Security("C:\Metastock Data\METAS\XAU",C);
D1:=Input("DAYS FOR REGRESSION",1,2000,300);
```

```
D2:=Input("ROC DAYS",1,100,15);
RS1:=ROC(C,D2,%);
RS2:=ROC(SEC2,D2,%);
b:=Correl(RS1,RS2,D1,0)*Stdev(RS1,D1)/Stdev(RS2,D1);
PRED:=b*RS2;
DIVERG:=(PRED-RS1);
Mov(DIVERG,3,E)
```

Intermarket Regression Divergence Indicator with Intercept

```
SEC2:=Security("C:\Metastock Data\METAS\XAU",C);
D1:=Input("DAYS FOR REGRESSION",1,2000,300);
D2:=Input("ROC DAYS",1,100,15);
RS1:=ROC(C,D2,%);
RS2:=ROC(SEC2,D2,%);
b:=Correl(RS1,RS2,D1,0)*Stdev(RS1,D1)/Stdev(RS2,D1);
a:=Mov(RS1,D1,S)-b*Mov(RS2,D1,S);
PRED:=b*RS2+a;
DIVERG:=(PRED-RS1);
Mov(DIVERG,3,E)
```

Intermarket Momentum Oscillator

The oscillator should be applied on the plot of the intermarket divergence indicator.

```
D1 := Input("Days for Oscillator", 2, 400, 200);

(Mov(INDICATOR - LLV(INDICATOR,D1), 3,S) * 100)/
(Mov(HHV(INDICATOR,D1) - LLV(INDICATOR,D1), 3,S))
```

Double LRS Divergence

You will need to change the first two lines of the code to point to the appropriate folder in your hard drive where data for the silver ETF (SLV) and the dollar index are located.

```
SEC1:=Security("C:\Metastock Data\METAS\SLV",C);
SEC2:=Security("C:\Metastock Data\METAS\DXY0",C);
D1:=Input("DAYS FOR DIVERG",1,200,15);
D2:=Input("DAYS FOR CORRELATION",1,1000,300);
sY:=Stdev(C,D2)/Mov(C,D2,S);
s1:=Stdev(SEC1,D2)/Mov(SEC1,D2,S);
s2:=Stdev(SEC2,D2)/Mov(SEC2,D2,S);
```

```
rY1:=Correl(SEC1,C,D2,0);
rY2:=Correl(SEC2,C,D2,0);
r12:=Correl(SEC1,SEC2,D2,0);
rY12:=(rY1-rY2*r12)/Sqrt(1-r12*r12);
rY21:=(rY2-rY1*r12)/Sqrt(1-r12*r12);
LRS1:=LinRegSlope(SEC1,D1)/Abs(Ref(SEC1,-D1+1))*100;
LRS2:=LinRegSlope(SEC2,D1)/Abs(Ref(SEC2,-D1+1))*100;
LRS:=LinRegSlope(C,D1)/Abs(Ref(C,-D1+1))*100;
DIVERG:=(rY12*sY/s1*LRS1+rY21*sY/s2*LRS2-LRS)*100;
Mov(DIVERG,3,E)
```

Intermarket Multiple Regression Divergence

The regression formula is only applicable for trading gold and the regression coefficients a and b_i in the fifth line should be modified for other markets. You will need to
change the first three lines of the code to point to the appropriate folder in your hard
drive where data for the XAU, silver and the dollar index are located.

```
SEC1:=Security("C:\Metastock Data\METAS\XAU",C);
SEC2:=Security("C:\Metastock Data\METAS\SLV",C);
SEC3:=Security("C:\Metastock Data\METAS\DXY0",C);
D2:=Input("DAYS FOR ROC",1,100,9);
a:=.071;b1:=.216;b2:=.166;b3:=-.43;
ROCY:=ROC(C,D2,%);
ROC1:=ROC(SEC1,D2,%);
ROC2:=ROC(SEC2,D2,%);
ROC3:=ROC(SEC3,D2,%);
PRED:=a+b1*ROC1+b2*ROC2+b3*ROC3;
DIVERG:=(PRED-ROCY)*10;
Mov(DIVERG,3,E)
```

Intermarket (Predicted) Moving Average

The formula is only applicable for gold. The regression coefficients a and b_i in the
fifth line should be modified for other markets. You will need to change the first three
lines of the code to point to the appropriate folder in your hard drive where data for
the XAU, silver and the dollar index are located.

```
SEC1:=Security("C:\Metastock Data\METAS\XAU",C);
SEC2:=Security("C:\Metastock Data\METAS\SLV",C);
SEC3:=Security("C:\Metastock Data\METAS\DXY0",C);
```

```
D1:=Input("MA DAYS",1,1000,13);
D2:=Input("DAYS FOR ROC",1,100,11);
a:=.16;b1:=.2;b2:=.175;b3:=-.5;
ROCY:=ROC(C,D2,%);
ROC1:=ROC(SEC1,D2,%);
ROC2:=ROC(SEC2,D2,%);ROC3:=ROC(SEC3,D2,%);
PR11:=a+b1*ROC1+b2*ROC2+b3*ROC3;
PRED:=Ref(C,-D2)*(1+PR11/100);
Mov(PRED,D1,S)
```

Intermarket (Predicted) Moving Average Universal

This formula can be used for all markets by changing the appropriate intermarket
security in the first line.

```
SEC2:=Security("C:\Metastock Data\METAS\XAU",C);
D3:=Input("MA DAYS",1,1000,13);
D1:=Input("DAYS FOR REGRESSION",1,2000,500);
D2:=Input("ROC DAYS",1,100,11);
RS1:=ROC(C,D2,%);
RS2:=ROC(SEC2,D2,%);
b:=Correl(RS1,RS2,D1,0)*Stdev(RS1,D1)/Stdev(RS2,D1);
a:=Mov(RS1,D1,S)-b*Mov(RS2,D1,S);
PR11:=b*RS2+a;
PRED:=Ref(C,-D2)*(1+PR11/100);
Mov(PRED,D3,S)
```

Congestion Index

```
D1:=Input("DAYS IN CONGESTION",1,500,15);
CI:=ROC(C,D1-1,%)/((HHV(H,D1)-LLV(L,D1))/(LLV(L,D1)+.01)+.000001);
Mov(CI,3,E)
```

A.2   METASTOCK CODE FOR THE GOLD COMPARISON TESTS IN CHAPTER 11

(Copyright Markos Katsanos 2008)

To recreate the tests, click on enhanced system tester, click on new system and type
the buy, sell, sell short and buy to cover code. Then to run the test, click on new

simulation, next, add securities, select GLD, select periodicity daily, click on next, type in initial equity 111111, select default size 90 % available equity, select both long trades and short trades. Click on more ..., fill in interest rate 4 %, and fill in 10 points per transaction for the commissions. Click on trade execution, uncheck realistic market prices and select buy price and sell price at open. Then fill in 1 day for the delay.

Gold bullion or World Gold Index data should be appended to GLD data before 18 November 2004 when the GLD first started trading in the NYSE.

Regression Divergence

Enter long
```
SEC2:=Security("C:\Metastock Data\METAS\XAU",C);
D1:=400; {REGRESSION DAYS}
D2:=12; {ROC DAYS}
RS1:=ROC(C,D2,%);
RS2:=ROC(SEC2,D2,%);
b:=Correl(RS1,RS2,D1,0)*Stdev(RS1,D1)/Stdev(RS2,D1);
a:=mov(RS1,D1,S)-b*MOV(RS2,D1,S);
pred:=b*RS2+a;
DIVERG1:=(PRED-RS1);
DIVERG:=Mov(DIVERG1,3,E);
IM:=(Mov(DIVERG - LLV(DIVERG,200), 3,S) * 100)/(Mov(HHV(DIVERG,
    200) - LLV(DIVERG,200), 3,S));

DIVERG>0 AND ALERT(CROSS(60,IM),4) AND
STOCH(5,3)>MOV(STOCH(5,3),3,S) AND ROC(SEC2,2,%)>1
```

Sell order
```
D1:=400; {REGRESSION DAYS}
D2:=12; {ROC DAYS}
RS1:=ROC(C,D2,%);
RS2:=ROC(SEC2,D2,%);
b:=Correl(RS1,RS2,D1,0)*Stdev(RS1,D1)/Stdev(RS2,D1);
a:=mov(RS1,D1,S)-b*MOV(RS2,D1,S);
pred:=b*RS2+a;
DIVERG1:=(PRED-RS1);
DIVERG:=Mov(DIVERG1,3,E);
IM:=(Mov(DIVERG - LLV(DIVERG,200), 3,S) * 100)/(Mov(HHV
    (DIVERG,200) - LLV(DIVERG,200), 3,S));

DIVERG<0 AND STOCH(5,3)<MOV(STOCH(5,3),3,S) AND LLV(IM,4)<15
    AND IM>REF(IM,-1)
```

Sell short
SEC2:=Security("C:\Metastock Data\METAS\XAU",C);
D1:=400; {REGRESSION DAYS}
D2:=12; {ROC DAYS}
RS1:=ROC(C,D2,%);
RS2:=ROC(SEC2,D2,%);
b:=Correl(RS1,RS2,D1,0)*Stdev(RS1,D1)/Stdev(RS2,D1);
a:=mov(RS1,D1,S)-b*MOV(RS2,D1,S);
pred:=b*RS2+a;
DIVERG1:=(PRED-RS1);
DIVERG:=Mov(DIVERG1,3,E);
IM:=(Mov(DIVERG - LLV(DIVERG,200), 3,S) * 100)/(Mov(HHV
    (DIVERG,200) - LLV(DIVERG,200), 3,S));

DIVERG<-1 AND STOCH(5,3)<MOV(STOCH(5,3),3,S)
AND ALERT(CROSS(IM,8),4) AND ROC(SEC2,2,%)<0

Buy to cover
SEC2:=Security("C:\Metastock Data\METAS\XAU",C);
D1:=400; {REGRESSION DAYS}
D2:=12; {ROC DAYS}
RS1:=ROC(C,D2,%);
RS2:=ROC(SEC2,D2,%);
b:=Correl(RS1,RS2,D1,0)*Stdev(RS1,D1)/Stdev(RS2,D1);
a:=mov(RS1,D1,S)-b*MOV(RS2,D1,S);
pred:=b*RS2+a;
DIVERG1:=(PRED-RS1);
DIVERG:=Mov(DIVERG1,3,E);
IM:=(Mov(DIVERG - LLV(DIVERG,200), 3,S) * 100)/(Mov(HHV
    (DIVERG,200) - LLV(DIVERG,200), 3,S));

ALERT(DIVERG>0,3)   AND   STOCH(5,3)>MOV(STOCH(5,3),3,S)   AND
    HHV(IM,4)>OPT6 AND IM<REF(IM,-1)

Relative Strength (Divergence)

Buy
SEC2:=Security("C:\Metastock Data\METAS\XAU",C);
RS:=MOV((C/SEC2),3,E);
IM:=Mov(RS - LLV(RS,300), 3,S) /(Mov(HHV(RS,300) - LLV(RS,300),
    3,S))*100;
LLV(IM,4)<20 AND IM >REF(IM,-1) AND IM>(1+10/100)*LLV(IM,4)
AND STOCH(5,3)>MOV(STOCH(5,3),3,S)

Sell
SEC2:=Security("C:\Metastock Data\METAS\XAU",C);
RS:=MOV((C/SEC2),3,E);
IM:=Mov(RS - LLV(RS,300), 3,S) /(Mov(HHV(RS,300) - LLV(RS,300), 3,S))*100;
(HHV(IM,4)>35 AND IM <REF(IM,-1)
AND STOCH(5,3)<MOV(STOCH(5,3),3,S))

Short
SEC2:=Security("C:\Metastock Data\METAS\XAU",C);
RS:=MOV((C/SEC2),3,E);
IM:=Mov(RS - LLV(RS,300), 3,S) /(Mov(HHV(RS,300) - LLV(RS,300), 3,S))*100;
HHV(IM,4)>85 AND IM <REF(IM,-1) AND IM<(1-10/100)*HHV(IM,4)
AND STOCH(5,3)<MOV(STOCH(5,3),3,S)

Cover
SEC2:=Security("C:\Metastock Data\METAS\XAU",C);
RS:=MOV((C/SEC2),3,E);
IM:=Mov(RS - LLV(RS,300), 3,S) /(Mov(HHV(RS,300) - LLV(RS,300), 3,S))*100;
LLV(IM,4)<20 AND IM >REF(IM,-1)
AND STOCH(5,3)>MOV(STOCH(5,3),3,S)

Relative Strength

Buy
SEC2:=Security("C:\Metastock Data\METAS\dxy0",C);
D1:=200; {REGRESSION}
D2:=15; {REF}
RS:=MOV((C/SEC2),3,E);

LR1:=REF(LinearReg(RS,D1+D2,E,3),-D2);
ALERT(CROSS(RS,LR1),8) AND RS>(1+3/100)*LR1
AND STOCH(5,3)>MOV(STOCH(5,3),3,S)

SELL
SEC2:=Security("C:\Metastock Data\METAS\dxy0",C);
D1:=50; {REGRESSION}
D2:=6; {REF}
RS:=MOV((C/SEC2),3,E);

```
LR1:=REF(LinearReg(RS,D1+D2,E,3),-D2);
ALERT(CROSS(LR1,RS),6) AND RS<(1-3/100)*LR1
AND STOCH(5,3)<MOV(STOCH(5,3),3,S)
```

Disparity (XAU)

Buy
```
SEC2:=Security("C:\Metastock Data\METAS\XAU",C);
D1:=15;
D2:=15;
D3:=1;
DIS1:=((C - Mov(C,D1,S)) / Mov(C,D1,S)) * 100;
DIS2:=((SEC2 - Mov(SEC2,D2,S)) / Mov(SEC2,D2,S)) * 100;
DIV1:=(D3*DIS2-DIS1);
DIVERG:=Mov(DIV1,3,E);
IM:=(Mov(DIVERG - LLV(DIVERG,200), 3,S) * 100)/(Mov(HHV(DIVERG,
   200) - LLV(DIVERG,200), 3,S));
DIVERG>0 AND ALERT(CROSS(80,IM),4) AND IM< REF(IM,-1) AND
   STOCH(5,3)>MOV(STOCH(5,3),3,S)
AND ROC(SEC2,2,%)>0
```

Sell
```
SEC2:=Security("C:\Metastock Data\METAS\XAU",C);
D1:=15;
D2:=15;
D3:=1;
DIS1:=((C - Mov(C,D1,S)) / Mov(C,D1,S)) * 100;
DIS2:=((SEC2 - Mov(SEC2,D2,S)) / Mov(SEC2,D2,S)) * 100;
DIV1:=(D3*DIS2-DIS1);
DIVERG:=Mov(DIV1,3,E);
IM:=(Mov(DIVERG - LLV(DIVERG,200), 3,S) * 100)/(Mov(HHV(DIVERG,
   200) - LLV(DIVERG,200), 3,S));
DIVERG<0 AND LLV(IM,4)<30 AND IM> REF(IM,-1)
AND STOCH(5,3)<MOV(STOCH(5,3),3,S)
```

Short
```
SEC2:=Security("C:\Metastock Data\METAS\XAU",C);
D1:=15;
D2:=15;
D3:=1;
DIS1:=((C - Mov(C,D1,S)) / Mov(C,D1,S)) * 100;
DIS2:=((SEC2 - Mov(SEC2,D2,S)) / Mov(SEC2,D2,S)) * 100;
```

DIV1:=(D3*DIS2-DIS1);
DIVERG:=Mov(DIV1,3,E);
IM:=(Mov(DIVERG - LLV(DIVERG,200), 3,S) * 100)/(Mov(HHV(DIVERG, 200) - LLV(DIVERG,200), 3,S));

DIVERG<-1 AND ALERT(CROSS(IM,25),3) AND IM> REF(IM,-1)
AND STOCH(5,3)<MOV(STOCH(5,3),3,S) AND ROC(SEC2,2,%)<0

Cover
SEC2:=Security("C:\Metastock Data\METAS\XAU",C);
D1:=15;
D2:=15;
D3:=1;
DIS1:=((C - Mov(C,D1,S)) / Mov(C,D1,S)) * 100;
DIS2:=((SEC2 - Mov(SEC2,D2,S)) / Mov(SEC2,D2,S)) * 100;
DIV1:=(D3*DIS2-DIS1);
DIVERG:=Mov(DIV1,3,E);
IM:=(Mov(DIVERG - LLV(DIVERG,200), 3,S) * 100)/(Mov(HHV(DIVERG, 200) - LLV(DIVERG,200), 3,S));
ALERT(DIVERG>0,3) AND HHV(IM,3)>60 AND STOCH(5,3)> MOV (STOCH(5,3),3,S)

Disparity (DXY)

Buy
SEC2:=Security("C:\Metastock Data\METAS\DXY0",C);
D1:=20;
D2:=15;
D3:=-1;
DIS1:=((C - Mov(C,D1,S)) / Mov(C,D1,S)) * 100;
DIS2:=((SEC2 - Mov(SEC2,D2,S)) / Mov(SEC2,D2,S)) * 100;
DIV1:=(D3*DIS2-DIS1);
DIVERG:=Mov(DIV1,3,E);
IM:=(Mov(DIVERG - LLV(DIVERG,200), 3,S) * 100)/(Mov(HHV(DIVERG, 200) - LLV(DIVERG,200), 3,S));
DIVERG>0 AND ALERT(CROSS(85,IM),4) AND IM< REF(IM,-1) AND STOCH(5,3)>MOV(STOCH(5,3),3,S)
AND ROC(SEC2,2,%)>0

Sell
SEC2:=Security("C:\Metastock Data\METAS\DXY0",C);
D1:=20;
D2:=15;
D3:=-1;

DIS1:=((C - Mov(C,D1,S)) / Mov(C,D1,S)) * 100;
DIS2:=((SEC2 - Mov(SEC2,D2,S)) / Mov(SEC2,D2,S)) * 100;
DIV1:=(D3*DIS2-DIS1);
DIVERG:=Mov(DIV1,3,E);
IM:=(Mov(DIVERG - LLV(DIVERG,200), 3,S) * 100)/(Mov(HHV(DIVERG,
    200) - LLV(DIVERG,200), 3,S));
DIVERG<0 AND {ALERT(CROSS(IM,OPT5),4)} LLV(IM,4)<25 AND IM>
    REF(IM,-1)
AND STOCH(5,3)<MOV(STOCH(5,3),3,S)

Short
SEC2:=Security("C:\Metastock Data\METAS\DXY0",C);
D1:=20;
D2:=15;
D3:=-1;
DIS1:=((C - Mov(C,D1,S)) / Mov(C,D1,S)) * 100;
DIS2:=((SEC2 - Mov(SEC2,D2,S)) / Mov(SEC2,D2,S)) * 100;
DIV1:=(D3*DIS2-DIS1);
DIVERG:=Mov(DIV1,3,E);
IM:=(Mov(DIVERG - LLV(DIVERG,200), 3,S) * 100)/(Mov(HHV(DIVERG,
    200) - LLV(DIVERG,200), 3,S));
DIVERG<-1 AND ALERT(CROSS(IM,25),3) AND IM> REF(IM,-1)
AND STOCH(5,3)<MOV(STOCH(5,3),3,S) AND ROC(SEC2,2,%)<0

Cover
SEC2:=Security("C:\Metastock Data\METAS\DXY0",C);
D1:=20;
D2:=15;
D3:=-1;
DIS1:=((C - Mov(C,D1,S)) / Mov(C,D1,S)) * 100;
DIS2:=((SEC2 - Mov(SEC2,D2,S)) / Mov(SEC2,D2,S)) * 100;
DIV1:=(D3*DIS2-DIS1);
DIVERG:=Mov(DIV1,3,E);
IM:=(Mov(DIVERG - LLV(DIVERG,200), 3,S) * 100)/(Mov(HHV(DIVERG,
    200) - LLV(DIVERG,200), 3,S));
ALERT(DIVERG>0,3)   AND   HHV(IM,3)>50   AND   STOCH(5,3)>MOV
    (STOCH(5,3),3,S)

LRS (XAU)

Buy
SEC2:=Security("C:\Metastock Data\METAS\XAU",C);
D1:=40;{LRS GOLD}

D2:=50;{LRS INTERMARKET}
D3:=STDEV(C,200)/STDEV(SEC2,200);
LRSI:=LinRegSlope(SEC2,D2)/Abs(Ref(SEC2,-D2+1))*100;
LRS:=LinRegSlope(C,D1)/Abs(Ref(C,-D1+1))*100;
DIV1:=(D3*LRSI-LRS)*100;
DIVERG:=Mov(DIV1,3,E);
IM:=(Mov(DIVERG - LLV(DIVERG,200), 3,S) * 100)/(Mov(HHV(DIVERG,
    200) - LLV(DIVERG,200), 3,S));
DIVERG>0 AND ALERT(CROSS(70,IM),4) AND IM< REF(IM,-1) AND
    STOCH(5,3)>MOV(STOCH(5,3),3,S)
AND ROC(SEC2,2,%)>0

Sell
SEC2:=Security("C:\Metastock Data\METAS\XAU",C);
D1:=40;{LRS GOLD}
D2:=50;{LRS INTERMARKET}
D3:=STDEV(C,200)/STDEV(SEC2,200);
LRSI:=LinRegSlope(SEC2,D2)/Abs(Ref(SEC2,-D2+1))*100;
LRS:=LinRegSlope(C,D1)/Abs(Ref(C,-D1+1))*100;
DIV1:=(D3*LRSI-LRS)*100;
DIVERG:=Mov(DIV1,3,E);
IM:=(Mov(DIVERG - LLV(DIVERG,200), 3,S) * 100)/(Mov(HHV(DIVERG,
    200) - LLV(DIVERG,200), 3,S));
DIVERG<0 AND LLV(IM,4)<15 AND IM> REF(IM,-1)
    AND STOCH(5,3)<MOV(STOCH(5,3),3,S)

Short
SEC2:=Security("C:\Metastock Data\METAS\XAU",C);
D1:=40;{LRS GOLD}
D2:=50;{LRS INTERMARKET}
D3:=STDEV(C,200)/STDEV(SEC2,200);
LRSI:=LinRegSlope(SEC2,D2)/Abs(Ref(SEC2,-D2+1))*100;
LRS:=LinRegSlope(C,D1)/Abs(Ref(C,-D1+1))*100;
DIV1:=(D3*LRSI-LRS)*100;
DIVERG:=Mov(DIV1,3,E);
IM:=(Mov(DIVERG - LLV(DIVERG,200), 3,S) * 100)/(Mov(HHV(DIVERG,
    200) - LLV(DIVERG,200), 3,S));
DIVERG<-1 AND ALERT(CROSS(IM,5),3) AND IM> REF(IM,-1)
AND STOCH(5,3)<MOV(STOCH(5,3),3,S) AND ROC(SEC2,2,%)<0

Cover
SEC2:=Security("C:\Metastock Data\METAS\XAU",C);
D1:=40;{LRS GOLD}

D2:=50;{LRS INTERMARKET}
D3:=STDEV(C,200)/STDEV(SEC2,200);
LRSI:=LinRegSlope(SEC2,D2)/Abs(Ref(SEC2,-D2+1))*100;
LRS:=LinRegSlope(C,D1)/Abs(Ref(C,-D1+1))*100;
DIV1:=(D3*LRSI-LRS)*100;
DIVERG:=Mov(DIV1,3,E);
IM:=(Mov(DIVERG - LLV(DIVERG,200), 3,S) * 100)/(Mov(HHV(DIVERG, 200) - LLV(DIVERG,200), 3,S));
ALERT(DIVERG>0,3) AND HHV(IM,3)>50 AND STOCH(5,3)> MOV(STOCH(5,3),3,S)

LRS (DXY)

Buy
SEC2:=Security("C:\Metastock Data\METAS\DXY0",C);
D1:=30;{LRS GOLD}
D2:=40;{LRS INTERMARKET}
D3:=-STDEV(C,200)/STDEV(SEC2,200);
LRSI:=LinRegSlope(SEC2,D2)/Abs(Ref(SEC2,-D2+1))*100;
LRS:=LinRegSlope(C,D1)/Abs(Ref(C,-D1+1))*100;
DIV1:=(D3*LRSI-LRS)*100;
DIVERG:=Mov(DIV1,3,E);
IM:=(Mov(DIVERG - LLV(DIVERG,200), 3,S) * 100)/(Mov(HHV(DIVERG, 200) - LLV(DIVERG,200), 3,S));
DIVERG>0 AND ALERT(CROSS(85,IM),4) AND IM< REF(IM,-1) AND STOCH(5,3)>MOV(STOCH(5,3),3,S)
AND ROC(SEC2,2,%)>0

Sell
SEC2:=Security("C:\Metastock Data\METAS\DXY0",C);
D1:=30;{LRS GOLD}
D2:=40;{LRS INTERMARKET}
D3:=-STDEV(C,200)/STDEV(SEC2,200);
LRSI:=LinRegSlope(SEC2,D2)/Abs(Ref(SEC2,-D2+1))*100;
LRS:=LinRegSlope(C,D1)/Abs(Ref(C,-D1+1))*100;
DIV1:=(D3*LRSI-LRS)*100;
DIVERG:=Mov(DIV1,3,E);
IM:=(Mov(DIVERG - LLV(DIVERG,200), 3,S) * 100)/(Mov(HHV(DIVERG, 200) - LLV(DIVERG,200), 3,S));
DIVERG<0 AND LLV(IM,4)<25 AND IM> REF(IM,-1)
AND STOCH(5,3)<MOV(STOCH(5,3),3,S)

Short
SEC2:=Security("C:\Metastock Data\METAS\DXY0",C);
D1:=30;{LRS GOLD}
D2:=40;{LRS INTERMARKET}
D3:=-STDEV(C,200)/STDEV(SEC2,200);
LRSI:=LinRegSlope(SEC2,D2)/Abs(Ref(SEC2,-D2+1))*100;
LRS:=LinRegSlope(C,D1)/Abs(Ref(C,-D1+1))*100;
DIV1:=(D3*LRSI-LRS)*100;
DIVERG:=Mov(DIV1,3,E);
IM:=(Mov(DIVERG - LLV(DIVERG,200), 3,S) * 100)/(Mov(HHV(DIVERG,
    200) - LLV(DIVERG,200), 3,S));
DIVERG<-1 AND ALERT(CROSS(IM,25),3) AND IM> REF(IM,-1)
AND STOCH(5,3)<MOV(STOCH(5,3),3,S) AND ROC(SEC2,2,%)<0

Cover
SEC2:=Security("C:\Metastock Data\METAS\DXY0",C);
D1:=30;{LRS GOLD}
D2:=40;{LRS INTERMARKET}
D3:=-STDEV(C,200)/STDEV(SEC2,200);
LRSI:=LinRegSlope(SEC2,D2)/Abs(Ref(SEC2,-D2+1))*100;
LRS:=LinRegSlope(C,D1)/Abs(Ref(C,-D1+1))*100;
DIV1:=(D3*LRSI-LRS)*100;
DIVERG:=Mov(DIV1,3,E);
IM:=(Mov(DIVERG - LLV(DIVERG,200), 3,S) * 100)/(Mov(HHV(DIVERG,
    200) - LLV(DIVERG,200), 3,S));
ALERT(DIVERG>0,3) AND HHV(IM,3)>60 AND STOCH(5,3)>
    MOV(STOCH(5,3),3,S)

Bollinger Band (XAU)

Buy
SEC2:=Security("C:\Metastock Data\METAS\XAU",C);
D1:=100;{BB PERIOD GOLD}
D2:=100;{BB PERIOD INTERMARKET}
sec1BOL:= 1+((C- Mov(C,D1,S)+2*Stdev(C,D1))/(4*Stdev(C,D1)));
sec2BOL:=1+((SEC2- Mov(SEC2,D2,S)+2*Stdev(SEC2,D2))/(4*Stdev
    (SEC2,D2)));
DIVERG1:=(sec2BOL-sec1BOL)/sec1bol*100;
diverg:=Mov(diverg1,3,E);
IM:=(Mov(DIVERG - LLV(DIVERG,200), 3,S) * 100)/(Mov(HHV(DIVERG,
    200) - LLV(DIVERG,200), 3,S));

DIVERG>0 AND ALERT(CROSS(70,IM),4) AND IM< REF(IM,-1) AND
STOCH(5,3)>MOV(STOCH(5,3),3,S)
AND ROC(SEC2,2,%)>0

Sell
SEC2:=Security("C:\Metastock Data\METAS\XAU",C);
D1:=100;{BB PERIOD GOLD}
D2:=100;{BB PERIOD INTERMARKET}
sec1BOL:= 1+((C- Mov(C,D1,S)+2*Stdev(C,D1))/(4*Stdev(C,D1)));
sec2BOL:=1+((SEC2- Mov(SEC2,D2,S)+2*Stdev(SEC2,D2))/(4*Stdev
(SEC2,D2)));
DIVERG1:=(sec2BOL-sec1BOL)/sec1bol*100;
diverg:=Mov(diverg1,3,E);
IM:=(Mov(DIVERG - LLV(DIVERG,200), 3,S) * 100)/(Mov(HHV(DIVERG,
200) - LLV(DIVERG,200), 3,S));
((DIVERG<-5 AND DIVERG>REF(DIVERG,-1)) OR (LLV(IM,4)<30 AND
IM> REF(IM,-1)))
AND STOCH(5,3)<MOV(STOCH(5,3),3,S)

Short
SEC2:=Security("C:\Metastock Data\METAS\XAU",C);
D1:=100;{BB PERIOD GOLD}
D2:=100;{BB PERIOD INTERMARKET}
sec1BOL:= 1+((C- Mov(C,D1,S)+2*Stdev(C,D1))/(4*Stdev(C,D1)));
sec2BOL:=1+((SEC2- Mov(SEC2,D2,S)+2*Stdev(SEC2,D2))/(4*Stdev
(SEC2,D2)));
DIVERG1:=(sec2BOL-sec1BOL)/sec1bol*100;
diverg:=Mov(diverg1,3,E);
IM:=(Mov(DIVERG - LLV(DIVERG,200), 3,S) * 100)/(Mov(HHV(DIVERG,
200) - LLV(DIVERG,200), 3,S));
DIVERG<-10 AND ALERT(CROSS(IM,5),3) AND IM> REF(IM,-1)
AND STOCH(5,3)<MOV(STOCH(5,3),3,S) AND ROC(SEC2,2,%)<0

Cover
SEC2:=Security("C:\Metastock Data\METAS\XAU",C);
D1:=100;{BB PERIOD GOLD}
D2:=100;{BB PERIOD INTERMARKET}
sec1BOL:= 1+((C- Mov(C,D1,S)+2*Stdev(C,D1))/(4*Stdev(C,D1)));
sec2BOL:=1+((SEC2- Mov(SEC2,D2,S)+2*Stdev(SEC2,D2))/(4*Stdev
(SEC2,D2)));
DIVERG1:=(sec2BOL-sec1BOL)/sec1bol*100;
diverg:=Mov(diverg1,3,E);

IM:=(Mov(DIVERG - LLV(DIVERG,200), 3,S) * 100)/(Mov(HHV(DIVERG,
    200) - LLV(DIVERG,200), 3,S));
ALERT(DIVERG>0,3) AND HHV(IM,3)>50 AND STOCH(5,3)>
    MOV(STOCH(5,3),3,S)

Z-Score (XAU)

Buy
SEC2:=Security("C:\Metastock Data\METAS\XAU",C);
D1:= 100;
r:=Correl(SEC2,C,D1,0);
Z1:=(C-Mov(C,D1,S))/Stdev(C,D1);
Z2:=(SEC2-Mov(SEC2,D1,S))/Stdev(SEC2,D1);
ZDIV:=(Z2*r/Abs(r)-Z1)*Abs(r);
diverg:=Mov(ZDIV,3,E);
IM:=(Mov(DIVERG - LLV(DIVERG,200), 3,S) * 100)/(Mov(HHV(DIVERG,
    200) - LLV(DIVERG,200), 3,S));
ALERT(CROSS(80,IM),4) AND IM< REF(IM,-1) AND STOCH(5,3)>
    MOV(STOCH(5,3),3,S)
AND ROC(SEC2,2,%)>0

Sell
SEC2:=Security("C:\Metastock Data\METAS\XAU",C);
D1:= 100;
r:=Correl(SEC2,C,D1,0);
Z1:=(C-Mov(C,D1,S))/Stdev(C,D1);
Z2:=(SEC2-Mov(SEC2,D1,S))/Stdev(SEC2,D1);
ZDIV:=(Z2*r/Abs(r)-Z1)*Abs(r);
diverg:=Mov(ZDIV,3,E);;
IM:=(Mov(DIVERG - LLV(DIVERG,200), 3,S) * 100)/(Mov(HHV(DIVERG,
    200) - LLV(DIVERG,200), 3,S));
LLV(IM,4)<50 AND IM> REF(IM,-1)
AND STOCH(5,3)<MOV(STOCH(5,3),3,S)

Short
SEC2:=Security("C:\Metastock Data\METAS\XAU",C);
D1:= 100;
r:=Correl(SEC2,C,D1,0);
Z1:=(C-Mov(C,D1,S))/Stdev(C,D1);
Z2:=(SEC2-Mov(SEC2,D1,S))/Stdev(SEC2,D1);
ZDIV:=(Z2*r/Abs(r)-Z1)*Abs(r);
diverg:=Mov(ZDIV,3,E);;

IM:=(Mov(DIVERG - LLV(DIVERG,200), 3,S) * 100)/(Mov(HHV(DIVERG, 200) - LLV(DIVERG,200), 3,S));
DIVERG<0 AND ALERT(CROSS(IM,10),3) AND IM> REF(IM,-1)
AND STOCH(5,3)<MOV(STOCH(5,3),3,S) AND ROC(SEC2,2,%)<0

Cover
SEC2:=Security("C:\Metastock Data\METAS\XAU",C);
D1:= 100;
r:=Correl(SEC2,C,D1,0);
Z1:=(C-Mov(C,D1,S))/Stdev(C,D1);
Z2:=(SEC2-Mov(SEC2,D1,S))/Stdev(SEC2,D1);
ZDIV:=(Z2*r/Abs(r)-Z1)*Abs(r);
diverg:=Mov(ZDIV,3,E);;
IM:=(Mov(DIVERG - LLV(DIVERG,200), 3,S) * 100)/(Mov(HHV(DIVERG, 200) - LLV(DIVERG,200), 3,S));
HHV(IM,3)>40 AND STOCH(5,3)>MOV(STOCH(5,3),3,S)

Z-Score (DXY)

Buy
SEC2:=Security("C:\Metastock Data\METAS\DXY0",C);
D1:= 500;
r:=Correl(SEC2,C,D1,0);
Z1:=(C-Mov(C,D1,S))/Stdev(C,D1);
Z2:=(SEC2-Mov(SEC2,D1,S))/Stdev(SEC2,D1);
ZDIV:=(Z2*r/Abs(r)-Z1)*Abs(r);
diverg:=Mov(ZDIV,3,E);
IM:=(Mov(DIVERG - LLV(DIVERG,200), 3,S) * 100)/(Mov(HHV(DIVERG, 200) - LLV(DIVERG,200), 3,S));
ALERT(CROSS(90,IM),4) AND IM< REF(IM,-1) AND STOCH(5,3)>
MOV(STOCH(5,3),3,S)
AND ROC(SEC2,2,%)>0

Sell
SEC2:=Security("C:\Metastock Data\METAS\DXY0",C);
D1:= 500;
r:=Correl(SEC2,C,D1,0);
Z1:=(C-Mov(C,D1,S))/Stdev(C,D1);
Z2:=(SEC2-Mov(SEC2,D1,S))/Stdev(SEC2,D1);
ZDIV:=(Z2*r/Abs(r)-Z1)*Abs(r);
diverg:=Mov(ZDIV,3,E);;

IM:=(Mov(DIVERG - LLV(DIVERG,200), 3,S) * 100)/(Mov(HHV(DIVERG,
    200) - LLV(DIVERG,200), 3,S));
LLV(IM,4)<50 AND IM> REF(IM,-1)
AND STOCH(5,3)<MOV(STOCH(5,3),3,S)

Short
SEC2:=Security("C:\Metastock Data\METAS\DXY0",C);
D1:= 500;
r:=Correl(SEC2,C,D1,0);
Z1:=(C-Mov(C,D1,S))/Stdev(C,D1);
Z2:=(SEC2-Mov(SEC2,D1,S))/Stdev(SEC2,D1);
ZDIV:=(Z2*r/Abs(r)-Z1)*Abs(r);
diverg:=Mov(ZDIV,3,E);;
IM:=(Mov(DIVERG - LLV(DIVERG,200), 3,S) * 100)/(Mov(HHV(DIVERG,
    200) - LLV(DIVERG,200), 3,S));
DIVERG<0 AND ALERT(CROSS(IM,5),3) AND IM> REF(IM,-1)
AND STOCH(5,3)<MOV(STOCH(5,3),3,S) AND ROC(SEC2,2,%)<0

Cover
SEC2:=Security("C:\Metastock Data\METAS\DXY0",C);
D1:=500;
r:=Correl(SEC2,C,D1,0);
Z1:=(C-Mov(C,D1,S))/Stdev(C,D1);
Z2:=(SEC2-Mov(SEC2,D1,S))/Stdev(SEC2,D1);
ZDIV:=(Z2*r/Abs(r)-Z1)*Abs(r);
diverg:=Mov(ZDIV,3,E);;
IM:=(Mov(DIVERG - LLV(DIVERG,200), 3,S) * 100)/(Mov(HHV(DIVERG,
    200) - LLV(DIVERG,200), 3,S));
HHV(IM,3)>50 AND STOCH(5,3)>MOV(STOCH(5,3),3,S)

Multiple Regression Divergence (XAU-SLV-DXY)

Buy
SEC1:=Security("C:\Metastock Data\METAS\XAU",C);
SEC2:=Security("C:\Metastock Data\METAS\SLV",C);
SEC3:=Security("C:\Metastock Data\METAS\DXY0",C);
D2:=11; {ROC DAYS}
a:=.16;b1:=.2;b2:=.175;b3:=-.5;
ROCY:=ROC(C,D2,%);
ROC1:=ROC(SEC1,D2,%);
ROC2:=ROC(SEC2,D2,%);
ROC3:=ROC(SEC3,D2,%);

```
PRED:=a+b1*ROC1+b2*ROC2+b3*ROC3;
DIVERG1:=(PRED-ROCY)*10;
DIVERG:=Mov(DIVERG1,3,E);
IM:=(Mov(DIVERG - LLV(DIVERG,300), 3,S) * 100)/(Mov(HHV(DIVERG,
   300) - LLV(DIVERG,300), 3,S));
DIVERG>1 AND ALERT(CROSS(70,IM),4) AND STOCH(5,3)>
   MOV(STOCH(5,3),3,S)
```

Sell
```
SEC1:=Security("C:\Metastock Data\METAS\XAU",C);
SEC2:=Security("C:\Metastock Data\METAS\SLV",C);
SEC3:=Security("C:\Metastock Data\METAS\DXY0",C);
D2:=11; {ROC DAYS}
a:=.16;b1:=.2;b2:=.175;b3:=-.5;
ROCY:=ROC(C,D2,%);
ROC1:=ROC(SEC1,D2,%);
ROC2:=ROC(SEC2,D2,%);
ROC3:=ROC(SEC3,D2,%);
PRED:=a+b1*ROC1+b2*ROC2+b3*ROC3;
DIVERG1:=(PRED-ROCY)*10;
DIVERG:=Mov(DIVERG1,3,E);
IM:=(Mov(DIVERG - LLV(DIVERG,300), 3,S) * 100)/(Mov(HHV(DIVERG,
   300) - LLV(DIVERG,300), 3,S));
STOCH(15,3)<MOV(STOCH(15,3),5,S) AND HHV(STOCH(15,3),3)>80 AND
   LLV(IM,4)<14
```

Short
```
SEC1:=Security("C:\Metastock Data\METAS\XAU",C);
SEC2:=Security("C:\Metastock Data\METAS\SLV",C);
SEC3:=Security("C:\Metastock Data\METAS\DXY0",C);
D2:=11; {ROC DAYS}
a:=.16;b1:=.2;b2:=.175;b3:=-.5;
ROCY:=ROC(C,D2,%);
ROC1:=ROC(SEC1,D2,%);
ROC2:=ROC(SEC2,D2,%);
ROC3:=ROC(SEC3,D2,%);
PRED:=a+b1*ROC1+b2*ROC2+b3*ROC3;
DIVERG1:=(PRED-ROCY)*10;
DIVERG:=Mov(DIVERG1,3,E);
IM:=(Mov(DIVERG - LLV(DIVERG,300), 3,S) * 100)/(Mov(HHV(DIVERG,
   300) - LLV(DIVERG,300), 3,S));
DIVERG<-4 AND STOCH(5,3)<MOV(STOCH(5,3),5,S)
   AND ALERT(CROSS(IM,7),4) AND IM>1.2*REF(IM,-2)
```

Cover
```
SEC1:=Security("C:\Metastock Data\METAS\XAU",C);
SEC2:=Security("C:\Metastock Data\METAS\SLV",C);
SEC3:=Security("C:\Metastock Data\METAS\DXY0",C);
D2:=11; {ROC DAYS}
a:=.16;b1:=.2;b2:=.175;b3:=-.5;
ROCY:=ROC(C,D2,%);
ROC1:=ROC(SEC1,D2,%);
ROC2:=ROC(SEC2,D2,%);
ROC3:=ROC(SEC3,D2,%);
PRED:=a+b1*ROC1+b2*ROC2+b3*ROC3;
DIVERG1:=(PRED-ROCY)*10;
DIVERG:=Mov(DIVERG1,3,E);
IM:=(Mov(DIVERG - LLV(DIVERG,300), 3,S) * 100)/(Mov(HHV(DIVERG,
   300) - LLV(DIVERG,300), 3,S)));
ALERT(DIVERG>0,3) AND STOCH(5,3)>MOV(STOCH(5,3),5,S) AND HHV
   (IM,4)>60 AND IM<REF(IM,-1)
```

LRS Double (SLV-DXY)

Buy
```
SEC1:=Security("C:\Metastock Data\METAS\SLV",C);
SEC2:=Security("C:\Metastock Data\METAS\DXY0",C);
D1:=20;{LRS SEC1};
D2:=30;{LRS SEC2};
D3:=20;{LRS GOLD};
sY:=Stdev(C,300)/Mov(C,300,S);
s1:=Stdev(SEC1,300))/Mov(SEC1,300,S);
s2:=Stdev(SEC2,300))/Mov(SEC2,300,S);
rY1:=Correl(SEC1,C,300,0);
rY2:=Correl(SEC2,C,300,0);
r12:=Correl(SEC1,SEC2,300,0);
rY12:=(rY1-rY2*r12)/Sqrt(1-r12*r12);
rY21:=(rY2-rY1*r12)/Sqrt(1-r12*r12);
LRS1:=LinRegSlope(SEC1,D1)/Abs(Ref(SEC1,-D1+1))*100;
LRS2:=LinRegSlope(SEC2,D2)/Abs(Ref(SEC2,-D2+1))*100;
LRS:=LinRegSlope(C,D3)/Abs(Ref(C,-D3+1))*100;
DIVERG1:=(rY12*sY/s1*LRS1+rY21*sY/s2*LRS2-LRS)*100;
DIVERG:=Mov(DIVERG1,3,E);
IM:=(Mov(DIVERG - LLV(DIVERG,200), 3,S) * 100)/(Mov(HHV(DIVERG,
   200) - LLV(DIVERG,200), 3,S)));
DIVERG>0 AND ALERT(CROSS(70,IM),4) AND STOCH(5,3)>
   MOV(STOCH(5,3),3,S)
```

Sell
SEC1:=Security("C:\Metastock Data\METAS\SLV",C);
SEC2:=Security("C:\Metastock Data\METAS\DXY0",C);
D1:=20;{LRS SEC1};
D2:=30;{LRS SEC2};
D3:=20;{LRS GOLD};
sY:=Stdev(C,300)/Mov(C,300,S);
s1:=Stdev(SEC1,300))/Mov(SEC1,300,S);
s2:=Stdev(SEC2,300))/Mov(SEC2,300,S);
rY1:=Correl(SEC1,C,300,0);
rY2:=Correl(SEC2,C,300,0);
r12:=Correl(SEC1,SEC2,300,0);
rY12:=(rY1-rY2*r12)/Sqrt(1-r12*r12);
rY21:=(rY2-rY1*r12)/Sqrt(1-r12*r12);
LRS1:=LinRegSlope(SEC1,D1)/Abs(Ref(SEC1,-D1+1))*100;
LRS2:=LinRegSlope(SEC2,D2)/Abs(Ref(SEC2,-D2+1))*100;
LRS:=LinRegSlope(C,D3)/Abs(Ref(C,-D3+1))*100;
DIVERG1:=(rY12*sY/s1*LRS1+rY21*sY/s2*LRS2-LRS)*100;
DIVERG:=Mov(DIVERG1,3,E);
IM:=(Mov(DIVERG - LLV(DIVERG,200), 3,S) * 100)/(Mov(HHV(DIVERG,
    200) - LLV(DIVERG,200), 3,S));

STOCH(15,3)<MOV(STOCH(15,3),5,S) AND HHV(STOCH(15,3),3)>80 AND
    LLV(IM,4)<7

Short
SEC1:=Security("C:\Metastock Data\METAS\SLV",C);
SEC2:=Security("C:\Metastock Data\METAS\DXY0",C);
D1:=20;{LRS SEC1};
D2:=30;{LRS SEC2};
D3:=20;{LRS GOLD};
sY:=Stdev(C,300)/Mov(C,300,S);
s1:=Stdev(SEC1,300)/Mov(SEC1,300,S);s2:=Stdev(SEC2,300)/Mov(SEC2,300,S);
rY1:=Correl(SEC1,C,300,0);
rY2:=Correl(SEC2,C,300,0);
r12:=Correl(SEC1,SEC2,300,0);
rY12:=(rY1-rY2*r12)/Sqrt(1-r12*r12);
rY21:=(rY2-rY1*r12)/Sqrt(1-r12*r12);
LRS1:=LinRegSlope(SEC1,D1)/Abs(Ref(SEC1,-D1+1))*100;
LRS2:=LinRegSlope(SEC2,D2)/Abs(Ref(SEC2,-D2+1))*100;
LRS:=LinRegSlope(C,D3)/Abs(Ref(C,-D3+1))*100;
DIVERG1:=(rY12*sY/s1*LRS1+rY21*sY/s2*LRS2-LRS)*100;
DIVERG:=Mov(DIVERG1,3,E);
IM:=(Mov(DIVERG - LLV(DIVERG,200), 3,S) * 100)/(Mov(HHV(DIVERG,
    200) - LLV(DIVERG,200), 3,S));

DIVERG<-1 AND STOCH(5,3)<MOV(STOCH(5,3),5,S)
AND ALERT(CROSS(IM,5),4) AND IM>REF(IM,-2)

Cover
SEC1:=Security("C:\Metastock Data\METAS\SLV",C);
SEC2:=Security("C:\Metastock Data\METAS\DXY0",C);
D1:=20;{LRS SEC1};
D2:=30;{LRS SEC2};
D3:=20;{LRS GOLD};
sY:=Stdev(C,300)/Mov(C,300,S);
s1:=Stdev(SEC1,300))/Mov(SEC1,300,S);
s2:=Stdev(SEC2,300))/Mov(SEC2,300,S);
rY1:=Correl(SEC1,C,300,0);
rY2:=Correl(SEC2,C,300,0);
r12:=Correl(SEC1,SEC2,300,0);
rY12:=(rY1-rY2*r12)/Sqrt(1-r12*r12);
rY21:=(rY2-rY1*r12)/Sqrt(1-r12*r12);
LRS1:=LinRegSlope(SEC1,D1)/Abs(Ref(SEC1,-D1+1))*100;
LRS2:=LinRegSlope(SEC2,D2)/Abs(Ref(SEC2,-D2+1))*100;
LRS:=LinRegSlope(C,D3)/Abs(Ref(C,-D3+1))*100;
DIVERG1:=(rY12*sY/s1*LRS1+rY21*sY/s2*LRS2-LRS)*100;
DIVERG:=Mov(DIVERG1,3,E);
IM:=(Mov(DIVERG - LLV(DIVERG,200), 3,S) * 100)/(Mov(HHV(DIVERG,
    200) - LLV(DIVERG,200), 3,S));
ALERT(DIVERG>0,3) AND STOCH(5,3)>MOV(STOCH(5,3),5,S) AND
    HHV(IM,4)>55 AND IM<ref(IM,-1)

LRS Double (XAU-DXY)

Buy
SEC1:=Security("C:\Metastock Data\METAS\XAU",C);
SEC2:=Security("C:\Metastock Data\METAS\DXY0",C);
D1:=20;{LRS SEC1};
D2:=30;{LRS SEC2};
D3:=20;{LRS GOLD};
sY:=Stdev(C,300)/Mov(C,300,S);
s1:=Stdev(SEC1,300))/Mov(SEC1,300,S);
s2:=Stdev(SEC2,300))/Mov(SEC2,300,S);
rY1:=Correl(SEC1,C,300,0);
rY2:=Correl(SEC2,C,300,0);
r12:=Correl(SEC1,SEC2,300,0);
rY12:=(rY1-rY2*r12)/Sqrt(1-r12*r12);
rY21:=(rY2-rY1*r12)/Sqrt(1-r12*r12);
LRS1:=LinRegSlope(SEC1,D1)/Abs(Ref(SEC1,-D1+1))*100;

```
LRS2:=LinRegSlope(SEC2,D2)/Abs(Ref(SEC2,-D2+1))*100;
LRS:=LinRegSlope(C,D3)/Abs(Ref(C,-D3+1))*100;
DIVERG1:=(rY12*sY/s1*LRS1+rY21*sY/s2*LRS2-LRS)*100;
DIVERG:=Mov(DIVERG1,3,E);
IM:=(Mov(DIVERG - LLV(DIVERG,300), 3,S) * 100)/(Mov(HHV(DIVERG,
    300) - LLV(DIVERG,300), 3,S));

DIVERG>0 AND ALERT(CROSS(70,IM),4) AND
    STOCH(5,3)>MOV(STOCH(5,3),3,S)
```

Sell

```
SEC1:=Security("C:\Metastock Data\METAS\XAU",C);
SEC2:=Security("C:\Metastock Data\METAS\DXY0",C);
D1:=20;{LRS SEC1};
D2:=30;{LRS SEC2};
D3:=20;{LRS GOLD};
sY:=Stdev(C,300)/Mov(C,300,S);
s1:=Stdev(SEC1,300))/Mov(SEC1,300,S);
s2:=Stdev(SEC2,300))/Mov(SEC2,300,S);
rY1:=Correl(SEC1,C,300,0);
rY2:=Correl(SEC2,C,300,0);
r12:=Correl(SEC1,SEC2,300,0);
rY12:=(rY1-rY2*r12)/Sqrt(1-r12*r12);
rY21:=(rY2-rY1*r12)/Sqrt(1-r12*r12);
LRS1:=LinRegSlope(SEC1,D1)/Abs(Ref(SEC1,-D1+1))*100;
LRS2:=LinRegSlope(SEC2,D2)/Abs(Ref(SEC2,-D2+1))*100;
LRS:=LinRegSlope(C,D3)/Abs(Ref(C,-D3+1))*100;
DIVERG1:=(rY12*sY/s1*LRS1+rY21*sY/s2*LRS2-LRS)*100;
DIVERG:=Mov(DIVERG1,3,E);
IM:=(Mov(DIVERG - LLV(DIVERG,300), 3,S) * 100)/(Mov(HHV(DIVERG,
    300) - LLV(DIVERG,300), 3,S));

STOCH(15,3)<MOV(STOCH(15,3),5,S) AND HHV(STOCH(15,3),3)>80 AND
    LLV(IM,4)<10
```

Short

```
SEC1:=Security("C:\Metastock Data\METAS\XAU",C);
SEC2:=Security("C:\Metastock Data\METAS\DXY0",C);
D1:=20;{LRS SEC1};
D2:=30;{LRS SEC2};
D3:=20;{LRS GOLD};
sY:=Stdev(C,300)/Mov(C,300,S);
s1:=Stdev(SEC1,300))/Mov(SEC1,300,S);
s2:=Stdev(SEC2,300))/Mov(SEC2,300,S);
rY1:=Correl(SEC1,C,300,0);
```

```
rY2:=Correl(SEC2,C,300,0);
r12:=Correl(SEC1,SEC2,300,0);
rY12:=(rY1-rY2*r12)/Sqrt(1-r12*r12);
rY21:=(rY2-rY1*r12)/Sqrt(1-r12*r12);
LRS1:=LinRegSlope(SEC1,D1)/Abs(Ref(SEC1,-D1+1))*100;
LRS2:=LinRegSlope(SEC2,D2)/Abs(Ref(SEC2,-D2+1))*100;
LRS:=LinRegSlope(C,D3)/Abs(Ref(C,-D3+1))*100;
DIVERG1:=(rY12*sY/s1*LRS1+rY21*sY/s2*LRS2-LRS)*100;
DIVERG:=Mov(DIVERG1,3,E);
IM:=(Mov(DIVERG - LLV(DIVERG,300), 3,S) * 100)/(Mov(HHV(DIVERG,
     300) - LLV(DIVERG,300), 3,S));

DIVERG<-1 AND STOCH(5,3)<MOV(STOCH(5,3),5,S)
     AND ALERT(CROSS(IM,15),4) AND IM>REF(IM,-2)
```

Cover
```
SEC1:=Security("C:\Metastock Data\METAS\XAU",C);
SEC2:=Security("C:\Metastock Data\METAS\DXY0",C);
D1:=20;{LRS SEC1};
D2:=30;{LRS SEC2};
D3:=20;{LRS GOLD};
sY:=Stdev(C,300)/Mov(C,300,S);
s1:=Stdev(SEC1,300))/Mov(SEC1,300,S);
s2:=Stdev(SEC2,300))/Mov(SEC2,300,S);
rY1:=Correl(SEC1,C,300,0);
rY2:=Correl(SEC2,C,300,0);
r12:=Correl(SEC1,SEC2,300,0);
rY12:=(rY1-rY2*r12)/Sqrt(1-r12*r12);
rY21:=(rY2-rY1*r12)/Sqrt(1-r12*r12);
LRS1:=LinRegSlope(SEC1,D1)/Abs(Ref(SEC1,-D1+1))*100;
LRS2:=LinRegSlope(SEC2,D2)/Abs(Ref(SEC2,-D2+1))*100;
LRS:=LinRegSlope(C,D3)/Abs(Ref(C,-D3+1))*100;
DIVERG1:=(rY12*sY/s1*LRS1+rY21*sY/s2*LRS2-LRS)*100;
DIVERG:=Mov(DIVERG1,3,E);
IM:=(Mov(DIVERG - LLV(DIVERG,300), 3,S) * 100)/(Mov(HHV(DIVERG,
     300) - LLV(DIVERG,300), 3,S));

ALERT(DIVERG>0,3) AND STOCH(5,3)>MOV(STOCH(5,3),5,S) AND
     HHV(IM,4)>70 AND IM<ref(IM,-1)
```

Regression Double (XAU-DXY)

Buy
```
SEC1:=Security("C:\Metastock Data\METAS\XAU",C);
```

```
SEC2:=Security("C:\Metastock Data\METAS\DXY0",C);
D1:=500; {REGRESSION DAYS}
D2:=11; {ROC DAYS}
ROCY:=ROC(C,D2,%);
ROC1:=ROC(SEC1,D2,%);
ROC2:=ROC(SEC2,D2,%);
sY:=Stdev(ROCY,D1);
s1:=Stdev(ROC1,D1);s2:=Stdev(ROC2,D1);
rY1:=Correl(ROC1,ROCY,D1,0);
rY2:=Correl(ROC2,ROCY,D1,0);
r12:=Correl(ROC1,ROC2,D1,0);
b1:=(rY1-rY2*r12)/(1-r12*r12)*(sY/s1);
b2:=(rY2-rY1*r12)/Sqrt(1-r12*r12)*(sY/s2);
a:=Mov(ROCY,D1,S)-b1*Mov(ROC1,D1,S)-b2*Mov(ROC2,D1,S);
PRED:=a+b1*ROC1+b2*ROC2;
DIVERG:=(PRED-ROCY)*10;
DIVERG:=Mov(DIVERG,3,E);
IM:=(Mov(DIVERG - LLV(DIVERG,200), 3,S) * 100)/(Mov(HHV(DIVERG,
    200) - LLV(DIVERG,200), 3,S));
R2:= b1*s1/sY*rY1+b2*s2/sY*rY2;

DIVERG>1 AND ALERT(CROSS(80,IM),4) AND STOCH(5,3)>MOV
    (STOCH(5,3),3,S) and R2>.46 AND (ADX(18) <28 or LinRegSlope
    (adx(18),5)<0)
```

Sell

```
SEC1:=Security("C:\Metastock Data\METAS\XAU",C);
SEC2:=Security("C:\Metastock Data\METAS\DXY0",C);
D1:=500; {REGRESSION DAYS}
D2:=11; {ROC DAYS}
ROCY:=ROC(C,D2,%);
ROC1:=ROC(SEC1,D2,%);
ROC2:=ROC(SEC2,D2,%);
sY:=Stdev(ROCY,D1);
s1:=Stdev(ROC1,D1);s2:=Stdev(ROC2,D1);
rY1:=Correl(ROC1,ROCY,D1,0);
rY2:=Correl(ROC2,ROCY,D1,0);
r12:=Correl(ROC1,ROC2,D1,0);
b1:=(rY1-rY2*r12)/(1-r12*r12)*(sY/s1);
b2:=(rY2-rY1*r12)/Sqrt(1-r12*r12)*(sY/s2);
a:=Mov(ROCY,D1,S)-b1*Mov(ROC1,D1,S)-b2*Mov(ROC2,D1,S);
PRED:=a+b1*ROC1+b2*ROC2;
DIVERG:=(PRED-ROCY)*10;
DIVERG:=Mov(DIVERG,3,E);
```

IM:=(Mov(DIVERG - LLV(DIVERG,200), 3,S) * 100)/(Mov(HHV(DIVERG, 200) - LLV(DIVERG,200), 3,S));
STOCH(15,3)<MOV(STOCH(15,3),5,S) AND LLV(IM,4)<15
OR (DIVERG<-25 AND ALERT(CROSS(MOV(STOCH(15,3),4,S), STOCH (15,3)), 3) AND ALERT(CROSS(MOV(STOCH(50,3),4,S), STOCH(50,3)), 3) AND HHV(STOCH(50,3),3)>80)

Short
SEC1:=Security("C:\Metastock Data\METAS\XAU",C);
SEC2:=Security("C:\Metastock Data\METAS\DXY0",C);
D1:=500; {REGRESSION DAYS}
D2:=11; {ROC DAYS}
ROCY:=ROC(C,D2,%);
ROC1:=ROC(SEC1,D2,%);
ROC2:=ROC(SEC2,D2,%);
sY:=Stdev(ROCY,D1);
s1:=Stdev(ROC1,D1);s2:=Stdev(ROC2,D1);
rY1:=Correl(ROC1,ROCY,D1,0);
rY2:=Correl(ROC2,ROCY,D1,0);
r12:=Correl(ROC1,ROC2,D1,0);
b1:=(rY1-rY2*r12)/(1-r12*r12)*(sY/s1);
b2:=(rY2-rY1*r12)/Sqrt(1-r12*r12)*(sY/s2);
a:=Mov(ROCY,D1,S)-b1*Mov(ROC1,D1,S)-b2*Mov(ROC2,D1,S);
PRED:=a+b1*ROC1+b2*ROC2;
DIVERG:=(PRED-ROCY)*10;
DIVERG:=Mov(DIVERG,3,E);
IM:=(Mov(DIVERG - LLV(DIVERG,200), 3,S) * 100)/(Mov(HHV(DIVERG, 200) - LLV(DIVERG,200), 3,S));

DIVERG<-4 AND STOCH(5,3)<MOV(STOCH(5,3),5,S)
   AND ALERT(CROSS(IM,5),4) AND IM>REF(IM,-2)

Cover
SEC1:=Security("C:\Metastock Data\METAS\XAU",C);
SEC2:=Security("C:\Metastock Data\METAS\DXY0",C);
D1:=500; {REGRESSION DAYS}
D2:=11; {ROC DAYS}
ROCY:=ROC(C,D2,%);
ROC1:=ROC(SEC1,D2,%);
ROC2:=ROC(SEC2,D2,%);
sY:=Stdev(ROCY,D1);
s1:=Stdev(ROC1,D1);s2:=Stdev(ROC2,D1);
rY1:=Correl(ROC1,ROCY,D1,0);
rY2:=Correl(ROC2,ROCY,D1,0);

```
r12:=Correl(ROC1,ROC2,D1,0);
b1:=(rY1-rY2*r12)/(1-r12*r12)*(sY/s1);
b2:=(rY2-rY1*r12)/Sqrt(1-r12*r12)*(sY/s2);
a:=Mov(ROCY,D1,S)-b1*Mov(ROC1,D1,S)-b2*Mov(ROC2,D1,S);
PRED:=a+b1*ROC1+b2*ROC2;
DIVERG:=(PRED-ROCY)*10;
DIVERG:=Mov(DIVERG,3,E);
IM:=(Mov(DIVERG - LLV(DIVERG,200), 3,S) * 100)/(Mov(HHV(DIVERG,
    200) - LLV(DIVERG,200), 3,S));

ALERT(DIVERG>0,3) AND STOCH(5,3)>MOV(STOCH(5,3),5,S) AND HHV
    (IM,4)>55 AND IM<REF(IM,-1)
```

A.3   METASTOCK CODE FOR THE S&P SYSTEMS DESCRIBED IN CHAPTER 12

SPY Daily Regression System

(Copyright Markos Katsanos 2007)

To recreate the tests click on enhanced system tester, click on new system and type the buy and sell code. Then to run the test, click on new simulation, next, add securities, select SPY, select periodicity daily, click on next, type in initial equity 40000, select transaction cost 20000, select only long trades. Click on more..., fill in interest rate 4%, and fill in 10 points per transaction for the commissions. Click on trade execution, uncheck realistic market prices and select buy price and sell price at open. Then fill in 1 day for the delay.

```
Long
SEC2:=Security("C:\Metastock Data\INTERMARKET\T2108",C);
D1:=400; {REGRESSION DAYS}
D2:=20; {ROC DAYS}
RS1:=ROC(C,D2,%);
RS2:=ROC(SEC2,D2,%);
b:=Correl(RS1,RS2,D1,0)*Stdev(RS1,D1)/Stdev(RS2,D1);
a:=mov(RS1,D1,S)-b*MOV(RS2,D1,S);
pred:=b*RS2+a;
DIVERG:=(PRED-RS1);
DIVERG:=Mov(DIVERG,3,E);
IM:=(Mov(DIVERG - LLV(DIVERG,40), 3,S) * 100)/(Mov(HHV(DIVERG,
    40) - LLV(DIVERG,40), 3,S));

HHV(DIVERG,2)>1 AND ALERT(CROSS(80,IM),5) AND STOCH(5,3)>
    MOV(STOCH(5,3),3,S) AND ROC(SEC2,3,%)>0
```

Sell

SEC2:=Security("C:\Metastock Data\INTERMARKET\T2108",C);
D1:=400; {REGRESSION DAYS}
D2:=20; {ROC DAYS}
RS1:=ROC(C,D2,%);
RS2:=ROC(SEC2,D2,%);
b:=Correl(RS1,RS2,D1,0)*Stdev(RS1,D1)/Stdev(RS2,D1);
a:=mov(RS1,D1,S)-b*MOV(RS2,D1,S);
pred:=b*RS2+a;
DIVERG1:=(PRED-RS1);
DIVERG:=Mov(DIVERG1,3,E);
IM:=(Mov(DIVERG - LLV(DIVERG,40), 3,S) * 100)/(Mov(HHV(DIVERG,
    40) - LLV(DIVERG,40), 3,S));

DIVERG<0 AND STOCH(5,3)<MOV(STOCH(5,3),4,S) AND LLV(IM,4)<15
    AND IM>REF(IM,-1) AND ROC(SEC2,3,%)<0

Sell short

SEC2:=Security("C:\Metastock Data\INTERMARKET\T2108",C);

HHV(SEC2,9)>72 AND SEC2<60 AND STOCH(15,3)<MOV(STOCH(15,3),
    4,S) AND SEC2<MOV(SEC2,15,E) AND C<MOV(C,15,E)

Buy to cover

SEC2:=Security("C:\Metastock Data\INTERMARKET\T2108",C);
STOP:=LLV(C,4)+2.2*ATR(8);

(STOCH(15,3)>MOV(STOCH(15,3),3,S) AND LLV(SEC2,9)<25
AND (SEC2>30 OR SEC2>MOV(SEC2,5,E)))
OR CROSS(C,STOP) OR (LLV(SEC2,9)<40 AND CROSS(C,MOV(C,5,E)))

S&P 500 E-mini 15-min Intraday System

(Copyright Markos Katsanos 2008)

To recreate the tests click on enhanced system tester, click on new system and type the buy, sell, sell short and buy to cover code. Then to run the test, click on new simulation, next, add securities, select ES, select periodicity 15 min, click on next, type in initial equity 40000, select Number of units 250 (5 contracts x 50), select both long and short trades. Click on more. . ., fill in interest rate margin 0 %, Money Market 0 %, and fill in 12 (2.4x5) points per transaction for the commissions, and then fill in the following margin requirements: Long Initial:5.5 %, Long Maintenance:4.4 %, Short Initial:105.5 %, Short Maintenance:104.4 %. Click on trade execution, uncheck realistic market prices and select buy price and sell price at open and then fill in 1 day for the delay. The first line of the code should be modified to point to the folder in your computer that Euro Stoxx futures data are located and the 12th line should be modified to your local time (e.g. if you are located in France this should be changed to HOUR()<=15).

Long
```
SEC2:=Security("C:\Metastock Data\RT\FESX",C);
D1:=9;{LRS ES}
D2:=9;{LRS ESTX}
D3:=Stdev(C,200)/(Stdev(SEC2,200)+.01);
LRSI:=LinRegSlope(SEC2,D2)/Abs(Ref(SEC2,-D2+1))*100;
LRS:=LinRegSlope(C,D1)/Abs(Ref(C,-D1+1))*100;
DIV1:=(D3*LRSI-LRS)*100;
DIVERG:=Mov(DIV1,3,E);
IM:=(Mov(DIVERG - LLV(DIVERG,250), 3,S) * 100)/(Mov(HHV(DIVERG,
  250)-LLV(DIVERG,250),3,S)+.01);
CI:=ROC(C,14,%)*100/((HHV(H,15)-LLV(L,15)+.001)/(LLV(L,15)+.1)*
  100);

(HOUR()<=9 AND HHV(DIVERG,2)>0 AND IM>70 AND IM<REF
  (IM,-1) AND Stoch(5,3)>Mov(Stoch(5,3),4,S) AND ROC(SEC2,5,%)>.2
  AND CI>REF(CI,-1)) {DIVERGENCE}
OR (ABS(CI)<20 AND Stoch(15,3)>Mov(Stoch(15,3),4,S) AND LLV
  (Stoch(15,3),3)<30 AND ROC(C,1,%)>.1 AND ROC(SEC2,1,%)>.1)
  {CONGESTION}
OR (IM>50 AND ROC(C,10,%)>.2 AND ROC(SEC2,9,%)>.4 AND
  C>MOV(C,40,E) AND MACD()>MOV(MACD(),9,E) AND CI>20 AND
  CI<85) {TRENDING}
```

Sell
```
SEC2:=Security("C:\Metastock Data\RT\FESX",C);
D1:=9;{LRS ES}
D2:=9;{LRS ESTX}
D3:=Stdev(C,200)/(Stdev(SEC2,200)+.01);
LRSI:=LinRegSlope(SEC2,D2)/Abs(Ref(SEC2,-D2+1))*100;
LRS:=LinRegSlope(C,D1)/Abs(Ref(C,-D1+1))*100;
DIV1:=(D3*LRSI-LRS)*100;
DIVERG:=Mov(DIV1,3,E);
IM:=(Mov(DIVERG - LLV(DIVERG,250), 3,S) * 100)/(Mov(HHV(DIVERG,
  250)-LLV(DIVERG,250),3,S)+.01);
STOP:=HHV(C,4)-1.6*ATR(8);
CI:=ROC(C,14,%)*100/((HHV(H,15)-LLV(L,15)+.001)/(LLV(L,15)+.1)*
  100);
```

(HOUR()<=9 AND DIVERG<0 AND STOCH(15,3)<MOV(STOCH(15,3),4,S)
   AND LLV(IM,4)<15 AND IM>REF(IM,-1) AND ROC(SEC2,2,%)<0)
   {DIVERGENCE}
OR (ABS(CI)<20 AND Stoch(15,3)<Mov(Stoch(15,3),4,S) AND HHV
   (Stoch(15,3),3)>90 AND IM<50) {CONGESTION}
OR (CI<-20 AND ROC(C,9,%)<-.4 AND ROC(SEC2,9,%)<-.4) {TRENDING}
OR (HHV(CI,3)>85 AND ABS(CI)<60 AND Stoch(15,3)<Mov(Stoch(15,3),
   4,S) AND HHV(Stoch(15,3),3)>80 AND ROC(C,1,%)<-.1) {REVERSAL}
OR CROSS(STOP,C)

Sell Short
SEC2:=Security("C:\Metastock Data\RT\FESX JUN 07",C);
D1:=9;{LRS ES}
D2:=9;{LRS ESTX}
D3:=Stdev(C,200)/(Stdev(SEC2,200)+.01);
LRSI:=LinRegSlope(SEC2,D2)/Abs(Ref(SEC2,-D2+1))*100;
LRS:=LinRegSlope(C,D1)/Abs(Ref(C,-D1+1))*100;
DIV1:=(D3*LRSI-LRS)*100;
DIVERG:=Mov(DIV1,3,E);
IM:=(Mov(DIVERG - LLV(DIVERG,250), 3,S) * 100)/(Mov(HHV(DIVERG,
   250)-LLV(DIVERG,250),3,S)+.01);
CI:=ROC(C,14,%)*100/((HHV(H,15)-LLV(L,15)+.001)/(LLV(L,15)+.1)*100);

(HOUR()<=9 AND LLV(DIVERG,2)<0 AND STOCH(15,3)<MOV(STOCH
   (15,3),4,S) AND LLV(IM,4)<5 AND IM>REF(IM,-1) AND ROC
   (SEC2,5,%)<0 AND CI<REF(CI,-1)) {DIVERGENCE}
OR (ABS(CI)<20 AND Stoch(15,3)<Mov(Stoch(15,3),4,S) AND HHV
   (Stoch(15,3),3)>80 AND ROC(C,1,%)<-.1 AND ROC(SEC2,1,%)<-.1 AND
   IM<50) {CONGESTION}
OR (IM<50 AND ROC(C,10,%)<-.2 AND ROC(SEC2,9,%)<-.4 AND
   C<MOV(C,40,E) AND MACD()<MOV(MACD(),9,E) AND CI<-20 AND
   CI>-85) {TREND}

Buy to Cover
SEC2:=Security("C:\Metastock Data\RT\FESX JUN 07",C);
D1:=9;{LRS ES}
D2:=9;{LRS ESTX}
D3:=Stdev(C,200)/(Stdev(SEC2,200)+.01);
LRSI:=LinRegSlope(SEC2,D2)/Abs(Ref(SEC2,-D2+1))*100;
LRS:=LinRegSlope(C,D1)/Abs(Ref(C,-D1+1))*100;
DIV1:=(D3*LRSI-LRS)*100;
DIVERG:=Mov(DIV1,3,E);
IM:=(Mov(DIVERG - LLV(DIVERG,250), 3,S) * 100)/(Mov(HHV(DIVERG,
   250)-LLV(DIVERG,250),3,S)+.01);

CI:=ROC(C,14,%)*100/((HHV(H,15)-LLV(L,15)+.001)/(LLV(L,15)+.1)*100);
STOP:=LLV(C,4)+1.6*ATR(8);

(HOUR()<=9 AND IM>75 AND ROC(SEC2,2,%)>0 AND
   Stoch(15,3)>Mov(Stoch(15,3),4,S)) {DIVERGENCE}
OR   (ABS(CI)<20   AND   Stoch(15,3)>Mov(Stoch(15,3),4,S)   AND   LLV
   (Stoch(15,3),3)<30) {CONGESTION}
OR (CI>20 AND ROC(C,9,%)>.4 AND ROC(SEC2,9,%)>.4) {TRENDING}
OR (LLV(CI,3)<-85 AND ABS(CI)<60 AND Stoch(15,3)>Mov(Stoch(15,3),
   4,S) AND LLV(Stoch(15,3),3)<30 AND ROC(C,1,%)>.1) {REVERSAL}
OR CROSS(C,STOP)

A.4   METASTOCK CODE FOR THE DAX SYSTEMS DESCRIBED IN CHAPTER 13

DAX Daily Disparity System

(Copyright Markos Katsanos 2008)

To recreate the tests click on enhanced system tester, click on new system and type the buy and sell code. Then to run the test, click on new simulation, next, add securities, select Dax Futures continuous (@:FDXc1), select periodicity daily, click on next, select points only test. Click on more..., and fill in the commissions 0.08 points per transaction (€2). Click on trade execution, uncheck realistic market prices and select buy price and sell price at open. Then fill in 1 day for the delay.

You will need also to change the first line of the code to point to the appropriate folder in your hard drive where CAC 40 futures are located.

Long
SEC2:=Security("C:\Metastock Data\REUTERSFUTURES\@:FCEc1",C);
CI:=ROC(C,39,%)/((HHV(H,40)-LLV(L,40))/(LLV(L,40)+.01)+.000001);
D1:=10;
DIS1:=((C-Mov(C,D1,S)) /Mov(C,D1,S))*100;
DIS2:=((SEC2-Mov(SEC2,D1,S))/Mov(SEC2,D1,S))*100;DIV2:=DIS2-DIS1;
DIVERG:=Mov(DIV2,3,E);
IM:=(Mov(DIVERG - LLV(DIVERG,200), 3,S) * 100)/(Mov(HHV(DIVERG,
   200) - LLV(DIVERG,200), 3,S));
LRS20:=LinRegSlope(C,20)/Abs(Ref(C,-19))*100;
LRS:=LinRegSlope(C,40)/Abs(Ref(C,-39))*100;
(HHV(DIVERG,2)>0 AND IM>65 AND IM<REF(IM,-1) AND
   Stoch(5,3)>Mov(Stoch(5,3),4,S) AND ROC(SEC2,6,%)>.4
   AND ROC(C,1,%)>0)
{**Buy Condition 1** -DIVERGENCE}

OR (ABS(CI)<35 AND LRS20< .2 AND LLV(STOCH(15,3),4)<30 AND
    STOCH(15,3)>30 AND STOCH(5,3)>MOV(STOCH(5,3),4,S))
{**Buy Condition 2** CONGESTION}

Sell
SEC2:=Security("C:\Metastock Data\REUTERSFUTURES\@:FCEc1",C);
CI:=ROC(C,39,%)/((HHV(H,40)-LLV(L,40))/(LLV(L,40)+.01)+.000001);
D1:=10;
DIS1:=((C - Mov(C,D1,S)) / Mov(C,D1,S))*100;
DIS2:=((SEC2 - Mov(SEC2,D1,S)) / Mov(SEC2,D1,S)) * 100;DIV2:=DIS2-
    DIS1;
DIVERG:=Mov(DIV2,3,E);
IM:=(Mov(DIVERG - LLV(DIVERG,200), 3,S) * 100)/(Mov(HHV(DIVERG,
    200) - LLV(DIVERG,200), 3,S));
(DIVERG<0 AND LLV(IM,4)<5 AND IM> REF(IM,-1)
    AND STOCH(5,3)<MOV(STOCH(5,3),3,S)) {**Sell Condition 1:** DIVER-
    GENCE}
OR (hhv(CI,3)-CI>40 AND DIV2<0 AND ROC(C,3,%)<-.1) {**Sell Condition
    2:** Trend reversal}

OR (MOV(C,10,S)<MOV(C,150,S) AND CROSS(MOV(MACD(),7,E),MACD())
    AND DIV2<0) {**Sell Condition 3-** Bear Market downtrend}

OR (DIVERG<-1 AND STOCH(5,3)<MOV(STOCH(5,3),3,S) AND ROC
    (C,2,%)<-.5 AND ROC(SEC2,2,%)<-.6) {**Sell Condition 4:** Intermarket}

Sell short
SEC2:=Security("C:\Metastock Data\REUTERSFUTURES\@:FCEc1",C);
CI:=ROC(C,39,%)/((HHV(H,40)-LLV(L,40))/(LLV(L,40)+.01)+.000001);
LRS20:=LinRegSlope(C,20)/Abs(Ref(C,-19))*100;
LRS:=LinRegSlope(C,40)/Abs(Ref(C,-39))*100;

(hhv(CI,3)-CI>50 AND LRS<0 AND MACD()<MOV(MACD(),7,E))
{**Short condition 1:** Trend reversal} OR
(ABS(CI)<30 AND LRS20< .1 AND HHV(STOCH(25,3),4)>85 AND
    STOCH(25,3)<70 AND STOCH(5,3)<MOV(STOCH(5,3),4,S)) {**Short con-
    dition 2:** CONGESTION}

Buy to cover
SEC2:=Security("C:\Metastock Data\REUTERSFUTURES\@:FCEc1",C);
CI:=ROC(C,39,%)/((HHV(H,40)-LLV(L,40))/(LLV(L,40)+.01)+.000001);
D1:=10;
DIS1:=((C - Mov(C,D1,S)) / Mov(C,D1,S)) * 100;
DIS2:=((SEC2 - Mov(SEC2,D1,S)) / Mov(SEC2,D1,S))*100;DIV2:=DIS2-
    DIS1;

DIVERG:=Mov(DIV2,3,E);
IM:=(Mov(DIVERG - LLV(DIVERG,200), 3,S) * 100)/(Mov(HHV(DIVERG, 200) - LLV(DIVERG,200), 3,S));
(DIVERG>0 AND HHV(IM,4)>60 AND IM< REF(IM,-1)
AND STOCH(5,3)>MOV(STOCH(5,3),3,S)) {**Cover condition 1: Divergence**}
OR (LLV(CI,3)-CI<-40) {**Cover condition 2: Trend reversal**}
OR (MOV(C,10,S)>MOV(C,150,S) AND CROSS(MACD(),MOV(MACD(),7,E)))
{**Cover condition 3: Trend**}
OR (ABS(CI)<30 AND LLV(STOCH(25,3),4)<30 AND STOCH(25,3)>40
AND STOCH(5,3)>MOV(STOCH(5,3),4,S)) {**Cover condition 4:** CONGES-TION}

DAX MA Crossover System

Long
CI:=ROC(C,39,%)/((HHV(H,40)-LLV(L,40))/(LLV(L,40)+.01)+.000001);

(CI>30 AND STOCH(5,3)>MOV(STOCH(5,3),3,S) AND MOV(C,15,S)>MOV
(C,20,S)) OR (ABS(CI)<25 AND STOCH(5,3)>MOV(STOCH(5,3),3,S) AND
LLV(STOCH(40,3),2)<30) {CONGESTION}

Sell
CI:=ROC(C,39,%)/((HHV(H,40)-LLV(L,40))/(LLV(L,40)+.01)+.000001);
(hhv(CI,3)-CI>40) OR (ABS(CI)<20 AND STOCH(5,3)<MOV(STOCH
(5,3),3,S) AND HHV(STOCH(40,3),4)>85 AND STOCH(40,3)<75)
{CONGESTION}

Short
CI:=ROC(C,39,%)/((HHV(H,40)-LLV(L,40))/(LLV(L,40)+.01)+.000001);
(CI<-30 AND ROC(CI,3,%)<0 AND STOCH(5,3)<MOV(STOCH(5,3),3,S)
AND MOV(C,10,S)<MOV(C,20,S) AND MOV(C,2,S)<MOV(C,150,S)) OR
(ABS(CI)<25 AND ROC(CI,3,%)<0 AND STOCH(5,3)<MOV(STOCH
(5,3),3,S) AND HHV(STOCH(40,3),2)>70) {CONGESTION}

Buy to cover
CI:=ROC(C,39,%)/((HHV(H,40)-LLV(L,40))/(LLV(L,40)+.01)+.000001);
LLv(CI,3)-CI<-40 OR (CROSS(MACD(),MOV(MACD(),7,E)) AND C>MOV
(C,7,E))

DAX Intermarket Enhanced MA Crossover System

Long
SEC2:=Security("C:\Metastock Data\REUTERSFUTURES\@:STXEc1",C);
CI:=ROC(C,39,%)/((HHV(H,40)-LLV(L,40))/(LLV(L,40)+.01)+.000001);

D1:=10;
DIS1:=((C - Mov(C,D1,S)) / Mov(C,D1,S)) * 100;
DIS2:=((SEC2 - Mov(SEC2,D1,S)) / Mov(SEC2,D1,S)) * 100;DIV2:=DIS2-
    DIS1;

(CI>30 AND STOCH(5,3)>MOV(STOCH(5,3),3,S) AND MOV(C,15,S)>
    MOV(C,20,S)) OR (ABS(CI)<25 AND STOCH(5,3)>MOV(STOCH(5,3),3,S)
    AND LLV(STOCH(40,3),2)<30 AND ROC(SEC2,1,%)>0 AND DIV2>0)
    {CONGESTION}

Sell
SEC2:=Security("C:\Metastock Data\REUTERSFUTURES\@:STXEc1",C);
CI:=ROC(C,39,%)/((HHV(H,40)-LLV(L,40))/(LLV(L,40)+.01)+.000001);
D1:=10;
DIS1:=((C - Mov(C,D1,S)) / Mov(C,D1,S)) * 100;
DIS2:=((SEC2 - Mov(SEC2,D1,S)) / Mov(SEC2,D1,S)) * 100;DIV2:=DIS2-
    DIS1;
(hhv(CI,3)-CI>40) OR (ABS(CI)<20 AND STOCH(5,3)<MOV(STOCH(5,3),
    3,S) AND HHV(STOCH(40,3),4)>85 AND STOCH(40,3)<75 AND DIV2<0)
    {CONGESTION}

Short
SEC2:=Security("C:\Metastock Data\REUTERSFUTURES\@:STXEc1",C);
CI:=ROC(C,39,%)/((HHV(H,40)-LLV(L,40))/(LLV(L,40)+.01)+.000001);
D1:=10;
DIS1:=((C - Mov(C,D1,S)) / Mov(C,D1,S)) * 100;
DIS2:=((SEC2 - Mov(SEC2,D1,S)) / Mov(SEC2,D1,S)) * 100;DIV2:=DIS2-
    DIS1;

(CI<-30 AND ROC(CI,3,%)<0 AND DIV2<0 AND ROC(SEC2,2,%)<-.5 AND
    STOCH(5,3)<MOV(STOCH(5,3),3,S) AND MOV(C,10,S)<MOV(C,20,S)
    AND MOV(C,2,S)<MOV(C,150,S))
OR (ABS(CI)<25 AND ROC(CI,3,%)<0 AND STOCH(5,3)<MOV(STOCH
    (5,3),3,S) AND HHV(STOCH(40,3),2)>70 AND ROC(SEC2,1,%)<0 AND
    DIV2<0 AND MOV(SEC2,10,S)<MOV(SEC2,20,S)) {CONGESTION}

Buy to cover
SEC2:=Security("C:\Metastock Data\REUTERSFUTURES\@:STXEc1",C);
CI:=ROC(C,39,%)/((HHV(H,40)-LLV(L,40))/(LLV(L,40)+.01)+.000001);
D1:=10;
DIS1:=((C - Mov(C,D1,S)) / Mov(C,D1,S)) * 100;
DIS2:=((SEC2 - Mov(SEC2,D1,S)) / Mov(SEC2,D1,S)) * 100;DIV2:=DIS2-
    DIS1;

LLv(CI,3)-CI<-40 OR (CROSS(MACD(),MOV(MACD(),7,E)) AND C>MOV (C,7,E))

MetaStock Code for Tradesim Simulation of the DAX Component Stock Disparity System

This test can only be run with Tradesim (a MetaStock plug-in) which can be obtained from http://www.compuvision.com.au/.

After running the MetaStock exploration open Tradesim and load the following DAX component stocks: ALV,BAS,BAY,DAI,DBK,DTE,EOA,SIE,RWE, SAP.

Check the Pyramid profits and Equal dollar units boxes and fill in the following trade parameters:

Initial trading capital: 28 000
Maximum open positions: 20
Transaction cost: 10
Margin: 50 %
Capital per trade: 20 000
Minimum trade size: 5000

```
SEC2:=Security("C:\Metastock Data\REUTERSFUTURES\@:FCEc1",C);
CI:=ROC(C,39,%)/((HHV(H,40)-LLV(L,40))/(LLV(L,40)+.01)+.000001);
D1:=10;STOP:=HHV(C,3)-2.2*ATR(10);
DIS1:=((C-Mov(C,D1,S)) /Mov(C,D1,S))*100;
DIS2:=((SEC2-Mov(SEC2,D1,S))/Mov(SEC2,D1,S))*100;DIV2:=DIS2-DIS1;
DIVERG:=Mov(DIV2,3,E);
IM:=(Mov(DIVERG - LLV(DIVERG,200), 3,S) * 100)/(Mov(HHV(DIVERG,
   200) - LLV(DIVERG,200), 3,S));
LRS20:=LinRegSlope(C,20)/Abs(Ref(C,-19))*100;
LRS:=LinRegSlope(C,40)/Abs(Ref(C,-39))*100;

ENTRYTRIGGER:=(HHV(DIVERG,2)>0 AND IM>65 AND IM<Ref(IM,-
   1) AND Stoch(5,3)>Mov(Stoch(5,3),4,S) AND ROC(SEC2,6,%)>.4 AND
   ROC(C,1,%)>0) {DIVERGENCE}
OR (Abs(CI)<35 AND LRS20< .2 AND LLV(Stoch(15,3),4)<30 AND
   Stoch(15,3)>30 AND Stoch(5,3)>Mov(Stoch(5,3),4,S)) {CONGESTION};

EXITTRIGGER:=(DIVERG<0 AND LLV(IM,4)<5 AND IM> Ref(IM,-1)
AND Stoch(5,3)<Mov(Stoch(5,3),3,S))
OR (HHV(CI,3)-CI>40 AND DIV2<0 AND ROC(C,3,%)<-.1)
OR (Mov(C,10,S)<Mov(C,150,S) AND Cross(Mov(MACD(),7,E),MACD())
   AND DIV2<0)
```

```
OR (DIVERG<-1 AND Stoch(5,3)<Mov(Stoch(5,3),3,S) AND ROC(C,2,%)<-.5
  AND ROC(SEC2,2,%)<-.6) OR Cross(STOP,L);
ExtFml("TradeSim.SetTimeStop",50);ExtFml("TradeSim.EnableDelayOfEntry
  ByOneBar");ExtFml("TradeSim.EnableDelayOfAllExitsByOneBar");
ExtFml("TradeSim.RecordTrades","DAX10DIS",LONG, EntryTrigger,OPEN,0,
  EXITTRIGGER,OPEN,START);
```

MetaStock Exploration of the DAX Component Stocks

To create the DAX Stock exploration, go to The Explorer and choose the New button. Enter in the following code in the filter column. To explore for possible hits, open the Explorer (click on binocular icon), click on Options and load 500 records, then click explore and select the folder in your hard drive with the 30 DAX component stocks. Be sure to change the first line of the code to point to the appropriate folder on your hard drive where the CAC 40 futures continuous data are located. Alternatively, if you don't have a futures data provider you can use data for the CAC 40 Index from Yahoo (ticker: ^FCHI) or other sources.

```
SEC2:=Security("C:\Metastock Data\REUTERSFUTURES\@:FCEc1",C);
CI:=ROC(C,39,%)/((HHV(H,40)-LLV(L,40))/(LLV(L,40)+.01)+.000001);
D1:=10;STOP:=HHV(C,3)-2.2*ATR(10);
DIS1:=((C-Mov(C,D1,S)) /Mov(C,D1,S))*100;
DIS2:=((SEC2-Mov(SEC2,D1,S))/Mov(SEC2,D1,S))*100;DIV2:=DIS2-DIS1;
DIVERG:=Mov(DIV2,3,E);
IM:=(Mov(DIVERG - LLV(DIVERG,200), 3,S) * 100)/(Mov(HHV(DIVERG,
  200) - LLV(DIVERG,200), 3,S)));
LRS20:=LinRegSlope(C,20)/Abs(Ref(C,-19))*100;
LRS:=LinRegSlope(C,40)/Abs(Ref(C,-39))*100;

(HHV(DIVERG,2)>0 AND IM>65 AND IM<Ref(IM,-1) AND Stoch(5,3)>
  Mov(Stoch(5,3),4,S)  AND  ROC(SEC2,6,%)>.4  AND  ROC(C,1,%)>0)
  {DIVERGENCE}
OR  (Abs(CI)<35  AND  LRS20< .2  AND  LLV(Stoch(15,3),4)<30  AND
  Stoch(15,3)>30 AND Stoch(5,3)>Mov(Stoch(5,3),4,S)) {CONGESTION};
```

A.5   METASTOCK CODE FOR THE FTSE SYSTEM DESCRIBED IN CHAPTER 14

FTSE System

(Copyright Markos Katsanos 2008)

To recreate the tests, click on enhanced system tester, click on new system and type the buy, sell, sell short and buy to cover code. Then to run the test, click on new simulation, next, add securities, select the FTSE (.FTSE), select periodicity daily, click on next, select points only test. Click on more..., and fill in the commissions 0.17 points per transaction (£1.7). Click on trade execution, uncheck realistic market prices and select buy price and sell price at open. Then fill in 1 day for the delay.

You will need also to change the first three lines of the code to point to the appropriate folder in your hard drive where the CAC 40, XOI and BIX data are located.

Long

```
CAC:=Security("C:\Metastock Data\REUTERSINDEX\.FCHI",C);
XOI:=Security("C:\Metastock Data\ REUTERSINDEX \.XOI",C);
BIX:=Security("C:\Metastock Data\ REUTERSINDEX \.BIX",C);
CI:=ROC(C,39,%)/((HHV(H,40)-LLV(L,40))/(LLV(L,40)+.01)+.000001);
CI:=Mov(CI,3,E);
RG:=-.11+.551*ROC(CAC,10,%)+.097*ROC(BIX,10,%)+.116*ROC(XOI,
    10,%);
PRED:=Ref(C,-10)*(1+RG/100);
DIVERG:=(PRED-C)/C*100;
IM:=(Mov(DIVERG - LLV(DIVERG,200), 3,S) * 100)/(Mov(HHV(DIVERG,
    200) - LLV(DIVERG,200), 3,S));

(ALERT(CROSS(50,IM),4) AND ALERT(CROSS(STOCH(10,3),20),3) AND
    CROSS(C,MOV(C,5,E)) AND STOCH(10,3)>MOV(STOCH(10,3),4,S))
OR
(IM>50 AND IM<REF(IM,-1) AND Stoch(5,3)>Mov(Stoch(5,3),4,S) AND
    ALERT(CROSS(Stoch(10,3),20),3) AND
ALERT(L<BBandBot(C,20,S,1),3) AND REF(100*LinRegSlope(C,80)/Ref(C,-
    79),-15)>.03)
```

Sell

```
CAC:=Security("C:\Metastock Data\REUTERSINDEX\.FCHI",C);
XOI:=Security("C:\Metastock Data\ REUTERSINDEX \.XOI",C);
BIX:=Security("C:\Metastock Data\ REUTERSINDEX \.BIX",C);
RG:=-.11+.551*ROC(CAC,10,%)+.097*ROC(BIX,10,%)+.116*ROC(XOI,
    10,%);
PRED:=Ref(C,-10)*(1+RG/100);
DIVERG:=(PRED-C)/C*100;
IM:=(Mov(DIVERG - LLV(DIVERG,200), 3,S) * 100)/(Mov(HHV(DIVERG,
    200) - LLV(DIVERG,200), 3,S));

(ALERT(CROSS(IM,30),4) AND ALERT(CROSS(80,STOCH(10,3)),3) AND
    ALERT(CROSS(MOV(C,10,E),C),2))
```

Short

CAC:=Security("C:\Metastock Data\REUTERSINDEX\.FCHI",C);
XOI:=Security("C:\Metastock Data\ REUTERSINDEX \.XOI",C);
BIX:=Security("C:\Metastock Data\ REUTERSINDEX \.BIX",C);
RG:=-.11+.551*ROC(CAC,10,%)+.097*ROC(BIX,10,%)+.116*ROC(XOI,
  10,%);
PRED:=Ref(C,-10)*(1+RG/100);
DIVERG:=(PRED-C)/C*100;
IM:=(Mov(DIVERG - LLV(DIVERG,200), 3,S) * 100)/(Mov(HHV(DIVERG,
  200) - LLV(DIVERG,200), 3,S));

(ALERT(CROSS(IM,30),4) AND ALERT(CROSS(80,STOCH(10,3)),3) AND
  ALERT(CROSS(MOV(C,10,E),C),2) AND STOCH(10,3)<MOV(STOCH
  (10,3),4,S))

Cover

CAC:=Security("C:\Metastock Data\REUTERSINDEX\.FCHI",C);
XOI:=Security("C:\Metastock Data\ REUTERSINDEX \.XOI",C);
BIX:=Security("C:\Metastock Data\ REUTERSINDEX \.BIX",C);
RG:=-.11+.551*ROC(CAC,10,%)+.097*ROC(BIX,10,%)+.116*ROC(XOI,
  10,%);
PRED:=Ref(C,-10)*(1+RG/100);
DIVERG:=(PRED-C)/C*100;
IM:=(Mov(DIVERG - LLV(DIVERG,200), 3,S) * 100)/(Mov(HHV(DIVERG,
  200) - LLV(DIVERG,200), 3,S));

ALERT(CROSS(50,IM),4) AND STOCH(10,3)>MOV(STOCH(10,3),4,E) AND
  C>MOV(C,10,E)

Note

As I have stressed in the book, the correlation between related markets is not static
but changes over time.

Although the regression coefficients used in the current FTSE multiple regression
system above were the best at the time of writing (December 2007), by the time this
book is published, correlations might have changed and the regression coefficients
might need adjustment.

Therefore, if you wish to use the multiple regression system you should first
check the correlations between the FTSE and the independent variables used in the
regression equation (CAC 40, BIX and XOI) and if any of the correlations have
changed (from the ones depicted in Table 14.1), you will have to make the necessary
adjustments in the regression coefficients.

A.6 METASTOCK CODE FOR THE OIL AND GOLD STOCK SYSTEMS DESCRIBED IN CHAPTER 15

Oil Stocks

MetaStock exploration code

To create the Oil Stock exploration, go to The Explorer and choose the New button. Enter in the following code in the filter column. To explore for possible hits, open the Explorer (click on binocular icon), click on Options and load 900 records, then click explore and select the folder in your hard drive with oil stocks. Be sure to change the first three lines of the code to point to the appropriate folders on your hard drive where the crude oil, S&P 500 and XOI data are located.

```
SEC1:=Security("C:\Metastock Data\REUTERSFUTURES\@:CLc1",C);
SEC2:=Security("C:\Metastock Data\REUTERSINDEX\.SPX",C);
SEC3:=Security("C:\Metastock Data\REUTERSINDEX\.XOI",C);
VFI:=Fml("VFI");
RS:=Mov((C/SEC3),3,E);
sY:=Stdev(C,300)/Mov(C,300,S);
s1:=Stdev(SEC1,300))/Mov(SEC1,300,S);
s2:=Stdev(SEC2,300))/Mov(SEC2,300,S);
rY1:=Correl(ROC(SEC1,10,%),ROC(C,10,%),300,0);
rY2:=Correl(ROC(SEC2,10,%),ROC(C,10,%),300,0);
r12:=Correl(ROC(SEC1,10,%),ROC(SEC2,10,%),300,0);
rY12:=(rY1-rY2*r12)/Sqrt(1-r12*r12);
rY21:=(rY2-rY1*r12)/Sqrt(1-r12*r12);
LRS1:=LinRegSlope(SEC1,25)/Abs(Ref(SEC1,-24))*100;
LRS2:=LinRegSlope(SEC2,25)/Abs(Ref(SEC2,-24))*100;
LRS:=LinRegSlope(C,20)/Abs(Ref(C,-19))*100;
DIVERG:=(rY12*sY/s1*LRS1+rY21*sY/s2*LRS2-LRS)*100;
DIVERG:=Mov(DIVERG,3,E);
IM:=(Mov(DIVERG - LLV(DIVERG,200), 3,S) * 100)/(Mov(HHV(DIVERG,
   200)-LLV(DIVERG,200),3,S));

Mov(RS,50,S)>Mov(RS,200,S) AND Mov(VFI,50,S)>Mov(VFI,200,S) AND
DIVERG>0 AND Alert(Cross(70,IM),5) AND Stoch(5,3)>Mov(Stoch(5,3),4,S)
   AND Correl(SEC3,C,200,0)>0.5
```

If you don't have the VFI and FVE custom (money flow) indicators you must first create them because they are being called by the oil exploration system.

To create the VFI Indicator in MetaStock, click on the indicator builder (fx), click on New..., type VFI in the Name box and the following code in the formula box. Use the same procedure to create the FVE indicator.

VFI formula

```
PERIOD:= Input("PERIOD FOR VFI",5,1300,130);
COEF:=.2;
VCOEF:=Input("MAX VOLUME CUTOFF",0,50,2.5);
INTER:=Log(Typical())-Log(Ref(Typical(),-1));
VINTER:=Stdev(INTER,30);
CUTOFF:=COEF*VINTER*C;
VAVE:=Ref(Mov(V,PERIOD,S),-1);
VMAX:=VAVE*VCOEF;
VC:=If(V<VMAX,V,VMAX);
MF:=Typical()-Ref(Typical(),-1);
VFI:=Sum(If(MF>CUTOFF, +VC, If(MF <-CUTOFF, -VC,0)),PERIOD)/
  VAVE;
Mov(VFI,3,E);
```

FVE formula

```
PERIOD:= Input("PERIOD FOR FVE",5,80,22);
COEF:=Input("COEF FOR CUTOFF",0,2,.1);
H1:=If(H>0,H,Mov(H,5,S));
L1:=If(L>0,L,Mov(L,5,S));
INTRA:=Log(H1)-Log(L1);
VINTRA:=Stdev(INTRA,PERIOD);
INTER:=Log(Typical())-Log(Ref(Typical(),-1));
VINTER:=Stdev(INTER,PERIOD);
CUTOFF:=COEF*(VINTER+VINTRA)*C;
MF:=C-(H+L)/2+Typical()-Ref(Typical(),-1);
FVE:= Sum(If(MF>CUTOFF, +V, If(MF <-CUTOFF, -V,0)),PERIOD)/
  (Mov(V,PERIOD,S)+1)/PERIOD*100;
FVE
```

MetaStock Expert Advisor

Oil stock system

MetaStock explorations only provide entry signals. To get exit signals you should create another expert advisor and attach it to the oil stocks that you bought.

To create the oil stock (bullish) expert advisor click on the binocular icon then click on new... , and fill in an appropriate name (e.g. oil stocks) in the name field and fill in the following in the Notes field: Oil stock system (see Chapter 15 of *Intermarket Trading Strategies* by Markos Katsanos). Then click on symbols, then fill in the appropriate action (BUY) and fill in the same code that you used for the oil stock exploration above. Then click on Graphic and select an appropriate graphic (e.g. green arrow below price plot).

Then click again on the new symbol, name it EXIT and fill in the following code:

```
SEC1:=Security("C:\Metastock Data\REUTERSFUTURES\@:CLc1",C);
SEC2:=Security("C:\Metastock Data\REUTERSINDEX\.SPX",C);
sY:=Stdev(C,300)/Mov(C,300,S);
s1:=Stdev(SEC1,300))/Mov(SEC1,300,S);
s2:=Stdev(SEC2,300)/Mov(SEC2,300,S);
rY1:=Correl(ROC(SEC1,10,%),ROC(C,10,%),300,0);
rY2:=Correl(ROC(SEC2,10,%),ROC(C,10,%),300,0);
r12:=Correl(ROC(SEC1,10,%),ROC(SEC2,10,%),300,0);
rY12:=(rY1-rY2*r12)/Sqrt(1-r12*r12);
rY21:=(rY2-rY1*r12)/Sqrt(1-r12*r12);
LRS1:=LinRegSlope(SEC1,25)/Abs(Ref(SEC1,-24))*100;
LRS2:=LinRegSlope(SEC2,25)/Abs(Ref(SEC2,-24))*100;
LRS:=LinRegSlope(C,20)/Abs(Ref(C,-19))*100;
DIVERG:=(rY12*sY/s1*LRS1+rY21*sY/s2*LRS2-LRS)*100;
DIVERG:=Mov(DIVERG,3,E);
IM:=(Mov(DIVERG - LLV(DIVERG,200), 3,S) * 100)/(Mov(HHV(DIVERG,
    200)-LLV(DIVERG,200),3,S));
(Stoch(15,3)<Mov(Stoch(15,3),5,S)    AND    HHV(Stoch(15,3),3)>80    AND
    LLV(IM,4)<7)
```

Don't forget to change the first two lines of the code to point to the folder in your hard drive where data for crude oil futures and the S&P 500 are located. Then click on Graphic and select an appropriate graphic (e.g. red EXIT sign above the price plot). All you have to do now is attach this expert to the stocks that you bought using the oil exploration.

MetaStock Code for Tradesim Simulation

Oil stocks
This test can only be run with Tradesim v. 4.2 2 (a MetaStock plug-in) which can be obtained from http://www.compuvision.com.au/.

After running the MetaStock exploration open Tradesim and load the OIL STOCKS file and fill in the following trade parameters:

Initial trading capital: $100 000
Maximum open positions: 20
Transaction cost: $10
Minimum trade size: $3000

Volume filter: Limit position to a maximum of 15 % of the traded volume.

Check the Pyramid profits and Equal percent dollar units boxes and fill in the following 10 % for the percentage.

The code for the Tradesim test is the same code used for the MetaStock exploration plus the additional Tradesim commands (beginning with ENTRYTRIGGER) which should be added at the end. The complete code should be copied in column A of the explorer.

```
SEC1:=Security("C:\Metastock Data\REUTERSFUTURES\@:CLc1",C);
SEC2:=Security("C:\Metastock Data\REUTERSINDEX\.SPX",C);
SEC3:=Security("C:\Metastock Data\REUTERSINDEX\.XOI",C);
VFI:=Fml("VFI");
RS:=Mov((C/SEC3),3,E);
sY:=Stdev(C,300)/Mov(C,300,S);
s1:=Stdev(SEC1,300))/Mov(SEC1,300,S);
s2:=Stdev(SEC2,300))/Mov(SEC2,300,S);
rY1:=Correl(ROC(SEC1,10,%),ROC(C,10,%),300,0);
rY2:=Correl(ROC(SEC2,10,%),ROC(C,10,%),300,0);
r12:=Correl(ROC(SEC1,10,%),ROC(SEC2,10,%),300,0);
rY12:=(rY1-rY2*r12)/Sqrt(1-r12*r12);
rY21:=(rY2-rY1*r12)/Sqrt(1-r12*r12);
LRS1:=LinRegSlope(SEC1,25)/Abs(Ref(SEC1,-24))*100;
LRS2:=LinRegSlope(SEC2,25)/Abs(Ref(SEC2,-24))*100;
LRS:=LinRegSlope(C,20)/Abs(Ref(C,-19))*100;
DIVERG:=(rY12*sY/s1*LRS1+rY21*sY/s2*LRS2-LRS)*100;
DIVERG:=Mov(DIVERG,3,E);
IM:=(Mov(DIVERG - LLV(DIVERG,200), 3,S) * 100)/(Mov(HHV(DIVERG,
   200)-LLV(DIVERG,200),3,S));

ENTRYTRIGGER:=Mov(RS,50,S)>Mov(RS,200,S) AND Mov(VFI,50,S)>
   Mov(VFI,200,S) AND
DIVERG>0 AND Alert(Cross(70,IM),5) AND Stoch(5,3)>Mov(Stoch(5,3),4,S)
   AND Correl(SEC3,C,200,0)>0.5;

EXITTRIGGER:=(Stoch(15,3)<Mov(Stoch(15,3),5,S) AND HHV(Stoch
   (15,3),3)>80
AND LLV(IM,4)<7)
(Alert(Cross(0,Fml("FVE")),7) AND Fml("FVE")<-5 AND
Cross(Mov(VFI,100,E),VFI));
ExtFml("TradeSim.Initialize");
ExtFml("TradeSim.SetVolumeMultiplier",100);
```

ExtFml("TradeSim.SetTimeStop",100);ExtFml("TradeSim.EnableDelayOfEntry
  ByOneBar");ExtFml("TradeSim.EnableDelayOfAllExitsByOneBar");
ExtFml("TradeSim.RecordTrades","OIL STOCKS",LONG,EntryTrigger,OPEN,
  0, EXITTRIGGER,OPEN,START);

Gold Stocks

MetaStock code for Tradesim simulation
SEC1:=Security("C:\Metastock Data\METAS\XGLD",C);
SEC3:=Security("C:\Metastock Data\METAS\XAU",C);
VFI:=Fml("VFI");
RS:=Mov((C/SEC3),3,E);
D1:=500; {REGRESSION DAYS}
D2:=11; {ROC DAYS}
RS1:=ROC(C,D2,%);
RS2:=ROC(SEC1,D2,%);
b:=Correl(RS1,RS2,D1,0)*Stdev(RS1,D1)/Stdev(RS2,D1);
a:=Mov(RS1,D1,S)-b*Mov(RS2,D1,S);
pred:=b*RS2+a;
DIVERG:=(PRED-RS)*10;
DIVERG:=Mov(DIVERG,3,E);
IM:=(Mov(DIVERG - LLV(DIVERG,200), 3,S) * 100)/(Mov(HHV(DIVERG,
  200)-LLV(DIVERG,200),3,S));

ENTRYTRIGGER:= Mov(RS,50,S)>Mov(RS,200,S) AND Mov(VFI,50,S)>
  Mov(VFI,200,S) AND
DIVERG>0 AND Alert(Cross(70,IM),5) AND Stoch(5,3)>Mov(Stoch(5,3),4,S)
  AND Correl(ROC(SEC1,10,%),ROC(C,10,%),200,0)>0.1;
EXITTRIGGER:=(Stoch(15,3)<Mov(Stoch(15,3),5,S) AND HHV(Stoch
  (15,3),3)>80 AND LLV(IM,4)<7)

ExtFml("TradeSim.Initialize");
ExtFml("TradeSim.SetVolumeMultiplier",100);
ExtFml("TradeSim.SetTimeStop",80);ExtFml("TradeSim.EnableDelayOfEntry
  ByOneBar");ExtFml("TradeSim.EnableDelayOfAllExitsByOneBar");
ExtFml("TradeSim.RecordTrades","GOLD STOCKS",LONG,EntryTrigger,
  OPEN,0, EXITTRIGGER,OPEN,START);

MetaStock exploration code
To create the Gold Stock exploration, go to The Explorer and choose the New button.
Enter in the following code in the filter column. To explore for possible hits, open the
Explorer (click on binocular icon), click on Options and load 900 records, then click

explore and select the folder in your hard drive with gold stocks. Be sure to change the first two lines of the code to point to the appropriate folders on your hard drive where gold bullion or GLD, and XAU data are located.

```
SEC1:=Security("C:\Metastock Data\METAS\XGLD",C);
SEC3:=Security("C:\Metastock Data\METAS\XAU",C);
VFI:=Fml("VFI");
RS:=Mov((C/SEC3),3,E);
D1:=500; {REGRESSION DAYS}
D2:=11; {ROC DAYS}
RS1:=ROC(C,D2,%);
RS2:=ROC(SEC1,D2,%);
b:=Correl(RS1,RS2,D1,0)*Stdev(RS1,D1)/Stdev(RS2,D1);
a:=Mov(RS1,D1,S)-b*Mov(RS2,D1,S);
pred:=b*RS2+a;
DIVERG:=(PRED-RS)*10;
DIVERG:=Mov(DIVERG,3,E);
IM:=(Mov(DIVERG - LLV(DIVERG,200), 3,S) * 100)/(Mov(HHV(DIVERG,
    200)-LLV(DIVERG,200),3,S));
Mov(RS,50,S)>Mov(RS,200,S) AND Mov(VFI,50,S)>Mov(VFI,200,S) AND
DIVERG>0 AND Alert(Cross(70,IM),5) AND Stoch(5,3)>Mov(Stoch(5,3),4,S)
    AND Correl(ROC(SEC1,10,%),ROC(C,10,%),200,0)>0.1
```

MetaStock Expert Advisor

Gold stock system
MetaStock explorations only provide entry signals. To get both entry and exit signals you should create an expert advisor and attach it to the gold stocks that you bought.

To create the gold stock expert advisor click on the appropriate icon then click on new.., and fill in a suitable name (e.g. Gold stocks) in the name field and fill in the following in the Notes field: Gold stock system (see Chapter 15 of *Intermarket Trading Strategies* by Markos Katsanos). Then click on symbols, then fill in the appropriate action (BUY) and fill in the same code that you used for the exploration above. Then click on Graphic and select an appropriate graphic (e.g. green arrow below price plot).

Then click again on new symbol, name it EXIT and fill in the following code :

```
SEC1:=Security("C:\Metastock Data\METAS\XGLD",C);
SEC3:=Security("C:\Metastock Data\METAS\XAU",C);
VFI:=Fml("VFI");
RS:=Mov((C/SEC3),3,E);
```

```
D1:=500; {REGRESSION DAYS}
D2:=11; {ROC DAYS}
RS1:=ROC(C,D2,%);
RS2:=ROC(SEC1,D2,%);
b:=Correl(RS1,RS2,D1,0)*Stdev(RS1,D1)/Stdev(RS2,D1);
a:=Mov(RS1,D1,S)-b*Mov(RS2,D1,S);
pred:=b*RS2+a;
DIVERG:=(PRED-RS)*10;
DIVERG:=Mov(DIVERG,3,E);
IM:=(Mov(DIVERG - LLV(DIVERG,200), 3,S) * 100)/(Mov(HHV(DIVERG,
    200)-LLV(DIVERG,200),3,S));

(Stoch(15,3)<Mov(Stoch(15,3),5,S) AND HHV(Stoch(15,3),3)>80 AND LLV
    (IM,4)<7)
```

Don't forget to change the first two lines of the code to point to the folder in your hard drive where data for gold spot prices (or the World Gold Index) and the XAU are located. Then click on Graphic and select an appropriate graphic (e.g. red EXIT sign above the price plot). All you have to do now is attach this expert to the stocks that you bought using the gold exploration.

A.7 METASTOCK CODE FOR THE FUTURES AND ETF SYSTEMS IN CHAPTER 16

1 Test II Relative Strength System (FUTURES)

MetaStock code for Tradesim simulation
This test can only be run with Tradesim v. 4.2 2 (a MetaStock plug-in) which can be obtained from http://www.compuvision.com.au/.

To run this test you should change the first line of the code to point to the appropriate folder on your hard drive where the S&P 500 data are located. Copy and paste the following code into column A of MetaStock's explorer and then click on options and load 2100 records.

After running the MetaStock exploration, open Tradesim and load the FUTURES file and fill in the following trade parameters:

Initial trading capital: $500 000
Maximum open positions: 30
Capital per trade: $30 000
Transaction cost: $10
Minimum trade size: $5000
Ignore volume filter

```
SEC2:=Security("C:\Metastock Data\REUTERSINDEX\.SPX",C);
D3:=150;{DAYS FOR SMOOTH RS}
RS:=Mov((C/SEC2),D3,E);

entrytrigger:= RS>Mov(RS,120,E) AND ROC(Mov(C,25,E),2,%)>0 AND
    LinRegSlope(RS,20)>0
AND Correl(C,SEC2,130,0)<.5 AND Stoch(100,3)<80
AND RS>Ref(HHV(RS,250),-20);
EXITTRIGGER:=Cross(Mov(RS,90,E),RS) OR ROC(RS,3,%)<-.5;

ExtFml("TradeSim.Initialize");
ExtFml("TradeSim.EnableDelayOfEntryByOneBar");ExtFml("TradeSim.Enable
    DelayOfAllExitsByOneBar");
ExtFml("TradeSim.RecordTrades","FUTURES",LONG,EntryTrigger,OPEN,0,
    EXITTRIGGER,OPEN,START);
```

MetaStock Exploration Code for the Relative Strength FUTURES System

To create the FUTURES exploration, go to The Explorer and choose the New button. Enter in the following code in the appropriate column. To explore for possible hits, open the Explorer (click on binocular icon), click on Options and load 500 records, then click explore and select the folders in your hard drive with Commodity, Index FUTURES and International Indices. Be sure to change the first line of the code to point to the appropriate folder on your hard drive where the S&P 500 data are located.

```
Column A:
Col. Name: Price
Code: C
Column B:
Col. Name: RS
Code:
SEC2:=Security("C:\Metastock Data\REUTERSINDEX\.SPX",C);
D3:=150;{DAYS FOR SMOOTH RS}
RS:=Mov((C/SEC2),D3,E);RS
Column C:
Col. Name: HHV RS
Code:
SEC2:=Security("C:\Metastock Data\REUTERSINDEX\.SPX",C);
D3:=150;{DAYS FOR SMOOTH RS}
RS:=Mov((C/SEC2),D3,E);Ref(HHV(RS,250),-20)
```

Column D:
Col. Name: RS-MA%
Code:
SEC2:=Security("C:\Metastock Data\REUTERSINDEX\.SPX",C);
D3:=150;{DAYS FOR SMOOTH RS}
RS:=Mov((C/SEC2),D3,E);(RS-Mov(RS,120,E))/Mov(RS,120,E)*100

Column E:
Col. Name: LRS(RS)
Code:
SEC2:=Security("C:\Metastock Data\REUTERSINDEX\.SPX",C);
D3:=150;{DAYS FOR SMOOTH RS}
RS:=Mov((C/SEC2),D3,E);LinRegSlope(RS,20)
Column F:
Col. Name: CORREL
Code:
SEC2:=Security("C:\Metastock Data\REUTERSINDEX\.SPX",C);
Correl(C,SEC2,130,0)

Filter
SEC2:=Security("C:\Metastock Data\REUTERSINDEX\.SPX",C);
D3:=150;{DAYS FOR SMOOTH RS}
RS:=Mov((C/SEC2),D3,E);

RS>Mov(RS,120,E) AND ROC(Mov(C,25,E),2,%)>0 AND LinRegSlope
  (RS,20)>0
AND Correl(C,SEC2,130,0)<.5 AND Stoch(100,3)<80
AND RS>Ref(HHV(RS,250),-20)

To close long positions you can either create another exploration and enter the following code in the filter column or create an expert and drop it on each security.

Sell exploration
To create the FUTURES sell exploration, go to The Explorer and choose the New button and name it: Sell Relative Strength (Futures). Then enter the following code in the filter column. To explore for sell signals, open the Explorer (click on binocular icon), click on Options and load 500 records, then click explore and select the folders in your hard drive with Commodity, Index FUTURES and International Indices. Be sure to change the first line of the code to point to the appropriate folder on your hard drive where the S&P 500 data are located.

Name: Sell Relative Strength (Futures)

Filter
SEC2:=Security("C:\Metastock Data\REUTERSINDEX\.SPX",C);
D3:=150;{DAYS FOR SMOOTH RS}
RS:=Mov((C/SEC2),D3,E);
Cross(Mov(RS,90,E),RS) OR ROC(RS,3,%)<-.5

Futures expert advisor

To create the Futures expert, go to the Expert advisor and choose the New expert.
Click on symbols, and choose New and enter the following code and appropriate
graphic symbols:

Name: Buy Futures (Relative Strength)
Graphic: Green Up arrow
Code:
SEC2:=Security("C:\Metastock Data\REUTERSINDEX\.SPX",C);
D3:=150;{DAYS FOR SMOOTH RS}
RS:=Mov((C/SEC2),D3,E);
RS>Mov(RS,120,E) AND ROC(Mov(C,25,E),2,%)>0 AND LinRegSlope
   (RS,20)>0
AND Correl(C,SEC2,130,0)<.5 AND Stoch(100,3)<80
AND RS>Ref(HHV(RS,250),-20)

Name: Sell Futures (RS)
Graphic: Red exit sign
Code:
SEC2:=Security("C:\Metastock Data\REUTERSINDEX\.SPX",C);
D3:=150;{DAYS FOR SMOOTH RS}
RS:=Mov((C/SEC2),D3,E);
Cross(Mov(RS,90,E),RS) OR ROC(RS,3,%)<-.5

2 Test II ETF Relative Strength

MetaStock Code for Tradesim Simulation
This test can only be run with Tradesim v. 4.2 2 (a MetaStock plug-in) which can be
obtained from http://www.compuvision.com.au/.

Change the first line of the code to point to the appropriate folder on your hard
drive where the S&P 500 data are located. Copy and paste the following code into
column A of MetaStock's explorer and then click on options and load 2100 records.

After running the MetaStock exploration open Tradesim and load the ETF file and
fill in the following trade parameters:

Initial trading capital: $500 000
Maximum open positions: 30

Capital per trade: $30 000
Transaction cost: $10
Minimum trade size: $5000
Volume filter: Limit position to a maximum of 20 % of the traded volume.

```
SEC2:=Security("C:\Metastock Data\REUTERSINDEX\.SPX",C);
D3:=150;{DAYS FOR SMOOTH RS}
RS:=Mov((C/SEC2),D3,E);
VFI:=Fml("VFI");
entrytrigger:=RS>Mov(RS,120,E)   AND   ROC(Mov(C,25,E),2,%)>0   AND
    LinRegSlope(RS,20)>0
AND Correl(C,SEC2,130,0)<.5 AND Stoch(100,3)<80 AND Mov(VFI,25,E)>0;
EXITTRIGGER:=Cross(Mov(RS,90,E),RS)  OR  ROC(RS,3,%)<-.5  OR  Mov
    (VFI,25,E)<0;

ExtFml("TradeSim.Initialize");
ExtFml("TradeSim.EnableDelayOfEntryByOneBar");ExtFml("TradeSim.Enable
    DelayOfAllExitsByOneBar");
ExtFml("TradeSim.RecordTrades","ETF",LONG,EntryTrigger,OPEN,0,
EXITTRIGGER,OPEN,START);
```

MetaStock Exploration Code for the Relative Strength ETF System

To create the ETF exploration, go to The Explorer and choose the New button. Enter in the following code in the filter column. To explore for possible hits, open the Explorer (click on binocular icon), click on Options and load 500 records, then click explore and select the folder in your hard drive with the ETF data. Be sure to change the first line of the code to point to the appropriate folder on your hard drive where the S&P 500 data are located.

Note: Before running the exploration you should first create the VFI indicator. The code for this indicator is included in A6 above.

Name: Buy ETF
Notes: Displays ETF where the comparative relative strength (i.e. between the ETF and the S&P 500) crosses above its signal line. This was discussed in Mr Katsanos' book *Intermarket Trading Strategies*. Column A displays the close of each security, Column B the Relative Strength between the security and index, Column C the VFI, Column D the % difference between the Relative Strength and its moving average, Column E the value of the 20-day linear regression slope of the relative strength and Column F the correlation between the security and the S&P 500. The filter does not rely on any of the column formulas so feel free to change the column formula to calculate any of your favorite indicators.

```
Filter
SEC2:=Security("C:\Metastock Data\REUTERSINDEX\.SPX",C);
D3:=150;{DAYS FOR SMOOTH RS}
RS:=Mov((C/SEC2),D3,E);
VFI:=Fml("VFI");
RS>Mov(RS,120,E) AND ROC(Mov(C,25,E),2,%)>0 AND LinRegSlope
  (RS,20)>0
AND Correl(C,SEC2,130,0)<.5 AND Stoch(100,3)<80 AND Mov(VFI,25,E)>0
```

```
Column A:
Col. Name: Price
Code: C
Column B:
Col. Name: RS
Code:
SEC2:=Security("C:\Metastock Data\REUTERSINDEX\.SPX",C);
D3:=150;{DAYS FOR SMOOTH RS}
RS:=Mov((C/SEC2),D3,E);RS
Column C:
Col. Name: VFI
Code:
Fml("VFI")
Column D:
Col. Name: RS-MA%
Code:
SEC2:=Security("C:\Metastock Data\REUTERSINDEX\.SPX",C);
D3:=150;{DAYS FOR SMOOTH RS}
RS:=Mov((C/SEC2),D3,E);(RS-Mov(RS,120,E))/Mov(RS,120,E)*100
```

```
Column E:
Col. Name: LRS(RS)
Code:
SEC2:=Security("C:\Metastock Data\REUTERSINDEX\.SPX",C);
D3:=150;{DAYS FOR SMOOTH RS}
RS:=Mov((C/SEC2),D3,E);LinRegSlope(RS,20)
Column F:
Col. Name: CORREL
Code:
SEC2:=Security("C:\Metastock Data\REUTERSINDEX\.SPX",C);
Correl(C,SEC2,130,0)
```

To close long positions you can either create the following exploration or create an expert and drop it on each security.

Sell exploration

To create the ETF sell exploration, go to The Explorer and choose the New button and name it: Sell Relative Strength (ETF). Then enter the following code in the filter column. To explore for sell signals, open the Explorer (click on binocular icon), click on Options and load 500 records, then click explore and select the folders in your hard drive with the ETF data. Be sure to change the first line of the code to point to the appropriate folder on your hard drive where the S&P 500 data are located.

```
Name: Sell ETF
Filter
SEC2:=Security("C:\Metastock Data\REUTERSINDEX\.SPX",C);
D3:=150;{DAYS FOR SMOOTH RS}
RS:=Mov((C/SEC2),D3,E);
VFI:=Fml("VFI");
Cross(Mov(RS,90,E),RS) OR ROC(RS,3,%)<-.5 OR Mov(VFI,25,E)<0
```

ETF Expert Advisor

To create the ETF expert, go to the Expert advisor and choose the New expert. Click on symbols, and choose New and enter the following code and appropriate graphic symbols:

```
Name: Buy ETF
Graphic: Green Up arrow
Code:
SEC2:=Security("C:\Metastock Data\REUTERSINDEX\.SPX",C);
D3:=150;{DAYS FOR SMOOTH RS}
RS:=Mov((C/SEC2),D3,E);
VFI:=Fml("VFI");
RS>Mov(RS,120,E) AND ROC(Mov(C,25,E),2,%)>0 AND LinRegSlope
   (RS,20)>0
AND Correl(C,SEC2,130,0)<.5 AND Stoch(100,3)<80 AND Mov(VFI,25,E)>0

Name: Sell ETF
Graphic: Red exit sign
Code:
SEC2:=Security("C:\Metastock Data\REUTERSINDEX\.SPX",C);
D3:=150;{DAYS FOR SMOOTH RS}
RS:=Mov((C/SEC2),D3,E);
VFI:=Fml("VFI");
Cross(Mov(RS,90,E),RS) OR ROC(RS,3,%)<-.5 OR Mov(VFI,25,E)<0
```

A.8   METASTOCK CODE FOR THE FOREX SYSTEMS DESCRIBED IN CHAPTER 17

Yen (USD/YEN) Daily Intermarket Volatilty System

(Copyright Markos Katsanos 2008)

To recreate the tests click on enhanced system tester, click on new system and type the buy and sell code. Then to run the test, click on new simulation, next, add securities, select the yen (USD/JPY), select periodicity daily, click on next, select transaction cost \$100 000. Click on more..., and fill in the exit commission = \$13 points per transaction (100 000 *0.015/average yen price during the test duration). Click on trade execution, uncheck realistic market prices and select buy price and sell price at open.

You will need also to change the first line of the code to point to the appropriate folder in your hard drive where the S&P 500 (SPX), 10-year Treasury yield (TNX) and dollar index (DXY) are located.

Long
```
SEC1:=Security("C:\Metastock Data\REUTERSINDEX\.SPX",C);
SEC3:=Security("C:\Metastock Data\REUTERSINDEX\.TNX",C);
SEC2:=Security("C:\Metastock Data\REUTERSINDEX\.DXY",C);
D1:=200; {REGRESSION DAYS} D2:=15;
RS1:=ROC(C,D2,%);RS2:=ROC(SEC2,D2,%);
b:=Correl(RS1,RS2,D1,0)*Stdev(RS1,D1)/(Stdev(RS2,D1)+.001);
a:=mov(RS1,D1,S)-b*MOV(RS2,D1,S);
pred:=b*RS2+a;DIVERG:=(PRED-RS1); DIVERG:=Mov(DIVERG,3,E);
IM:=(Mov(DIVERG - LLV(DIVERG,200), 3,S) * 100)/(Mov(HHV(DIVERG,
    200) - LLV(DIVERG,200), 3,S));
SDC:=Stdev(C,15)/Mov(C,15,S);SDADX:=SDC*ADX(15);
DISY:=(C-Mov(C,10,E))/Mov(C,10,E)*100;
DIS3:=(SEC3-Mov(SEC3,10,E))/Mov(SEC3,10,E)*100;
DIS:=MOV((DIS3-DISY),3,E);

(HHV(IM,4)>70 AND IM<HHV(IM,4)-4 AND MOV(C,2,S)>MOV(C,10,S)
    AND (DIS>0 OR ROC(SEC1,1,%)>2) AND C>O)
OR (HHV(DIS,4)>4 and DIS <HHV(DIS,4) AND CROSS(STOCH(5,3),20))
OR (LLV(SDADX,3)<0.11 AND CROSS(C, BBandTop(C,20,S,1.8)) AND
    (DIS>0 OR SEC2>MOV(SEC2,20,S)))
```

Sell
```
SEC2:=Security("C:\Metastock Data\REUTERSINDEX\.DXY",C);
SEC3:=Security("C:\Metastock Data\REUTERSINDEX\.TNX",C);
D1:=200; {REGRESSION DAYS} D2:=15; {ROC DAYS}
```

RS1:=ROC(C,D2,%); RS2:=ROC(SEC2,D2,%);
b:=Correl(RS1,RS2,D1,0)*Stdev(RS1,D1)/(Stdev(RS2,D1)+.001);
a:=mov(RS1,D1,S)-b*MOV(RS2,D1,S);
pred:=b*RS2+a;
DIVERG1:=(PRED-RS1); DIVERG:=Mov(DIVERG1,3,E);
IM:=(Mov(DIVERG - LLV(DIVERG,200), 3,S) * 100)/(Mov(HHV(DIVERG,
   200) - LLV(DIVERG,200), 3,S));
SDC:=Stdev(C,15)/Mov(C,15,S);SDADX:=SDC*ADX(15);
DISY:=(C-Mov(C,10,E))/Mov(C,10,E)*100;
DIS3:=(SEC3-Mov(SEC3,10,E))/Mov(SEC3,10,E)*100;
DIS:=MOV((DIS3-DISY),3,E);
MA:=MOV(C,4,E)-MOV(C,4,E)*1.2/100;

CROSS(BBandBOT(C,10,S,2.5),C)

OR (LLV(IM,4)<30 and IM >LLV(IM,4) AND MACD()<MOV(MACD(),7,E))
OR (LLV(DIS,4)<-4 and DIS >LLV(DIS,4) AND CROSS(80,STOCH(5,3)))

Sell short
SEC1:=Security("C:\Metastock Data\REUTERSINDEX\.SPX",C);
SEC2:=Security("C:\Metastock Data\REUTERSINDEX\.DXY",C);
SEC3:=Security("C:\Metastock Data\REUTERSINDEX\.TNX",C);
D1:=200; D2:=15; RS1:=ROC(C,D2,%); RS2:=ROC(SEC2,D2,%);
b:=Correl(RS1,RS2,D1,0)*Stdev(RS1,D1)/(Stdev(RS2,D1)+.001);
a:=mov(RS1,D1,S)-b*MOV(RS2,D1,S);
pred:=b*RS2+a; DIVERG1:=(PRED-RS1); DIVERG:=Mov(DIVERG1,3,E);
IM:=(Mov(DIVERG - LLV(DIVERG,200), 3,S) * 100)/(Mov(HHV(DIVERG,
   200) - LLV(DIVERG,200), 3,S));
SDC:=Stdev(C,15)/Mov(C,15,S);SDADX:=SDC*ADX(15);
DISY:=(C-Mov(C,10,E))/Mov(C,10,E)*100;
DIS3:=(SEC3-Mov(SEC3,10,E))/Mov(SEC3,10,E)*100;
DIS:=MOV((DIS3-DISY),3,E);

(LLV(IM,4)<30 and IM >LLV(IM,4)+4 AND MOV(C,2,S)<MOV(C,10,S)
   AND (DIS<0 OR ROC(SEC1,1,%)<-2) AND C<O)
OR (LLV(DIS,4)<-4 and DIS >LLV(DIS,4) AND CROSS(80,STOCH(5,3)))
OR (LLV(SDADX,3)<.11 AND CROSS(BBandBOT(C,20,S,1.8),C) AND
   DIS<0)

Buy to cover
SEC2:=Security("C:\Metastock Data\REUTERSINDEX\.DXY",C);
SEC3:=Security("C:\Metastock Data\REUTERSINDEX\.TNX",C);
D1:=200; {REGRESSION DAYS} D2:=15; {ROC DAYS}

```
RS1:=ROC(C,D2,%); RS2:=ROC(SEC2,D2,%);
b:=Correl(RS1,RS2,D1,0)*Stdev(RS1,D1)/(Stdev(RS2,D1)+.001);
a:=mov(RS1,D1,S)-b*MOV(RS2,D1,S);
pred:=b*RS2+a;
DIVERG1:=(PRED-RS1);
DIVERG:=Mov(DIVERG1,3,E);
IM:=(Mov(DIVERG - LLV(DIVERG,200), 3,S) * 100)/(Mov(HHV(DIVERG,
    200) - LLV(DIVERG,200), 3,S));
SDC:=Stdev(C,15)/Mov(C,15,S);SDADX:=SDC*ADX(15);
DISY:=(C-Mov(C,10,E))/Mov(C,10,E)*100;DIS3:=(SEC3-
    Mov(SEC3,10,E))/Mov(SEC3,10,E)*100;
DIS:=MOV((DIS3-DISY),3,E);
MA:=REF(MOV(C,4,E),-1)+MOV(C,4,E)*1.2/100;

CROSS(C, BBandTop(C,10,S,2.5))
OR (HHV(IM,4)>70 AND IM<HHV(IM,4) AND MACD()>MOV
    (MACD(),9,E))
OR (HHV(DIS,4)>4 and DIS <HHV(DIS,4) AND ((CROSS(C,MOV(C,10,S))
    AND SEC2>MOV(SEC2,20,S)) or CROSS(STOCH(5,3),20)))
```

Yen Futures (GLOBEX:6J) Daily Intermarket Volatilty System

(Copyright Markos Katsanos 2008)

This is the inverse of the system above. To simulate futures trading with MetaStock you will have to do a points only test and then multiply the trade results by the point value which in the case of yen futures is 12 500 000.

You will need also to change the first line of the code to point to the appropriate folder in your hard drive where the S&P 500 (SPX), 10-year Treasury yield (TNX) and dollar index (DXY) are located.

Long
```
SEC1:=Security("C:\Metastock Data\REUTERSINDEX\.SPX",C);
SEC2:=Security("C:\Metastock Data\REUTERSINDEX\.DXY",C);
SEC3:=Security("C:\Metastock Data\REUTERSINDEX\.TNX",C);
D1:=200; D2:=15; RS1:=ROC(C,D2,%);RS2:=ROC(SEC2,D2,%);
b:=Correl(RS1,RS2,D1,0)*Stdev(RS1,D1)/(Stdev(RS2,D1)+.001);
a:=mov(RS1,D1,S)-b*MOV(RS2,D1,S);pred:=b*RS2+a;DIVERG:=MOV
    ((PRED-RS1),3,E);
IM:=(Mov(DIVERG - LLV(DIVERG,200), 3,S) * 100)/(Mov(HHV(DIVERG,
    200) - LLV(DIVERG,200), 3,S));
SDC:=Stdev(C,15)/Mov(C,15,S);SDADX:=SDC*ADX(15);
DISY:=(C-Mov(C,10,E))/Mov(C,10,E)*100;
```

DIS3:=(SEC3-Mov(SEC3,10,E))/Mov(SEC3,10,E)*100;
DIS:=MOV((-DIS3-DISY),3,E);

(HHV(IM,4)>70 AND IM<HHV(IM,4)-4 AND MOV(C,2,S)>MOV(C,10,S)
   AND (DIS>0 OR ROC(SEC1,1,%)<-2) AND C>O)
OR (LLV(SDADX,3)<0.11 AND CROSS(C, BBandTop(C,20,S,1.8)) AND
   DIS>0)
OR (HHV(DIS,4)>2 and DIS <HHV(DIS,4) AND ALERT
   (CROSS(STOCH(10,3),20),3) AND STOCH(10,3)>MOV(STOCH(10,3),4,S)
   AND ROC(SEC2,4,%)<0)

Sell
SEC2:=Security("C:\Metastock Data\REUTERSINDEX\.DXY",C);
SEC3:=Security("C:\Metastock Data\REUTERSINDEX\.TNX",C);
D1:=200; {REGRESSION DAYS} D2:=15; {ROC DAYS}
RS1:=ROC(C,D2,%); RS2:=ROC(SEC2,D2,%);
b:=Correl(RS1,RS2,D1,0)*Stdev(RS1,D1)/(Stdev(RS2,D1)+.001);
a:=mov(RS1,D1,S)-b*MOV(RS2,D1,S);
pred:=b*RS2+a;
DIVERG1:=(PRED-RS1); DIVERG:=Mov(DIVERG1,3,E);
IM:=(Mov(DIVERG - LLV(DIVERG,200), 3,S) * 100)/(Mov(HHV(DIVERG,
   200) - LLV(DIVERG,200), 3,S));
SDC:=Stdev(C,15)/Mov(C,15,S);SDADX:=SDC*ADX(15);
DISY:=(C-Mov(C,10,E))/Mov(C,10,E)*100;
DIS3:=(SEC3-Mov(SEC3,10,E))/Mov(SEC3,10,E)*100;
DIS:=MOV((-DIS3-DISY),3,E);

CROSS(BBandBOT(C,10,S,2.5),C)
OR (LLV(IM,4)<30 and IM >LLV(IM,4) AND MACD()<MOV(MACD(),9,E))
OR (LLV(DIS,4)<-2 and DIS >LLV(DIS,4) AND (CROSS(80,STOCH(5,3)) OR
   SEC2>MOV(SEC2,20,S)))

Sell short
SEC1:=Security("C:\Metastock Data\REUTERSINDEX\.SPX",C);
SEC2:=Security("C:\Metastock Data\REUTERSINDEX\.DXY",C);
SEC3:=Security("C:\Metastock Data\REUTERSINDEX\.TNX",C);
D1:=200; D2:=15; RS1:=ROC(C,D2,%); RS2:=ROC(SEC2,D2,%);
b:=Correl(RS1,RS2,D1,0)*Stdev(RS1,D1)/(Stdev(RS2,D1)+.001);
a:=mov(RS1,D1,S)-b*MOV(RS2,D1,S);
pred:=b*RS2+a; DIVERG1:=(PRED-RS1); DIVERG:=Mov(DIVERG1,3,E);
IM:=(Mov(DIVERG - LLV(DIVERG,200), 3,S) * 100)/(Mov(HHV(DIVERG,
   200) - LLV(DIVERG,200), 3,S));
SDC:=Stdev(C,15)/Mov(C,15,S);SDADX:=SDC*ADX(15);

DISY:=(C-Mov(C,10,E))/Mov(C,10,E)*100;
DIS3:=(SEC3-Mov(SEC3,10,E))/Mov(SEC3,10,E)*100;
DIS:=MOV((-DIS3-DISY),3,E);
(LLV(IM,4)<30 and IM >LLV(IM,4)+4 AND MOV(C,2,S)<MOV(C,10,S)
    AND (DIS<0 OR ROC(SEC1,1,%)>2) AND C<O)
OR (LLV(SDADX,3)<.11 AND CROSS(BBandBOT(C,20,S,1.8),C) AND
    (DIS<0 OR SEC2<MOV(SEC2,20,S)))
OR (LLV(DIS,4)<-2 and DIS >LLV(DIS,4) AND ALERT(CROSS
    (80,STOCH(10,3)),3) AND STOCH(10,3)<MOV(STOCH(10,3),4,S) AND
    ROC(SEC2,4,%)>0)

Buy to cover
SEC2:=Security("C:\Metastock Data\REUTERSINDEX\.DXY",C);
SEC3:=Security("C:\Metastock Data\REUTERSINDEX\.TNX",C);
D1:=200; {REGRESSION DAYS} D2:=15; {ROC DAYS}
RS1:=ROC(C,D2,%); RS2:=ROC(SEC2,D2,%);
b:=Correl(RS1,RS2,D1,0)*Stdev(RS1,D1)/(Stdev(RS2,D1)+.001);
a:=mov(RS1,D1,S)-b*MOV(RS2,D1,S);
pred:=b*RS2+a;
DIVERG1:=(PRED-RS1);
DIVERG:=Mov(DIVERG1,3,E);
IM:=(Mov(DIVERG - LLV(DIVERG,200), 3,S) * 100)/(Mov(HHV(DIVERG,
    200) - LLV(DIVERG,200), 3,S));
SDC:=Stdev(C,15)/Mov(C,15,S);SDADX:=SDC*ADX(15);
DISY:=(C-Mov(C,10,E))/Mov(C,10,E)*100;
DIS3:=(SEC3-Mov(SEC3,10,E))/Mov(SEC3,10,E)*100;
DIS:=MOV((-DIS3-DISY),3,E);

CROSS(C, BBandTop(C,10,S,2.5))
OR (HHV(IM,4)>70 AND IM<HHV(IM,4) AND MACD()>MOV
    (MACD(),7,E))
OR (HHV(DIS,4)>2 and DIS <HHV(DIS,4) AND CROSS(C,MOV(C,10,S))
    AND (CROSS(STOCH(5,3),20) OR SEC2<MOV(SEC2,20,S)))

Yen (USD/YEN) Daily Intermarket Regression System

(Copyright Markos Katsanos 2008)

You can't simulate actual forex trading with MetaStock and get an accurate result but there are two ways that you can get around it.

The first one is to select a points-only simulation and convert the profit/loss for each transaction manually to your base currency according to the formula:

Profit/loss=((Sell price−Buy price)−(min move*spread pips))*units/home currency.

In the yen test with USD as the home currency this reduces to:

Profit/loss=((Sell price−Buy price)−(0.01*1.5))*100000/Sell price.

You'll then have to calculate the test statistics manually.

A quicker way is to select transaction cost=$100 000 and exit commission=$13 (100 000 *0.015/average yen price during the test duration).

In this case you will get a good enough approximation of the actual test statistics. I used the second method with the following code.

You will need also to change the first line of the code to point to the appropriate folder in your hard drive where the S&P 500 (SPX), 10-year Treasury yield (TNX) and dollar index (DXY) are located.

Long

```
SEC1:=Security("C:\Metastock Data\REUTERSINDEX\.SPX",C);
SEC3:=Security("C:\Metastock Data\REUTERSINDEX\.TNX",C);
SEC2:=Security("C:\Metastock Data\REUTERSINDEX\.DXY",C);
D1:=200; {REGERSSION DAYS} D2:=15; {ROC DAYS}
RS1:=ROC(C,D2,%);RS2:=ROC(SEC2,D2,%);
b:=Correl(RS1,RS2,D1,0)*Stdev(RS1,D1)/(Stdev(RS2,D1)+.001);
a:=mov(RS1,D1,S)-b*MOV(RS2,D1,S);
pred:=b*RS2+a;DIVERG:=(PRED-RS1); DIVERG:=Mov(DIVERG,3,E);
IM:=(Mov(DIVERG - LLV(DIVERG,200), 3,S) * 100)/(Mov(HHV(DIVERG,
    200) - LLV(DIVERG,200), 3,S));
SDC:=Stdev(C,15)/Mov(C,15,S);SDADX:=SDC*ADX(15);
DISY:=(C-Mov(C,OPT1,E))/Mov(C,OPT1,E)*100;
DIS3:=(SEC3-Mov(SEC3,OPT1,E))/Mov(SEC3,OPT1,E)*100;
DIS:=MOV((DIS3-DISY),3,E);

HHV(IM,4)>65 AND IM<HHV(IM,4)-10 AND
REF(MOV(C,2,S),-1)>REF(MOV(C,15,S),-1) AND MOV(C,2,S)>MOV
    (C,15,S) AND (DIS>0 OR roc(sec1,1,%)>1.2)
```

Sell

```
SEC3:=Security("C:\Metastock Data\REUTERSINDEX\.TNX",C);
SEC2:=Security("C:\Metastock Data\REUTERSINDEX\.DXY",C);
D1:=200; {REGRESSION DAYS} D2:=15; {ROC DAYS}
RS1:=ROC(C,D2,%); RS2:=ROC(SEC2,D2,%);
b:=Correl(RS1,RS2,D1,0)*Stdev(RS1,D1)/(Stdev(RS2,D1)+.001);
a:=mov(RS1,D1,S)-b*MOV(RS2,D1,S);
pred:=b*RS2+a;
DIVERG1:=(PRED-RS1); DIVERG:=Mov(DIVERG1,3,E);
IM:=(Mov(DIVERG - LLV(DIVERG,200), 3,S) * 100)/(Mov(HHV(DIVERG,
    200) - LLV(DIVERG,200), 3,S));
```

DISY:=(C-Mov(C,OPT1,E))/Mov(C,OPT1,E)*100;
DIS3:=(SEC3-Mov(SEC3,OPT1,E))/Mov(SEC3,OPT1,E)*100;
DIS:=MOV((DIS3-DISY),3,E);

(LLV(IM,4)<30 and IM >LLV(IM,4) AND MACD()<MOV(MACD(),9,E))
OR   (ALERT(CROSS(80,STOCH(20,3)),3)   AND   STOCH(20,3)<78   AND
    STOCH(20,3)<mov(STOCH(20,3),4,S)   AND   LLV(DIS,2)<0   AND
    DIS>REF(DIS,-1))

Sell short
SEC3:=Security("C:\Metastock Data\REUTERSINDEX\.TNX",C);
SEC2:=Security("C:\Metastock Data\REUTERSINDEX\.DXY",C);
D1:=200; {REGERSSION DAYS}
D2:=15; {ROC DAYS}
RS1:=ROC(C,D2,%); RS2:=ROC(SEC2,D2,%);
b:=Correl(RS1,RS2,D1,0)*Stdev(RS1,D1)/(Stdev(RS2,D1)+.001);
a:=mov(RS1,D1,S)-b*MOV(RS2,D1,S);
pred:=b*RS2+a; DIVERG1:=(PRED-RS1); DIVERG:=Mov(DIVERG1,3,E);
IM:=(Mov(DIVERG - LLV(DIVERG,200), 3,S) * 100)/(Mov(HHV(DIVERG,
    200) - LLV(DIVERG,200), 3,S));
SDC:=Stdev(C,15)/Mov(C,15,S);SDADX:=SDC*ADX(15);
DISY:=(C-Mov(C,OPT1,E))/Mov(C,OPT1,E)*100;
DIS3:=(SEC3-Mov(SEC3,OPT1,E))/Mov(SEC3,OPT1,E)*100;
DIS:=MOV((DIS3-DISY),3,E);
(LLV(IM,4)<30 and IM >LLV(IM,4)+10 AND
REF(MOV(C,2,S),-1)<REF(MOV(C,15,S),-1) AND MOV(C,2,S)<MOV
    (C,15,S))

Buy to cover
SEC3:=Security("C:\Metastock Data\REUTERSINDEX\.TNX",C);
SEC2:=Security("C:\Metastock Data\REUTERSINDEX\.DXY",C);
D1:=200; {REGERSSION DAYS} D2:=15; {ROC DAYS}
RS1:=ROC(C,D2,%); RS2:=ROC(SEC2,D2,%);
b:=Correl(RS1,RS2,D1,0)*Stdev(RS1,D1)/(Stdev(RS2,D1)+.001);
a:=mov(RS1,D1,S)-b*MOV(RS2,D1,S);
pred:=b*RS2+a;DIVERG1:=(PRED-RS1);DIVERG:=Mov(DIVERG1,3,E);
IM:=(Mov(DIVERG - LLV(DIVERG,200), 3,S) * 100)/(Mov(HHV(DIVERG,
    200) - LLV(DIVERG,200), 3,S));
DISY:=(C-Mov(C,OPT1,E))/Mov(C,OPT1,E)*100;
DIS3:=(SEC3-Mov(SEC3,OPT1,E))/Mov(SEC3,OPT1,E)*100;
DIS:=MOV((DIS3-DISY),3,E);

(HHV(IM,4)>65 AND IM<HHV(IM,4) AND MACD()>MOV(MACD(),9,E))

OR (ALERT(CROSS(STOCH(20,3),20),3) AND STOCH(20,3)>22 AND
STOCH(20,3)>mov(STOCH(20,3),4,S) and HHV(DIS,2)>0 AND
DIS<REF(DIS,-1))

Euro (EURO/USD) Daily MA-intermarket System

(Copyright Markos Katsanos 2008)

In this case select no. of units=100 000 and exit commission=10 (1 pip).

You will need also to change the first line of the code to point to the appropriate
folder in your hard drive where the CRB Index and the 10-year Treasury yield (TNX)
data are located.

Long
SEC1:=Security("C:\Metastock Data\REUTERSINDEX\.CRB",C);
SEC3:=Security("C:\Metastock Data\REUTERSINDEX\.TNX",C);
PC:=Log(MOV(C,10,S)/Ref(MOV(C,10,S),-1));
FILT:=Stdev(PC,20);
CI:=ROC(C,40-1,%)/((HHV(H,40)-LLV(L,40))/(LLV(L,40)+.01)+.000001);
CI:=Mov(CI,7,E);

MOV(C,10,S)>LLV(MOV(C,10,S),3)+.7*FILT   AND   C>SAR(.04,.1)   AND
    SEC1>MOV(SEC1,35,S) AND SEC3<MOV(SEC3,5,S) AND ABS(CI)>40
    AND CI>LLV(CI,3)+3

Sell
C<SAR(.04,.1)

Sell short
SEC1:=Security("C:\Metastock Data\REUTERSINDEX\.CRB",C);
SEC3:=Security("C:\Metastock Data\REUTERSINDEX\.TNX",C);
PC:=Log(MOV(C,10,S)/Ref(MOV(C,10,S),-1));
FILT:=Stdev(PC,20);
CI:=ROC(C,40-1,%)/((HHV(H,40)-LLV(L,40))/(LLV(L,40)+.01)+.000001);
CI:=Mov(CI,7,E);

MOV(C,10,S)<HHV(MOV(C,10,S),3)-.7*FILT   AND   C<SAR(.04,.1)   AND
    (SEC1<MOV(SEC1,35,S) AND SEC3>MOV(SEC3,5,S)) AND ABS(CI)>40
    AND CI<HHV(CI,3)-3

Buy to cover
C>SAR(.04,.1)

Appendix B
Neural Network Systems

There are two primary ways we make money trading; catching a big price move with a small position or having a large position and catching a small move.

—Bill Meehan

The following is a detailed procedure for recreating the neural network systems described in Chapter 14, using NeuroShell Trader.

B.1 ROC

All neural network systems were developed using Ward's NeuroShell Day Trader Professional v. 5.4 (www.neuroshell.com).

To recreate this test open the FTSE chart and load data from 27 April 1993 to 27 February 2008. Then load data for the French CAC 40, the Amex Oil Index (XOI) and the S&P Bank Index (BIX).

Next, from the Insert menu select New prediction and add the following inputs that the neural network is going to use for the prediction. Press Add Input/Indicator and select Change/Percent Change (%) from the change category.

To modify the input's default parameters click on the small "+" beside the input. This will cause it to expand to show the parameters and range of variables that are going to be tested. In this case modify the Time Series to CAC 40 Close and the Periods search space from 1 to 10 and click on Finish.

Repeat the above procedure for the XOI and the BIX. You should now have the following inputs for each intermarket security.

%Change(Time Series,Periods)(Time Series, Periods)
Time Series Search Space = CAC 40 INDEX Close
Periods Search Space = 1 to 10

%Change(Time Series,Periods)(Time Series, Periods)
Time Series Search Space = S&P BANK INDEX Close
Periods Search Space = 1 to 10

%Change(Time Series,Periods)(Time Series, Periods)
Time Series Search Space = AMEX Oil Index Close
Periods Search Space = 1 to 10

The next step is to modify the default parameters that the prediction will use when training. Among other things, parameters are used to determine the number and type of walk-forward tests, as well as the training set size and the training objective (training by profit or error).

To modify the parameters press next/Modify Prediction Parameters and press the first from the left (output) tab. On the top of the dialog box a list lets you select the "Indicator whose future value is to be predicted for each index in the current chart". Select the "Optimal percent change in open" option from the dropdown list and fill in 20 trading days to the "How far into the future this indicator should be predicted" question at the bottom of the dialog box.

Next select the input tab and choose the Full optimization option.

The next (date) tab allows you to set the samples and dates for training and optimization, testing the optimized parameters or, as NeuroShell calls it, "paper trading" and out-of-sample testing.

To use all three samples you should first check the "save optimization which performs best on later paper trading" and "Start before last chart date" boxes. Then fill in the dates for the Optimization sample (in grey) from 4/27/1993 to 1/1/2003, for the Paper Trading sample (in orange) from 1/1/2003 to 1/1/2005 and for the Trading sample (green) from 1/1/2005 to the last chart date.

The next tabs (shares and costs) allow you to set the number of shares, commissions and margins.

Select "Buy a Fixed Number of 1 Contract" and fill in the entry and exit commission of 1.7 per trade, the margin to £3000 per contract and the point value to £10 per FTSE point.

Next press the positions tab and select "Both long and short" and "Find the optimal trading rules".

The next (training) tab allows you to optimize against return on account, net profit, minimum drawdown, return on trades, error, etc.

Choose "Maximize Return on Trades" from the drop down list. At the bottom of the dialog box you can also specify the maximum hidden neurons used by the training process. I have limited the maximum number of hidden neurons to seven. Then select the last (Optimization) tab and fill in seven bars for the shortest average trade span. The number of inputs should be left unchanged to the default value of 10. The progress of the training and optimization process is displayed as you go along and lets you know the approximate amount of time remaining until completion. This progress is continually updated, and because of the way genetic algorithms evolve, a remaining time of 15 minutes could change and take longer if the genetic algorithm suddenly finds a better solution and decides to continue on the new path. You can retrain the neural network at any time if you are not satisfied with the results but you should first save the chart with the final system before proceeding to the next test.

Please note that it is very unlikely that you will get exactly the same results with the ones presented in the book as I had to retrain the neural network a number of times before obtaining a satisfactory output.

B.2 ROC (RELATIVE)

The test procedure is similar to the one described above. The only difference is in the Inputs parameters. In this test I used the intermarket minus the FTSE percentage change instead of just the intermarket security percentage change. The difference was then smoothed by a moving average.

To recreate this test, choose "Edit/Modify Prediction Selection" from the pop-up menu. Then remove all inputs from the previous (ROC) test and insert the new ones as follows:

- Press Add Input/Indicator and select Indicator/Averages/Simple Moving Average.
- Change the time periods to Arithmetic/subtract.
- Set the parameters for Operand #1 by selecting from the Indicator list Change/Percent Change(%).
- To modify the input's default parameters press modify input and modify the Time Series to CAC40 Close.
- Modify the No. of Periods to search space 1 to 10.
- Click on Finish.
- Repeat the same procedure for Operand #2, this time leaving the default parameters (Time series=close, periods 1 to 10).

Repeat the above procedure for the XOI and the BIX. You should now have three inputs, one for each intermarket security.

Then click on the Modify Prediction Parameters tab and change the output tab the "How far into the future this indicator should be predicted" from 20 to 15 trading days.

You are now ready to start the training process.

If you are satisfied with the results, and before proceeding with the next test, you should first save this chart with a different name.

B.3 DISPARITY

The test procedure is similar to the ones described above. The only difference is in the input parameters. In this test I used the disparity indicator instead of percentage change.

You will need first to create the disparity indicator as follows:

- Select "New Indicator" from the Insert menu.
- Using the Indicator Wizard, select "Arithmetic/Divide" from the indicator list. The formula for the Numerator should be:

Mul2(Sub(close,Avg(close,10)),100)

and for the denominator:

Avg(Close,10).

- After, inserting both formulas, click Finish and name the new indicator "Disparity" and save it in the custom indicator list.
- Choose Edit/modify Prediction Selection from the pop-up menu, remove all inputs from the first (ROC) test and insert the new ones as follows.
- Press Add Input/Indicator and select Subtract from the Arithmetic indicator category.
- Set the parameters for both Operands by selecting from the custom Indicator category the disparity indicator.
- To modify the indicator default parameters, press Modify Input and modify the Time Series to CAC40 Close and the search space from 2 to 30 for the first Operand of the subtraction only. You should modify the search space of the second Operand from 2 to 30 but leave the time series to the default (FTSE) close.
- Repeat the above procedure for the XOI and the BIX. You should now have three inputs, one for each intermarket security.
- Click on the Modify Prediction Parameters tab and in the output field change the "How far into the future this indicator should be predicted" from 20 to 15 trading days.

You are now ready to start the training process. The training and optimization process should take a little more time than the first two systems as there are more parameters to optimize.

- If you are satisfied with the results, and before proceeding with another test you should first save this chart with a different name.
- If you have any problems you can always phone or email NeuroShell technical support at support@wardsystems.com. The quality of their technical support is very high and the replies are prompt and to the point.

B.4   COMBINED TRADING STRATEGY

To recreate this strategy select New Trading Strategy from the Insert menu and enter the following entry and exit conditions in the appropriate locations of the Trading

Strategy Wizard:

- Press on Add Condition\Indicator and from the menu select Relational A>B (A>B).
- Then press Next and Finish.
- Press Add Condition and click on the small + sign next to ROC Optimal % Change in Open as predicted 20 bars ago. This will cause it to expand to show more choices.
- From these choices select Pred >Long Entry Threshold: Predicted 20 bar Optimal % Change in Open.
- Repeat the same procedure to add the prediction signals for the ROC relative and disparity conditions and then click Finish.
- Modify the B search space as follows:

Long Entry

A>B(A,B)
A Search Space= Prediction Signal: 20 bar Optimal % Change in Open
B Search Space= 0 to 0.5

A>B(A,B)
A Search Space= Prediction Signal: 15 bar Optimal % Change
B Search Space= 0 to 0.5

A>B(A,B)
A Search Space= Prediction Signal: 15 bar Optimal % Change #2
B Search Space= 0 to 1
Finally select "Generate a buy long MARKET order if all of the following are true"

Repeat the same procedure to enter the rest of the conditions.

For the Short Entry and Long Exit conditions you should reverse the inequality from A>B to A<B and choose the appropriate Thresholds from the Predicted outputs.

You should now have the following conditions and associated threshold Search Spaces:

Long Exit

A<B(A,B)
A Search Space= Prediction Signal: 20 bar Optimal % Change in Open
B Search Space= −0.5 to 0

A<B(A,B)
A Search Space= Prediction Signal: 15 bar Optimal % Change
B Search Space= −0.5 to 0

A<B(A,B)
A Search Space= Prediction Signal: 15 bar Optimal % Change #2
B Search Space= −1 to 0

Short Entry

A<B(A,B)
A Search Space= Prediction Signal: 20 bar Optimal % Change in Open
B Search Space= −1 to 0

A<B(A,B)
A Search Space= Prediction Signal: 15 bar Optimal % Change
B Search Space= −1 to 0

A<B(A,B)
A Search Space= Prediction Signal: 15 bar Optimal % Change #2
B Search Space= −1 to 0

Short Exit

A>B(A,B)
A Search Space= Prediction Signal: 20 bar Optimal % Change in Open
B Search Space= 0 to 0.5

A>B(A,B)
A Search Space= Prediction Signal: 15 bar Optimal % Change
B Search Space= 0 to 0.5

A>B(A,B)
A Search Space= Prediction Signal: 15 bar Optimal % Change #2
B Search Space= 0 to 1

The next step is to modify the default Trading Strategy Parameters used for the optimization process.

- To modify the parameters press next/Modify Prediction Parameters.
- Press the first from the left (Rules) tab
- Select Full Optimization from the bottom of the dialog box.
- Select the Trading tab and check the "Long/Short entries exit existing short/long positions" and "Match date ranges to the out of sample data ranges of predictions used in the trading strategy" boxes.
- The next tabs (costs) allow you to set the number of shares, commissions and margins.

- Fill in the entry and exit commissions of 1.7 per trade, the margin to £3000 per contract and the point value to £10 per FTSE point.
- The next (Optimization) tab allows you to optimize against return on account, net profit, minimum drawdown, return on trades, error, etc.
- Choose "Maximize Return on Trades" from the drop down list.

After backtesting the trading strategy, use the "Detailed Analysis ..." button to view the results for the combined system.

B.5   HYBRID STRATEGY

The test procedure is similar to the Combined Strategy described above. The only difference is the addition of the Stochastic Crossover and Moving Average Conditions. To recreate this strategy, copy the Combined Strategy and paste it in the same chart. Then change the name to Hybrid and add the additional conditions to the appropriate locations after the prediction signal conditions. You should now have the following entry and exit conditions:

Long Entry: Generate a buy long MARKET order if 3 of the following are true

A>B(A,B)
A Search Space= Prediction Signal: 20 bar Optimal % Change in Open
B Search Space= 0 to 0.5

A>B(A,B)
A Search Space= Prediction Signal: 15 bar Optimal % Change
B Search Space= 0 to 0.5

A>B(A,B)
A Search Space= Prediction Signal: 15 bar Optimal % Change #2
B Search Space= 0 to 1

A>B(A,ExpAvg(TimeSeries, ExpAvgPeriods))
A Search Space=Close
Time Series Search Space=Close
Search Space=Close
ExpAvg Search Space= 5 to 15

CrossAbove(%KAvg(High Price,Low Price,Closing Price,Stochastic Periods,Avg Periods),Time Series #2)
High Price Search Space=High

Low Price Search Space=Low
Closing Price Search Space=Close
Stochastic Periods Search Space= 5 to 20
Avg Periods Search Space=3 to 3
Time Series #2 Search Space= 20 to 40

Long Exit: Generate a sell long MARKET order if 2 of the following are true:

A<B(A,B)
A Search Space= Prediction Signal: 20 bar Optimal % Change in Open
B Search Space= −0.5 to 0

A<B(A,B)
A Search Space= Prediction Signal: 15 bar Optimal % Change
B Search Space= −0.5 to 0

A<B(A,B)
A Search Space= Prediction Signal: 15 bar Optimal % Change #2
B Search Space= −1 to 0

CrossBelow(%KAvg(High Price,Low Price,Closing Price,Stochastic Periods,Avg
Periods),Time Series #2)
High Price Search Space=High
Low Price Search Space=Low
Closing Price Search Space=Close
Stochastic Periods Search Space=5 to 20
Avg Periods Search Space=3 to 3
Time Series #2 Search Space= 70 to 90

CrossBelow (Time Series #1,ExpAvg(TimeSeries, ExpAvgPeriods))
Time Series #1 Search Space=Close
Time Series Search Space=Close
ExpAvg Search Space= 5 to 15

Short Entry: Generate a sell short MARKET order if 3 of the following are true

A<B(A,B)
A Search Space= Prediction Signal: 20 bar Optimal % Change in Open
B Search Space= −1 to 0

A<B(A,B)
A Search Space= Prediction Signal: 15 bar Optimal % Change
B Search Space= −1 to 0

A<B(A,B)
A Search Space= Prediction Signal: 15 bar Optimal % Change #2
B Search Space= −1 to 0

A<B(A,ExpAvg(TimeSeries, ExpAvgPeriods))
A Search Space=Close
Time Series Search Space=Close
Search Space=Close
ExpAvg Search Space= 5 to 15

Short Exit: Generate a cover short MARKET order if 2 of the following are true:

A>B(A,B)
A Search Space= Prediction Signal: 20 bar Optimal % Change in Open
B Search Space= 0 to 0.5

A>B(A,B)
A Search Space= Prediction Signal: 15 bar Optimal % Change
B Search Space= 0 to 0.5

A>B(A,B)
A Search Space= Prediction Signal: 15 bar Optimal % Change #2
B Search Space= 0 to 1

A>B(A,ExpAvg(TimeSeries, ExpAvgPeriods))
A Search Space=Close
Time Series Search Space=Close
Search Space=Close
ExpAvg Search Space= 5 to 15

The only trading parameter that you will need to modify is the Rules tab where you should select "parameters search " instead of full optimization.

Appendix C
Rectangles

To measure is to know. If you can not measure it, you can not improve it.

–Lord Kelvin

This has nothing to do with intermarket trading but I decided to include it here because since the publication of my article on rectangles in the June 2007 issue of *Technical Analysis of STOCKS & COMMODITIES*, I have received numerous emails from magazine readers asking for the MetaStock code of a rectangle pattern recognition system, obviously wanting to cash in on the article concepts.

I always wanted my articles to be of some practical use to trading professionals and active investors and the emails were all the motivation I needed to develop the MetaStock exploration which follows. But first, for the benefit of readers who have not read the article, I thought it would be useful to include the following information on rectangles.

Rectangles consist of a sideways price action or congestion area bounded by two horizontal or nearly horizontal parallel trendlines at top and bottom. At least two points are required to define each line but three points are more common. Rectangles can be either continuation or reversal patterns depending on the direction of the breakout in relation to the price trend before entering the formation. As reversals, rectangles appear more commonly at bottoms.

In the article, I presented some useful rectangle statistics and also a statistically derived formula to estimate the breakout price target objective. I used the statistics in the article to come up with the following code for a MetaStock exploration that will detect rectangles of up to two peaks and troughs. On trying to extend the code to include more than two peaks or troughs I came up with all sorts of problems as the MetaStock formula language is not the best for pattern recognition systems. Nevertheless, even with only two peaks, the system produced outstanding results.

C.1   RECTANGLE EXPLORATION

MetaStock Code

Col B: Target

```
A1:=5;
PK1:=Peak(1,H,A1);PK2:=Peak(2,H,A1);TR1:=Trough(1,L,A1);TR2:=Trough
    (2,L,A1);
H1:=Max(PK1,PK2);L1:=Min(TR1,TR2);
RH:=H1-L1;H1+2.3*Power(RH,.8)
```

Col C: StopLoss

```
A1:=5;PK1:=Peak(1,H,A1);PK2:=Peak(2,H,A1);
H1:=Max(PK1,PK2);H1*.98
```

Col D: ProfStop

```
A1:=5;PK1:=Peak(1,H,A1);PK2:=Peak(2,H,A1)
H1:=Max(PK1,PK2);1.55*H1
```

Filter

(Copyright Markos Katsanos 2007)

```
D1:=180;
A1:=5;
PK1:=Peak(1,H,A1);PK2:=Peak(2,H,A1);TR1:=Trough(1,L,A1);TR2:=Trough
    (2,L,A1);
H1:=Max(PK1,PK2);L1:=Min(TR1,TR2);H2:=.98*H1;
CI:=((HHV(C,140)-LLV(C,140))/LLV(C,140))*100; {CONGESTION INDEX}
P12:=PK1>.97*PK2 AND PK1<1.03*PK2 AND PeakBars(2,H,A1)<D1;
T12:=TR1>.97*TR2 AND TR1<1.03*TR2 AND TroughBars(2,L,A1)<D1;

Fml("FVE")>8 AND LinRegSlope(Fml("FVE"),22)>.5 AND
Ref(LinRegSlope(C,100)/Ref(C,-99),-2)*100<.12 AND
Ref(LinRegSlope(C,100)/Ref(C,-99),-2)*100>-.09 AND Cross(C,H1) AND
V>Ref(Mov(V,100,S),-2) AND Ref(CI,-1)/Ref(CI,-D1-1)<1 AND
(P12 AND T12)
```

If you don't have FVE in your indicators list then you should create a custom indicator named FVE with the following code:

```
PERIOD:= Input("PERIOD FOR FVE",5,80,22);
COEF:=Input("COEF FOR CUTOFF",0,2,.1);
H1:=If(H>0,H,Mov(H,5,S));
L1:=If(L>0,L,Mov(L,5,S));
INTRA:=Log(H1)-Log(L1);
VINTRA:=Stdev(INTRA,PERIOD);
INTER:=Log(Typical())-Log(Ref(Typical(),-1));
VINTER:=Stdev(INTER,PERIOD);
CUTOFF:=COEF*(VINTER+VINTRA)*C;
MF:=C-(H+L)/2+Typical()-Ref(Typical(),-1);
FVE:= Sum(If(MF>CUTOFF, +V, If(MF <-CUTOFF,
-V,0)),PERIOD)/(Mov(V,PERIOD,S)+1)/PERIOD*100;
FVE
```

Target Formula

In my article published in the June 2007 issue of *Technical Analysis of STOCKS & COMMODITIES*, I derived statistically the following formula for calculating the average price objective of rectangle formations:

$$\text{Target} = 2.3h^{.8}$$

where target = the breakout price objective in points or dollars which is the vertical distance measured from the formation upper boundary trendline to the first short term top. If this is measured on the chart with a ruler then the preferences should be set to display the chart in arithmetic and not logarithmic scale; h = rectangle height in points or dollars.

In the following example the target was exceeded by only \$0.6 or 0.7 %. On 18 May 2007 Royal Dutch Shell Plc. (RDS.A) broke out from a 9-month rectangle and never looked back until it peaked on 9 July 2007 at \$85.34.

Rectangle height $h = 71.87$ (upper rectangle boundary) $- 63.28$ (lower boundary) $= 8.59$

Substituting for h in the above formula we get:

$$\text{Breakout} = 2.3^*(8.59)^{.8} = 2.3^*5.59 = 12.85$$

and therefore the predicted target price is $71.87 + 12.85 = 84.72$ vs. the actual breakout price of 85.34.

Exit Rules

Of course nothing is certain in the stock market and potential rectangles can some-times fail to reach the expected profit target or breakouts fail to follow through and reverse direction to enter below the rectangle upper boundary.

My research on rectangles (presented in my article in the June 2007 issue of *Technical Analysis of STOCKS & COMMODITIES*) was used to derive the following conditions to close long positions detected by the exploration formula above:

- Profit target: The stock reaches the profit target according to the formula calculated in Column B of the exploration) or 55 % whichever comes first.
- Inactivity stop: The stock fails to reach the profit target in 95 calendar days (65 trading days).
- Stop loss: The price crosses below the rectangle upper boundary (calculated in Column C of the exploration).

Glossary

Advance-decline line

One of the most widely used indicators to measure the breadth of the stock market. To calculate the A/D line the number of declining issues is subtracted from the number of advancing issues each day and the net total is added to the previous cumulative total.

American Depository Receipts (ADRs)

ADRs are negotiable receipts for the securities of a foreign company which are kept in the vaults of an American bank, allowing Americans to trade foreign securities in the United States.

Arbitrage

The simultaneous buying and selling of assets in different markets or in derivative forms, taking advantage of the price difference.

Artificial neural networks

Nonlinear statistical modeling tools that can be used to model complex relationships between inputs and outputs or to find patterns in data.

Autocorrelation

Correlation between values of a series and others from the same series separated by a given interval.

Average True Range (ATR)

The True Range indicator was first introduced by J. Welles Wilder in his book, *New Concepts in Technical Trading Systems* (see Bibliography). Wilder defined the true range to be the greatest of the following for each period:

- The distance from today's high to today's low.
- The distance from yesterday's close to today's high.
- The distance from yesterday's close to today's low.

The Average True Range is simply the average of the true ranges over the past x periods.

Black box
A proprietary trading system whose rules are password protected and not disclosed.

Bollinger Bands
Developed by John Bollinger, this indicator plots trading bands two standard deviations above and below a 20-day moving average.

Central Limit Theorem
This theorem states that as the number of cases in the sample increases, the distribution of the data approaches normality.

Correlation coefficient
The correlation coefficient indicates the strength and direction of a linear relationship between two variables. A correlation coefficient of 1 (or -1) indicates a perfect linear relationship. A correlation coefficient of zero indicates that there is no straight line relationship between the two variables.

Covariance
Covariance is the measure of how much two random variables change together. The covariance is calculated by taking the cross product of the deviations from the mean, and then dividing by the number of observations.

Cover
Purchasing back a contract or a stock sold earlier to profit from a price decline.

Chaos Theory
Describes the behavior of nonlinear systems. In the stock market, Chaos Theory seeks to forecast the future path of stock prices, using non parametric methods.

Drawdown
The reduction in account equity from a previous high as a result of a trade loss or a series of losses.

Efficient Market Theory
The Efficient Market Theory states that at any given time, security prices fully reflect all available information.

Exchange-traded funds (ETFs)
Investment funds that can be bought and sold as a package on an exchange. Typically, ETFs try to replicate a stock market index such as the S&P 500 (e.g. SPY) or a market sector such as energy or technology, or a commodity such as gold or crude oil.

Exponential moving average

An exponential (or exponentially weighted) moving average places more weight on the most recent closing prices by applying weighting factors which decrease exponentially. It is calculated by applying a percentage of today's closing price to yesterday's moving average value. The formula for calculating EMA is:

EMA = (Today's closing price* k) + (Yesterday's EMA* $(1 - k)$), where $k = 2/(n + 1)$; n = no. of periods.

Finite Volume Element Indicator (FVE)

This indicator was developed by Markos Katsanos and introduced in the April 2003 issue of *Technical Analysis of STOCKS & COMMODITIES* magazine. It was modified for volatility in the September 2003 issue of the magazine. FVE is a money flow indicator but with two important differences from existing money flow indicators:

1. It resolves contradictions between intraday money flow indicators (such as Chaikin's money flow) and inter-day money flow indicators (like Granville's On Balance Volume) by taking into account both intra- and inter-day price action.
2. Unlike other money flow indicators which add or subtract all volume even if the security closed just 1 cent higher than the previous close, FVE uses a volatility threshold to exclude the volume on days of minimal price changes.

The FVE provides three types of signals:

1. The strongest signal is divergence between price and the indicator. Divergence can provide leading signals of breakouts or warnings of impending corrections. The classic method for detecting divergence is for FVE to make lower highs while price makes higher highs (negative divergence). An alternative method is to draw the linear regression line on both charts, and compare the slopes. A logical buy signal would be for the FVE, diverging from price, to rise sharply and make a series of higher highs and/or higher lows.
2. The most obvious and coincident signal is the slope of the FVE line. An upward slope indicates that the bulls are in control and the opposite for downward slope. This indicator level is a unique and very important property of FVE. Values above zero are bullish and indicate accumulation while values below zero indicate distribution. FVE crossing the zero line indicates that the short to intermediate balance of power is changing from the bulls to the bears or vice versa.
3. The best scenario is when a stock is in the process of building a base, and the FVE diverges from price and rises to cross the zero line from below, at a sharp angle. Conversely the crossing of the zero line from above is a bearish signal to liquidate positions or initiate a short trade.

Genetic algorithm

This is an alternative method to the "brute force" approach that seeks to solve optimization problems using the methods of evolution, or survival of the fittest.

Hidden neurons
Used to connect the input and output layer of a neural network. They are built during the learning process and use weighting transform functions to serve as connectors.

Historic volatility
Measures how much a security price has fluctuated over a period of time in the past; usually calculated by taking the standard deviation of price changes over a time period.

Historical data
A series of past intraday or daily market prices.

Kolmogorov-Smirnov normality test
The Kolmogorov-Smirnov test can be used to test that a variable is normally distributed by comparing the observed distribution function with a specified theoretical normal distribution.

Kurtosis
Descriptive measure of the sharpness of the peak of a frequency-distribution curve.

Lag
The time difference or shift between one value of a time series and a previous value of the same time series.

Least-squares method
Fitting a line or curve to data so as to minimize the sum of the squares of the differences between the observed values and the estimated values.

Linear regression line
A statistical technique for fitting a straight line to a set of data points using the least squares method.

Market breadth
Internal market statistics which are calculated by counting stocks that meet certain criteria. The "Percentage of stocks above their 40-day moving average" for example, counts the number of stocks currently trading above their 40-day price moving average and then plots this as a percentage. So if the daily value of this statistic is 70, you know that 70 % of the stocks on the NYSE are above their 40-day MA.

Maximum adverse excursion
The most equity lost intraday by any single position.

Momentum
The change of today's price from some fixed number of days in the past.

Momentum indicator

A technical analysis indicator showing the distance the current close is relative to the recent x-period high/low range. Momentum indicators are useful for predicting overbought or oversold conditions, and possible turning points within the market.

Money flow

A technical indicator that incorporates volume and price action to measure buying or selling pressure.

Monte Carlo Simulation

A procedure used to repeatedly analyze a system by rearranging the trades randomly (hence the name).

Moving average crossover system

One of the most popular trading systems. A dual moving average crossover system generates a buy signal when the shorter of two moving averages exceeds the longer one; a sell signal is generated when the shorter moving average falls below the longer moving average.

Moving average convergence/divergence (MACD)

The MACD is a trend-following momentum indicator that shows the relationship between two moving averages and is calculated by subtracting the value of the 26-period exponential moving average from the 12-period exponential moving average. A 9-period dotted exponential moving average (the "signal line") is usually displayed on top of the MACD indicator line. The MACD was developed by Gerald Appel, publisher of *Systems and Forecasts*.

Multicollinearity

A case of multiple regression in which the predictor variables are themselves highly correlated with result of two variables explaining the same portion of variation whereas either would be sufficient.

Multiple linear regression

Linear regression where more than one predictor variable is involved.

Neural networks

See Artificial neural networks.

Normal distribution

A probability distribution for a continuous random variable that forms a symmetrical bell-shaped curve around the mean.

Normalized
A price series adjusted so that the data vary within a prescribed standard range (usually between 0 and 100).

Null hypothesis
The hypothesis that an observed difference (as between the means of two samples) is due to chance alone and not due to a fundamental cause.

On-balance volume (OBV)
This is a money flow indicator developed by Joe Granville. It seeks to show if volume is flowing into or out of a security and is calculated by adding today's volume to a cumulative total when the security's price closes up, and subtracting the day's volume when the security's price closes down.

Oscillator
An indicator used to identify oversold or overbought levels.

Out-of-sample data
Price data that haven't been used in developing or optimizing a mechanical system.

Over-fitting or curve-fitting
Optimizing the parameters of a trading model to return the highest profit over the historical data. An absurd and false model may fit perfectly if the model has enough complexity by comparison to the amount of data available. Over-fitting is generally recognized to be a violation of Occam's razor principle.

Pairs trading
Taking a long position and a short position at the same time on two stocks in the same sector, creating a hedge.

Pessimistic rate of return
A statistic that adjusts the usual wins/loss statistic to estimate the worst return from trading results by reducing the number of wins by the square root of the actual number and increasing the number of losses by the square root of the actual number of losses.

Pip
The smallest price increment of change in a currency. The last digit after the decimal point of the exchange rate is a pip: for example, in a EUR/USD exchange rate quote, a change from 1.4715 to 1.4716 is one pip.

Pyramid
A technique of adding additional positions to a winning trade based on a certain criteria as the trend grows.

Random walk

Theory that stock daily price changes are random and there is no sequential correlation between prices from one day to the next. Many believers of the random walk theory believe that it is impossible to outperform the market consistently without taking additional risk.

Range

The difference between the high and low price during a given period.

Rate of change

Calculates the n period price change of a security expressed as a percentage according to the following formula:

$$(\text{Ctoday} - Cn)/Cn^* \, 100$$

where Ctoday and Cn are the closing prices today and n days ago respectively.

Relative strength

A price comparison of two securities. It is calculated by taking the ratio of their prices.

Risk-adjusted return

It is calculated by dividing the annualized rate of return on equity by the standard deviation of equity changes.

Shapiro-Wilk's test

The Shapiro-Wilk's W test is used in testing for normality. If the W statistic is significant, then the hypothesis that the distribution is normal should be rejected.

Sharpe ratio

This is a measure of the mean excess return per unit of risk and describes how much excess return you are receiving for the extra volatility of trade results and is calculated according to the following simple formula:

$$SR = (r - R)/\sigma$$

where r is the asset return, R is the return on a benchmark asset, such as US T-bills, and σ is the standard deviation of the excess return.

S&P e-mini

Electronically traded, smaller-sized ($50 times the S&P 500) contracts of the Standard & Poor's 500 index.

Standard deviation

A widely-used statistical concept indicating the spread of the data set around the mean, equal to the square root of the sum of squares of the deviations from the arithmetic mean according to the following formula:

$$\sigma = \text{sqrt}\left(\sum (x_{i..n} - \mu)^2\right)$$

where: μ = arithmetic mean of the series.

Sterling ratio method
Another measure of risk/return given by:

$$SR = R\,(\%)/(D\,(\%) + 10\,\%)$$

where R = three-year average annual return; D = three-year average maximum annual drawdown.

Stochastics oscillator
An overbought/oversold momentum indicator that compares where a security's price closed relative to its trading range over the last x-time periods. The formula for the %K parameter of the Stochastic is:

(today's close − x period lowest close)/(x period highest − x period lowest)

Values of %K are then transformed into a range between zero and 100 and smoothed by their three-period moving average.

Stock index futures
A futures contract that uses a market index as the underlying instrument. The delivery is usually in cash.

Tradesim®
A MetaStock plug-in used for portfolio back-testing of a large number of stocks. More information is available at http://www.compuvision.com.au/.

Trailing stop
A stop-loss order that follows the prevailing price trend. The stop attempts to exit at the price that would value the position at the highest profit over the historical period less the trailing value.

T-test
This analysis is used when comparing the means of two groups to assess whether one group is statistically different than the other.

Volume Flow Indicator (VFI)

The VFI is a money flow indicator based on the popular On Balance Volume (OBV) but with three very important modifications:

- Positive readings indicate a bullish state and negative ones a bearish state.
- The calculation is based on the day's mean instead of the closing price.
- A threshold is introduced to eliminate the volume on minimal price changes and another threshold to trim excessive volume.

The VFI was first introduced by Markos Katsanos in the June 2004 issue of *Technical Analysis of STOCKS & COMMODITIES*. A simplified interpretation of the VFI is that values above zero indicate a bullish state and the crossing of the zero line is the trigger or buy signal.

METASTOCK® FUNCTIONS

I thought it would be helpful to include the MetaStock functions used in this book, for the benefit of the readers who are not familiar with the MetaStock formula language.

ABS(DATA ARRAY)
Calculates the absolute value of the data array.

ADX(PERIODS)
Calculates Wilder's Average Directional Movement indicator.

ALERT()
The alert function is used in conjunction with other functions to extend a true signal for a specified number of periods. The following example illustrates the use of the alert() function:

Buy: STOCH(10,3)>MOV(STOCH(10,3),4,S)) AND
ALERT(CROSS(STOCH(10,3),20),3)

If these were entered as the Enter Long rule, the system would enter a long position when the stochastic was greater than its moving average and had crossed over 20 at any time over the previous three time periods.

ATR(PERIODS)
Calculates the Average True Range indicator (see also Glossary).

BBANDTOP(DATA ARRAY, PERIODS, METHOD, DEVIATIONS)
Calculates the top Bollinger Band of DATA ARRAY using METHOD calculation method and shifted upward DEVIATION standard deviations. Example:

BBANDTOP(C, 10, S, 2) calculates the top Bollinger Band 2 standard deviations from the 10-day simple moving average.

BBANDBOT(DATA ARRAY, PERIODS, METHOD, DEVIATIONS)
Similar to the above. It calculates the bottom band.

C
C is the closing price of the base security on test.

CI(PERIODS)
This calculates the Congestion Index (a custom indicator described in Chapter 9).

CORREL(DATA ARRAY, DATA ARRAY, PERIODS, SHIFT)
Calculates the correlation between two data arrays over PERIODS time periods, after shifting the second data array to the right SHIFT periods. Example:
The formula CORREL(SEC1, SEC2, 30, 0) calculates the 30-day correlation between securities SEC1 and SEC2.

CROSS(DATA ARRAY 1, DATA ARRAY 2)
Returns 1 or "true" when DATA ARRAY 1 crosses above DATA ARRAY 2. Example: CROSS(C, MOV(C,10,E)) is true when the closing price crosses over its 10-day exponential moving average.

FML("FORMULA_NAME")
Calculates the value of a custom formula. The formula can be referenced using the FORMULA_NAME in quotes. Example:
FML("FVE") calculates the value of the custom formula FVE using the default period of 22 days.

H
This is today's extreme high price of the base security on test.

HHV(DATA ARRAY, PERIODS)
Calculates the highest value in the DATA ARRAY over the preceding PERIODS (PERIODS includes the current day). Example:
The formula "HHV(C, 5)" returns the highest closing price over the preceding five periods.

HOUR()
On an intraday test, returns the number of hours that have passed during the day using a 24-hour clock. For example, if the current time is 14:15:20, the hour() function will return "14".

L

This is today's extreme low price of the base security on test.

LINREGSLOPE(DATA ARRAY, PERIODS)

Calculates the slope of the linear regression line.

LLV(DATA ARRAY, PERIODS)

Calculates the lowest value in the DATA ARRAY over the preceding PERIODS (PERIODS includes the current day). Example:

The formula "LLV(C, 5)" returns the lowest closing price over the preceding five days.

MACD()

Calculates the MACD indicator (for more information on the MACD see also the Glossary).

MOV(DATA ARRAY, PERIODS, METHOD)

Calculates a PERIODS moving average of DATA ARRAY using METHOD calculation method. Valid methods are:

EXPONENTIAL, SIMPLE, TIMESERIES, TRIANGULAR, WEIGHTED, VARIABLE, AND VOLUMEADJUSTED (these can be abbreviated as E, S, T, TRI, W, VAR, and VOL). Example:

The formula "MOV(C, 30, E)" returns the value of a 30-period exponential moving average of the closing prices.

SAR(STEP, MAXIMUM)

Calculates the predefined Parabolic SAR indicator (for a description of the parabolic see also the Glossary and Chapter 17). Example:

SAR(0.02, 0.20) calculates the parabolic function using an acceleration factor of 0.02 and a maximum value of 0.2.

STDEV(DATA ARRAY, PERIODS)

Calculates the standard deviation of a data array for PERIODS days. Example:

STDEV(C, 21) calculates the one month (21 trading day) standard deviation of the closing price of the security on test.

STOCH(%K PERIODS, %K SLOWING)

Calculates the stochastic oscillator. Example:

The formula "STOCH(10, 3)" returns the value of the 3-day moving average of a 10-period stochastic.

ABBREVIATIONS

ADX	Wilder's Average Directional Index
AMEX	American Stock and Options Exchange
AORD	Australian All Ordinaries Index
ATG	Athens General Stock Index
ATR	Average True Range
AUD	Australian Dollar
CAC	French Stock Market Index
CACF	CAC 40 Futures
CI	Congestion Index
CME	Chicago Mercantile Exchange
CRB	Commodity Research Bureau Index
DAX	German Stock Exchange Index
DJ-30	Dow Jones Industrial Average
DJIA	Dow Jones Industrial Average
DXY	Dollar Index
EMA	Exponential moving average
ES	Standard & Poor 500 e-mini futures
ESTX	Euro Stoxx 50 Index
ETF	Exchange Traded Fund
EUREX	European Derivatives Exchange
FDAX	DAX Index Futures
FOREX	Foreign Exchange
FTSE	London Stock Exchange FTSE-100 Index
GLD	Gold ETF
GLOBEX	CME electronic trading system for futures
GSCI	The Goldman Sachs Commodity Index
HUI	AMEX's Gold BUGS Index
IMO	Intermarket Momentum Oscillator
LRS	Linear regression slope
LSE	London Stock Exchange
MA	Moving average
MACD	Moving Average Convergence/Divergence
N225	Tokyo Stock Exchange Nikkei 225 Index
NQ	Nasdaq 100 futures
NYMEX	New York Mercantile Exchange
NYSE	New York Stock Exchange
OIX	CBOE Oil Index
Pred	Predicted
RJ/CRB	Reuters/Jefferies CRB Index
RS	Relative Strength
S&P 500	Standard & Poor 500
SD	Standard deviation
SEC	Security
SPX	Standard & Poor 500

StDev   Standard deviation
TNX   10-year Treasury Note yield
TSX   S&P/TSX Composite Canadian Stock Index
VHF   Vertical horizontal filter
VIX   The CBOE Volatility Index
XAU   Philadelphia Gold & Silver Sector
XOI   AMEX Oil Index
YM   Dow Jones Industrial Average e-mini futures
Z   Z-Score or FTSE futures
ZN   10-year Treasury Note E-CBOT futures

Bibliography

ARTICLES

Angle, K.D. (1993). "Asset Allocation: Stocks, Bonds, Futures." *Technical Analysis of STOCKS & COMMODITIES*, Volume 11: February.

Barrie, Scott (1997). "Trend-Following the Corn/Wheat Spread." *Technical Analysis of STOCKS & COMMODITIES*, Volume 15: October.

Chan, William K.N. (2001). "A Critical Study on the Efficacy of Stop-Loss." *Market Technician's Association Journal*, Spring–Summer 2001.

Fishman, Mark B. (1991). "Artificial Intelligence and Market Analysis." *Technical Analysis of STOCKS & COMMODITIES*. Volume 9: March.

Fishman, Mark B. (1991). "Using Neural Nets in Market Analysis." *Technical Analysis of STOCKS & COMMODITIES*. Volume 9: April.

Giampaolo, G., Ruggero, C., Riccardo, B., et al. (1999). "Predicting the Exchange Rate: A Comparison of Econometric Models, Neural Networks and Trading Systems." *Market Technician's Association Journal*. Issue 52, Summer 1999.

Gopalakrishnan, Jayanthi (1999). "Trading the MACD." *Technical Analysis of STOCKS & COMMODITIES*. Volume 17: October.

Gopalakrishnan, Jayanthi (2006). "Correlation Reports: CSI Data." *Technical Analysis of STOCKS & COMMODITIES*. Volume 24: December.

Gopalakrishnan, Jayanthi (2006). "Before Commodities Were King." *Technical Analysis of STOCKS & COMMODITIES*. Volume 24: Bonus issue.

Harris, Michael (2002). "Improve Your System with the Profitability Rule." *Technical Analysis of STOCKS & COMMODITIES*. Volume 20: September.

Huebotter, Paul and Huebotter, Carole (1997). "The Fundamentals of Sector Rotation." *Technical Analysis of STOCKS & COMMODITIES*. Volume 15: February.

Jones, Donald L. (1986). "Commodity Futures Add Value." *Financial Analysis Journal*, May–June.

Karczewski, Jack (1997). "Using Multiple Regression Analysis." *Technical Analysis of STOCKS & COMMODITIES*. Volume 11: August.

Kase, Cynthia Ann (1993). "The Kase Dev-Stop –Accounting for Volatility, Variance and Skew in Managing Trading Risk." *Market Technician's Association Journal*. Issue 41, Summer 1993.

Katsanos, Markos (2003). "Detecting Breakouts." *Technical Analysis of STOCKS & COM-MODITIES*. Volume 21: April.

Katsanos, Markos (2003). "Detecting Breakouts in Intraday Charts." *Technical Analysis of STOCKS & COMMODITIES*. Volume 21: September.

Katsanos, Markos (2004). "Using Money Flow to Stay with the Trend." *Technical Analysis of STOCKS & COMMODITIES*. Volume 22: June.

Katsanos, Markos (2004). "Volume Flow Performance." *Technical Analysis of STOCKS & COMMODITIES*. Volume 22: July.

Katsanos, Markos (2005). "Las Vegas or Los Nasdaq?" *Technical Analysis of STOCKS & COMMODITIES*. Volume 23: January.

Katsanos, Markos (2005). "Flags and Pennants." *Technical Analysis of STOCKS & COM-MODITIES*. Volume 23: April.

Katsanos, Markos (2005). "Detecting Breakouts from Flags and Pennants." *Technical Analysis of STOCKS & COMMODITIES*. Volume 23: May.

Katsanos, Markos (2006). "Bear Flags." *Technical Analysis of STOCKS & COMMODITIES*. Volume 24: May.

Katsanos, Markos (2007). "How Effective are Rectangles?" *Technical Analysis of STOCKS & COMMODITIES*. Volume 25: June.

Katz, Jeffrey Owen (1992). "Developing Neural Network Forecasters for Trading." *Technical Analysis of STOCKS & COMMODITIES*. Volume 10: April.

Kean, John (1992). "Using Neural Nets for Intermarket Analysis." *Technical Analysis of STOCKS & COMMODITIES*. Volume 10: November.

Kim, J.-H., Park, S.-J., et al. (2003). "Stock Price Prediction using Backpropagation Neural Network in KOSPI." International Conference on Artificial Intelligence IC-AI'03. 200–203.

Kim, K.-J. and Lee, W. B. (2004). "Stock Market Prediction using Artificial Neural Networks with Optimal Feature Transformation". *Neural Computing and Applications* 13(3): 255–260.

Lo, Andrew W. and MacKinlay, A.C. (1988). "Stock Market Prices do not Follow Random Walks: Evidence from a Simple Specification Test." *The Review of Financial Studies*. Vol. 1, No. 1.

Long, Erik (2003). "Making Sense of Fractals." *Technical Analysis of STOCKS & COMMODI-TIES*. Volume 21: May.

Meyers, Dennis (1997). "The T-Bond Futures and Stock Market Breadth System." *Technical Analysis of STOCKS & COMMODITIES*. Volume 15: November.

Meyers, Dennis (1995). "Modifying the Parabolic Stop and Reversal." *Technical Analysis of STOCKS & COMMODITIES*. Volume 13: July.

Meyers, Dennis (1995). "The Utility Average Stock Market Indicator." *Technical Analysis of STOCKS & COMMODITIES*. Volume 13: August.

Meyers, Dennis (1996). "The Electric Utility Bond Market Indicator." *Technical Analysis of STOCKS & COMMODITIES*. Volume 14: January.

Meyers, Dennis (1996). "The GMI Bond Market System." *Technical Analysis of STOCKS & COMMODITIES*. Volume 14: April.

Meyers, Dennis (1996). "The Gold and Silver Bond Fund System." *Technical Analysis of STOCKS & COMMODITIES*. Volume 14: May.

Meyers, Dennis (1996). "A/D Volume, New-High, New-Low System." *Technical Analysis of STOCKS & COMMODITIES*. Volume 14: July.

Meyers, Dennis (1997). "A New Utility Average Stock Market System." *Technical Analysis of STOCKS & COMMODITIES*. Volume 15: March.

Meyers, Dennis (1997). "Walk Forward with the Xau Bond Fund System." *Technical Analysis of STOCKS & COMMODITIES*. Volume 15: May.

Meyers, Thomas (1992). "Four Common Errors in Testing Trading Systems." *Technical Analysis of STOCKS & COMMODITIES*. Volume 10: September.

Murphy, J. John and Hirschfield, J. David (1988). "Spread Trading the CRB Index." *Technical Analysis of STOCKS & COMMODITIES*. Volume 6: May.

Murphy, J. John (1992). "The Link between Bonds and Commodities." *Technical Analysis of STOCKS & COMMODITIES*. Volume 10: May.

Murphy, J. John (1992). "The Link between Bonds and Stocks." *Technical Analysis of STOCKS & COMMODITIES*. Volume 10: July.

Murphy, J. John (1992). "The CRB Index/Bond Ratio." *Technical Analysis of STOCKS & COMMODITIES*. Volume 10: August.

Murphy, J. John (1992). "Utilities and Stocks." *Technical Analysis of STOCKS & COMMODITIES*. Volume 10: October.

Murphy, J. John (1992). "Interest Rates and the US Dollar." *Technical Analysis of STOCKS & COMMODITIES*. Volume 10: October.

Murphy, J. John (1992). "Gold and the US Dollar." *Technical Analysis of STOCKS & COMMODITIES*. Volume 10: December.

Nauzer, Balsara (1992), "Using Probability Stops in Trading." *Technical Analysis of STOCKS & COMMODITIES*. Volume 10: May.

Parkinson, Michael (1980). "The Extreme Value Method for Estimating the Variance of the Rate of Return." *The Journal of Business* 53: 1, January.

Penn, D. (2003). "Intermarket Relationships." *Technical Analysis of STOCKS & COMMODITIES*. Volume 21: July.

Peterson, Dennis (2002). "Moving Averages." *Technical Analysis of STOCKS & COMMODITIES*. Volume 20: June.

Peterson, Dennis (2002). "Developing a Trading System." *Technical Analysis of STOCKS & COMMODITIES*. Volume 20: August.

Rothschild, Raymond (1991). "Diversification and Risk." *Technical Analysis of STOCKS & COMMODITIES*. Volume 9: May.

Ruggiero, M. (1996). "Build a Real Neural Net." *Futures*. June.

Stake, James (1995). "Designing a Personal Neural Net Trading System." *Technical Analysis of STOCKS & COMMODITIES*. Volume 13: January.

Sweeny, John (1992). "Where to Put your Stops." *Technical Analysis of STOCKS & COMMODITIES*. Volume 10: December.

Vakkur, Mark (1996). "Treasury Bond Yields and the S&P 500." *Technical Analysis of STOCKS & COMMODITIES*. Volume 14: August.

Weiss, Eric (1980). "ARIMA Forecasting." *Technical Analysis of STOCKS & COMMODITIES*. Volume 1: February.

BOOKS

Achelis, Steven B. (1995). *Technical Analysis from A to Z*. Chicago, IL: Probus Publishing Company.

Appel, Gerald (1979). *The Moving Average Convergence-Divergence Method*. Great Neck, NY: Signalert.

Azoff, M. E. (1994). *Neural Network Time Series Forecasting of Financial Markets*. John Wiley & Sons Ltd.

Balsara, Nauzer J. (1992). *Money Management Strategies for Futures Traders*. John Wiley & Sons Inc.

Chande, Tushar S. (1997). *Beyond Technical Analysis*. J. Wiley & Sons Inc.

Chande, Tushar and Kroll, Stanley (1994). *The New Technical Trader*. John Wiley & Sons Inc.

Colby, Robert W. and Meyers, Thomas A. (1988). *The Encyclopedia of Technical Market Indicators*. McGraw-Hill.

DeMark, R. Thomas (1994). *The Science of Technical Analysis*. J. Wiley & Sons Inc.

Granville, Joseph E. (1976). *New Strategy of Daily Stock Market Timing for Maximum Profit*. Englewood Cliffs, NJ: Prentice-Hall.

Hinkle D. Wiersma, W. and Jurs, S. (1989). *Applied Statistics for the Behavioral Sciences*. Houghton Mifflin.

Kaufman, Perry (1995). *Smarter Trading*. New York: McGraw-Hill.

Kaufman, Perry (2005). *New Trading and Methods*, J. Wiley & Sons Inc.

Krutsinger, Joe (1997). *Trading Systems Secrets of the Masters*. New York: McGraw-Hill.

Lebeau, Charles and Lucas, David (1991). *Technical Trader's Guide to Computer Analysis of the Futures Market*. Homewood, IL: Business One Irwin.

Lefevre, Edwin (1994). *Reminiscences of a Stock Operator*. John Wiley & Sons Inc.

Meyers, Thomas (1989). *The Technical Analysis Course*. Probus Publishing.

Murphy, John J. (1991). *Intermarket Technical Analysis: Trading Strategies for the Global Stock, Bond, Commodity, and Currency Markets*. John Wiley & Sons Inc.

Murphy, John J. (2004). *Intermarket Analysis: Profiting from Global Market Relationships*. New York: John Wiley & Sons, Inc.

Murphy Joseph E. (1988). *Stock Market Probability*. Irwin.

Nison, Steve (1994). *Beyond Candlesticks: New Japanese Charting Techniques Revealed*. John Wiley & Sons Inc.

O'Niel, William (1995). *How to Make Money in Stocks*, Second edition. New York, NY: McGraw-Hill.

Pardo, R. (1992). *Design, Testing, and Optimization of Trading Systems*. New York, John Wiley & Sons Inc.

Pedhazur, Elazar J. (1997). *Multiple Regression in Behavioral Research*. Wadsworth.

Pring, Martin J. (1991). *Technical Analysis Explained, Third edition*. New York, NY: McGraw-Hill, 1991.

Pruit G. and Hill, J. (2003). *Building Winning Trading Systems with Trade Station*. J. Wiley & Sons Inc.

Ruggiero, Murray A. (1997). *Cybernetic Trading Strategies*. John Wiley & Sons Inc.

Sperandeo, Victor (1991). *Trader Vic: Methods of a Wall Street Master*. John Wiley & Sons, Inc.

Sperandeo, Victor (2008). *Trader Vic on Commodities: What's Unknown, Misunderstood, and Too Good to Be True*. John Wiley & Sons, Inc.

Schwager, Jack D. (1992). *The New Market Wizards*. John Wiley & Sons, Inc.

Schwager, Jack D. (1995). *Schwager on Futures: Technical Analysis*. John Wiley & Sons, Inc.

Taleb, Nassim Nicholas (1997). *Fooled by Randomness*. Texere, New York.

Taleb, Nassim Nicholas (2007). *The Black Swan: The Impact of the Highly Improbable*. Random House

Vince, R. (1990). *Portfolio Management Formulas: Mathematical Trading Methods for the Futures, Options and Stock Markets*. John Wiley & Sons Inc.

Wilder, J. Welles. (1978). *New Concepts in Technical Trading Systems*. Greensboro, NC: Trend Research.

Zweig, Martin (1986). *Martin Zweig's Winning on Wall Street*. Warner Books.

Index

Lightning Source UK Ltd.
Milton Keynes UK
UKOW06n2001101215

264487UK00009B/71/P